The Political Geography of Inequality
Regions and Redistribution

This book is a study of redistribution and inequality in political unions. It addresses two questions: why some political systems have more centralized systems of interpersonal redistribution than others, and why some political unions make larger efforts to equalize resources among their constituent units than others. This book presents a new theory of the origin of fiscal structures in systems with several levels of government. The argument points to two major factors to account for the variation in redistribution: the interplay between economic geography and political representation on the one hand, and the scope of interregional economic externalities on the other. To test the empirical implications derived from the argument, the book relies on in-depth studies of the choice of fiscal structures in unions as diverse as the European Union, Canada, and the United States in the aftermath of the Great Depression; Germany before and after reunification; and Spain after the transition to democracy.

Pablo Beramendi is an Associate Professor of Political Science at Duke University. His research focuses on the political economy of redistribution and inequality. Previously, he has taught at the Maxwell School of Syracuse University and in the Department of Politics at the University of Oxford. He is also a research associate at the Juan March Institute (Madrid) and a former research Fellow at the Science Center (Berlin). Among his published works are articles on the determinants of taxation and inequality; the role of inequality in shaping electoral turnout; and the relationship between federalism, inequality, and redistribution.

Cambridge Studies in Comparative Politics

General Editor
Margaret Levi   *University of Washington, Seattle*

Assistant General Editors
Kathleen Thelen   *Massachusetts Institute of Technology*
Erik Wibbels   *Duke University*

Associate Editors
Robert H. Bates   *Harvard University*
Stephen Hanson   *University of Washington, Seattle*
Torben Iversen   *Harvard University*
Stathis Kalyvas   *Yale University*
Peter Lange   *Duke University*
Helen Milner   *Princeton University*
Frances Rosenbluth   *Yale University*
Susan Stokes   *Yale University*
Sidney Tarrow   *Cornell University*

Other Books in the Series
David Austen-Smith, Jeffry A. Frieden, Miriam A. Golden, Karl Ove Moene, and Adam Przeworski, eds., *Selected Works of Michael Wallerstein: The Political Economy of Inequality, Unions, and Social Democracy*
Andy Baker, *The Market and the Masses in Latin America: Policy Reform and Consumption in Liberalizing Economies*
Lisa Baldez, *Why Women Protest: Women's Movements in Chile*
Stefano Bartolini, *The Political Mobilization of the European Left, 1860–1980: The Class Cleavage*
Robert Bates, *When Things Fell Apart: State Failure in Late-Century Africa*
Mark Beissinger, *Nationalist Mobilization and the Collapse of the Soviet State*
Nancy Bermeo, ed., *Unemployment in the New Europe*
Carles Boix, *Democracy and Redistribution*
Carles Boix, *Political Parties, Growth, and Equality: Conservative and Social Democratic Economic Strategies in the World Economy*

Continued after the Index

The Political Geography of Inequality

Regions and Redistribution

PABLO BERAMENDI
Duke University

CAMBRIDGE
UNIVERSITY PRESS

32 Avenue of the Americas, New York NY 10013-2473, USA

Cambridge University Press is part of the University of Cambridge.

It furthers the University's mission by disseminating knowledge in the pursuit of education, learning and research at the highest international levels of excellence.

www.cambridge.org
Information on this title: www.cambridge.org/9781107637214

© Pablo Beramendi 2012

This publication is in copyright. Subject to statutory exception and to the provisions of relevant collective licensing agreements, no reproduction of any part may take place without the written permission of Cambridge University Press.

First published 2012
First paperback edition 2014

A catalogue record for this publication is available from the British Library

Library of Congress Cataloguing in Publication data
Beramendi, Pablo.
The political geography of inequality : regions and redistribution / Pablo Beramendi.
p. cm. – (Cambridge studies in comparative politics)
Includes bibliographical references and index.
ISBN 978-1-107-00813-7 (hardback) – ISBN 978-1-107-40046-7 (pbk.)
1. Regionalism. 2. Equality. 3. European Union countries – Economic conditions – Regional
disparities. 4. North America – Economic conditions – Regional disparities. 5. Comparative
government. I. Title. II. Series.
JF197.B47 2011
320.011–dc22   2011010908

ISBN 978-1-107-00813-7 Hardback
ISBN 978-1-107-63721-4 Paperback

Cambridge University Press has no responsibility for the persistence or accuracy of URLs for external or third-party internet websites referred to in this publication, and does not guarantee that any content on such websites is, or will remain, accurate or appropriate.

To Marta, for the hours stolen

Contents

List of Tables		*page* x
List of Figures		xii
Acknowledgments		xv
1	Regions and Redistribution: Introduction and Overview	1
2	A Theory of Fiscal Structures in Political Unions	23
3	The Road Ahead: The Empirical Strategy	46
4	The European Union: Economic Geography and Fiscal Structures under Centrifugal Representation	67
5	North America's Divide: Distributive Tensions, Risk Sharing, and the Centralization of Public Insurance in Federations	103
6	Germany's Reunification: Distributive Tensions and Fiscal Structures under Centripetal Representation	135
7	Endogenous Decentralization and Welfare Resilience: Spain, 1978–2007	175
8	The Legacy of History	206
9	The Political Geography of Inequality: Summary and Implications	234
Appendix A Chapter 2		249
Appendix B Chapter 4		253
Appendix C Chapter 7		257
Appendix D Chapter 8 – Sources and Descriptive Statistics		258
References		263
Index		283

Tables

2.1	The Geography of Income Inequality and Preferences for Fiscal Structures	page 31
3.1	Case Selection and Empirical Strategy	57
5.1	Intercensus Net Migration Ratios, by Province, Canada 1901–1921	112
5.2	Interstate Mobility in the United States	114
5.3	Intercensus Net Migration Ratios, by Province, Canada 1921–1941	115
5.4	The Legislative Process of the American Social Security Act	131
6.1	The Allocation of Tax Sources by Level of Government	139
6.2	Interregional Redistribution before Reunification, 1979–1989	140
6.3	Interregional Redistribution in Germany with and without Eastern Länder	147
6.4	Incorporating the East: A Multidimensional Effort	152
6.5	The Effort to Incorporate the East: Map of Preferences	154
6.6	The Allocation of Interregional Transfers in Germany, 1991–1994	161
6.7	The Redistributive Impact of the FA System	163
6.8	Partisan Composition of Regional Parliaments since 1990	165
6.9	The Allocation of Interregional Transfers in Germany, 1995–2002	173
7.1	The Limits of the Federalization Process	178
7.2	General Elections: Distribution of Seats in the Spanish Central Parliament – Lower Chamber	181
7.3	The Geography of Income and Inequality in Spain: An Overview	188
7.4	The Structure of ACs' Revenues, 1986–2002	191
7.5	The Income Tax and the Evolution of Fiscal Decentralization, 1993–2009	193
7.6	The Legislative Production of the New Constitution of Catalonia	200

7.7	The ACs Before the Reform of Regional Financing in Spain, 2008–2009	201
8.1	Dimensions of the Geography of Income Inequality, 1980–2000	210
8.2	Decentralization of Interpersonal Redistribution in Advanced Democracies, 1980–2000	213
8.3	Determinants of Interregional Inequalities in Political Unions around the World: Dimensions of the Geography of Income Inequality, 1980–2000	214
8.4	Decentralization of Interpersonal Redistribution in Political Unions around the World, 1978–2001	222
8.5	Does Inequality Reproduce Itself? Determinants of Overall Economic Inequality in OECD Countries (1980–2000)	225
8.6	Interregional Redistribution in Political Unions	231
B.1	Mixed Level Estimates of Individual Preferences for the Harmonization of Social Welfare Systems within the European Union	253
B.2	Logit and Probit Estimates of Support for Welfare Centralization among European Social Democratic Parties and Trade Unions	254
B.3	OLS Estimation of Countries' Position over the EU's role in Social Policy during the Constitutional Convention	255
D.1	Economic Geography, Interpersonal Redistribution, and Income Inequality in Advanced Industrial Societies (Tables 8.1, 8.2, and 8.5 in text)	258
D.2	Economic Geography, Interpersonal Redistribution, and Interregional Redistribution around the World (Tables 8.3 and 8.4 in text)	259
D.3	Advanced Industrial Societies (Tables 8.1, 8.2, and 8.5 in text)	259
D.4	Sample Including Advanced and Developing Countries (Tables 8.2 and 8.4 in text)	261

Figures

1.1	Fiscal Structures and Income Inequality in Political Unions	page 7
2.1	The Political Process	26
2.2	The Geography of Income and Institutional Preferences	30
2.3	Preferences for Fiscal Structures When the Poor Region Is Highly Specialized	36
2.4	The Conditional Relationship between Economic Geography and Representation	44
2.5	Determinants of Targeted Interregional Transfers: Expected Relationships	45
4.1	Unbalanced Policy Integration in the European Union (1957–2004)	69
4.2	Relative Composition of EU Expenditure, 1958–2001 (percent)	70
4.3	Distribution of CAP Expenditure by Country (as a percentage of total CAP expenditures)	72
4.4	Distribution by Country of Structural and Cohesion Funds	73
4.5	The Geography of Income Inequality in the European Union	78
4.6	Labor Markets and Mobility in the European Union	80
4.7	Preferences about Social Policy Centralization in the European Union	86
4.8	Attitudes toward Welfare Centralization among European Social Democratic Parties and Labor Unions	88
4.9	The EU's Role in Social Policy as a Function of the Geography of Inequality	92
4.10	Interregional Redistribution and Mobility in the EU: 1990–2003	100
5.1	Evolution of GNP per Capita in Canada and the United States (1926–1945)	108
5.2	Evolution of the Unemployment Rate in Canada and the United States (1926–1945)	109
5.3	The Geography of the Depression in the United States and Canada	110

5.4	The Timing of Migration out of the South	115
6.1	The Geography of Unemployment before and after Reunification	144
6.2	The Geography of Income Inequality before and after Reunification	145
6.3	The Evolution of Inequality in Germany	148
6.4	The Evolution of Social Security Transfers in Germany	157
6.5	The Growing Leverage of Smaller Parties in the Federal Parliament	164
7.1	Evolution of Spain's Fiscal Structure	183
7.2	Net Balance in Total Fiscal Flows (1991–2005)	186
7.3	Net Balance in Social Security Flows (1991–2005)	187
7.4	Income per Capita and Inequality across Regions in Spain	187
8.1	Economic Geography and Interpersonal Redistribution: Political Contingencies	211
8.2	Conditional Effect of the Geography of Inequality I	217
8.3	Conditional Effect of the Geography of Inequality II	217
8.4	Predicted Levels of Decentralization of Interpersonal Redistribution as a Function of the Geography of Income Inequality and Representation	218
8.5	The Conditional Effect of Income Geography on the Decentralization of Redistribution	222
8.6	Income Geography and Representation as Determinants of the Level of Decentralization of Redistribution in Political Unions Worldwide (predicted values)	223
8.7	Representation and the Self-Reproduction of Inequality	227
8.8	Impact of Representation and Mobility on Interregional Transfers (predicted values)	232

Acknowledgments

That this book has taken a long time to see light is by no means attributable to lack of help. Several people deserve special mention. Tony Atkinson and Gosta Esping-Andersen supervised the dissertation that provided the seeds of this book. Their encouragement, and especially their many theoretical and methodological lessons, remains and will continue to be a major source of guidance. Jonas Pontusson examined the dissertation rigorously and constructively, offering comments and questions that helped a great deal in developing my research agenda thereafter. Carles Boix and Alberto Diaz-Cayeros generously took apart the very first draft in a workshop at the Maxwell School of Syracuse University in the spring of 2006. Their feedback since then has proved invaluable. In addition, Suzanne Mettler, Matt Cleary, Brian Taylor, and Hans Peter Schmitz offered very helpful criticisms. As a result, the book underwent a massive transformation, most of which has taken place at Duke.

During this process, Erik Wibbels has read and commented on every version of this manuscript. He is not only the sharpest of critics but also a most loyal friend. Jonathan Rodden has seen this project evolve since its inception and has been a constant source of encouragement and advice. Herbert Kitschelt has read the full manuscript twice and offered pointed and constructive criticisms. David Soskice's help to develop the model and his insistence on simplifying the argument have proved invaluable. Finally, since we became friends in the late 1990s, David Rueda has patiently listened to and commented on different parts of the project, always combining constructive criticism and support. This book owes a great deal to their generous friendship, as does my quality of life as an academic.

In addition, many other colleagues and friends have helped at different stages of the project with data, comments, and/or suggestions over the years: John Aldrich, Francesc Amat, Christopher Anderson, Ben Ansell, Krishna Ayyangar, Keith Banting, Marius Busemeyer, Thomas Cusack, Alex Downes, Jose Fernandez-Albertos, Rob Franzese, Sarah Hobolt, Florian Hollenbach, Lisbet Hoogue, Torben Iversen, Seth Jolly, Karen Jusko, Judith Kelley, Desmond King,

Kai Konrad, Thomas Konig, Anirudh Krishna, Dan Kselman, Alexander Kuo, Ignacio Lago, Santiago Lago, Sandra León, Bahar Leventoglu, Johannes Lindvall, Julia Lynch, Isabela Mares, Gary Marks, Kimberly Morgan, Rafael Morillas, Luc Perkins, Jan Pierskalla, Thomas Pluemper, Adam Przeworski, Philipp Rehm, Karen Remmer, Wolfgang Renzsch, Berthold Rittberger, Nicholas Sambanis, Ken Scheve, Tim Smeeding, David Stasavage, Dan Stegarescu, Ernesto Stein, John Stephens, James Struthers, William Sundstrom, Duane Swank, Kathy Thelen, Daniel Treisman, Guillermo Trejo, Pieter van Houten, the late Michael Wallerstein, Barry Weingast, and Chris Wleizan.

At Cambridge two anonymous readers provided excellent and detailed reviews. I am most grateful for the care they took and for requesting a number of modifications that have clearly improved the book. I am also indebted to Margaret Levi and Lew Bateman for their insights, guidance, and nurturing patience. Last but not least, my thanks to Caroline Lees and especially Heidi Young for making sure that the book is understandable to people other than myself.

On a more personal note, I wish to thank my parents. I owe much of my approach to politics to my father, a rare historian with the mindset of a social scientist, and much of my approach to the world to their exemplary fights against the struggles of life. Finally, my deepest thanks go to the true heroine in this story: my wife, Marta. Her unreserved support, patience, and spark as this project stole more and more time from her and our daughter (also Marta) made it all possible. The Martas are the only two people in this world that do not need to open this book to suffer from it. It is for their presence and for my far too long absences that I dedicate it to them.

1

Regions and Redistribution

Introduction and Overview

> Yes, when – not if – when we get a chance, the Federal Government will assume bold leadership in distress relief. For years Washington has alternated between putting its head in the sand and saying there is no large number of destitute people in our midst who need food and clothing, and then saying the States should take care of them, if there are. [...] I say that while the primary responsibility for relief rests with localities now, as ever, yet the Federal Government has always had a still and continuing responsibility for the broader public welfare. It will soon fulfill that responsibility.
>
> Franklin D. Roosevelt, Nomination Acceptance Speech, 1932

> Now, if Spain were an American state rather than a European country, things would not be so bad [...] Spain would be receiving a lot of automatic support in the crisis: Florida's housing boom has gone bust, but Washington keeps sending the Social Security and Medicare checks. [...]
>
> Now what? A breakup of the euro is very nearly unthinkable, as a sheer matter of practicality [...] So the only way out is forward: to make the euro work, Europe needs to move much further toward political union, so that European nations start to function more like American states.
>
> Paul Krugman, *New York Times*, February 14, 2010

Economic downturns challenge governments and institutions. The Great Depression dramatically exposed the limitations of earlier approaches to social and welfare issues in the United States. Roosevelt's 1932 pledge to strengthen the role of federal government was a response to the failing paradigm, then dominant in federations, that state and local governments should fend for themselves. In striking parallelism, today's financial crisis presents a similar challenge to the European Union (EU). Krugman's plea for a stronger Europe highlights the tensions of a monetary union without a coherent fiscal policy. The presidential candidate in the 1930s, like the economist today, recognized the importance of fiscal structures in political unions.[1] This book defines fiscal structures as a combination of two factors: the level of centralization of income taxes and transfers; and the extent of redistribution between regional governments.

Fiscal structures are crucial to economic welfare during periods of hardship. Anyone driving around America today is likely to encounter constant reminders of a failed economy. Empty buildings, formerly busy car dealerships that once harbored a frenzy of transactions, now stand neglected. When the illusion of endless credit vanished in 2007 many Americans faced unemployment. Yet they did so on a very unequal basis. According to data from the U.S. Bureau of Labor, a sales agent in Arkansas, facing dismissal in the last quarter of 2007, would have expected a level of benefits equal to 30% of his wage for an average of fourteen weeks. A similar worker in California would have been entitled to about one-half of his previous salary for twenty weeks. In Pennsylvania, he would have received 60% of his previous earnings for eighteen weeks.

Across America, workers doing similar jobs are treated differently. These inequalities are partly due to the constraints Roosevelt faced in fulfilling his nomination pledge. However, political unions elsewhere did not encounter the same obstacles. Whereas Roosevelt could only pass legislation to incentivize states to launch their own unemployment insurance systems, the government of Canada adopted a national system in 1941. Similarly, workers in Germany can expect the same amount of unemployment insurance benefits regardless of where they live. I consider these differences in the territorial organization of taxes and public insurance systems to be differences in the organization of interpersonal redistribution.[2]

Both national and subnational (state, local, or regional) governments face increasing economic pressures during periods of rising unemployment. Naturally it is in their interests to help ailing sectors in times of crisis where possible. In the car industry, for example, major companies routinely lobby national and regional governments in France, Germany, and Spain for help to keep struggling plants operational. Likewise, states in the United States can subsidize production via tax incentives, as many Southern states have done. This has facilitated the entry of European and Japanese car makers into the American market, and altered the geography of car production in the United States. Alternatively, subnational governments may choose to facilitate a shift in their economic structures and bid for new investments at the expense of declining sectors.

---

[1] I define political unions broadly as entities where citizens are ruled by national and regional governments within a common economic space. The concept includes confederations, such as the European Union, all of the world's democratic federations, as well as countries undergoing processes of political and fiscal decentralization, such as Spain.

[2] The underlying assumption here is that most redistribution occurs through programs that are meant to provide insurance over the life course (such as unemployment benefits and pensions) and that the tools used to finance them (direct and indirect income taxes, insurance contributions) are, in part and to varying degrees, progressive. To the extent that for large sectors of society the benefits received exceed the amount justified by earlier contributions, insurance programs are also redistributive programs (Atkinson 1995; Moene and Wallerstein 2001; Varian 1980).

Whichever approach they adopt, subnational governments need resources. To the extent that they differ in the size of their tax bases, subnational governments are not equally equipped to face the challenge of sustaining employment levels. Wealthier states will be more able to cope with economic uncertainties and to secure new employment opportunities for their residents. Because subnational governments need resources to develop their own policies, the interregional transfers of resources between rich and poor areas is a central aspect of the politics of redistribution in political unions. Some federations, such as Germany, have instruments aimed at reducing the resource gap between subnational governments, thereby enabling them to provide equally for their residents.[3] Other federations, such as the United States, lack such instruments and either preserve or exacerbate the disparities in fiscal capacity among the union members. I consider differences in the reallocation of fiscal resources between subnational governments differences in levels of interregional redistribution.

The organization of fiscal structures determines how much redistribution, both interpersonal and interregional, there is in political unions, ultimately shaping the scope and profile of inequality. The distinctive feature of political unions, as opposed to centralized democracies, lies in the trade-off between the pursuit of equality and the protection of political autonomy. The fundamental dilemma at the heart of modern, democratic, political unions is how to reconcile the two goals of equality and autonomy. In an era in which social insurance and redistribution occupy the lion's share of governments' budgets, the tension between equality and autonomy manifests itself in a conflict over the design of fiscal structures. About one-third of the world's population lives in democratic political unions today. Hence, a real understanding of inequality requires a better grasp of the politics behind public insurance systems (interpersonal redistribution) and interregional transfers in political unions.

These are timely and understudied issues. Renegotiation of the fiscal contract is a prominent item on the political agenda in Spain, Italy, Belgium, and even the United Kingdom (with the ongoing discussions about Scotland and Wales). Beyond Europe, democracies as diverse as Bolivia, Russia, and India face similar conflicts. The way unions solve them illustrates an important, and largely overlooked, aspect of the political economy of inequality and redistribution.

To fill this gap this book develops a new political geography of inequality. I ask why some political unions show less redistribution and more inequality than others. In seeking an answer to this question, I develop a new comparative analysis of the politics of fiscal structures in political unions. I argue that the observable variation in fiscal structures and outcomes across political unions results from the combined effect of economic geography and political representation. By economic geography I refer to cross-regional differences in terms of income inequality and economic specialization. By political representation

---

[3] Here I make no judgment about the efficiency effects associated with the way these resources are actually spent.

I refer to the set of institutions, most notably party systems, electoral rules, and legislatures, which translate political preferences into policy choices. The former explains the set of contending preferences regarding the organization of interpersonal redistribution and levels of interregional redistribution. The latter explains the transitions to actual institutional choices and outcomes. This book shows how the combination of economic geography and representation illuminates the long-term foundations of inequality in political unions, thereby accounting for the observable differences between them.

My analysis provides an alternative framework beyond the simplistic reasoning that has dominated the field so far. In the rest of this chapter, I present the puzzles motivating this study, outline its main arguments, discuss how the book contributes to existing literature, and finally, address the challenges involved in pursuing these arguments empirically and how the book's structure responds to them.

PUZZLES: THE DOMINANT VIEW AND ITS LIMITS

The notion that federalism, and more generally fragmented political structures, necessarily means less redistribution and more inequality runs deep in comparative politics and political economy. A quarter of a century ago, Wildavsky proclaimed that "there is no escape from a compelling truth: federalism and equality of result cannot coexist" (Wildavsky 1984: 68). In a similar spirit, the notion that "in the American context, Madison, not Marx, seems to be having the last word" (Lowi 1984: 379) remains a widely held belief.[4] After all, the United States remains the most unequal among advanced democratic societies, and many countries with even more uneven distributions of wealth, such as Brazil or Mexico, have federal forms of government.

An overview of the intellectual history of the organization of power within political unions reveals that Lowi and Wildavsky are in excellent company. Welfare economists see federalism and decentralization as particularly adequate to balance the need to attend to both heterogeneous local preferences and cross-jurisdictional externalities.[5] Local provision of public goods copes better with informational asymmetries, preference revelation, and issues of adequacy between policy instruments and people's needs, whereas a central ruler

---

[4] See, among others, Huber, Ragin and Stephens (1993); Peterson (1995); Peterson and Rom (1990); Prud'homme (1995) as well as recent insights from institutional economic history by Alston and Ferrie (1999). On the role of federalism in the development of the American welfare state, see also Alesina and Glaeser (2004). For arguments elaborating on the efficiency gains associated with federalism, see Buchanan (1950, 1995); Inman and Rubinfield (1997a, 1997b); Oates (1999); Prud'homme (1995); Qian and Weingast (1997); and Weingast (1995). For positive analyses of the impact of federalism on the economy, see Brennan and Buchanan (1980) Cai and Treisman (2005); Rodden (2006); Treisman (2004, 2007); and Wibbels (2005a).
[5] See Gramlich (1973, 1987); Musgrave (1997); Oates (1972); Oates and Brown (1987, 1991, 1999); Wildasin (1991).

is supposed to achieve more efficient outcomes in those policy realms affected by cross-jurisdictional externalities.

In contrast, public choice theorists advocate federalism because it provides an institutional arena for different levels of government to interact strategically to maximize political returns and economic rents. Deeply anchored in these tenets, the literature on market-preserving federalism provides a prominent example of this line of reasoning: federalism is market friendly because it restrains the predatory nature of the public sector through citizens' ability to punish incumbents either with their ballot or "with their feet."[6]

As federalism sets incumbents at different levels of government to compete for economic factors, the interplay between mobility and the behavior of subnational leaders becomes critical. Welfare economists and public choice theorists see in the mobility of economic factors an important engine behind the alleged benefits of federalism, though again, from rather different angles. For welfare economists, as illustrated by the seminal work by Tiebout (1956), the mobility of citizens and capital is for the most part a mechanism of preference revelation for incumbents who are assumed to be driven only by aggregate welfare considerations.[7]

For public choice theorists, both the ability of productive factors to exit and the risk of a welfare magnet effect work to constrain Leviathan's economic appetite. In sum, the interplay between federalism and factor mobility promotes economic efficiency because the reduction in the size of government is essentially reflected in lower levels of distortionary redistribution. The key implication of these analyses is that the informational and efficiency advantages of federal structures come at the expense of the social union. More inequality becomes, yet again, the price tag of better markets.[8]

In addition to this largely normative literature, the conventional view also draws on empirical work on the origins and evolution of the welfare state as well as on the more recent increase in attention to the institutional foundations of inequality (Alesina and Glaeser 2004; Persson and Tabellini 2003). The constraints on redistribution here do not come just from the expected behavior of economic factors, but from the political system itself. Federalism institutionalizes a system of veto points that enables defenders of specific territorial interests to object to, and eventually block, nationwide redistributive

---

[6] Buchanan (1950, 1995: 19–27); Buchanan and Wagner (1970); Inman and Rubinfield (1997: 73–105); Weingast, Montinola and Qian (1995); Qian and Weingast (1997: 83–92); Weingast (1993: 286–311; 1995: 1–31).

[7] Provided that the demand for local public services is income elastic, that these services are financed by income taxes (Oates 1972, 1991), and that there is perfect mobility, Tiebout's model predicts that communities become homogeneous in income and heterogeneous in capacities. For a systematic discussion of the usefulness and analytical limitations of Tiebout's work, see Bewley (1981: 713–740); Panizza (1999: 97–139); Rose-Ackermann (1983: 55–85); Stiglitz (1983: 17–55).

[8] For discussions on the relationship between mobility and redistribution, see Crémer et al. (1996) and Epple and Romer (1991).

endeavors. As such, fragmented political structures crystallize multidimensionality, thereby priming second dimensions (such as identity, territory, or race) and limiting the feasibility of large redistributive coalitions (Iversen 2006).[9] A similar logic guides many analyses of welfare policy reform in North American federations, where scholars tend to interpret proposals in favor of decentralization as masked efforts to curtail the welfare state.[10]

More recently, a third stream of research has come to confirm the association between inequality and decentralized political institutions, though this time reversing the direction of causality. Starting with the seminal work by Bolton and Roland (1997), a number of contributions have emphasized the shape and territorial specificities of income distribution as a key determinant of political integration and constitutional choices in federations (Alesina and Spolaore 2003; Beramendi 2007; Sambanis and Milanovic 2009; Wibbels 2005b). The argument goes as follows: federalism and decentralization are associated with particular distributive outcomes not because they exogenously generate them[11], but because distributional concerns play a fundamental role in shaping the organization of fiscal structures in political unions.[12]

There is no doubt that these lines of research have provided important insights on both the economics and the politics of decentralization. Moreover, there is much to like about the elegance and parsimony of these approaches to the association between federalism, decentralization, and inequality. However, they are unable to account for the observable variation in fiscal structures across political unions. Figure 1.1 provides an overview of the relationship between fiscal structures and inequality in political unions. In the left panel, the x axis ranks countries according to their level of decentralization of interpersonal redistribution, and the y axis ranks countries according to their level of disposable household income inequality (Gini coefficients).[13] In turn, the

---

[9] For studies on the United States, see; Amenta and Carruthers (1988: 661–678); Pierson (1995: 449–478); Quadagno (1994); Skocpol (1992); and Skocpol and Orloff (1984: 726–750) as well as the recent insights from institutional economic history by Alston and Ferrie (1999: 49–74, 118–152). For a recent formalization on the determinants of the welfare state in the United States see Alesina, Glaeser, and Sacerdote (2001); and Alesina and Glaeser (2004). For similar, albeit older, insights see Lowi (1984: 37–55). For quantitative cross-national comparisons, see, among others, Hicks and Kenworthy (1998: 1631–1673); Hicks and Swank (1992: 658–674); Huber, Ragin and Stephens (1993); and Huber and Stephens (2001).

[10] This claim builds upon devolution to the provinces/states in Canada and the United States. On the former, see Banting (1987, 1992: 149–170, 1995); Courchene (1993: 83–135; 1994); and Kenneth (1998). On the latter, see Peterson (1995); Peterson, Rom and Scheve (1998); and Volden (1997: 65–97).

[11] As an example, see the logic underlying the conclusions Huber, Ragin and Stephens (1993: 711–750); and Huber and Stephens (2001) draw from their index of constitutional structure.

[12] This literature is part of a broader trend that places tensions associated with the distribution of income as major determinants of institutional choices such as the nature of the political regime (Acemoglu and Robinson 2006; Boix 2003), or the design of electoral rules (Cusack, Iversen and Soskice 2007; Rogowski and MacRae 2008; Tichi and Vindigni 2003).

[13] Household income per equivalent adult as defined by the Standardized Income Distribution Database (Babones 2008) and the Luxembourg Income Study.

Regions and Redistribution: Introduction 7

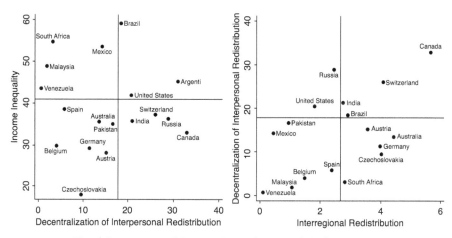

FIGURE 1.1. Fiscal Structures and Income Inequality in Political Unions

right panel ranks countries along the two dimensions of fiscal structures identified previously, namely, interpersonal and interregional redistribution.[14] Thus, the y axis ranks countries along the same indicator of decentralization of interpersonal redistribution (x axis in the previous panel), and the x axis now ranks unions according to their level of interregional redistribution.

Two important points follow from the left panel in Figure 1.1. First, the United States, the case on which the conventional view is largely based, is indeed the most prominent example of a positive association between fiscal decentralization and income inequality. Yet it clearly seems to be more the exception than the rule, particularly among advanced industrial political unions. Canada, Belgium, Germany, Austria, and Spain offer a wide range of variation in both distributive outcomes and levels of decentralization of interpersonal redistribution.[15] Moreover, the variation becomes even larger if developing federations are considered.

This diversity of outcomes, largely at odds with the conventional view, motivates the leading question in this study: why is it that some political unions show less redistribution and more inequality than others? The key, I argue, lies in the organization of their fiscal structures. A comparison between the two panels in Figure 1.1 illustrates this point. The top left quadrant of the left panel includes a group of countries (Venezuela, Malaysia, South Africa, Mexico, and Brazil) with exceedingly high levels of inequality and very little decentralization of interpersonal redistribution. Interestingly, this subgroup also shows very low levels of interregional redistribution as reflected by their concentration in the bottom left quadrant of the right panel.

---

[14] Interregional distribution is defined as transfers to other levels of government as a percentage of GDP. For additional details on sources, see Appendix D.
[15] See also Lindert (2004); Linz and Stepan (2000); Obinger, Leibfried and Castles (2005).

Unsurprisingly, this subgroup of countries shares one other feature – the underdevelopment of effective social and public insurance policies at the national level (Beramendi and Diaz-Cayeros 2008; Wibbels 2006). Variation increases as we move beyond this quadrant. Remarkably, even in the noisy context of these bivariate relationships, a discernable pattern emerges. The incidence of inequality appears to be larger in those unions with high levels of decentralization of interpersonal redistribution and low levels of interregional redistribution.

In contrast, those unions able to combine relatively decentralized systems of interpersonal redistribution with significant efforts to redistribute resources across territories, such as Canada, manage to avoid the *distributive curse* associated with the conventional view. Put simply, the organization of fiscal institutions within political unions dictates how egalitarian these are. Logically, then, any solution to the puzzle of diversity of outcomes lies in achieving a better understanding of the origins and evolution of fiscal structures themselves.

A careful consideration of several cases helps substantiate this claim. I shall return to Roosevelt for a moment. Following the Great Depression, distributive tensions among states in the United States and among provinces in Canada became starker, triggering a myriad of competing proposals for institutional adjustment on both sides of the frontier. Interestingly enough, similar regional patterns of inequality yielded very different responses in the two North American federations. While Canada developed a centralized system of unemployment insurance in 1941, the U.S. Social Security Act (1935) included provisions leaving the ultimate design and implementation of unemployment insurance in the hands of the states.[16] This diversity of responses is puzzling because the two unions confronted the Depression from very similar positions. During the first decades of the century, the United States and Canada were alike in their approach to the issue of unemployment. In fact, until the Depression their systems of social protection were equally fragmented, both politically and organizationally. In addition, both systems were exposed to a similar set of external influences. Hence the question: why did the paths of these two rather similar systems diverge during the late 1930s and early 40s? Moreover, the case of the United States is particularly interesting because it shows relatively poorer regions actively resisting and ultimately blocking a centralized system that would have generated significant transfers toward them. This case, and others such as present-day Scotland, present the puzzle of low income regions opposing integration despite significant potential transfers. In turn, the

---

[16] Though eventually transformed into a hybrid regime (Lieberman 1998; Mettler 2002), the U.S. system remained one in which states can differ in terms of prerequisites, generosity, and duration of unemployment benefits. Throughout most of the twentieth century this has been one of the most prominent *small differences that matter* to explain why distributive outcomes differed between the two North American federations (Banting 1987, 2005; Card and Freeman 1993).

Canadian response presents the puzzle of rich regions endorsing a centralized fiscal structure despite significant income losses.

The contrasting dynamics in the United States and Canada are echoed more recently in the EU, Spain, and Germany. As the European Economic Community evolved from an entity built primarily around geopolitical considerations toward a progressively integrated market, the question of whether fiscal integration ought to parallel monetary integration has gained salience. A large empirical literature substantiates Krugman's concerns about the unbalanced nature of policy integration in the EU (Scharpf 1998). Regarding fiscal and social policy, the EU remains pretty much a "hollow center" (Pierson and Leibfried 1995; Streeck 1995). The European center engages only in modest attempts to ameliorate inequality among European citizens and only moderately constrains interregional differences in terms of fiscal resources. As a result, the EU is today a very inegalitarian union. Why?

Germany provides important counterexamples to the dynamics in the EU in particular, and the conventional view more generally. Germany is the most obvious example of a large and highly redistributive welfare state and large levels of interregional redistribution being perfectly compatible with federalism and decentralization (Manow 2005). Indeed, Germany's political evolution after Reunification shows a federation incorporating five new poorer *länder* and twenty million new citizens. The system did not change, despite a massive alteration in the geography of income and labor markets. It also assimilated the new members in a short period of time, triggering an unprecedented redistributive effort from the West to the East. The German experience is puzzling for its institutional stability in light of major structural change, and for the fact that rich regions endorsed an assimilation strategy involving large levels of redistribution toward poorer members.

Finally, the Spanish experience is probably the one most clearly at odds with the predictions of the consensus view. Over the last two decades of the twentieth century the Spanish welfare state has expanded at the same time that the state structure has undergone a far-reaching process of political decentralization (Espina 2007; Gallego, Goma and Subirats 2003). While virtually every important public policy in Spain, including health, education, infrastructure development, policing, and industrial development is now decentralized, the bulk of social security transfers expands and remains in the hands of the central government (Subirats and Gallego 2002). If distributive tensions associated with the geography of inequality are to bring about more decentralized fiscal structures, as the literature on endogenous institutions contends, what explains the remarkable levels of resilience of Spain's central government against the notion of engaging a territorial partition of the welfare state? Why has fiscal decentralization in Spain taken the form of reticent partial concessions on the revenue side and virtually no concessions on the expenditure side (Espina 2007; León 2007; Moreno and McEwen 2005)?

More broadly, why does European inequality map neatly onto anemic social effort at the EU level, while geographic distribution of inequality seems weakly linked to fiscal dynamics in Spain and Germany?

OVERVIEW OF THE ARGUMENT

As a strategy to solve these puzzles, this book analyzes the origins and evolution of fiscal structures in political unions. Political unions organize their fiscal systems according to one of three designs: a *centralized* design (C) in which the national government controls income taxes and transfers as well as the allocation of resources across regions; a *decentralized* design (D) in which regions control income transfers and taxes and there is very little redistribution between regions; and, finally, a hybrid design (H), in which a partially decentralized system of interpersonal redistribution coexists with significant levels of interregional redistribution. These are obviously ideal types in a continuum in which actual unions fall in different positions. The situation in Spain in the aftermath of its democratic transition exemplifies a political union with a centralized fiscal structure (C). The European Union is a case of a very decentralized fiscal structure (D). Finally, Germany's fiscal structure during the post-war period offers an example of a hybrid regime (H).

In explaining variation among these designs, I build on the premise that electoral concerns drive the choice of fiscal structures (O'Neill 2005). An important part of gaining and retaining office lies in acquiring a position to forge successful electoral coalitions, an endeavor for which fiscal redistributive policies constitute a powerful tool. Thus, political elites will support the specific fiscal structure that best serves their electoral interest. This book highlights two factors shaping politicians' choices between the three types: the combined effect of economic geography and the organization of political representation on the one hand, and the role of mobility as a source of cross-regional economic externalities on the other. These factors, I argue, are the mechanisms driving the political geography of inequality. I outline the argument in four steps.

Decentralizing fiscal structures matters for inequality because it activates the underlying economic geography of the union.

The distributive consequences of allowing subnational governments to control taxes and transfers are a function of the preexisting levels of inequality between and within regions. This being the case, it is reasonable to assume that political actors are aware of the structure of inequality within the different territories and their relative position within it, from which they derive an expectation about the distributive implications associated with any alternative institutional design. Put simply, actors deciding on the design of fiscal structures are at the same time making a choice regarding income redistribution. By implication, the prospect of any institutional change concerning the territorial allocation of the powers to tax and transfer triggers a distributive conflict both between and within units. This conflict unfolds along two dimensions: income differences among individuals within regions, and income differences between regions.

The economic geography of the union shapes actors' preferences about the organization of redistribution in political unions.

In the context of the two-dimensional space defined by income and regions, this book establishes that economic geography works through three mechanisms that jointly shape actors' preferences. These are: the geography of income, the geography of economic specialization, and the scope of cross-regional externalities (i.e., individual geographical mobility).

As I show in detail in the next chapter, the distribution of income in any political union breaks into four groups: rich citizens in rich regions, poor citizens in rich regions, rich citizens in poor regions, and poor citizens in poor regions. These groups' preferences, I argue, reflect the underlying geography of inequality. Provided that the level of inequality within regions is lower than that of the union, wealthy citizens in richer regions have no incentive to agree to a fiscal structure that transfers resources to other areas of the country. Thus, they have much to fear from either a centralized system of interpersonal redistribution or large levels of interregional redistribution.

Poor citizens in poor regions by contrast are the natural beneficiaries of integrated fiscal structures. They support centralized fiscal structures that transfer rents directly to them, paid for by wealthier citizens in other regions. However, poor citizens in rich regions do not have the same incentives. They are better off pursuing a decentralized system of interpersonal redistribution in which they are the beneficiaries of fiscal transfers occurring only within their region than engaging in class solidarity with the rest of the union. Simply put, region trumps class for this subgroup of citizens.

The same principle applies to the rich citizens of poor regions. While they might rather not directly finance a national system of public insurance, they have incentives to extract as many resources as possible from their counterparts from other regions. As a result, they support a decentralized fiscal structure with significant levels of interregional redistribution, additional resources that will benefit the local economy and ease their own fiscal burden.

In sum, when income and regional ascriptions overlap, actors' preferences are defined by their individual redistributive motives. In contrast, in the presence of a mismatch between individual and regional ascriptions, the latter dominate the former. This yields a rather intuitive scenario in which both rich and poor regions within the union aim to maximize their political autonomy and the amount of resources at their disposal.

On the basis of this template, I take one step further to try to understand the set of circumstances under which regions behave counterintuitively. I identify the conditions under which poor regions sacrifice income to preserve autonomy and rich regions willingly engage in redistribution of resources toward other members of the union. In doing so, the book pays close attention to both the possibility of alternative geographies of income, and, more importantly, to the geography of risk within the union. I argue that the patterns of economic specialization (Krugman 1991) determine the geography of labor market risk in the union, thereby introducing a new set of motives behind the selection of public insurance systems and fiscal structures (Mares 2003; Moene and Wallerstein 2001; Varian 1980).

Regionally specialized economies may be harmed by nationally uniform public insurance systems. Centralization in the presence of highly specialized regional economies creates what Alesina and Perotti (1998) called "political risks," that is, the risk of a functional mismatch between the needs of the local economy and the design of public insurance.

This logic helps explain why sometimes poor regions opt for less fiscal integration. They face a trade-off between the interregional income transfers inherent to centralization and their capacity to maintain their preferred policy choice in order to cope with their own specific labor market risks. Indeed, sufficiently high levels of specialization may shape the preferences of relevant actors even up to the point of overcoming the procentralization incentives of lower income regions. As a result, elites in a specialized poor region may choose to stay autonomous to protect the region's capacity to design fiscal policy as they see fit (Beramendi 2007). A prominent example of this counterintuitive behavior is provided by the southern American states during the debates over the institutional design of the Social Security Act (1935), analyzed in detail in Chapter 5.

More generally, the book shows that as the geographies of income and risk grow apart, so do preferences for the design of insurance systems, thereby nurturing the political demand for more fragmented fiscal structures. This diversity of preferences about the design of interpersonal redistribution, in turn, exacerbates the distributive conflict over resources between regions. How these conflicts resolve depends to a large extent on two factors: the organization of political representation and the level of labor mobility across regions.

Political representation conditions the way in which contending preferences translate into the actual organization of fiscal structures.

Representation matters because it determines the balance of power between the regional and national elites, thus meditating distributive disagreements among them.[17] To illuminate this process, I introduce a distinction between systems of representation that understand conflicts over the nature of fiscal structures as an affair between units and systems of representation that see redistribution as a conflict among individuals across regions. I refer to the former as centrifugal representation and to the latter as centripetal representation. In empirical terms, a centrifugal system of representation is the joint outcome of highly malapportioned legislative chambers, relatively weak national elections, and, as a consequence, highly fragmented party organizations with a weak national leadership. In turn, lower malapportionment and relatively stronger national

---

[17] Cox (1990, 1997); Iversen and Soskice (2006); Rodden (2008).

party organizations are correlates of centripetal representation.[18] Contingent on the system of representation, a similar set of distributive tensions associated with economic geography lead to different fiscal structures, ultimately explaining the variation in distributive outcomes across unions.

This interaction between economic geography and political representation works as follows. Under centrifugal representation there is little or no salience of national elections and virtually no cost for regional elites to challenge the national party. Local leaders focus, almost exclusively, on the mandates of their respective principals. The protection of unit-specific interests dominates the political agenda. Politics becomes a conflict about the distribution of resources among jurisdictions, and territorial interests (preferences over interregional redistribution) outweigh class interests (preferences over the centralization of interpersonal redistribution).

Unsurprisingly, these political and institutional circumstances facilitate the direct impact of unequal economic conditions on the politics of institutional choice. A heterogeneous economic geography translates into very decentralized fiscal structures with a very narrow window for redistributive efforts and inequality reproduces itself by contributing to the selection of institutional arrangements that, in turn, will protect existing territorial inequalities. Ultimately, under centrifugal representation, economic geography limits the feasibility of radical alterations of the interpersonal distribution of income via public policy, thus fostering an observable association between decentralized political structures and inegalitarian distributive outcomes. In addition to facilitating the decentralization of interpersonal redistribution, centrifugal representation, for instance in the form of a malapportioned senate, also fosters the capacity to extract interregional transfers by local strongholds. As we shall see in Chapter 4, the very lack of a proper set of redistributive policies in the EU illustrates this dynamics.

Things work differently under centripetal representation. National party elites are stronger and respond to pivotal groups of voters that cut across regional boundaries. Accordingly, the main lines of political competition tend to follow income groups as opposed to regions. When centripetal representation is at its highest, outcomes depend much less on the preferences of regions and much more on how parties target population subgroups that cut across regional boundaries. If representation operates under plurality in a common national circumscription, parties will target the union's median voter. If representation works to preserve proportionality, national elites will devise a combination of interpersonal and interregional redistribution as close as possible to the interests of the median legislature of the winning coalition (Austen-Smith and Banks 1988). This combination will generate relatively large levels of overall redistribution within the union, but this will result mostly from the territorial incidence of centralized policies of interpersonal redistribution, and less from

---

[18] Gibson (2004); Rodden (2006); Wibbels (2005a).

specific transfers of resources from wealthier to poorer regional governments (interregional redistribution).[19]

In either case, the disaggregating push of an uneven geography of inequality is contained by a set of political incentives to either build or sustain a proredistributive coalition that cuts across territorial boundaries. As a result, this book argues, centripetal representation limits the extent to which an uneven economic geography undermines redistributive efforts and reproduces itself over time.

> Given some level of decentralization of interpersonal redistribution, interregional labor mobility conditions regional preferences for interregional redistribution; high levels of mobility create incentives for wealthier regions to accept larger interregional transfers toward poorer areas.

This book contends that interregional mobility is a key factor in the process of selection of fiscal structures. The idea of a *race to the bottom* constraining the growth of government is a popular image that presents incumbents as individuals subject to the constraints imposed by highly mobile economic factors. Yet mobility is not an option for everyone. Highly specialized workers find it hard to move outside their industries. Because industries tend to be clustered geographically, labor mobility is inversely related to asset specificity and economic specialization (Boix 2003; Krugman 1991; Lucas 1990). In contrast, unskilled workers and those citizens permanently dependent on public transfers, such as low- to middle-income pensioners, are more likely to move in response to welfare and income differences between territories.[20] High levels of mobility, in particular of workers and long-term dependents, do not operate as an external constraint on the behavior of regional and federal incumbents. Instead, high levels of mobility work as a multiplier of social risks across regions, thereby creating political incentives to increase levels of redistribution between regions.

Specifically, I posit (and show empirically) that the threat of a large inflow of dependents can cause rich regions, rather counterintuitively, to accept more interregional redistribution. This is particularly the case when richer regions are also specialized, and therefore perceive mobility as an undesirable shock

---

[19] As we shall see in the case of Germany, it may be the case that the pivotal group of voters is itself concentrated in specific regions (the East). Under these circumstances the union will redistribute resources to its poorer members in two ways: indirectly, by virtue of the geographical concentration of beneficiaries of interpersonal redistribution, and directly, via interregional transfers.

[20] Under certain circumstances this may trigger a race to the bottom. For instance, Rom, Peterson, and Scheve (1996) find evidence of such processes in the United States during 1976–1994 concerning Aid to Families with Dependent Children (AFDC). In other policies, however, the race turns toward the *top*: when the region of Catalonia (Spain) decided to pass a supplement to the pensions of those residents in Catalonia who had not previously contributed to social security, the national government matched the increase nationwide shortly thereafter (Arriba 1999). Clearly, with selective patterns of mobility, the magnitude and direction of whatever race states enter becomes a policy-specific, group-specific phenomenon (Volden 2004, 2005).

against which interregional redistribution provides insurance. In this sense, mobility operates both as a mechanism muting the decentralizing effects of large interregional income and labor market disparities and as an engine behind the support for more redistribution between territories.

To summarize, this book identifies the interaction between economic geography and representation and the level of cross-regional mobility as the two mechanisms driving the political geography of inequality. In the next section I discuss the main difficulties ahead in identifying their effects, theoretically and empirically.

CHALLENGES AND THE ROAD AHEAD

The relationship between fiscal structures and economic geography is a long-term, dynamic one in which feedback processes play an important role. By feedback I mean a process by which institutions alter their environment in ways that either contribute to their stability or facilitate change (Greif and Laitin 2004; Pierson 2004; Thelen 2004). Over time, the very distributive consequences of fiscal arrangements nurture contentions about their stability and condition their institutional environment.[21]

This raises a critical issue in this study: fiscal structures, political representation, and inequality are jointly endogenous in the long run. As detected by three recent reviews of the field (Beramendi 2007b; Rodden 2006; Wibbels 2006b), issues of reverse causality and selection have become more and more prominent as the literature has managed to find causal arrows running in all possible directions. That is, fiscal structures, political representation (or dimensions thereof), and inequality appear as both causes and effects at different stages of history. This triggers a number of challenges concerning the theoretical and empirical identification of the relationship between fiscal structures and their economic and political determinants. If fiscal structures are themselves endogenous with respect to preexisting distributions of income, do they really have causal effects of their own, or do they operate as mechanisms that merely reproduce preexisting economic conditions? In what sense are political representation or mobility exogenous? In other words, how can one differentiate empirically the conditions under which institutions are created from the institutional effects themselves?

A tempting response is to argue, in line with venerable traditions in classical political economy, that insofar as institutions are endogenous, their effects are self-selected and therefore essentially superfluous. If institutions just reproduce the underlying tastes of the relevant political coalition, they do not really matter per se. Through a different route, we would revisit the early, and rather

---

[21] As elaborated in detailed in Chapter 3, a growing body of literature suggests that more decentralized fiscal structures lead to: demands for changes in electoral rules, the increase of territorial chambers' power, and more decentralized political parties (Amat, Jurado and Leon 2010; Beramendi and Maiz 2004; Brancatti 2009; Chhibber and Kollman 2004).

disconcerting, Rikerian assessment of the significance of federalism (Riker 1964). Reasoning along this path one quickly reduces the relationship between institutions and economic outcomes to one in which the latter determine the former, rendering politics irrelevant.[22] This book challenges this view.

Arguably, the very reason why institutions are contested, in this case, the reason why political actors engage in conflict about fiscal structures, is that they have effects on their political and economic environment. In other words, the motivations and preferences of the actors involved in the process of institutional choice derive from the expected impact of institutions, that is, from counterfactual exercises about what the institutional effects will be. Political contentions over fiscal structures occur because they have distributive implications that cumulate over time.

These implications may be consistent with previous expectations, in which case institutions become a mechanism by which a particular dimension of reality becomes self-perpetuating. Alternatively, institutions may work in directions unexpected and/or unintended by their designers, in which case institutions become a factor of change. From the fact that the actual effects of any given institution are consistent with what the designer anticipated it does not follow logically that that institution has no impact. Symmetrically, from the fact that a particular institution has unintended effects it does not follow that this institution is exogenous. It simply means that its designers had the "wrong" expectations about (or could not foresee) its institutional effects. Whether designers have the right expectations is a different issue from the existence and influence of the expectations themselves.

On these premises, I argue that the *neo-Rikerian* claim that endogenous institutions necessarily lack an impact of their own is misleading because it conflates the methodological difficulties of distinguishing the causal effects of institutions with an alleged theoretical impossibility for these effects to exist. It is precisely to avoid this confusion that we need to "sort out institutional effects from the conditions under which they function" (Przeworski 2004).[23] With this goal in mind, this book combines attention to the long-term dynamics of the relationship between fiscal structures and economic geography with the identification of the marginal effects of economic geography, mobility, and representation posited in the argument. This agenda imposes a number of conditions, both theoretical and empirical. Theoretically, it requires a model in which the different elements of the argument and their roles in the political process of adopting different fiscal structures are clearly identified. Critically, this implies treating fiscal structures and representation as two different and

---

[22] For a related discussion on the institutional determinants of economic developments, see Acemoglu, Johnson and Robinson (2002); and Przeworski (2004, 2004b, 2004c).
[23] As Przeworski himself reminds us (2007a), causality refers to the identification of the mechanisms behind the observed impact of a particular factor or institution on the basis of 1) a theoretical argument and, ideally, 2) a comparison between the observable world and a counterfactual scenario in which all other elements but the factor of interest remain unchanged (Fearon 1991).

separable aspects of political unions, even though they partially coevolve over time. Empirically, the goal of evaluating the causal role of economic geography, mobility, and representation imposes a number of constraints on the selection of cases.

First, in gaining historical perspective and leverage over causality, it is essential to stop somewhere. Hence, this book is not concerned with the formation of unions. While the role of economic geography in the formation of unions is a fascinating issue (Beramendi and Wibbels 2010), it falls outside the empirical realm of this study. This book focuses on unions whose existence predates the conflict over fiscal structures.

Second, there needs to be variation in the organization of political representation. To evaluate the process by which changes in economic geography impact fiscal structures over time under different systems of representation, it is essential to have cases with different status quo (centrifugal versus centripetal). This facilitates the study of how status quo in terms of representation mediates the effects of a changing economic geography. In addition, it also facilitates the analysis of how deviations over time with respect to the status quo in terms of representation affect the evolution of fiscal structures. Finally, the identification of marginal effects requires stricter conditions, namely, a quasi-experimental setting in which an exogenous change in the variable of interest (say, the geography of income or mobility) occurs when other elements of the analysis (for example, political representation) can credibly be considered given.

The implementation of these criteria, which I discuss in detail in Chapter 3, yields five cases of interest: the European Union, the United States, Canada, Germany, and Spain. The investigation of these cases, combined with a set of cross-national statistical analyses, constitute the empirical core of the book. I close this section by outlining how they speak to each of the elements of the argument: the impact of economic geography on preferences for fiscal structures, the role of mobility in shaping interpersonal and interregional redistribution in political unions, and finally, how political representation mediates the transition from preferences to outcomes.

Economic Geography and Preferences

To establish the effect of the geography of income and economic specialization on preferences for fiscal structures this book combines several approaches. Whenever possible, alas only in the case of the EU, I resort to statistical analyses. The goal is to provide sound evidence that macrolevel indicators of crossregional differences in terms of income and specialization do predict individual preferences for fiscal structures. In the case of the EU, I also explore quantitatively the impact of economic geography on the preferences of, on the one hand, political parties and trade unions, and on the other government executives. This latter analysis focuses on countries' positions during the Constitutional Convention. It produces direct quantitative evidence for the first element of the argument. And it is then complemented with a more historical, qualitative approach regarding the preferences of key players during specific historical experiences: the response of the two North American federations to the Great Depression, the fiscal response to Reunification in Germany, and the more recent attempts to decentralize the organization and provision of social security in Spain.

Mobility and Fiscal Structures

The five cases studies in this book offer good leverage to evaluate the empirical plausibility of the argument's predictions. Recall that depending on its level and composition, mobility affects the design of fiscal structures in two ways. First, it operates as a risk multiplier across regions, therefore exposing all regions equally to people's demand for redistribution, and reducing the incentives to sustain separate systems of interpersonal redistribution. Second, precisely for this reason, in unions with rich and specialized local economies, mobility creates incentives to increase interregional redistribution. The idea is to use the latter to limit mobility and preserve the workings of local economies.

This book addresses the role of interregional labor mobility in several ways. The comparison between the EU and Germany offers preliminary evidence on the relationship between the scope of mobility and the scope of redistribution. This comparison is further substantiated with a quantitative analysis of the impact of mobility on interregional redistribution. In turn, I pursue the identification of the marginal effects of mobility through two natural experiments[24]: a comparison of the responses of Canada and the United States to the Great Depression, and an analysis of the way Germany responded to the fiscal challenge of Reunification. The former illuminates the importance of mobility on decisions about the centralization of interpersonal redistribution. The latter illuminates the role of mobility in shaping rich regions' incentives to engage in cross-regional redistribution. As I argue in detail in Chapter 3, both events were the result of processes unrelated to preexisting fiscal structures and resulted in differential patterns of mobility across the three unions. Together these analyses shed considerable light on the role of mobility in shaping fiscal structures across political unions.

From Preferences to Outcomes: The Mediating Role of Political Representation

In addressing the transition from preferences to outcomes, this book takes three steps. First, the comprehensive overview of fiscal structures in the EU and

---

[24] Throughout this book I use the term natural experiment loosely, referring to situations in which an exogenous phenomenon results in the allocation of two cases that receive a differential treatment of an independent variable of interest and are otherwise very similar. The idea is to exploit history to locate case comparisons "as if" they were randomly assigned to different treatments (Dunning 2008).

Spain targets the interplay over time between economic geography and fiscal structures in two unions with opposite status quo in terms of political representation. With the analysis of the EU the book explores the fate of demands to centralize fiscal policy and increase interregional redistribution in a very centrifugal political system. In turn, the Spanish experience from 1978 onward allows us to trace the fate of growing demands for more decentralized fiscal structures and less interregional redistribution in a union with a much more centripetal system of representation. These two cases elucidate the complexity of the relationship between fiscal structures, political representation, and inequality over time. However, with this strength also comes a weakness: it is hard to identify natural experiments for the purpose of establishing causal effects.

Natural experiments require, among other things, that changes in patterns of economic geography must by and large respond to exogenous factors, and that the system of representation at the time the exogenous transformation of economic geography occurs must be credibly taken *as given*. In other words, in the short run, representation itself is not part of the renegotiation of the fiscal contract. Again, the comparative analysis of the Canadian and U.S. responses to the Depression and the analysis of Germany's fiscal structure before and after Reunification, provide two natural experiments to assess the causal mechanisms involved in the transition from preferences to outcomes.

As I elaborate in detail in Chapter 3, both the Depression and Reunification, and their implications for economic geography, are exogenous, and in neither case did the system of representation itself become the object of political contention during the subsequent period. In combination, these experiences help explore the effect of distributive tensions associated with economic geography at different points of the continuum between centrifugal and centripetal representation. Finally, a set of cross-sectional statistical analyses explores whether the conditional relationship between economic geography and political representation holds for a larger number of political unions.

THE BOOK'S CONTRIBUTIONS

The intellectual context of this book is best delineated with reference to two literatures, both of which have gained prominence in political economy research in the last two decades: the first concerns redistribution (Beramendi and Anderson 2008; Iversen 2005; Lindert 2004)[25]; the second concerns the origin of institutions (Acemoglu and Robinson 2006; Boix 2003; Bolton and Roland 1997). The former has highlighted institutions such as electoral systems or the contrast between presidential and parliamentary regimes as key factors accounting for the variation in public good provision and redistributive outcomes. The latter has developed an understanding of those same institutions, including democracy itself, as the outcome of distributive conflicts. The former treats institutions as exogenous; the latter, as endogenous. As discussed earlier,

---

[25] For a more detailed review of the literature, see Iversen (2006).

in isolation, either approach fails to account for the observable patterns of variation in this relationship. There is an obvious, yet largely unresolved, tension between theorizing institutions as a cause of redistribution and inequality, and theorizing redistributive conflicts as the driver behind the selection of institutions themselves. This tension lies at the heart of the relationship between political institutions and social outcomes. Focusing on the specific issue of redistribution in political unions, this book's contributions bridge these two streams of work, ultimately yielding a better understanding of the institutional underpinnings of redistribution and inequality. In what follows I outline the book's main contributions.

The book brings to the fore the role of economic geography and territorial politics in shaping public insurance systems and distributive outcomes. For a long time the median voter theory of redistribution (Meltzer and Richard 1981) dominated the field. Though elegant and simple, the median voter approach proved too straight a jacket to understand empirical patterns of public insurance systems and redistribution. As a result, the field set out to address its limitations by focusing on how partisanship and institutions shape public insurance systems (Iversen 2006). The dominant assumption throughout though is that economies and polities are both monolithic entities: one economy, one government, one nation. This does not reflect a commitment to ignore reality but a pressing need to simplify dimensions other than those of theoretical interest. The necessary consequence, however, is the underdevelopment of theoretical and empirical work on the role of economic geography and territorial politics in the politics of redistribution.[26] By developing a theory of how economic geography, political representation, and mobility interact to shape fiscal structures and distributive outcomes in political unions this book contributes to fill this gap.

In addition, such a theory helps bring politics into the literature on endogenous fiscal institutions. Largely in the hand of economists so far, earlier models of endogenous fiscal institutions are devoid of politics. With very few exceptions (O'Neill 2005, Weingast 2006), politics either disappears in the idyllic world of welfare economics or falls, again, victim of the constraining charm of the median voter. Unsurprisingly, existing accounts consistently overlook one crucial step, namely, the interplay between the distribution of preferences that emerges from economic geography and the existing set of rules and procedures governing the relations between different levels of government. For instance, Bolton and Roland's (1997) account of the breakup of nations, is far too anchored in the median voter theorem to incorporate the impact of the institutional complexities of different political unions. Political representation as a mechanism of aggregation of preferences is simply assumed away. By exploring

---

[26] Useful empirical efforts against this trend are Ferrera's (2005) study of the role of European Integration as a source of change in European social systems and Obinger, Leibfried and Castles' (2005) collection of case studies of the interplay between federalism and social policy.

the way representation shapes incumbents' strategic interests, this book puts the focus on a largely overlooked aspect of the politics of fiscal institutions.

I explain the relationship among political representation, fiscal structures, and inequality as the result of long-term historical processes rather than as the exogenous effect of a set of intrinsically inegalitarian institutions. I show that the association between federalism, decentralization, and inequality, far from being a historical imperative, reflects a particular combination of socioeconomic and institutional variables. In doing so, I identify the specific societal and institutional circumstances under which federalism and decentralization can coexist with egalitarian redistribution. And thus, I challenge both the notion that decentralized political structures are necessarily inegalitarian institutions and the reductionist view that fiscal institutions simply follow directly from income differences between regions.

The book also speaks to the issue of institutional stability in federations. The interplay between economic geography and representation emerges as an important clue to understand why federal fiscal arrangements tend to be "unstable by design" (Bednar 2008). Whether of external or endogenous origin, this book points to distributive conflicts as a major engine of change in political unions. In this context, the book offers a different perspective on the interplay between mobility and redistribution in political unions. By explaining how mobility of unskilled labor and welfare dependents alter the incentives behind the selection of fiscal structures, the book provides an alternative to the ways in which conventional economic theories of federalism have understood the interplay between institutions and the behavior of economic factors. Mobility, I argue, is not so much a factor that constrains redistribution in a decentralized setting but a factor that facilitates the centralization of fiscal structures and works to increase levels of interregional redistribution.

Empirically, the book presents one of the first systematic analyses of the politics behind the origins of fiscal structures in political unions. Such an analysis combines multilevel survey analysis of individual preferences, historical analyses, and time-series cross-sectional analyses at the macro level. In the context of these analyses the book makes a novel use of microlevel household income surveys to map out the contours of economic geography in the unions of interest, and to calculate measures of dispersion in the geography of inequality, subsequently used as a predictor of the level of decentralization of interpersonal redistribution. The use of household income surveys to capture economic geography is embedded both in the historical analyses of the European Union, Canada, the United States, Germany, and Spain, and in a series of cross-national statistical analyses of the political and economic determinants of fiscal structures.

Last but not least, the book contributes to the literature on comparative institutions and institutional change. The book theorizes fiscal structures as the outcome of political agency. Actors are, in turn, constrained by economic geography and political representation. The book shows how, in the long run, pressure for change can result either from long-term cumulative feedback effects (Spain) or from short-term external alterations in economic geography (United States, Canada). In so doing, it proves the contrast between "punctuated equilibrium theory" and long-term, cumulative sources of change to be a false dilemma. A full understanding of the origins and evolution of fiscal structures requires both perspectives. A historical perspective is critical to appreciate the importance of initial conditions and to properly grasp endogenous sources of change such as feedback effect. Attention to historical processes allows us to identify natural experiments, that is, situations in which an external event alters economic geography and forces political agents to engage the possibility of adjusting fiscal structures. Natural experiments cannot be identified without a genuine historical perspective (Diamond and Robinson 2010). And the determinants of political agency cannot be properly identified without natural experiments, leaving the engines of history in the dark. These perspectives are complements, not opposites. This book illustrates the benefits of combining them as a way to better grasp the links between actors, contextual factors, and institutions over time.

ORGANIZATION OF THE BOOK

Chapter 2 develops the theoretical framework of the book. It approaches the choice of fiscal institutions as a process in which different members of the union show contending preferences over both the decentralization of interpersonal redistribution and the level of interregional redistribution. Such a choice, I show, is driven by the interplay between economic geography and political representation on the one hand, and the scope of mobility on the other. Chapter 3 bridges the theoretical and empirical parts of the book by motivating the research strategy to evaluate the empirical implications of the argument.

Chapters 4 through 7 present a series of in-depth case studies in the spirit outlined previously. Chapter 4 focuses on the origins and evolution of the European Union's fiscal structures. Chapter 5 Applies the theoretical argument of the book to the puzzle of the differing responses by Canada and the United States to the challenges posed by the Great Depression. Chapter 6 takes on the remarkable continuity of Germany's fiscal structure after the Reunification in the early 1990s. Finally, Chapter 7 studies the evolution of Spain's fiscal structure since the transition to democracy in 1978.

The variation along the representation scale between the EU, the United States, Canada, Spain, and Germany sheds light on the determinants of fiscal structures. As a necessary complement to these efforts, Chapter 8 addresses the problem of generalizability by developing a rigorous statistical scrutiny of the main empirical implications of the theory. Finally, Chapter 9 draws together the central findings of the project, elaborates on their implications, both theoretical and practical, and discusses the project's limitations as potential lines for further scholarly inquiry.

2

A Theory of Fiscal Structures in Political Unions

Fiscal structures result from political choice. They are the outcome of a process in which political elites and citizens interact. Politicians care about votes and approach the process concerned about their electoral fate. Citizens care about their welfare and evaluate alternative fiscal structures by the cost and benefits they bring about. This chapter analyzes this process.

I begin by laying out the basic elements and the premises of my model. Second, I analyze how economic geography shapes the preferences for fiscal structures. Third, I focus on how cross-regional economic externalities, in particular mobility, mediate the distributive conflicts associated with economic geography, and shape preferences for interregional redistribution. In a later section I analyze the role of political representation as a mediating factor between contending preferences and the choice of fiscal structures. Finally, the last section summarizes the empirical implications of the argument.

THE ANALYTICAL FRAMEWORK: ELEMENTS AND PREMISES

The interaction between national and regional elites in political unions is complex. If the analysis that follows attempted to capture everything political within unions, the book would deteriorate into complexity for the sake of complexity. To prevent this, the model builds on a number of simplifying assumptions.

The first concerns the relationship between the two dimensions of fiscal structures under study. In the political process, interpersonal and interregional redistribution are deeply intertwined. For example, where a system of taxes and transfers is centralized there are distributive consequences across regions, driven by the dispersal of taxpayers and welfare recipients. Wealthier regions within the union see themselves exploited by less prosperous regions – as seen in ongoing disputes in Belgium, Italy, or Spain. In contrast, in a decentralized system poor regions demand more resources to meet their obligations. These examples demonstrate the interdependency of interpersonal and interregional redistribution. However, to analyze the origin of fiscal structures these two dimensions must be separated and the hierarchy between them understood.

In this book, I assume that the design of fiscal structures involves: first, a choice about the decentralization of taxes on and transfers to individuals; and then a choice about the amount of resource redistribution between regions. Interregional redistribution derives from decentralization in the allocation of resources between regions. It only becomes an issue if regional governments are, at least partly, involved in interpersonal redistribution. At the end of the process, there are three possible outcomes of political contentions over fiscal structures:

- A centralized fiscal structure, henceforth denoted as C, where the central government controls all taxes and transfers exclusively.
- A decentralized fiscal structure, henceforth denoted as D, where regions are in charge of interpersonal redistribution, and there is very little redistribution of resources between the regions.
- Finally, a hybrid system, henceforth denoted as H, consisting of a decentralized fiscal structure with significant interregional redistribution.

This chapter analyzes the choice between these options as the joint outcome of (1) the political demand for change in fiscal structures associated with economic geography and (2) a given set of mechanisms for political representation. The main elements of the model are as follows. In unions with several levels of government, the interplay between local and national elites drives the political process. Local elites value regional government positions but also benefit from their party winning the national election. Likewise, national elites gain utility from holding the national executive as well as when their party wins regional elections. Accordingly, their respective utility functions are defined as follows:

The utility of the any given party (P) leader in a district (r) is defined by:

$$U_r^P = p_r^P \lambda_r^P + \Phi \left(q_n^P \phi_r^P \right) \tag{1}$$

where p_r^P represents the probability of party P conquering the regional executive, and λ_r^P represents the rewards obtained by regional party elites holding office at the regional level. The second half of the expression captures the benefits that regional party leaders obtain from having their national elites win the national elections. Thus, q_n^P represents the probability of party P conquering the national executive and ϕ_r^P captures the utility gains derived from having the same party control the national executive.

In turn, the utility of P's national leadership is captured by:

$$U_n^P = q_n^P \lambda_n^P + (1 - \Phi) \sum \left(p_r^P \chi_r^P \right) \tag{2}$$

where λ_n^P represents the rewards obtained by national party elites from holding office at the national level and χ_r^P captures the benefits that the national elite of party P derive from winning elections in region r.

A Theory of Fiscal Structures in Political Unions

Analytically, the key elements of the model are the relationship between citizens' individual preferences, the probability of winning the election, and the system of representation.

Citizens' institutional preferences, as driven by economic geography, play a key role in determining the probability of office holding at both levels of government. The probabilities of national and local elites gaining office are assumed to be a direct reflection of the need of both to minimize the distance between their proposals and citizens' optimal institutional preferences. Let X_r^* and X_n^* represent the optimal institutional preference of the pivotal group of voters at, respectively, the regional and national levels of government. In turn, X_r^P and X_n^P define the proposals made by the regional and national elites of party P. By assumption, the distance between voters' ideal points and elites' proposals are constrained between 0 and 1. Assume the probability that the national elite will win the national election (q_n^P) is given by $(1 - (X_r^* - X_r^P)^2) = (1 - \Omega_r)$ under fiscal decentralization and by $(1 - (X_n^* - X_n^P)^2) = (1 - \Omega_n)$ otherwise. Similarly, the probability that the regional elite wins the regional election (p_r^P) is given by $(1 - (X_r^* - X_r^P)^2) = (1 - \varphi_r)$ under decentralization and by $(1 - (X_r^* - X_n^P)^2) = (1 - \varphi_n)$ under centralization.

The system of representation is captured by Φ, a parameter that captures the importance that party elites give to the result of elections held at a level of government other than their own. This parameter ranges between 0 and 1. A high level of Φ indicates that national elections are of great importance in local leaders' calculations, whereas low values of Φ (and consequently, high values of $(1 - \Phi)$) indicate that the results of regional elections are an important concern for national elites.

Throughout the book, I refer to systems with high (low) values of Φ as centripetal (centrifugal). While for the sake of tractability, I incorporate representation as a set of parameters capturing the importance of national elections and their implications for intraparty relationships across territories, I proceed on the assumption that the latter is closely correlated with other institutional aspects of representation. For instance, a directly elected senate with strong legislative powers increases the importance of regional politics relative to where such an institution does not exist. Likewise, a strongly malapportioned lower house that facilitates the formation of local strongholds would limit the party discipline of (at least some) local leaders, thus lowering the value of Φ in the model.

To simplify, I assume that party systems at local and national levels are similar. That is, the parties (P) competing across regions (indexed by r = 1...r) and the national level (N) are the same. This assumption purposefully rules out the presence of identity parties. The explicit goal is to avoid yet another dimension in the model. This may seem restrictive (after all a majority of unions have regional identity parties); however it does not critically reduce the realm of applicability of the model. The key issue concerns the channels through which identity affects the selection of fiscal structures. Identity is both a major source of demand for political autonomy and a factor that changes the

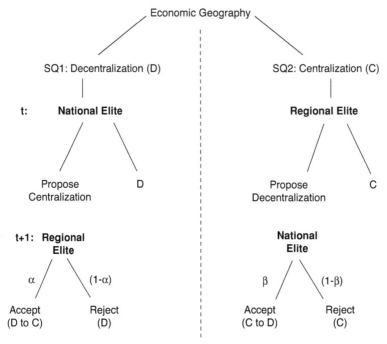

FIGURE 2.1. The Political Process

structure of party competition by altering both the political space in the union and the effective number of parties in specific regions.

These two channels are clearly important, but they do not require an additional parameter in the model. The effect of identity on preferences can be partially captured, indirectly, through economic geography. The effect of identity on representation is implicit to the centripetal-centrifugal continuum: if identity parties have a strong presence in the party system, representation is more likely to be centrifugal. I shall revisit this point in Chapter 3.

Figure 2.1 displays the two possible patterns of strategic interactions between the two levels of government, as determined by the status quo. Under SQ1 the distributive conflicts associated with the geography of inequality emerge when fiscal structures are decentralized (D). Under these circumstances, the national elites evaluate whether to pursue centralization. If they opt not to, the game ends. National elites operate under uncertainty. When they evaluate the pursuit of centralization, they are not sure what the response of the regional elites will be. Should national elites launch a proposal to move from a system of fragmented solidarity to a system of fiscal integration, regional elites will choose at $t + 1$ between accepting (with probability α) or rejecting such move (with probability $1 - \alpha$). This captures the fact that the national government does not know the type of regional elite. It simply knows that there is an α probability that it will accept a change in the direction of centralization. After

A Theory of Fiscal Structures in Political Unions

the decision by the regional elites, the game ends either with an institutional change (D → C) or with the preservation of the status quo in the aftermath of a conflict between national and regional elites. As a result of such conflict, the electoral chances of the national government (q_n^P) are reduced by a factor of $\mu = (1 - \frac{1}{\varepsilon})$ with $\varepsilon > 1$.

The sequencing of the game has a similar structure under SQ2, that is to say, when distributive tensions become politically relevant in a context of fiscal centralization. The mover at t is now the regional elite, and must decide whether to pursue fiscal decentralization (D → C). As before, it does so with some uncertainty about the response by the national elite at time t + 1 (as captured by probabilities β and $1 - \beta$). A potential conflict between regional and national elites also reduces the electoral chances of the first mover (p_r^P) by a factor of $\mu = (1 - \frac{1}{\varepsilon})$.

Solving the model requires an understanding of the incentives of the first movers to challenge the status quo given the expected response of the other party level. Accordingly, the decision rule for first movers is[1]:

For the national elite under SQ1 (decentralization) to pursue centralization if:

$$U_n^P(D) \leq \alpha \left(U_n^P(C)\right) + (1 - \alpha) \left(U_n^P(D \mid challenge)\right) \quad (4)$$

For the regional elite under SQ2 (centralization) to pursue decentralization:

$$U_r^P(C) \leq \beta \left(U_r^P(D)\right) + (1 - \beta) \left(U_r^P(C \mid challenge)\right) \quad (5)$$

As shown in the Appendix, solving both expressions produces the conditions under which either will pursue a change in the organization of fiscal structures:

$$1 \leq \frac{\alpha}{(1 - \alpha)} \frac{\left[(\Omega_r - \Omega_n)\lambda_n^P + (1 - \Phi)(\varphi_r - \varphi_n)\chi_r^P\right]}{(1 - \Omega_r)(1 - \mu)\lambda_n^P} \quad (6)$$

Under SQ1 (decentralization), the national elite will pursue centralization if the right-hand side term of (6) is greater than one. Otherwise, it has no incentive to do so. A number of insights follow for the expression above:

1. A rise in α, the probability that the regional elite accepts centralization, increases the payoff of going for centralization.
2. A rise in the top square bracket term measures exactly the expected gain from centralization (C) over decentralization (D). So if $(\Omega_r - \Omega_n) = (\varphi_r - \varphi_n) = 0$ it would never pay to change. In other words, if the economic geography in the region and the union are the same, there is no pressure/incentive for institutional change.

---

[1] A full formal development of the decision by the national government to pursue centralization under SQ1 and of the decision of the regional government to pursue decentralization under SQ2 is available in Appendix A.

3. $(1 - \Omega_r)$ is the probability of the national elite winning in a decentralized world. So when it goes to zero it always pays the national elite to challenge the status quo.
4. There is a relationship between the cost of challenge and institutional change. The closer is μ to 1, the smaller the cost of change; the smaller μ, the lower the incentives for change.
5. Finally, expression (6) also captures the link between the system of representation and the behavior of regional elites: if national politicians are indifferent between challenging or not SQ1, that is if (6) is an equality given the values of the parameters, then an increase in the importance of national elections for local leaders (Φ) requires an increase in the probability that regional elites accepts a proposal to centralize (α) for the equality to hold.

$$1 \leq \frac{\beta}{(1-\beta)} \frac{\left[(\varphi_n - \varphi_r)\lambda_r^P + \Phi(\Omega_n - \Omega_r)\phi_r^P\right]}{(1-\varphi_n)(1-\mu)\lambda_r^P} \qquad (7)$$

Under SQ2 (centralization), the regional leaders will pursue decentralization if the right hand side term of (7) is greater than one. It follows then that:

1. A rise in β, the probability that the national level accepts decentralization, increases the payoff of going for decentralization.
2. A rise in the top square bracket term measures exactly the expected gain from decentralization (D) over centralization (C). So if $(\varphi_n - \varphi_r) = (\Omega_n - \Omega_r) = 0$, it would never pay to change. Again, if the economic geography in the region and the union are the same, there is no pressure to challenge the status quo.
3. $(1 - \varphi_n)$ is the probability that the regional elite wins in a centralized world. So when it goes to zero it always pays the regional elite to challenge.
4. There is a relationship between the cost of challenge and institutional change that is similar to that in SQ1. The closer is μ to 1, the smaller the cost of change; the smaller μ, the lower the incentives for change.
5. Finally, expression (7) similarly captures the link between the system of representation and the behavior of regional elites in a status quo of centralization: if regional politicians are indifferent between challenging or not SQ2, that is if (7) is an equality given the values of the parameters, then an increase in the importance of national elections for local leaders (Φ) requires a decrease in the probability that national elites accepts a proposal to decentralize (β) for the equality to hold.

These results speak directly to the research questions at the core of this book. They highlight two important mechanisms underpinning the origin of fiscal structures:

1. The first one concerns the link between economic geography and citizens' institutional preferences. As regional economies grow apart, so do the

institutional preferences of voters, thereby shaping the calculations of political elites.
2. The second mechanism lies in the way in which the political interaction between national and regional elites plays out under different systems of representation. The weight of economic geography on elites' incentives is muted by the balance between national and regional interests in politicians' calculations, as captured by the importance attached by regional elites to winning national elections (Φ) and the cost of intraparty conflict (μ). These two parameters vary along systems of representation thereby mediating the impact of economic geography on institutional preferences.

These factors relate to the constraints faced by the political elites in charge of adjusting fiscal structures to changing distributive scenarios. The first constraint is electoral as, under democracy, politicians are largely bound by their constituencies' preferences. The second one is institutional. I analyze them in detail in the following sections.

ECONOMIC GEOGRAPHY AND PREFERENCES FOR FISCAL STRUCTURES

In sum, distributive conflicts associated with the geography of inequality drive elites' preferences apart through their impact on the electoral constraints they face. As these tensions exacerbate, the probability that either level of government responds favorably to the possibility of institutional change diminishes.

Understanding how economic geography shapes the gap between voters and political elites requires a more nuanced understanding of voters' preferences (X_i^*). The analysis proceeds in two steps. In the first, actors just care about income because levels of economic specialization are similar across regions. Accordingly, the choice of fiscal structures reflects only the geography of income of the union. In the second, I analyze a more realistic case where one of the two regions is intensely specialized in one area of production while the other is not.[2] Accordingly, the choice of fiscal structures reflects the geography of both income and risk associated with regional patterns of economic specialization. The contrast between these two unions illuminates how economic geography shapes preferences for fiscal structures.

The Geography of Income Inequality and Preferences for Fiscal Structures

I begin by considering a union with just two regions (A and B), where individuals care about their final consumption capacity and vary in their pretax

---

[2] Examples of concentrations of economic activity include fishing, farming, mining, manufacturing of particular goods (e.g. cars), or IT specialized industries such as hardware and software development.

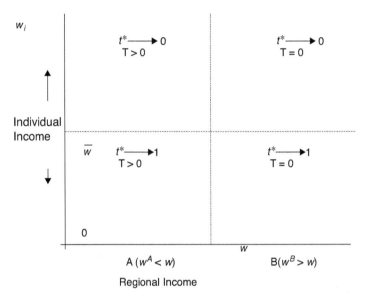

FIGURE 2.2. The Geography of Income and Institutional Preferences

income. A is poorer than B, that is, it has a lower aggregate income per capita ($w^A < w < w^B$).[3] As a result income varies along two dimensions: individuals and regions. Individuals, at any given time, may be employed or unemployed. The former have a final income defined by their posttax work earnings. The latter enjoy an income equal to the benefits received while being unemployed. This approach implies that redistributive concerns exclusively drive individuals.

In addition, citizens are affected by an interregional transfer that, when in place, is a function of the regional average income vis-à-vis the union. As a result, citizens face a decision about two policy instruments, namely, the level of interpersonal redistribution (t), and the level of interregional transfers of resources among members of the union, that is to say the level of interregional redistribution (T). On the basis of these premises, one can map out how the geography of inequality conditions the institutional preferences of different groups defined by their income level and regional location. Figure 2.2 summarizes the geographical distribution of preferences for redistribution that follows from the analysis of individual preferences over interpersonal (t) and interregional (T) redistribution.[4]

Figure 2.2 captures the key aspect of the geography of income in political unions: the coexistence of a redistributive conflict among individuals within regions and a redistributive conflict between regions within income groups. As

---

[3] No interregional externalities apply in the analysis in this section. Later in the chapter, I relax this assumption.
[4] The following discussion relies on an analysis of individual preferences that is presented formally in Appendix A.

A Theory of Fiscal Structures in Political Unions

TABLE 2.1. *The Geography of Income Inequality and Preferences for Fiscal Structures*

	Geography of Inequality	
	Region Has Less Inequality	Region Has More Inequality
Poor people in poor regions	C > H > D	H > D > C
Rich people in rich regions	D > H > C	C > D > H
Rich people in poor regions	H > D > C	C > H > D
Poor people in rich regions	D > H > C	C > D > H

a result, four groups with distinctive preferences emerge: poor people in poor regions, rich people in rich regions, rich people in poor regions, and poor people in rich regions. Critically, how these groups' preferences for redistribution map onto preferences for fiscal structures is in turn contingent on the regional patterns of inequality in the union. Table 2.1 summarizes the predictions concerning individuals' preferences as a function of their individual income, the income of their region, and the geography of income inequality in the union.

Consider first poor individuals in poor regions. Their desire for redistribution increases as the distance from the average income within the region increases (as established in Appendix A, $t^* \to 1$ as $w_i \to 0$) and they want to increase the tax base from which they extract their rents as much as possible (T > 0). Their institutional preferences are going to depend on the combination of the size of the tax base and the expected level of redistribution under different regimes. This in turn depends on the geography of inequality. If the poor region is more equal than the union, full fiscal centralization (C) is their first preference. Both the tax base and the expected level of redistribution will be larger. Their second best option would be a hybrid system of redistribution (H), in which interregional transfers out of the base of the rich region (T > 0) take place, thereby increasing resources to allow local interpersonal redistribution. Finally, they would be worst off under fiscal independence (D).

In the case of a poor region, such as A, this would imply that, even if they were able to impose a moderately high t, the actual amount of resources extracted would be limited by the size of the tax base. Assuming that the poor region is more equal than the union, poor people's institutional preferences would rank C > H > D. If, however, the poor region is more unequal than the union, and the gap in terms of regional wealth is not large, then the optimal choice may not be full centralization. Instead, it may be a hybrid regime in which the increase of the size of tax base is only partial but is compensated by the local pursuit of larger levels of redistribution. This would yield the following ranking of preferences: H > D > C.

Equally contingent are the preferences of rich people in rich regions. For moderate levels of inequality within the region, their preference ranking is

D > H > C. As one moves up in the income scale, the desire for redistribution among this particular subset of citizens declines ($t^* \to 0$ as $w_i \to \infty$). In addition, they have no incentive to accept any transfer of their regional tax base toward the government and citizens of the poorer region (T = 0). Thus, they are better off under a fully decentralized system (D) in which t is kept as low as possible.

Under these circumstances, their second best option is a system that minimizes the centralization of interpersonal redistribution, even if it is at the expense of side payments to other regions (H). Obviously, the smaller these side payments the better, as they would optimally like to see T = 0. Ultimately, any system that involves sharing the tax base with the poorer region and/or allowing the poor across the different regions to coalesce in support of redistribution makes them worse off. Therefore, full fiscal centralization (C) would be their last choice.

Other scenarios emerge depending on the geography of inequality. If a region is more unequal and only moderately wealthier than the rest of the union, and provided that the poor are politically engaged, the marginal cost of sharing nation-wide the burden of redistribution with the rich falls below the marginal cost of coping with a larger number of poor people under decentralization. Under these circumstances, the ranking for rich people in the rich region would, counterintuitively, become C > D > H.

A similar logic applies to rich people in poor regions, though their approach is driven by the fact that their individual and regional ascriptions do not overlap. On the one hand, they want to minimize the amount of taxes they pay ($t^* \to 0$ as $w_i \to \infty$) and on the other hand, they want to extract as much rent from the wealthier region as possible (T > 0). This combination triggers a dilemma for this group of citizens. A fully centralized system will liberate them from some of their fiscal burden. This benefit, however, may be offset by the need to cope with a larger dependent population, which may result in a scenario in which the tax burden they face is actually higher. The balance between these concerns will again be dictated by the skew of the regional distributions of income and the demands for redistribution emerging from it.

If levels of inequality were moderate, the optimal fiscal structure for richer citizens in poorer regions would be one that minimizes the central government's control over interpersonal redistribution and maximizes redistribution of resources between regions in a hybrid system (H). This would bridge the gap in terms of tax bases and increase the amount of resources for both public goods provision and rent extraction.

Assuming moderate levels of inequality, the worst case scenario for this subgroup of citizens would be a centralized fiscal design (C) in which they are exposed to the redistributive demands of a coalition of recipients across the union that limits the resources at their discretion. Therefore, under moderate levels of regional inequality, their preferences rank H > D > C. In contrast, as with wealthier citizens in rich regions, there are circumstances in which the

A Theory of Fiscal Structures in Political Unions

rich among the poor would prefer centralization. If the political process is such that poor people are mobilized to threaten regional elites under conditions of very high inequality, then it is possible that the fiscal burden for the rich within the poor region is potentially higher. In this case the cost of resisting vertical redistribution would outweigh the benefits.[5] The new ranking would then be C > H > D.

Finally, poor people within the rich region also face a dilemma, although of a different nature. They need to balance the amount of additional resources they would be able to extract from the rich by coalescing with the poor in the low-income region against the loss they would incur because of a change in their relative position within the new, union-wide, income distribution. Such loss would take the form of an implicit transfer of resources from the poor in the rich region to the poor in the poorer areas of the union.

In determining the size of this loss the key factor is, again, the skew of the regional income distributions. If the rich region is relatively equal, an increase in the centralization of interpersonal redistribution would imply that a large proportion of the poor in the rich region shift from net recipients to net contributors. As a result, given a relatively equal regional income distribution, the ranking of preferences among the poor in the rich region changes.

Because the poor in the rich region will want to protect their relative position, fiscal decentralization (D) would be preferred to any system implying any kind of transfer out of the region. Should a fully decentralized system of redistribution not be an option, their second choice would be to continue their alliance with the rich in support of fiscal structures that place more weight on interregional than on interpersonal redistribution (H). In the presence of a more egalitarian distribution of income within the region, the ranking would then be D > H > C. In contrast, if the rich region were very unequal, then a large share of the poor would remain net beneficiaries under a centralized redistributive system. More formally, insofar as the income of the median poor is equal or less than the income of the median voter of the union, a majority among the poor would support full fiscal centralization (C). Their preference ranking would be C > D > H.

In conclusion, a central insight emerges from this analysis of the preferences of the different groups in Table 2.1. Preferences for fiscal structures depend critically on the geography of income inequality. As the incidence of inequality between and within regions becomes more diverse, so do the preferences for fiscal structures, thereby rendering the emergence of a centralized system of interpersonal redistribution less feasible in political terms. As captured by expressions (4) and (5), a larger diversity of preferences feeds into increasing electoral costs for both national and regional elites should they deviate from the preferences of the pivotal group within their constituency.

---

[5] If however, the poor are disenfranchised, then rich citizens in poor regions are still better off under a decentralized system of redistribution.

The Geography of Risk and Preferences for Fiscal Structures

Unpacking the geography of risks and insurance demands attention to two factors: regional economic specialization and the scope of labor mobility across regions. The former, I will argue, works to exacerbate geographical differences in insurance demands. The latter works to mute these differences by fostering levels of risk sharing between regions. In this section, I analyze how the geography of risks and demands for insurance affect the politics of selection of fiscal structures.

Literature in political economy repeatedly identifies risks, that is the possibility of a future income loss, as a key factor in driving people's redistributive preferences (Atkinson 1995, 1999; Moene and Wallerstein 2001; Varian 1980). This being the case, risk and risk aversion, as well as the territorial distribution of risk, becomes a primary mechanism for other aspects of economic geography to condition the selection of fiscal institutions.

The concentration of different types of economic activities across territories is particularly relevant. This applies both to the existence of a division of labor in the world economy between countries, and to the concentration of different types of economic activity across the regions of any given union (Cai and Treisman 2005; Krugman 1991; Venables 2001). There are examples of this sort of process throughout economic history. As industrialization and deruralization develop, territorialization of different economic activities intensifies. Manufacturing industries are concentrated where there is easy access to transport, whereas extraction industries (fisheries, coal, etc.) are located close to natural resources, including fertile ground. Most countries have three or four areas of economic development that attract large masses of workers, thereby altering their social and economic geography.

In this context, it is possible to argue that workers vary in their ability to move across industries and regions. Their mobility is dependent on the fit between their abilities and the skills demanded by different sectors. For example, the oversupply of rural workers in nineteenth century Europe was largely absorbed by emerging manufacturing industries in Europe and beyond. Historically, masses of unskilled workers would be responsive to new employment opportunities in different territories, or, in times of crisis, to the supply of social protection in different localities. In contrast, when there is no fit between workers' skills and alternative opportunities, mobility is not an option and, arguably, employees become more aware of the possibility of a future income loss. So the trade-off between geographical mobility and the level of specialization of the economy (Boix 2003) speaks directly to the levels of risk aversion among workers.

To capture these processes I broaden the model of individual preferences to include an insurance element. This captures the importance of differences across regions in terms of economic specialization. The key analytical result is that the demand for redistribution increases with risk aversion, which reflects the level of economic specialization of the regional economy.[6] This is consistent with earlier contributions and, in substantive terms, implies that individuals working in more specialized industries, concentrated in particular territories (for example, wineries, fisheries, and coal mining), are less transferable to other regional labor markets, and therefore are more averse to economic risks than individuals with the ability to relocate and readjust professionally.

Finally, and critically, the introduction of risk aversion means that the demand for insurance also increases with income. Taken together, these predictions yield a pattern of preferences that differs significantly with respect to the geography of income inequality and helps elucidate the connection between the geography of risks and preferences over fiscal structures. The introduction of an insurance dimension in the model brings about significant implications for the formation of political coalitions in support of alternative institutional designs.

In contrast to the purely redistributive case, wealthier individuals in regions with specialized economic activities, have incentives to accept a public insurance system that will shelter them against a potential downturn of their regional political economy. Elites of highly specialized regions have incentives to preserve their own system of interpersonal redistribution, although it leads to taxation on their income. As a result, the policy preferences of different income classes within the region become more similar, which makes the formation of a political coalition in support of regional interests more likely to emerge.

More importantly, the analysis also implies that this dynamics is orthogonal to the level of wealth of different regions. An interesting implication of this result is that with sufficiently high levels of regional risk specificity, the citizens of a region poorer than the union may forego the income benefits of centralizing interpersonal redistribution to protect its ability to design an insurance system better tailored to their specific risk profiles.[7] To illustrate this point, Figure 2.3 displays the map of preferences for redistribution in a union in which the specialized region is relatively poorer.[8] Individual's preferences for redistribution within the specialized region grow closer despite income differences. In political terms, this implies that the poor and the rich within the specialized region prefer a system that complements the functioning of local economies, rather than a system that plays exclusively to their individual interests, as defined by their relative position in the income distribution.

In conclusion, an uneven geography of risk reinforces the polarizing effects of an uneven geography of income inequality. Risk differentials associated with

---

[6] On the relationship between skills, risks, and preferences, see Cusack, Iversen and Rehm (2006); Iversen and Soskice (2006); Moene and Wallerstein (2001); and Rehm (2009).
[7] A related analysis of this particular case is provided by Beramendi (2007). On the relationship between income gains and what they call "political risks" associated with centralization, see also Alesina and Perotti (1998); and Perotti (2001). For an argument in which centralization works in the opposite direction, reducing the policy risks among voters, see Crémer and Palfrey (1999).
[8] This corresponds to the formal analysis included in Appendix A.

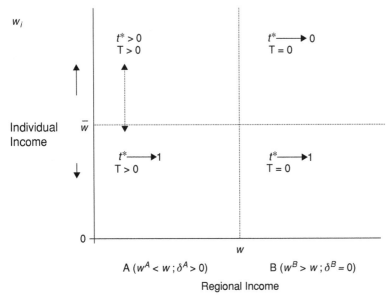

FIGURE 2.3. Preferences for Fiscal Structures When the Poor Region Is Highly Specialized

the diversity of economic activities across regions facilitate the formation of intra-regional cross-class coalitions and, conversely, undermine the likelihood of interregional class-based coalitions. This pattern of alliances links to preferences about the territorial articulation of the fiscal system: other things being equal, a diverse geography of risk increases the pressure in favor of a decentralized system of interpersonal redistribution and tilts political contentions toward a conflict over the scope of interregional redistribution. How these contentions are resolved depends not only on the geography of risks but also on the level and nature of mobility across regional borders.

MOBILITY AND THE ORGANIZATION OF FISCAL STRUCTURES: INTERREGIONAL REDISTRIBUTION AS INSURANCE TO PROTECT AUTONOMY

Cross-regional economic externalities emerge from events, such as external shocks, whose consequences transcend specific members of the union. To the extent that there are cross-regional economic externalities, the risk profiles of different regions become less distinctive from one another. This affects their preferences for the design of fiscal structures. As follows, I investigate the connection between externalities, economic specialization, and the selection of fiscal structures.[9]

---

[9] In this section, I rely on the same model of individual preferences as in the previous section (see Appendix A for a formal presentation).

The risk of external economic shocks creates political demand for a common pool of resources, that is, in favor of relatively more integrated fiscal structures (Alesina and Perotti 1998; Crémer and Palfrey 2000). This is because the prospect of an external shock works to reduce the distance among regions in terms of their risk profiles. Neither the poor nor the wealthy region know ex ante whether they will be affected by the shock. What they both know, however, is that if a negative shock hits them, they would be worse off without a common insurance scheme.[10] By contrast, insofar as there is a cross-regional fiscal structure at work, the region negatively affected by the shock can transfer some of the cost to the common pool. Otherwise, it must fend for itself. The possibility of an external shock creates a risk that cuts across regional boundaries, thereby compensating the effect of specific risks associated with the uneven geography of labor markets. As a result, they create incentives for the formation of coalitions in support of a more integrated fiscal system.

So, which specific form should this fiscal system take? Will people support a fully centralized system (C)? Or would they prefer a combination of decentralized interpersonal redistribution and large scale interregional transfers (H)? The answer to these questions depends on the nature of cross-regional economic externalities.

Economic shocks are bound to have differential effects on regional economies. A sudden drop in the demand for agricultural or manufacturing products is unlikely to affect all regional economies equally. Likewise, the deindustrialization associated with transitioning to a service economy is likely to have a stronger impact on those regions with a larger concentration of manufacturing industries. For example, the 1929 international financial crisis affected North American states and provinces in different ways. The Great Depression hit some areas, particularly rural areas, harder than others.

In this context, the key issue is whether the negative socioeconomic effects associated with the common shock of the financial crisis spanned across regions or remained geographically concentrated. If the latter, the redistributive and institutional contentions among citizens in different regions will exacerbate. The polarizing effects of the geography of risks will be enhanced by the shock.

However, if the social consequences of the crisis cut across regional boundaries, the dynamics of preference formation might change dramatically. This brings us to the geographical mobility of redundant workers and their dependents as a key engine behind cross-regional externalities. In the event of a negative shock affecting their local economy, laid-off workers will seek alternatives in areas of the country less affected by the crisis. At the same time, in the absence of a centralized welfare system, the unemployed and their dependents

---

[10] To see this in terms of the model in Appendix A, consider the economic effects of a negative shock on regions A or B. Any region affected by a negative shock faces simultaneously a loss of tax base (w) and an increase in the demand for redistribution (via the ratio between the employed and the unemployed populations, $\alpha/(1-\alpha)$.

will also seek the welfare offered in other localities (Peterson 1995; Peterson and Rom 1990).

The geographical mobility of the unemployed and their dependents has several effects. It reduces the distance across regions in terms of the tax base[11] and the size of the dependent population.[12] The region expelling unemployed poor people increases its employment rate and average output, whereas the recipient region sees both magnitudes drop. As a result, both regions also come closer in terms of the nature of the distributive conflict among their citizens.

As the poor travel across regional boundaries, net welfare recipients in wealthier regions lose their ability to protect their tax base by keeping a decentralized insurance system and reducing interregional redistribution. Therefore, their incentives to support a more centralized fiscal structure (C) increase. Interregional mobility of dependents from economically depressed to economically prosperous areas implies by definition an interregional transfer of resources between the regions of the union. As a result, as the policy preferences of different groups grow closer, the political pursuit of a fiscally centralized system becomes more feasible.[13] An important requirement for mobility to map onto a centralized fiscal structure (C) is that levels of economic specialization should be similar across different regions of the union. Only then will the different groups involved find common ground regarding interpersonal redistribution (t) in a context in which mobility has created high levels of interregional redistribution (T).

In contrast, the distribution of preferences is more heterogeneous when high levels of mobility among dependents combines with differential patterns of regional economic specialization. While citizens from a poor, non-specialized region would have a lot to gain from a fully centralized system, citizens in a wealthy, economically specialized region face a complex set of motives that work in opposite directions. They need some form of common pool of resources against the prospect of an external negative shock. Yet they also want to preserve policy autonomy to design interpersonal redistribution in ways that disrupt their regional economy least.

Due to high levels of regional economic specialization, the possibility of a large contingent of dependent immigrants affects not only the regional tax base, but also the existing fit between decentralized redistributive efforts and the organization of local labor markets. As a result, I argue, those who have more to fear from a centralized system of interpersonal redistribution (spurred by large levels of dependents' mobility) have incentives to act strategically. That is to say the elites of the wealthier region, in anticipation of undesired population inflows, have strong incentives to help fund decentralized redistribution in other regions through larger interregional transfers (T).

---

[11] In the preference formation model this is formally captured by w_r.
[12] In the preference formation model this is formally captured by $(1 - \alpha)$.
[13] For other analyses where increasing labor mobility facilitates the adoption of common social policies, see Bolton and Roland (1996); and Perotti (2001).

So, rich and poor citizens of the wealthier region will coalesce with the rich citizens of the poor region on an exchange in which interregional transfers (T) are used to limit the extent of interpersonal redistribution (t), even if at the expense of the poorest members of society. That way, they limit the scope of migration that would undermine the viability of more decentralized interpersonal redistribution. This will be the optimal strategy until an additional marginal increase in interregional redistribution (T) equates to the net loss due to changes in interpersonal redistribution (t) motivated by larger levels of cross-regional mobility of dependents.

In conclusion, support for a combination of decentralized interpersonal redistribution and generous interregional transfers is likely to grow stronger where high levels of dependents' mobility and regional economic specialization co-exist. The resulting fiscal structure would be dominated by interregional redistribution (H). The underlying logic of prospective self-insurance is also at work in the international arena: the privileged prefer to pay to keep the poor away rather than risk allowing undesired dependents into their economies.

To summarize, mobility works to reduce risk differentials across regions, thereby creating the conditions for more integrated fiscal structures. Whether such integration adopts the form of a hybrid (H) or a fully centralized system (C) depends on the patterns of regional economic specialization. The coexistence of high specialization in wealthy areas and large levels of mobility creates incentives for wealthier regions to accept interregional redistribution to preserve the nature of their local systems of production and interpersonal redistribution.

This analysis of mobility completes the study of the determinants of preferences for fiscal structures. While cross-regional variation in inequality and economic specialization work to facilitate more decentralized systems of redistribution, large levels of mobility create pressure in the opposite direction. Together, economic geography and mobility determine the map of contending institutional preferences within the union. The system of representation, in turn, determines which of these contending preferences ultimately prevails.

FROM PREFERENCES TO CHOICES: REPRESENTATION AND THE CHOICE OF FISCAL STRUCTURES

One of two mechanisms identified in the analysis of the interplay between national and regional elites is that of the electoral constraints associated with economic geography. The second concerns the balance of power between local and national interests in the political process, as determined by the system of representation. In combination with the distribution of preferences emerging from economic geography, this mechanism conditions both the probability (α) that the regional party elite accepts the centralization attempts of national party elites under SQ1 and the probability (β) that the national elite will accept decentralization attempts by the regional party elites under SQ2.

Recall the key predictions from expressions (6) and (7). First, the probability of agreeing to an institutional change increases the electoral price of intraparty conflict (μ). Second, as the value attached by regional leaders to the incumbency of the national executive increases, the probability that they accept a change toward higher levels of fiscal integration also increases. In contrast, as the importance of national political contests rises, the probability that the national party elite agrees to decentralize redistribution declines.

These results have important implications for the patterns of coalition formation among the groups identified earlier. Building on the seminal contributions by Crémer and Palfrey (1999, 2000), the parameters capturing the electoral cost of cross-jurisdictional conflict (μ) and the balance between the interests of national and local elites (Φ) define the political playing field in the event of increasing distributive tensions among territories and income groups. A key distinction here is whether the way coalitions are formed is *centrifugal*, that is tailored toward the representation of territorialized interests, or *centripetal*, that is set up to increase the incentives of political actors to mobilize the interests of social groups that cut across subnational territorial boundaries. Centrifugal representation corresponds to very low values of both μ and Φ. In contrast, centripetal representation implies the preeminence of political competition at the national level (high values of Φ) and very high electoral costs for conflictive regional elites.

At the extreme of centrifugal representation ($\Phi = 0$; low μ), there is little or no salience of national elections and virtually no cost for regional elites to challenge the national party. As centrifugal representation situates geography at the center of the political stage, the constraints imposed by regional inequalities on institutional changes grow stronger. At the extreme, the electoral constraints emerging from the geography of inequality dominate the strategy of regional political leaders. Politics becomes a conflict about the distribution of resources among jurisdictions, and territorial interests (preferences over the value of T) outweigh class interests (intraregional contentions over the value of t).

As regional incomes diverge ($w^A \neq w^B \neq w^C \ldots$), the distance between the optimal preferences of different regions increases (in terms of the model ($\varphi_r - \varphi_n$) tends to 1), thereby reducing the incentives of regional elites to accept any fiscal structure other than the one that maximizes their electoral survival. The analysis above suggests that any deviation from the ideal fiscal structure of the region's median voter brings about a disutility for the regional party leader.[14] Through this mechanism the diversity of preferences, determined by

---

[14] Assuming a standard democratic setup in which two parties compete for a majority of the voters within the district, and given the structure of this model, the probability of gaining and retaining office becomes a function of how closely the platforms offered by either party j approaches the ideal institutional configuration of the pivotal group of voters within the district. In accordance with previous contributions (Beramendi 2007; Bolton and Roland 1997; Crémer and Palfrey 1999) it is straightforward to see that such a position corresponds to the median voter within the district. As a result, the preferences of the median voter within each district become the criteria according to which regional elites will evaluate alternative institutional designs.

A Theory of Fiscal Structures in Political Unions

an uneven geography of inequality, drives exclusively the selection of fiscal structures. As the process of coalition formation occurs primarily within districts, provided that regional leaders have the institutional ability to veto any change against their core supporters' interests (SQ1), the polarizing effects of the economic geography imply a conflict of interests between districts that will yield, as a result, a more fragmented fiscal structure. For example, consider the pattern of preferences summarized in Table 2.1. Under SQ1, assuming that the region is relatively more equal than the rest of the union, it is straightforward that the elites of the wealthier region of the union (B) have no reason to give up fiscal independence. In turn, a reduction in the value of Φ under conditions of centralization (SQ2) will increase the likelihood of success of the political push to decentralize redistribution led by the leaders of B. In conclusion, under centrifugal representation a diverse economic geography translates directly into the adoption of more decentralized systems of redistribution.

The nature of coalition formation changes as the electoral weight of national elections (Φ) and the cost of intra-party conflict increase. Accordingly, national party elites are stronger and need to respond to a pivotal voter group that cuts across specific regional boundaries. In turn, as political conflict revolves around a group that is not territorially localized, the main lines of political competition are drawn along income groups as opposed to regions.

When centripetal representation is at its highest ($\Phi = 1$), the formation of the political will depends much less on the previously articulated preferences of regions, and much more on how parties target population subgroups that cut across regional boundaries. If representation operates under plurality in a common national circumscription, parties will target the union's median voter. If representation works to preserve proportionality, national elites will devise a combination of interpersonal and interregional redistribution as close as possible to the interests of the median legislature of the winning coalition (Austen-Smith and Banks 1988; Iversen and Soskice 2006).

In either case, centripetal representation downplays differences in terms of territorial interests within income groups on both sides of a divide along the lines of interpersonal redistribution. As a result, the diversity of institutional preferences across territories is dominated by contentions that occur mainly along class lines. In terms of the model, as political alliances are much more likely to be class based, specific distributive interests of certain regions are much less likely to be the primary concern when adjusting redistributive institutions to changes in the geography of economic inequality. Party strategies are driven by national elites with lesser incentives to accommodate their institutional proposals to the interests of the pivotal voter of any particular region. This is consistent with the predictions emerging from the results in (6) and (7).

In a status quo of decentralized redistribution (SQ1), centripetal representation works to overcome the resistance of local elites to centralize redistribution. In contrast, in a status quo of centralized redistribution (SQ2), centripetal representation reinforces the likelihood that national elites will reject fiscal decentralization in the presence of diverging preferences across regions, in turn associated with large economic geographical disparities.

If, under these conditions, changes in the geography of inequality facilitate the mobilization of a regionalist platform, the latter will meet the resistance of a political system organized around national, income classes-based, political parties. This resistance is a matter of electoral survival for national elites. As shown previously, a growing gap between national and regional distributions of income ($\Omega_n - \Omega_r$) increases the electoral cost of decentralizing redistribution for the national elite. By implication, centripetal representation limits the extent to which territorial inequalities manage to constrain redistributive efforts and reproduce themselves over time. An important implication for the study of inequality follows from this analysis.

The scenarios in between ($0 < \Phi < 1$) vary significantly in the balance of regional and national electoral concerns, and therefore in the extent to which pressures to either retain or move toward more decentralized fiscal structures succeed. Strongly malapportioned chambers (upper and lower) work hand in hand with heterogeneous and fragmented party systems to reduce the salience of national electoral contests as opposed to regional, territorialized, ones.[15] To the extent that this is the case, the institutional implications of a more diverse and polarizing geography of inequality will be more visible.

Consider the case, for instance, of wealthier elites in poorer regions. The above analysis suggests that these elites have incentives to both prevent the development of interpersonal redistribution and seek the extraction of resources via interregional redistribution. Under most distributional scenarios, H is their first preference.

In federations with powerful senates and/or strongly malapportioned lower houses, these elites will constitute a blocking minority able to steer the design of fiscal structures towards their own interests. This logic of *local strongholds* is particularly feasible under institutional conditions, such as strong malapportionment in the legislature, leaning toward centrifugal representation.[16]

In contrast, insofar as the system of representation offers fewer opportunities for local representatives to act as brokers of local interests, their imprint on the design of fiscal structures will be less marked. This has implications for understanding both the centralization of interpersonal redistribution and the level of interregional transfers. To the extent that the wealthy elites of poorer areas enjoy a privileged position in the system of representation, they will block any attempt to launch a comprehensive and fully centralized system of interpersonal redistribution. In turn, the size of interregional transfers (T) is a

---

[15] For an empirical analysis of the effects of these features on the economic performance of federations, see Rodden and Wibbels (2002). For an empirical analysis of the scope of electoral coattails in federations see Rodden and Wibbels (2010).

[16] For an empirical example of this logic in the study of macroeconomic performance in Latin America, see Gibson, Calvo and Falleti (2004). For an application of this analysis to developing federations, see Beramendi and Diaz-Cayeros (2008).

A Theory of Fiscal Structures in Political Unions

positive function of the ability of regional barons to extract resources and, by implication, a negative function of the ability of national parties to resist their pressure.

Finally, a word on the relationship between interregional economic externalities and different systems of representation. Whereas uneven geographies of inequality and risk are magnified by centrifugal representation and muted by centripetal representation, mobility and representation seem to have an orthogonal relationship.

Mobility fosters interregional redistribution at any point of the representation scale. Indeed, large economic externalities undermine the incentives of regional elites to protect their fiscal structures even under conditions of centrifugal representation that grant these elites effective veto power. To see how this process works, it is useful to compare the expected behavior of the elites of the wealthier region of the union (B) in the absence of economic externalities with their expected behavior when these externalities are at work.

Under institutional conditions that favor the relative power of regional versus national elites in a status quo of fragmented solidarity (SQ1), the absence of interregional economic externalities implies that the leaders of wealthier regions will reject proposals that limit their fiscal autonomy (D). However, under the same institutional conditions, the emergence of large levels of interregional mobility of dependents creates the conditions for them to accept an institutional change from fiscal independence (D) to a hybrid system with large levels of interregional transfers (H).

More generally, by fostering the levels of regional risk sharing, externalities work to reduce the terms $(\varphi_r - \varphi_n)$ in SQ1 and $\Omega_n - \Omega_r$ in SQ2. As a result, externalities work either to increase the probability that regional elites accept a move toward more integrated fiscal structures (α) in SQ1 or to reduce the probability that the national elites accept a proposal to move toward more decentralized fiscal structures in SQ2. Indeed, for sufficiently large levels of regional risk sharing, the incentives of regional leaders to challenge a centralized fiscal system decline decisively. In conclusion, higher levels of mobility facilitate the adoption of more centralized redistributive systems regardless of the system of representation in place.

To summarize, this section has analyzed in detail the process by which different systems of representation mediate the effects of economic geography on the decentralization of redistribution. I have also illustrated how the impact of mobility on fiscal structures is orthogonal to the nature of the system of representation.

SUMMARY OF HYPOTHESES

This concludes the theoretical study of the determinants of centralization of interpersonal redistribution and the level of interregional redistribution. With an eye toward the empirical sections of the book, I close the chapter with a summary of the main hypotheses emerging from the analysis.

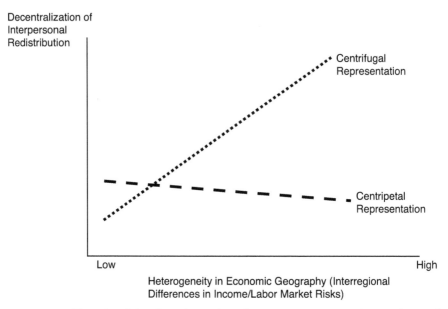

FIGURE 2.4. The Conditional Relationship between Economic Geography and Representation

What drives the (de)centralization of interpersonal redistribution?

Hypothesis 1: Economic geography shapes preferences for the (de)centralization of interpersonal redistribution. A heterogeneous geography of income and risk drives apart preferences for redistribution within and between regions, thereby fostering the demand for decentralized systems of interpersonal redistribution. By contrast, in the absence of high levels of regional economic specialization, large levels of mobility contribute to the homogeneization of redistributive preferences across regions and, through this route, to the centralization of interpersonal redistribution.

Hypothesis 2: Decentralization of interpersonal redistribution results from the interaction between economic geography and political representation. Empirically, the following expectations should be substantiated:

A. Under centrifugal systems of representation, cross regional differences in terms of inequality and risk translate directly into the adoption of decentralized systems of redistribution.
B. In contrast, under centripetal systems of representation, the nature of political competition mutes the impact of cross-regional differences in inequality and risk on the level of decentralization of redistribution. If anything, under centripetal representation, one should expect inequality between regions to facilitate either the adoption or the continuity of centralized systems of redistribution.

A Theory of Fiscal Structures in Political Unions

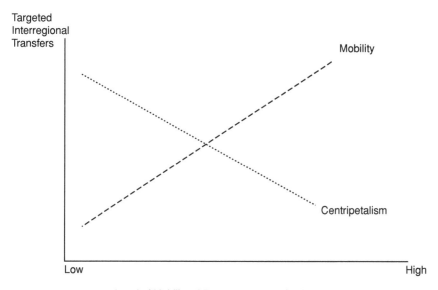

FIGURE 2.5. Determinants of Targeted Interregional Transfers: Expected Relations

C. As a result, the association between interregional inequality and overall income inequality in the union should be strongest in unions with centrifugal systems of representation.

Figure 2.4 displays the expected relationships graphically.

What explains the levels of interregional redistribution?

Hypothesis 3: Given a decentralized system of interpersonal redistribution, the level of interregional redistribution is: a positive function of the levels of mobility; and negatively related to systems of representation that weigh down the influence of specific regions (centripetal). Figure 2.5 displays the expected relationships graphically.

Chapter 3 introduces the empirical strategy for assessing these hypotheses.

3

The Road Ahead

The Empirical Strategy

This book studies the nature of redistribution in political unions. As reflected in my hypotheses, summarized in Chapter 2, the nuts and bolts behind the selection of fiscal structures lie in the interplay between economic geography and political representation on the one hand, and the scope of mobility on the other. Varying combinations of these factors are expected to yield different fiscal structures, and thereby different patterns of association between economic geography, the scope of fiscal redistribution, and overall levels of inequality in society.

The chapters ahead approach these mechanisms in two ways: first, as causal factors whose marginal effects ought to be identifiable empirically[1]; second, as elements of a dynamic process in which economic geography, mobility, representation, and fiscal structures condition each other over time. The endogenous nature of this process is a double-edge sword. Mapping out the process itself becomes necessary to understand how the different elements of the argument interact over time to shape redistribution in political unions. At the same time, however, the very nature of the process makes identifying marginal causal effects especially challenging.

To test the argument of the book, the empirical chapters (Chapters 4 to 8) develop a dual strategy that combines both natural experiments to facilitate the causal identification of marginal effects and attention to endogenous processes in two political unions with very different starting conditions. The natural experiments include the North American responses to the Great Depression, and Germany's response to Reunification. These cases pin down whether the causal logic posited in this book bears any resemblance with actual historical experiences and illustrate the workings of the main mechanisms in the model. I complement this study with attention to the evolution of contentions about fiscal structures in the European Union and Spain. These unions fail to meet

---

[1] On the requirements for causal identification and its implications for research design see Fearon (1991); and Manski (1995).

the requirements of a natural experiment, but allow me to capture the interplay between the different elements of the argument over time. The contrast between these two unions is also interesting because they vary in terms of the their political and institutional status quo at the onset of the process. Finally, the empirical strategy also includes a set of medium to large N statistical analyses (Chapter 8) to transcend a handful of historical cases, and assess whether the analysis applies more broadly to the universe of political unions.

This chapter motivates the selection of cases and explains how they serve the purpose of testing the central contentions of the book. The empirical evaluation of my hypotheses requires the following conditions:

1. The formation of the union itself does not result from the distributive conflicts of interest in this book.
2. The changes in economic geography or in the patterns of mobility that trigger the political conflict occur for reasons independent of the pre-existing fiscal structures and system of representation.
3. The set of cases allows for sufficient variation in terms of the organization of political representation.
4. Finally, the identification of the conditional relationship between economic geography and political representation requires that, in the event of an exogenous change in economic geography, the system of representation in place can be considered as given. Symmetrically, given a geography of income inequality, causal identification demands that changes in the system of representation follow from reasons independent of pre-existing fiscal structures. The same requirement of exogenous variation applies to the identification of the impact of mobility as well.

The remainder of this chapter discusses how the different cases stand in relation to each of these conditions. The first section shows how all five unions under consideration meet the first condition. The second focuses on the sources of change in economic geography and their implications for political contentions over the organization of redistribution (condition 2). Finally, the third section analyzes the variation among the cases in terms of the centrifugal-centripetal continuum, and the conditions under which political representation can be considered exogenous (conditions 3 and 4).

UNION FORMATION AND FISCAL STRUCTURES

Political integration, understood as the decision to remain within the political union or secede, conditions directly the size and shape of political unions. The link between the choice to secede and conflicts over who gets what within the union has been the focus of theoretical (Alesina and Spolaore 2003; Bolton and Roland 1997) as well as empirical research (Bakke and Wibbels 2006). There is little doubt that these two things are directly linked. In thinking about case selection, it is important to establish that the claims about the origins of fiscal structures made in this book assume that the process of state formation is complete, that is, locked in by a set of broadly accepted constitutional provisions, well before contentions about the design of fiscal structures unfold. Note that this does not necessarily imply that unions do not alter their size over time. What it means, though, is that the decision to form the union in the first place, and the procedures ruling contentions within the union, were adopted before the emergence of political conflicts over fiscal structures. Moreover, the reasons why the union was initially formed ought to be independent of the subsequent distributive conflicts over the design of its fiscal structures. This qualification is of particular importance for one of the cases of interest in this book, the European Union, to which I shall return.

A cursory overview of the geopolitical conditions surrounding the formation of these five unions suggests that none of them was originally formed in response to distributional concerns among potential members. This is not to say that distributional contentions did not matter subsequently for the specific arrangements ultimately made. They were actually rather important, for instance, during the drafting and ratification of the US Constitution (Beard 1913; Beramendi and Wibbels 2010; McGuire 2003; Wibbels 2005a). But the decision to form these unions in the first place was not driven by distributional concerns nor because its members shared common economic interests, a form of the "reductionist fallacy" ably denounced by Riker (1964: 15). Rather, geopolitical motives and the need of protection against a foreign enemy drove the process. Put simply, geopolitics explains whether the union is pursued or not; distributive conflicts help explain, I argue, how the union is ultimately organized, and how it evolved.

Building on the American experience, Riker famously pointed to the presence of an external threat as the key reason behind the formation of federations. Facing either exploitation from or war against the British Empire, the colonies faced a choice between integration and defeat. And they chose the former, thus confirming Riker's necessary conditions for the federal bargain to occur. First, a set of political elites want to expand their territorial control to meet a military or diplomatic threat. They, however, do not want to do it *manu militari*, but rather through a bargain with other territories, which leads to a second condition; that the politicians that accept the bargain and give up some power do so because of some external military threat as well. They either want protection or a share in the rewards from the aggression by the larger unit (Riker 1964: 11–14). The formation of the United States in turn triggered a process out of which Canada itself emerged. Indeed, the formation of Canada is best understood in terms of the geopolitical dynamics that unfolded between the Treaty of Paris (1783), in which the borders between Canada and the United States are recognized for the first time, the 1812 war between Britain and the United States, in which Canadian provinces were used either as pawns or bargaining chips, (thus acquiring awareness of the need to become a larger and stronger political entity), and the formal establishment of the confederation between Ontario, Quebec, Nova Scotia, and New Brunswick in the British North America Act (1867). Similarly, the shadow of the Soviet Union played a major role in shaping the way Germany emerged after the Second World War. To be sure, both the allies and the post-war German political elites had in mind the lessons emerging from the collapse of the Weimar Republic throughout the process leading to the Constitution of 1949. In particular, the legacy of Weimar weighed heavily on specific constitutional provisions directly bearing on the organization of fiscal structures, as well as the adoption of a more centripetal, consensus-oriented, architecture of representation. But again those concerns do not explain the decision to form two countries, one under the influence of Moscow, the other under the allies' supervision.

Geopolitical motives also help explain both the origins of European integration and the highly centrifugal system of governance adopted by its early members (Rosato 2011), a system whose fundamental traces remain despite the large steps made toward the parliamentarization of the Union (Rittberger 2005). Put briefly, "the construction of European integration is best understood not as an effort to foster peace and prosperity, but as an attempt by the major West European States to balance against the Soviet Union and one another" (Rosato 2011: 6). The latter, the need to balance against one another, ultimately explains the highly restrictive unanimity requirement imposed on any major decision concerning the economic union as designed by the European Coal and Steal Community (1951) and the European Economic Community (1957) treaties.[2] The preeminence of geopolitical concerns underpinning the formation of these four unions suggests that none of them resulted from bargains driven by mutually beneficial distributional advantages. As a result, there is no risk of circularity.

No such risk exists in the case of Spain either. The process of democratization in Spain resulted from the new sociopolitical conditions generated by economic development, the fragmentation of the coalition supporting Franco's regime, and a favorable international environment, both in Europe and across the Atlantic (Maravall 1997; Przeworski 2001). In this context, the origins of the Estado de las Autonomias (EA) reflect less distributive pressure on its constituent members and more a political strategy to accommodate, in a context of democratization, contending national identities. Centralism had been a

---

[2] Rosato's view stands as an alternative to what is conventionally seen as the standard theory of European integration, Moravcsik's "liberal intergovernmentalism." His core proposition holds that "European integration was a series of rational adaptations by national leaders to constraints and opportunities stemming from the evolution of an interdependent world economy, the relative power of states in the international system, and the potential for international institutions to bolster credibility of interstate commitments." (2011: 472) The debate seems to be about the relative weight of geopolitical vs. economic motives. The point to note though is that the latter do not refer to internal distributional conflicts, but to the need to seize new opportunities in a more integrated world economy. As a result, the controversy is orthogonal to our concerns. Even if geopolitical motives were less dominant than Rossato suggests, the sort of economic motives Moravcsik's account privileges do not necessarily violate condition one above.

dominant characteristic in the institutional organization of Spanish politics since its early modern days in 1810. Thus, the process of decentralization initiated with the Constitution implied a clear historical break, especially after nearly forty years of strongly centralized dictatorship. In fact, the EA represents the first enduring noncentralized polity in Spanish history. The union as such, however, and its main constituent elements, had a long historical tradition and did not emerge out of distributive concerns at the time of democratization. As we shall see in detail in Chapter 7, the Spanish constitutional design left many aspects of the process of decentralization open for future political negotiation, but not the formation of the political union itself, nor the definition of its system of political representation.

Once the unions formed out of military and geopolitical considerations, acute trade-offs over the design of their fiscal structures emerge. Conflicts between trade oriented and domestic oriented states, between urban and rural areas, between natural resource intensive and manufacturing intensive regions, between advanced and laggard areas – all conflicts at the center of this book's argument – unfolded very early in the history of these political unions. On the basis of these conflicts Beard (1933) produced an economic interpretation of the Constitution of the United States, recently vindicated and extended by McGuire (2003). Similar tensions are observable since the early days of the history of the European Union, as illustrated for instance by the conflicts over agricultural subsidies to producers potentially at risk as a result of the process. More generally, the history of federations is very rich in conflicts about who gets what. Any decision about tariffs, price levels, entry restrictions to imports or exports; any regulation on standards (let alone any decision on taxes) by either a state or the federal government is bound to generate massive distributive effects. Out of this large universe of cases, I have decided to focus more precisely on the design of fiscal structures, that is, taxes and transfers either between individuals or between territories, in historical periods in which a systematic intervention of the state in the economy was either demanded for the first time (such as the Great Depression) or a well known reality (Reunification, Spain). Under these circumstances, the stakes are higher, and any change in patterns of economic geography gain political saliency much faster.

Within this latter subset though, additional requirements limit the number of appropriate cases for the purposes of causal identification. As stated previously in conditions 2 to 4, the evaluation of the conditional relationship between economic geography and representation requires a set of cases with established systems of representation that vary along the continuum ranging from centrifugal to centripetal representation. The cases under scrutiny in the following chapters span the range of the centrifugal-centripetal representation scale, with the EU being the most centrifugal union in the subset, and Germany and Spain being the most centripetal ones in origin. This variation in constitutional structures and systems of representation is a necessary condition to assess how different systems react to transformations in economic geography and patterns of mobility. But it is not sufficient. In addition, the alteration in the patterns of economic geography and mobility must occur for reasons other than the distributive consequences of pre-existing fiscal arrangements. Finally, the identification of the effects of economic geography (and mobility) on fiscal structures requires that in the event of an exogenous modification of the former, the latter can be considered as given. Similarly, given a fixed economic geography, the empirical identification of the impact of a change in the system of representation is only feasible if such a change is, at least to some extent, independent from the preexisting fiscal structure. The remainder of this chapter elaborates in detail the extent to which the unions analyzed in the empirical chapters of the book meet these conditions.

EXOGENOUS CHANGES IN ECONOMIC GEOGRAPHY AND MOBILITY

The second condition above concerns the process through which the geography of economic inequality and patterns of mobility become politically salient. Causal identification requires that the change in the geography of inequality and labor market risk be exogenous. This is not always the case. The geography of economic inequality may become salient due to external, exogenous factors such as an external economic shock, or it may become politicized endogenously, that is to say, as a result of the distributive consequences emerging from existing fiscal structures themselves. Fiscal arrangements in political unions tend to be contested by net contributing members as expropriatory. This distinction is important for the purposes of hypothesis testing as it applies to the empirical cases in this study.

Consider first the exposure of the two North American federations to the Great Depression. In the very rich debate about its causes, it is hard to find the nature of the existing fiscal structures during the 1920s as a prominent factor. Whether one endorses the monetarist interpretation put forward by Friedman (Friedman and Schwartz 1963), or any other alternative (Temin 1976), it seems fair to argue that neither the extreme decentralization of interpersonal redistribution nor the lack of any major system that characterized the welfare systems of both Canada and the United States were major causes of the Depression that provoked a massive, and territorially uneven, economic contraction in both unions. Obviously, the lack of an effective system of taxes and transfers exacerbated the social consequences of the Depression. But that does not make it a cause of the Depression in the first place. The collapse of the financial system transcended national borders. It fell upon domestic fiscal systems as an unexpected burden. Hoover's initial reaction exacerbated the social consequences of the crash but it was hardly its cause (Bernacke 2004; Krugman 2008). The Depression was a major source of change in America's economic geography, one that also directly affected patterns of mobility within the union before changes in public insurance programs took place (Rosenbloom and Sundstrom 2004). In this sense, the patterns of mobility and distributive tensions that followed meet the exogeneity condition: they do not exclusively reflect the distributive impact of pre-existing fiscal structures.[3]

Similarly, Reunification as a historical process is largely the result of the sudden redrawing of Europe's political map, and not a response to the way the fiscal system in the Federal Republic had been operating up to that point. Again, the latter is bound to be of significance to our understanding of the way the new Germany responds to the many challenges posed by the process, but that does not make it a cause of the process itself. It was the collapse of the Soviet Union and, as a result, its system of satellite states that launched the process and shaped Western Germany's approach to it. Indeed, it is commonly recognized that the coup in Russia in 1990 was a major factor in driving western elites to speed up the process of incorporating Eastern Germany as much as possible (Wiesenthal 1995, 1996). This decision, in turn, triggered an overnight, and very extreme, alteration of Germany's economic geography and potential patterns of mobility. The sudden economic union of two areas with radically different levels of income, human capital, productivity, and pay created the conditions for potential massive population outflows from the East and increased the burden on the existing systems of interpersonal and interregional redistribution (Streeck 2009). As in the case of the North American federations, the distributive tensions associated with Reunification do not result only from the preexisiting fiscal arrangements. Rather, they largely reflect political choices imposed by external factors. In this sense, the German experience also meets the exogeneity condition.

In contrast to these three experiences, the processes of European integration and decentralization in Spain seem less straightforward. Notably, throughout the history of European integration, all major alterations of the union's economic geography result from enlargement decisions on which current members have veto power. Though a careful look at the timing and sequence of the enlargement decisions reveals a strong geopolitical impact again, enlargement negotiations were very much shaped by the distributive conflicts between current and potential members (Schneider 2009). This is particularly apparent in the cases of Southern and Eastern Europe. Negotiations about integration for Portugal, Spain, and Greece started shortly after the latter transitioned to democracy. European powers at the time saw the integration of these three countries as a necessary move toward the consolidation of their new democratic institutions (Gunther, Diamandouros and Puhle 1995). A concern about the evolution and stability of three major players in the Mediterranean flank of Europe was also in play at a time in which the end of the Cold War was not nearly in sight. In turn, the prospect of opening the Union to

---

[3] Obviously this does not rule out that, once in place, the eventual reorganization of the fiscal structure had a subsequent impact on regional inequalities and patterns of mobility. The point to note here is that the Great Depression constitutes a breaking point that allows for the identification of the causes underlying different responses.

The Road Ahead: The Empirical Strategy

South European democracies created deep distributive trade-offs, both between and within countries. Similarly, the wave of democratization that followed the collapse of the Soviet Union triggered the most recent enlargement to the East. Following the end of the Cold War tensions, and troubled by the political instability in Russia, the former European Free Trade Association (EFTA) states bordering the Union applied for membership. Naturally, the core members of the EU were worried about the income gap between the current and potential members of the union, and thus pushed for discriminatory membership and temporary restrictions to the mobility of workers (Schneider 2007). But they decided to pursue the enlargement anyway to expand their area of economic influence and ensure that the belt of countries separating them from the new Russia was economically and politically stable.[4]

At this point, it is critical to distinguish again between the *factors that trigger* the process from the factors that *drive how the process subsequently evolves*. There is clearly an exogenous element in the fact that external circumstances altered the pre-conditions for the Union's enlargement. Before the collapse of the Berlin Wall, none of these countries could choose their political regime, and therefore the process ultimately leading to enlargement could not start in the first place. But EU members linked their negotiation strategies during enlargement itself to their relative position within the existing fiscal structure of the Union. By implication, the risk of large population movements within the Union is also part of the same endogenous process. Concerns about mobility were central to the enlargement process and, as shown in Chapter 4, played an important role in the design of redistribution within the EU. Contrary to the cases of Germany, Canada, and the United States there is no external event, such as the Depression or Reunification, over which members of the Union have no effective veto. In consequence, the case for truly exogenous changes in economic geography proves much harder to make.

The same ambiguity about the sources of contentions over fiscal structures applies to the case of Spain (León-Alfonso 2007). The democratic regime inherited a fully centralized system of public insurance provision, and a fully centralized tax system. At the same time, the Constitution of 1978 set in motion a highly asymmetric process of decentralization. By virtue of historical precedent, two regions, the Basque Country and Navarra, enjoyed full fiscal autonomy and control over a wide range of policies from the outset. A second group (Galicia, Catalonia, and Andalusia), allegedly those regions with some historical pedigree derived from a tradition of nationalist political mobilization, could use a fast track to establish their regional institutions and assume control over an increasing array of policies. Finally, the rest of the seventeen regions would follow the "normal" track. Over time, all three groups gained control over policies such as education, health, or infrastructure development. Virtually, every public policy involving service provision (including health, education,

---

[4] On the politics of enlargement, see also Schimmelfennig (2001); and Plümper, Schneider and Troeger (2005).

and social service provision) was decentralized except one that still remains under central control, Social Security. As policy decentralization increased, so did their claim for fiscal transfers to sustain them.

Over the last three decades, political and fiscal decentralization in Spain have entered a spiral with no apparent end. The Basque nationalists, in power since the transition until 2009, aspire to assume control over the few policy areas still directed from Madrid, including social security. In turn, Catalonia displays an unanimous voice in demand of its homogenization with the Basque Country and Navarra, denouncing what they deem as an unjustifiable discrimination. Thus, they demand to have the same level of fiscal autonomy as the Basque Country and Navarra have enjoyed since the very beginning of the process. Being a wealthy region under the common framework, Catalan elites feel, much like Baden-Württemberg in Germany, that the level of redistribution implied by the status quo is excessive.

The status quo involves a centralized system of interpersonal redistribution, originally established by Franco and massively expanded by the Socialists during the mid 1980s and early 1990s, and central control until the early 1990s of the bulk of revenue collection and distribution of resources across regions. This system generates large levels of redistribution by centrally raising revenues from the areas with a larger tax base (Catalonia, Madrid, and Baleares) and transferring a large share of those revenues to less developed regions (Galicia, Extremadura, and Andalucia). Contentions over fiscal structures in Spain are clearly endogenous: what the former group denounces as excessive extraction, the latter celebrates as solidarity.

Unsurprisingly, conflicts over the allocation of fiscal resources across territories became increasingly prominent over the years. These conflicts concern two issues: how much revenue is to be raised centrally as opposed to regionally, and how the money collected by Madrid is to be allocated across regions. An overview of the dynamics of fiscal federalism in Spain reveals the impossibility of reaching a stable, self-enforcing arrangement (Beramendi and Máiz 2004; León-Alfonso 2007). Since 1993, when Catalonia extracted for the first time control over 15% of the income tax revenues in its territory in exchange for supporting the Socialists' minority government in Madrid, the system has been in constant flux. 1996 saw the 15% grow to 30%. When this 30% was generalized, new demands reached 50%. When the Conservatives gained an absolute majority in 2000, the process stalled, to restart in 2004–2008, a period in which Catalonia traded its support to Zapatero's minority government for the opportunity to pass in Madrid a new state constitution and impose a new fiscal federal agreement that implies a fundamental overhaul of the current system and a reduction in previous levels of redistribution. And so forth and so on.

This succinct overview suggests that, as in the case of the EU, some *given* factors shape processes of decentralization: to a significant extent, the constitutional arrangements of 1978 reflect special deals secured by some regions, in particular the historical fiscal privileges that the Basque Country and Navarra managed to keep even under Franco's dictatorship (1939–1975). It is also the case that the existence of nationalist parties pushing for fiscal autonomy predates both the constitutional agreement of 1978 and the subsequent conflicts around the concretion of fiscal arrangements between Madrid and the different regions. At the same time, however, once the status quo is in place after the transition and consolidation of democracy (1978–1981), virtually every conflict about the reform of fiscal federalism in Spain derives from the distributional consequences of earlier choices. In political terms, the evolution of fiscal decentralization in Spain is an endogenous process with no critical juncture of external origin. The initial arrangements shape the patterns of political decentralization; these feed back into the system of representation, most notably on the levels of decentralization of the party system, which in turn shapes the evolution of fiscal federal arrangements. This dynamics speaks directly to the third condition for causal identification, to which I turn now.

POLITICAL REPRESENTATION AND THE STATUS QUO: WHEN CAN POLITICAL REPRESENTATION BE TAKEN AS GIVEN?

This section is concerned with the final conditions for identifying the effect of economic geography and mobility on fiscal structures (Hypotheses 1 and 2), namely that the system of representation can be taken as given at the time conflicts over the design of fiscal structures erupt.

Chhibber and Kollman (2004) have exploited the experiences of Canada, India, the United States and the United Kingdom to argue that fiscal and administrative centralization is an important cause behind the centralization of the party system. Their focus is on cases of policy and national party integration: "as governments centralize authority, taking powers away or imposing new conditions on lower levels of government, voters will naturally have more incentives to try to influence politics at higher levels. And candidates will be more inclined to take positions on policy issues being dealt with at the higher levels of government and make those positions centerpieces of their campaign for office" (p.78). The same logic should apply as well in the opposite direction: as countries decentralize policy provision, political parties are expected to decentralize their organizational structures and candidates' nomination procedures. In terms of the argument developed in the previous chapter, then, the parameter on the importance of national elections (Φ) is itself endogenous with respect to the organization and evolution of the fiscal structure.

These findings pose a potential problem for an argument that is centered around the interplay between economic geography, in particular the geography of income inequality, and the structure of political representation. Specifically, they pose a problem for condition 3. If both representation and economic geography change at the same time, it would be simply impossible to identify the marginal effects posited by the argument. Hence the question: when can political representation be taken as given?

The political architecture of unions includes representation of regional interests at the national level, the articulation and organization of the party system, judicial review, and political decentralization (Falleti 2005; Hooghe, Marks and Schakel 2008; Rodden 2004). All of these are dimensions of the territorial distribution of power. Despite the fact that the causal arrows between them may flow in multiple directions over time, not all of them necessarily co-vary across space and time. This is partly because some aspects of decentralization are part of the constitution and others not.

Constitutional rules and procedures regulate strategic interaction between different levels of government. Independent judicial review systems and special requirements governing constitutional reform tend to protect constitutions from the instability of normal politics. In turn, the distribution of political authority across levels of government reflects the outcome of such a bargaining process. Ultimately, it reflects the equilibrium of forces within the federation at a particular moment in time.

In between, extra-constitutional institutions, such as the party system, shape the incentives of political elites and connect constitutional constraints to political preferences and outcomes. Loosely following Filippov, Ordeshook and Shvetsova (2004), these three layers correspond to three levels of institutional analysis. In principle, constitutional rules and procedures are more resistant to change, whereas political decentralization in different policy fields, including redistributive policy, appears more malleable.

The possibility of change in the characteristics of the party system is likely to fall between the two. As a result, the different dimensions of federations are unlikely to *move* at the same time. They are not equally fluid. For this reason the multidimensionality of political institutions becomes an asset worth exploiting. The relationship between different elements of federalism and decentralization can be approached by assuming that some of the other factors/dimensions are given. The possibility that institutions can, over time, be endogenous as well as the source of independent effects only becomes meaningful on the basis of this assumption. Otherwise, partial equilibrium relationships could not be identified. Hence the question: when can political representation be taken as given?

The answer is simple, not very often: (1) when history provides natural experiments in which unions with different systems of representation are *suddenly* exposed to *exogenous* shocks that require a change in the design of their fiscal structures. Among the cases in this book, these conditions apply only to the situation created after the Great Depression in North America and to the challenge of Reunification in Germany; (2) when the constitutional design is independent of and prior to distributive conflicts over fiscal structures that originate endogenously. These two situations differ in that they allow us to capture empirically different aspects of the interaction between economic geography and political representation.

Table 3.1 classifies the cases according to the nature of the system, or representation, either when the exogenous shock occurs (*natural experiments*) or at the onset of processes in which the different elements of the argument are jointly endogenous over time (*endogenous processes*). Table 3.1 conveys one

TABLE 3.1. *Case Selection and Empirical Strategy*

Representation in Status Quo	Research Design Conditions	
	Natural Experiments	Endogenous Processes
Centrifugal	US and Canada's responses to the Great Depression	The European Union
Centripetal	Germany's response to Reunification	Contentions over fiscal structures in Spain

important fact, namely there is variation in the organization of political representation within both groups of cases. In the rest of this section, I introduce the systems of representation in the cases within each group and discuss how comparison across the different cases helps the empirical evaluation of the argument.

Endogenous Processes

The European Economic Community (1957) was born a highly centrifugal political union (Dinan 1999; Moravcsik 1998; Rosato 2011). And it remains today a union in which decision making powers remain largely under the control of its constituent members, the national states. Undoubtedly, the Commission as an agenda setter (Garrett and Tsebelis 1996; Tsebelis and Garrett 2001), and the Parliament as a co-decider in a wider range of policy areas (Rittberger 2005), have increased their relative power over time. Yet, despite all these advances, Delors' dream of a "federation of nation states" remains an unrealized aspiration (European Parliament, Minutes of the Committee on Constitutional Affairs, Brussels, September 18, 2000).

Even after the relative empowering of the Parliament in the Treaty of Amsterdam, the legislative process in the EU remains as follows[5]: the Commission, after a long process of canvassing and consultation with both the Council and the Parliament, proposes legislation. This proposal is then evaluated and decided upon by the Council, either by qualified majority voting or by unanimity. This essentially gives any member or small group of members effective veto power on any proposal (Tsebelis 2002). Once the Council has decided, the proposal is either *consulted* or *co-decided* with the Parliament. In the first case, the Parliament lacks veto power but issues a nonbinding position on the proposal. In the latter case, approval of the Parliament is required for the proposal to become law. In case of disagreement, both parts resort to the Conciliation Committee. In the absence of an agreement in this committee, the proposal is moot. Overall, the balance of power between local and "federal" elites in the

---

[5] For a more detailed description of this process, see Hix (2005); and Thomson and Holsi (2006).

EU is clearly tilted towards the former when it comes to deciding about the organization of policy fields.

Central to the concerns in this chapter is the fact that any move toward policy integration in Europe requires simultaneously changes in the allocation of power across levels of government and changes in the voting procedures with the Council, as well as modifications in the balance of power between the latter and the Parliament (Hix 2005; Thomson et al. 2006).

In the specific policy areas of interest to this study, interpersonal redistribution via taxes and transfers, and interregional redistribution via policies such as the Structural Funds, institutional change is subject to the strictest control by national governments. Decisions by the Council on these matters follow the unanimity rule and the Parliament lacks co-decision powers. Any movement away from the status quo toward the centralization of interpersonal redistribution would entail not only a transfer of powers within the policy domain to Brussels but a removal of the unanimity voting rule and a modification of the balance of power between the latter and the Parliament. In this instance, the endogeneity between the choice of fiscal structures and political representation becomes particularly apparent: by centralizing interpersonal redistribution, EU member states would also be contributing to undermine the centrifugal nature of the system of representation. Within this dynamics, the notion that representation is exogenous at the time contentions over fiscal structures unfold appears particularly extravagant.

The experience of Spain over the last three decades provides yet another illustration of this logic. As outlined previously, Spain was designed to function and remain a centripetal political union. The Senate was conceived of and remains an empty shell, undermining the effective representation of territorial interests during the legislative process at the national level. More importantly, the Spanish electoral system is one of proportional representation, built upon the D'Hondt Law. Proportional representation is well known to generate incentives to build broad political appeals, platforms across cleavages transcending specific territorial interests (Austen-Smith and Banks 1988; Crémer and Palfrey 1999; Dixit and Londregan 1998) that materialize in encompassing coalition governments. In the case of Spain, the adoption of the D'Hondt version pursued the overrepresentation of rural provinces, with lower levels of population density and a higher likelihood to opt for conservative forces, and to ensure the generation and stabilization of a two-party political system at the national level (Montero 1998: 53–80). The goal was to keep the number of parties at bay and limit the scope of influence of regional, identity based parties. The political game was to be played by two strong and centralized national party organizations, never to be held at ransom by local barons of any sort. The presence of territorially integrated organizations on each side of the ideological spectrum constituted a key element of the centripetal design of representation. Only the existence of important nationalist parties in Catalonia and the Basque Country counterbalanced this design.

Over time, the initial decision to decentralize major public services, such as health, education, and infrastructure building has empowered the capacity of regional governments as political actors.[6] As a result, political party organizations have become regionalized, not least in some cases, such as Catalonia, Galicia, or Andalusia, because of the presence of *nationalist* (local) competitors. This, in turn, has exacerbated the demand for further decentralization of policies and resources, triggering a process in which the decentralization of political representation and fiscal decentralization are jointly endogenous. Over time, policy decentralization undermines the political sustainability of centripetal representation as part of a self-sustained dynamic with no obvious end in sight.[7] Again, key elements of the system of representation and fiscal decentralization appear to be jointly endogenous.

Given the tight links over time between decisions about policy decentralization and important aspects of the system of representation, the question arises as to what sort of leverage these chapters provide for the empirical evaluation of the argument. Clearly these two cases do not serve the purpose of isolating the marginal causal effects of changes in economic geography, mobility, or representation. They do, however, serve a related purpose, directly linked to the role of political representation in shaping fiscal structures.

Put shortly, the analysis of the politics behind the choice of fiscal structures in the EU and Spain does allow us to capture the importance of the status quo, that is, of the starting conditions in terms of political representation (centrifugal vs. centripetal) under which contentions about fiscal structures subsequently unfold. The relationship between representation and fiscal structures is clearly endogenous over time, but this does not render the initial choices in terms of political representation endogenous as well. Recall from earlier discussion that factors other than distributional considerations, such as geopolitical considerations or historical legacies, did shape the original articulation of representation in these two unions. The initial balance of power between the center and the regions in the Treaty of Rome (1957) or the Spanish Constitution (1978) is in this sense exogenous. As a rich literature on historical legacies and institutional inertia documents (Pierson 2004), and the model formalizes, these initial conditions determine who moves first and who holds the possibility of vetoes over the status quo in terms of fiscal structures. Exploring the dynamics of

---

[6] I offer a more detailed outline of this process in Chapter 7.
[7] Focusing on a different case, Diaz-Cayeros (2006) provides additional evidence of the difficulties of disentangling institutional choices, electoral concerns, and distributive politics. His innovative analysis of the institutional dynamics of the Mexican federation reveals that the centralization of the party system and the centralization of tax policy are jointly endogenous. In this and other Latin American cases, centralization of tax policy emerges as the outcome of bargaining with local political elites. The key to the process was to allow rich regions to become richer while using centralized redistribution to buy the support of the leaders of backward regions. This coalition between leaders of rich and poor regions alike, Diaz-Cayeros argues, was forged through the articulation of a national party system.

contention over fiscal structures in two unions with fundamentally different starting points contributes to a better understanding of the origins and evolution of fiscal structures, even if the cases under consideration do not meet all the requirements for the causal identification of marginal effects. Endogenous distributive tensions operate under very different institutional conditions in the EU and Spain. The argument predicts that in the EU the initial design of representation will exacerbate the decentralizing effect of economic geography on fiscal structures. In Spain, the argument predicts that the initial centripetal arrangements will constrain such effects and lag the process of decentralization of redistribution. Establishing whether these expectations hold is an important part of the empirical agenda in this book that complements the tighter grasp on causal mechanisms facilitated by natural experiments.

Natural Experiments

At different times in history, the Great Depression and Germany's Reunification created a set of circumstances that make capturing the causal link between economic geography and political representation and the role of mobility in shaping interpersonal redistribution a feasible endeavor. The contrast between the way the United States and Germany responded to radical transformations in their economic geography facilitates the evaluation of the mediating role of the systems of representation that in both cases can be considered as given. In turn, the contrast between the responses in Canada and the United States to the changing geography of income and labor market risk controls for a set of relatively similar political and institutional circumstances, thereby facilitating the assessment of the influence of mobility in shaping public insurance systems. In what follows, I discuss in detail the nature of representation in these three political unions before they were subject to a sudden transformation of their economic geography.

As opposed to the EU, the process of federalization in the United States and Canada was already completed during the early decades of the twentieth century. The federal government of the United States enjoyed a much more prominent political position. It controlled the political agenda, the army, trade policy, regulation of the economy, foreign policy, the bulk of the law and order system, and many other policy domains. In both cases, the federal government is the leading political institution in the federation: it sets the political agenda and controls the largest share of government resources. Accordingly, there was a system to ensure direct accountability from the federal government to the citizenry. This is particularly the case in the U.S.'s presidential system, but also in Canada, where the prime minister is determined by the majority in the House of Commons. Both unions used a majoritarian system to translate votes into either delegates to the electoral college (United States) or seats to the House (Canada). As a result, the system of representation is relatively closer to the centripetal end of the scale. Politics was much more federal in North America in the 1930s than it is in the European Union today. However, several aspects of the system of governance of both unions make the move towards the nationalization of politics before the Great Depression a moderate one.

The constitutional protection of states' rights is inherent to federalism. Such a protection works as a powerful source of centrifugalism in any policy domain recognized (whether explicitly or implicitly) under states' authority by the constitution. Essentially, any attempt to redraw the original allocation of policy responsibilities requires either a constitutional reform or, in previously underdeveloped policy domains, a careful political balance between national needs and states' rights. Such was the case in both Canada and the United States before the Great Depression. Social welfare was a residual, subsidiary task to be undertaken by lower levels of government and charitable institutions. Written at a time when public welfare was a rather inexpensive tool for public order and contention of the most destitute sectors of society, the Canadian Constitution explicitly left these matters to municipalities and provincial governments. Similarly, state and local authorities were in charge of organizing relief in the United States (the dole system), as social assistance did not belong to the policy domains under federal control (Banting 1987; Skocpol 1992). In addition, in both cases, launching a national public welfare system would require raising additional revenues, which in turn would trigger a constitutional conflict over the appropriate instruments and level of government to do so. In sum, the constitutionalization of states and provinces' authority over public welfare provision before the Great Depression enhances their relative position in any potential reform.

Along with the protection of *self-rule*, the second defining feature of federations concerns the organization of *shared rule* (Elazar 1987). The idea of shared rule refers to a panoply of political and institutional mechanisms that facilitates the representation of territorial interests in forming the national will. In the United States the primary mechanism is a highly malapportioned upper chamber, the Senate. The Senate is composed of two representatives directly elected by the population of each of the fifty states, empowered with a tight grip over the legislative process. By contrast, the Canadian Senate is an empty shell. Provincial executives, through a system of institutionalized intergovernmental relations, provide a functional equivalent for the representation of provincial interests in Ottawa. Regardless of their specific form, the impact of these representative provisions on the balance of power between the federal government and the states (Φ) is not obvious ex ante. A third mechanism, the organization of the party system, mediates the leverage granted to subnational units within the system of representation. Rodden (2006) illustrates this logic in the case of fiscal discipline. Under unclear divisions of authority, governments at different levels have incentives to transfer the cost of their policies to other levels. Subnational governments, for instance, have an incentive to incur debt and hope to be bailed out by the center whenever the financial crisis reaches its limit. Because regional governments do not know how committed to fiscal discipline the central government is, they will adjust their political behavior according to their expectations regarding the central government's resoluteness. Integrated national party systems make the resoluteness of the central government more credible and facilitate the enforcement of discipline by reducing incentives for regional incumbents to behave irresponsibly. An integrated party system affects the incentives of subnational incumbents in two different ways. First, local elites regarded as a liability for the overall electoral profile of the party face severe consequences in terms of their own political careers. As a result, opportunistic behavior by local incumbents is likely to be constrained (Enikolopov and Zhuravskaya 2003; Rodden and Wibbels 2002; Wibbels 2001). Second, an integrated national party system helps solve the commitment problem between incumbents at different levels of government by intertwining their political fates. In turn, partisan harmony and electoral coattails feed back on each other, facilitating the long-term cooperation between different levels of government and the party's organization. This renders commitments between local and national elites more credible, and facilitates policy coordination between levels of government, thus muting the centrifugal tendencies in the union.

From this perspective, the assessment of the balance of power between the federal government and the states in the United States and Canada depends upon the characteristics of the party system in the period preceding the Great Depression. Historical studies on both sides of the border convey a very similar picture, one of extremely fragmented political organizations controlled by local barons mostly responsive to the interests of their local constituencies. Describing the "brokerage politics" era in Canada, Carty, Cross and Young (2000) refer to the 1920s as "the golden age of political regionalism in Canada. The dominant politicians of the period were regional political bosses articulating regional interests and carrying their regions with them as they practiced a politics of accommodation [...] The preeminent party structure of this era has been described by Whitaker as the *ministerialist* party– an organization run by powerful regional chieftains whose control of the cabinet offices of the national government allowed them to engage in the political bargaining necessary to maintain their electoral support" (p. 17). In turn, Finegold and Skocpol (1995) describe the Democratic Party of the pre-New Deal years as one "of southerners and city bosses" (p. 41). Earlier, the progressives had failed to "dethrone the political bosses who in alliance with the holders of concentrated economic power defended the status quo [...], to eliminate the intermediate points where the public will was corrupted, and restore the power of the people" (Sundquist 1983: 43). Put simply, national parties were rather weak organizations on both sides of the border.[8] The "one party factionalism" in the South (Key 1949) was

---

[8] The Liberal Party in Canada eventually grew more centralized than the Democratic Party in the United States. This development, however, took place primarily after the Great Depression occurred, not before. For a detailed history of the Liberal Party in Canada and the timing of its territorial integration, see Whitaker (1977). Indeed, even during the late 1930s, when dicussions over the redesign of public insurance programs were well underway, there was quite a bit of conflict within the liberal party itself (Struthers 1983). I return to this issue in Chapter 5.

perhaps the most extreme case of a widespread phenomenon: "factional fluidity and discontinuity probably make a government especially susceptible to individual pressures and especially disposed toward favoritism. Or to put the reverse of the proposition, *the strength of organization reflecting something of a group or class solidarity creates conditions favorable to government according to rule or general principle* (Key 1949: 305). [...] Organization is not always necessary to obstruct; it is essential, however, for the promotion of a sustained program in behalf of the have nots[...]" (p. 307). As we shall see in detail in Chapter 5, the beneficiaries of this factionalist policy, Southern democratic elites, also had a privileged position in the Senate due to the seniority system, exercising a very strong influence on the formation of the political will (Hacker and Pierson 2002). Finally, the political fragmentation of state and local elites in both unions also meant that the Depression overcame by large factors their limited capabilities. Thus, the Depression opened an era of confusion on both sides of the border, staggering local and state officials, and setting the stage for a political conflict over the launching of new comprehensive public insurance programs. At the onset of this process both Canada and the United States were decentralized federations, unions in which the formation of the political will retained strong centrifugal components.

The organization of political will in Germany's "semi-sovereign state" (Katzenstein 1987) offers a contrasting case, one much closer to the centripetal end of the continuum, capturing the balance of power between central governments and subnational units. Centripetalism emerges in several features of the German political system. Chief among them is the system of proportional representation governing both federal and state elections (Schmidt 2003). According to Lijphart (1999: 162), the resulting gap between seats and votes in the Bundestag elections during the second half of the twentieth century was significantly lower than that observed, for instance, in the British House of Commons. In addition, the existence of a 5% entry threshold, again at the federal and state level, guarantees moderate levels of party system fractionalization. What is more, the organization of shared rule in Germany contrasts sharply with the one in North America in the 1930s. Germany's "*unitarian* federalism [...] emphasizes the preservation of the legal and economic unity... [...] Furthermore, Germany's federalism is characterized by extensive cooperation and interlocked politics between the federal government and the state governments, as well as by no less extensive horizontal coordination between the states" (Schmidt 2003: 15–16). In this context, the political weight of the *länder* during the legislative process is not based on their full legislative and administrative capacities in a number of policy areas, but on the role that the Bundesrat, the territorial upper chamber, has in passing national legislation.[9] The Bundesrat is composed of delegations from each land, appointed by the

---

[9] On this point, a distinction between *Einspruchsgesetz* (the Bundesrat can veto but the Bundestag (the Parliament) can overrule) and *Zustimmungsgesetz* (in which the majority of the Bundesrat has to consent) is in order. More than 50% of federal legislation belongs to the second category.

regional executives and led by the *Länder Ministerpräsidenten* (Gunlicks 2003). As opposed to the U.S. Senate, the number of representatives per region is a function of the number of inhabitants.

This design was directly intended to foster cooperation and stability between the different units of the federation. After Weimar's experience, perceived as overcentralized, the dominant view was that the new constitution should ensure that different levels of government cooperate in the design and implementation of any given program. The alternative design, allocating full and exclusive responsibilities to specific levels of government was thought to facilitate institutional conflict and ultimately political instability (Jeffery and Savigear 1991; Lehmbruch 1990: 462–486). The idea of "cooperation" permeated the design of public policies as well in such a way that it is very hard for citizens to attribute responsibilities for policy outcomes to a particular level of government. This procedure breeds consensus and prevents innovation (Scharpf 1988). In turn, this form of cooperative federalism bears important implications on the behavior of political parties and regional incumbents (Rodden 2006; Schmidt 2003). The importance of the Bundesrat in the legislative process demands that national parties coordinate their regional leaders to pass any major piece of legislation. To act as potential veto players in the Bundesrat, parties must first coordinate across länder (Saalfeld 2002). Thus, when a piece of legislation is discussed in the Budestag, national party elites are at the same time coordinating their strategies with "their" regional incumbents, represented in the Bundesrat. In turn, the behavior of regional leaders in office, but most importantly in the upper chamber, may condition the electoral chances of parties in federal elections. As a result, national parties have little incentive to support rent-seeking behavior on the part of their regional elites. The electoral costs for doing that might be politically devastating. Under these circumstances, party labels and organizations become ever more important for regional incumbents to win office. In sum, the shadow of Weimar was very much present in the design of political representation in the 1949 Constitution, yielding a highly centripetal political system. Such a system, combined with the unexpected process of Reunification, provides a natural experiment that allows us to observe how unions with centripetal systems of political representation respond to sudden transformations in their economic geography. The German case complements the natural experiment created by the Great Depression by broadening the range of systems of representation subject to exogenous economic pressures.

SUMMARY: EMPIRICAL STRATEGY AND HYPOTHESIS TESTING

The chapters that follow turn to study the politics of fiscal structures in the five unions included in Table 3.1. Chapter 4 analyzes the distributive conflicts over fiscal structures throughout the history of the European Union. Chapter 5 focuses on the reaction of Canada and the United States to the Great Depression in the realm of unemployment insurance. I concentrate on unemployment insurance because it is a policy that is fiscally and politically salient, and deals with risks that vary across territories as much as across social groups. Other programs, such as old-age insurance, deal with universal risks (Atkinson 1995; Varian 1980), and hence are less prone to conflicts articulated along territorial lines.[10] Thereafter, Chapter 6 examines Germany's response to the challenge of Reunification. Finally, Chapter 7 analyzes the design of interpersonal and interregional redistribution in the context of Spain's decentralization process. As a complement to the case studies, Chapter 8 provides a statistical evaluation of the main implications of the argument.

The organization of the chapters around specific unions as opposed to themes (interregional vs. interpersonal redistribution) or causal mechanisms (representation, mobility) follows from the premise that it makes the material more accessible to the non-specialized reader. However, the empirical evaluation of the theory rests on the lessons to be drawn across the five unions under study. By way of summarizing the research strategy outlined in this chapter, I finish with a discussion of the way the different chapters address the main hypotheses of the argument and conclude with an overview of how the different chapters contribute to the evaluation of the book's leading hypotheses.

Hypothesis 1: In the absence of high levels of regional economic specialization, large levels of mobility contribute to the homogeneization of redistributive preferences across regions and, through this route, to the centralization of interpersonal redistribution.

Two chapters speak directly to this hypothesis. The inquiry into the reasons behind the varying responses by Canada and the United States to the Great Depression provides a good setup to evaluate this expectation: both countries confronted the Depression from fairly similar starting points in terms of both political representation and the geography of income inequality, and yet Canada decided to centralize unemployment insurance whereas the United States did not. Do the reasons behind this divergence reflect differences in the patterns of crossregional mobility as predicted by the argument? In addition, Chapter 8 offers a test of the claim that higher levels of mobility work to homogenize distributive tensions across territories, thereby facilitating the centralization of redistribution.

Hypothesis 2: The decentralization of interpersonal redistribution results from the interaction between economic geography and political representation.

The empirical chapters of this book provide insights on this hypothesis in three different ways: (1) the natural experiments, in particular the contrast

---

[10] Thus it is not surprising that old-age insurance is effectively the responsibility of the federal government in all advances industrial democratic federations. Even in the highly fragmented US welfare system, old-age became the responsibility of the federal government. Consistent with this reasoning, it is equally noticeable that public health insurance in the United States is only available to the very poor (Medicaid) and citizens over 65 (Medicare).

between the United States's response to the Great Depression, and Germany's response to Reunification (Chapters 5 and 6), allow us to draw some inferences about the causal impact of a heterogeneous economic geography under different institutional conditions; (2) in addition, the contrast between the political conflicts over fiscal structures in the EU and Spain (Chapters 4 and 7) produces insights about the extent to which the organization of representation at the starting point shapes these processes; (3) finally, the quantitative analyses in Chapter 8 take on the empirical implications of this hypothesis directly and ponder whether the conclusions derived from the case studies bear some generalizability.

Hypothesis 3: Given a decentralized system of interpersonal redistribution, the level of interregional redistribution is positively related to levels of mobility and negatively related to centripetal representation.

The decentralization of interpersonal redistribution enhances conflicts over interregional transfers. Hypothesis 3 concerns the determinants of such transfers. The contrast between the European Union (Chapter 4) and Germany (5) brings to light interesting implications for the relationship between the scope of interregional mobility and the level of interregional redistribution. Similarly, a comparative overview of all five unions illuminates the question of what system of representation is more capable of weighing down the extractive capacity of territorially localized political strongholds. Finally, Chapter 8 includes a multivariate analysis of the determinants of interregional redistribution in political unions.

4

The European Union
Economic Geography and Fiscal Structures under Centrifugal Representation

European Union specialists note regularly that Brussels is gaining a prominent role in shaping the policies of the member states. However, there is an important exception to this trend: fiscal policy (Börzel 2005). Direct income taxes and transfers remain local in the EU despite the fact that labor regulations, VAT, trade policy, citizens' mobility, agricultural production, and monetary policy, among others, fall under the grip of EU officials. This imbalance became particularly apparent in debates over the proposal for a European Constitution in 2004.

From Rome (1957) to Lisbon (2009), European social policy has been characterized by numerous programmatic statements and open-ended prescriptions. Without the unanimous consent of the EU's members, these initiatives have had little practical impact. However, although there are no policy mechanisms for *interpersonal redistribution* implemented from Brussels, there are a number of initiatives that redistribute resources between countries. Considered together, these programs of *interregional redistribution* – such as structural funds – account for much of the current EU budget.

Why have so many EU policy realms integrated, but not interpersonal redistribution? Why do the few instances of redistributive effort within the EU take the form of interregional – or intercountry – transfers? In addressing these questions this chapter serves two purposes. First, it provides a detailed analysis of the way economic geography shapes preferences and choices concerning the centralization of interpersonal redistribution in a context of centrifugal representation. In doing so it provides an analysis of one of the extremes in the centrifugal-centripetal representation continuum and contributes to the testing of one of the leading hypotheses in this study, namely that *under centrifugal systems of representation, cross regional differences in terms of inequality and risk translate directly into the adoption of decentralized systems of redistribution* (H.2.A). In addition, by developing a study of how economic geography shapes individual preferences for the centralization of redistribution, this chapter offers a partial empirical evaluation of the microfoundations of the theoretical model.

Second, the chapter addresses the interplay between interpersonal and interregional redistribution in a union with a very heterogeneous economic geography. A major implication of this book's argument is that, given high levels of economic specialization across regions and high levels of decentralization of interpersonal redistribution, interregional transfers operate as an insurance mechanism to protect the political and economic autonomy of different areas. Therefore, the size and direction of interregional transfers should reflect concerns about mobility within the union.

As the risk of undesired inflows increases, so should interregional transfers, particularly toward areas where migrants originate. This chapter evaluates this contention by analyzing the relationship between mobility and interregional redistribution in the process of European integration.

The nature of the European Union's fiscal structure, I argue, is a function of the combined effect of three factors: a very heterogeneous economic geography; a centrifugal system of political representation; and the use of interregional transfers as part of a broader strategy to limit population flows from labor intensive, less productive economies to wealthier, skill-intensive ones. In building this case, I proceed as follows.

First, I present an overview of the origins and evolution of the EU's fiscal structure. The second section maps out how different elements of the theoretical model operate in the EU context. It also outlines the logic behind Europe's fiscal structure. The third and fourth sections analyze empirically the two dimensions of the EU's fiscal structure. Relying on a variety of micro and macro data, the third section links Europe's geographies of insurance and inequality to the decentralization of interpersonal redistribution. In doing so, particular attention is given to the effect of geography of inequality on political actors' institutional preferences. The fourth section addresses the relationship between mobility and interregional redistribution in the European Union. Finally, the last section brings together the core empirical findings of the chapter and discusses its theoretical implications.

THE EUROPEAN UNION'S FISCAL STRUCTURE

The specialized literature points almost unanimously to the unbalanced nature of policy integration of the European Union. Whether the analysis focuses on legislative output (Pollack 2003), policy dynamics (Hix 2001; Hooghe and Marks 2001; Majone 1996) or the asymmetric adoption of alternative decision making procedures (Börzel 2005; Cram 1997;), a consistent picture emerges. While market-oriented regulations have triggered the development of a more integrated framework of internal security, such a spillover is yet to reach the realm of interpersonal redistribution.

Figure 4.1 presents a summary of the patterns of integration across policy domains. I use data from Börzel (2005). These data measure both the level

The European Union

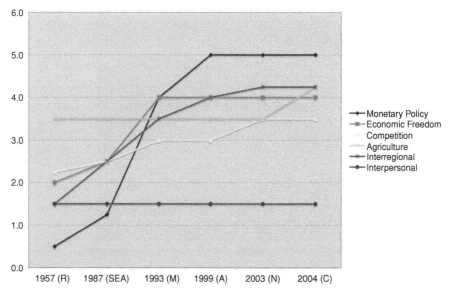

FIGURE 4.1. Unbalanced Policy Integration in the European Union (1957–2004) (*Source:* Author's elaboration on the basis of Börzel 2005)

(whether the issue falls under EU competence) and the scope (what decision making procedure applies to each policy) to ascertain the extent of integration across policy domains.[1] Figure 4.1 averages the scores for level and scope across six areas: economic freedom, competition and industry, monetary policy, judicial affairs, territorial economic and social cohesion (i.e., interregional redistribution), and taxes (i.e., interpersonal redistribution).

Lower values indicate lower levels of integration within a particular policy realm, and vice versa. Observations across time reflect the key legislative moments throughout the process of integration: the Treaty of Rome, the Single European Act, the Maastricht Treaty, the Amsterdam Treaty, the Nice Treaty, and the draft European Constitution (2004).

Figure 4.1 brings out two important aspects of the dynamics of integration. First, policy integration is very unbalanced in the EU. While market integration spills over some policy realms, such as judicial affairs, others, such as taxes and transfers, remain sheltered at the national level. Second, and central to

---

[1] The scale for *level* is as follows: 1 = exclusive national competence; 2 = shared competences dominated by national states; 3 = shared competences with equal level of responsibility between the union and the member states; 4 = shared competences dominated by the EU; and 5 = competence at the EU level. The *scale* for scope is as follows: 0 = no coordination; 1 = unanimity rule, there is coordination but each nation state has veto power; 2 = same as 1, but the commission may have legislative initiative and there is consultation with the European Parliament; 3 = the Commission has exclusive right of initiative and there is either consultation or codecision with the Parliament. Restricted judicial review by the European Court of Justice; 4 = co-legislation between the Council and the Parliament. Full judicial review by the European Court of Justice; and 5 = supranational centralization at the EU level. See Börzel (2005: 221).

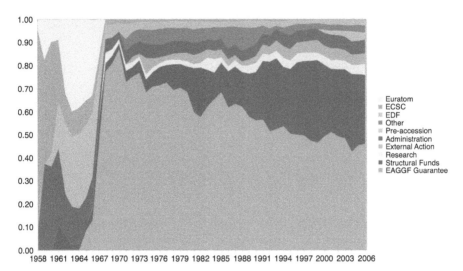

FIGURE 4.2. Relative Composition of EU Expenditure, 1958–2001 (percent) (*Source:* Author's elaboration on the basis of European Commission (2007: 53–57))

this book's concerns, interpersonal redistribution is barely existent at the EU level. Scores around 1–1.5 indicate both that the commission has hardly any influence in these policy realms vis-à-vis the member states and that even in those few instances in which the EU has initiated a social agenda of its own (to be discussed later in more detail), member states retain veto power. The decentralized nature of interpersonal redistribution within the EU is even more striking when one considers the size of the federal government relative to the size of the economy. Whereas the EU budget accounts for about 1% of GDP of the EU economy in 2004, the general government expenditure of the federal government in the United States that same year accounted for 35.7% of America's GDP (Hix 2005: 272). Indeed, the size of the EU government relative to the size of the European economy is much smaller than the size of any federal government of any federation in the world relative to the size of their respective economy.

Figure 4.1 conveys a third point, one that partially vindicates the logic of compensation discussed above. The analysis of interpersonal redistribution within the union constitutes just one aspect of the fiscal structure of the EU. A number of programs devoted to social and economic cohesion across territories have developed alongside market integration. Indeed, the lion's share of the EU budget goes to redistribution of resources between countries.

Redistribution in the EU is both limited and between countries (regions) as opposed to between individuals. Figure 4.2 delves deeper into this point by graphically depicting the relative composition of EU expenditure during 1958–2006. Of all the budgetary components captured by Figure 4.2, two stand out: the Common Agricultural Policy expenditures (EAGG Guarantee) and the Structural Funds. Both these programs constitute elements of interregional redistribution between members of the union. I present a brief overview of these programs in turn.

In the early 1960s, the members of the European Economic Community set out to implement the provisions of the Treaty of Rome, title II, article 33, which read as follows:

"The objectives of the common agricultural policy shall be:

(a) to increase agricultural productivity by promoting technical progress and by ensuring the rational development of agricultural production and the optimum utilization of the factors of production, in particular labor;
(b) thus to ensure a fair standard of living for the agricultural community, in particular by increasing the individual earnings of persons engaged in agriculture;
(c) to stabilize markets;
(d) to assure the availability of supplies;
(e) to ensure that supplies reach consumers at reasonable prices."

The pursuit of these goals was articulated around three basic measures (Hix 2005: 282): *protection against low internal prices* (by having the European Agricultural Guidance and Guarantee Fund (EAGGF) buy surplus goods when prices fall below the guarantee price in the European market); *protection against low import prices* (by imposing levies on imported agricultural goods when world prices fall below an agreed price); and *subsidies to achieve a low export price* (by paying out refunds to producers when the world price falls below an agreed price).

This policy originated as a way of compensating French farmers for opening the French economy to external competition, particularly German industries. Throughout the 1990s, the policy suffered a number of reforms, as a result of which the balance between the different elements of the policy has reversed. Until the early 1990s, price protection, to support the farmers, was the primary strategy. A series of reforms (1992, 2000) turned the policy into a direct income support program (about 45% of all agricultural expenditures were direct payments to farmers in 2005), concentrated in particular areas of the EU.

The last of these reforms took place in February 2006, when EU members agreed to cut the guaranteed minimum sugar price by 36%, in exchange for funds to encourage uncompetitive sugar producers to leave the industry. Funded through either VAT collections (collected by national governments) or direct contributions from member states (European Commission 2004), the EAGGF operates as a system of transfers targeted to agricultural producers concentrated in specific areas of the Union: hence its importance as an interregional transfer.

Figure 4.3 displays the percentage of agriculture expenditures received by different European countries. Payments and benefits are unevenly distributed by country, depending on the size of the agricultural sector and the structure of

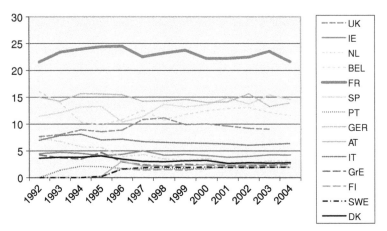

FIGURE 4.3. Distribution of CAP Expenditure By Country (as a percentage of total CAP expenditures) (*Source:* Author's elaboration on data from European Commission (2004))

production. France is the biggest beneficiary of community agricultural expenditure, largely because of the size of its share of agricultural employment and output.[2] As a result, CAP reforms are as much about redistribution between countries as they are about transfers to individual farmers.

The second major component of the EU budget corresponds to the Structural and Cohesion Funds (SCF). This rubric includes a plethora of programs designed to reduce economic disparities within the union. The SCF are the European Union's main instruments for supporting social and economic restructuring across the Union. They account for over one third of the European Union budget and are used to tackle regional disparities and support regional development through actions including developing infrastructure and telecommunications, developing human resources, and supporting research and development.[3] More recently, the objectives of these programs have been reduced to three: (1) to promote development and structural adjustment in regions that have a

---

[2] Obviously, causality here is a tricky matter in that the CAP has generated incentives to concentrate production in certain sectors and sustain an otherwise economically inefficient agricultural sector.

[3] These include: the European Regional Development Fund, set up in 1975, to promote development in the following areas: transport, communication technologies, energy, the environment, research and innovation, social infrastructure, training, urban redevelopment and the conversion of industrial sites, rural development, the fishing industry, and tourism and culture. In turn, created in 1957, the ESF is the EU's main source of financial support for efforts to develop employability and human resources. It helps Member States combat unemployment, prevent people from dropping out of the labor market, and promote training to make Europe's workforce and companies better equipped to face new, global challenges.; and the Financial Instrument for Fisheries, established in 1994, for the structural reform of the fisheries sector. In addition, the structural funds also include the guidance section of the European Agricultural Guidance and Guarantee Fund (EAGGF), devoted to rural development.

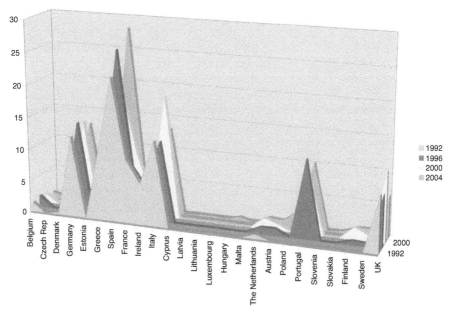

FIGURE 4.4. Distribution by Country of Structural and Cohesion Funds (*Source:* Author's elaboration on data from European Commission (2004))

per capita GDP below 75% of EU average; (2) to ameliorate the costs of structural adjustment in regions with industrial, service, or fisheries sectors facing major change, or deprived urban areas; and (3) for those areas not affected by (1) or (2), to improve human capital, through support for improvement of education and training systems. In addition, the implementation of the European Monetary Union as a result of the Maastricht Treaty brought the Cohesion Funds into play. To be able to join the euro, member countries had to meet a series of tight fiscal and budgetary criteria.[4] Since the reforms necessary to meet these criteria could potentially harm the growth potential of the poorest members of the Union at that time (Greece, Ireland, Spain, and Portugal), the Cohesion Funds were adopted to overcome this possibility. Over the years, the Irish economic miracle and the enlargement to the East in 2004 have altered the list of potential beneficiaries of these funds, which now include Greece, Spain, Portugal, Cyprus, Czech Republic, Estonia, Hungary, Latvia, Lithuania, Malta, Poland, Slovakia, and Slovenia. Figure 4.4 presents a detailed break

---

[4] These *convergence criteria* included (Hix 2005: 315): Price Stability (an average inflation rate no greater than 1.5% above the inflation rates of the three best-performing member states); Interest Rates (an average nominal long-term interest rate no greater than 2% above the interest rates of the three best performing member states); Government Budgetary Position (an annual current account deficit not exceeding 3% of GDP and a gross public debt ratio not exceeding 60% of GDP); and Currency Stability (fluctuations of less that 2.5% around the central rate of the narrow band of the Exchange Rate Mechanism for at least two years, with no devaluations).

down of the distribution of the Structural and Cohesion Funds during the period 1992–2004.

Considering Figures 4.2 to 4.4 together, it is clear that the budgetary expansion of the SCF increases in response to the growing size and the increasing disparities in terms of income per capita within the Union. Indeed, the members' GDP per capita is an excellent (negative) predictor of the share of structural actions to be received by any given country member (Mattila 2004). Figure 4.4 in particular shows how the bigger beneficiaries of structural actions are the lower income countries during the period 1986–1994, when the Union expanded to fifteen members and the monetary union crystallized. From the early 1990s onwards, these programs provide a significant amount of redistribution within the Union.

As a large body of literature has documented, the design of the EU budget is the product of a long series of intergovernmental bargains between the constituent members of the Union (Carruba 1997; Lange 1993; Mattila 2004; Mattli 1999; Moravcsik 1998; Rodden 2002; Weber 1999). In the context of these bargains, those areas in which the EU plays a role in redistributing resources across members develop as a compensation to the "losers" of the creation of a common market. In other words, the CAP and the Structural Actions are normally theorized as side payments without which further market or political integration would not be feasible (Moravcsik 1998). For instance, the creation of the Cohesion Fund is generally accepted as a direct compensation to Ireland and the South European countries for joining the European Monetary Union, modeled after German Bundesbank, and essentially giving up their monetary policy autonomy (Lange 1993). Yet these payments did not come at the cost of member states' fiscal policy autonomy. However compelling, the notion of horizontal redistribution as a mechanism to expand and preserve European markets does not explain the lack of centralization, or even coordination, of public social insurance and redistributive policies in the EU.[5]

In sum, the fiscal design of the European Union presents a clear dual structure. The absence of anything resembling a conventional system of interpersonal redistribution (with the exception of some of the income support components associated with the CAP) is accompanied by a complex web of programs of interregional redistribution that constitute a very significant and increasing share of the total EU budget. Countries remain overly protective of their fiscal policy capabilities even after five decades of economic integration. The diversity of Europe's economic geography helps explain the absence of vertical fiscal integration, but it does not speak to the second main aspect of the fiscal structure of the Union, namely the increasing presence of programs

---

[5] I should underscore that the lack of fiscal centralization in Europe by no means implies an absence of fiscal effects of the EU. A rich literature has focused on the effects of market and monetary integration on the fiscal policies of the member states. For an excellent overview, see Hallerberg (2002). The analysis of these indirect effects, though, is outside the scope of this book.

devoted to the transfer of resources between countries, that is, of programs of interregional redistribution. I turn now to explain these developments.

SUSTAINING AUTONOMY, MANAGING RISKS: THE LOGIC BEHIND EUROPE'S FISCAL STRUCTURE

A central theme in this book is that the specific design of fiscal structures in political unions reflects the balance between the decentralizing effects associated with economic geography and the centralizing push associated with large-scale cross-regional externalities. When both these factors are strong political elites face a trade-off between their need to protect their political autonomy and their need to cope with cross-regional externalities. The solution to this trade-off, this book argues, lies precisely in increasing the effort in interregional redistribution as a way to protect a decentralized system of interpersonal redistribution.

The evolution of interregional redistribution within the European Union fits this logic quite closely. The economic and political differences between the members limit the feasibility of a centralized system of interpersonal redistribution. In turn, the integration of markets creates room for significant economic externalities between the Union's members, such as the mobility of large contingents of unskilled labor or the increase in competition for producers. These externalities affect all members of the newly created market, albeit in different ways. The fears of the British, Danish, or German government are likely to be different from the fears of the Spanish, Greek, or Portuguese governments. Fears are largely associated not only with the level of economic growth of different countries, but also with the specificities of their political economies and labor markets. Scandinavian citizens see in Europe a risk to their welfare states (Sánchez-Cuenca 2002). Likewise, many French citizens perceive market integration to threaten the peculiarities of their respective social and economic models (Hobolt and Brouard 2010). At the same time, South European citizens see with a mix of hope and concern the adjustment of their economies to the standards imposed by the largest and more advanced European economies (European Commission 2002, 2003, 2004b).

The integration of fiscal structures is meant to deal with these concerns and facilitate the functioning of larger markets (Mattli 1999). Whether such integration affects primarily policy instruments devoted to interpersonal or interregional redistribution ultimately depends on the economic geography of the Union. In the absence of large differences in income levels, economic specialization or demographic structures, fiscal integration is expected to occur via interpersonal redistribution.

The difference between Europe and other experiences lies precisely in the constraints that emerge from the commitment of member states to fiscal policy autonomy. I will show that such commitment derives directly from the heterogeneous nature of Europe's geography of income and labor market risk. The EU represents a case of confederation in which the existence of potential externalities between members of the Union, as well as a common exposure to an increasingly integrated economy (Adsera and Boix 2002), create incentives toward pooling risks via some common fiscal institution, whereas significant disparities in income, risks, and shares of dependent population prevent the adoption of a fully integrated system of interpersonal redistribution. This creates a dilemma for member states in that failing to respect fiscal policy autonomy of constituent units and failing to cope with the externalities derived from market integration both jeopardize the existence of the economic union itself.

Under such conditions, the solution envisioned by "functional" theories of federalism, namely an initial phase of fiscal integration to overcome transaction costs followed by a process of functional adaptation to different needs, is unlikely to emerge.[6] Instead, a set of rather sticky domestic systems of redistribution and insurance limit the available strategies to cope with the risks and fears brought along by the process of market integration. Put simply, efforts concentrate on bridging resource capabilities across local governments, as opposed to income among citizens. The key intuition behind this expectation is that, in the context of a very heterogeneous economic geography, richer regions have a political incentive to transfer resources to poorer ones precisely to "protect" the specificities of their local political economies from a potential undesired inflow of dependents or labor surplus. The incentive works as follows.

An undesired inflow of immigrants would reduce the tax base and increase the preferred level of redistribution. More poor people implies lower contributions and higher demand for welfare. At the extreme, if levels of inequality in the rich region overcome those of the union, a decentralized system of redistribution becomes too costly. As a result, rich regions, especially those that are also economically specialized, would benefit from reacting to the possibility of an unwanted inflow of dependents before it actually happens. The issue at stake is how to contain the amount of risk-sharing between regions, such that fiscal centralization remains an unwanted option. To prevent such a

---

[6] Standard economic treatments would suggest that, insofar as social policy operates as an insurance mechanism that plays an important role in the functioning of efficiently designed labor markets, the mismatch between an integrated European market and a fragmented system of social protection is a short-term anomaly, bound to be eliminated by the passing of time. Cassella's work relates the design of public good provision in integrated markets to issues of allocative efficiency (Casella 2005; Cassella and Frey 1992; Cassella and Weingast 1995). In her view, as markets begin to integrate, centralized institutions are necessary to overcome transaction costs. As markets integrate more deeply, the boundaries for the provision of public goods must be redrawn to ensure a more efficient provision or a wider range of public goods. In light of this argument, and to the extent that public social insurance can be considered a public good, social policy integration should accompany market integration in the early stages, only to be decentralized again once the design of the union requires fine-tuning. Functionalist and neofunctionalist interpretations of European regional integration argue along similar lines. Mattli points out that "economic integration is likely to raise questions as to how the winners will compensate the losers. The ensuing need for compensatory mechanisms is bound to widen the fiscal responsibility of the central authority in a region." (1999: 39).

scenario, it makes sense for richer regions to devote resources to improve poor regions' economies.

The amount of interregional transfers will be larger the higher the expected level of population mobility. The creation of internally heterogeneous markets such as the Single European Act facilitates potential migratory movements by dependents, surplus labor, and transient minorities (such as Roma). The actual realization of such migration depends primarily on the gap in terms of economic performance between different regions of the Union. The wider this gap the more likely it is for richer regions to face an inflow of migrants in search of work, better welfare services, or even better charities. By transferring resources to poorer regions, richer ones would improve their economic conditions, and reduce the probability of suffering a demographic shock that would alter, as analyzed previously, the distribution of income and the preferred level of redistribution of the recipient region. In performing this function, large levels of interregional redistribution become a tool for the preservation of decentralized systems of interpersonal redistribution in contexts where a common market encompasses very heterogeneous regions. Interregional redistribution operates as a political and economic buffer that increases the incentives of *all* members to remain in the Union. The italics in "all" highlight the fact that the system of interregional redistribution reduces the risks faced by both rich and poor member states, thereby making compatible an integrated market and a set of highly heterogeneous systems of fiscal redistribution. Analyzed through this prism, interregional redistribution in the EU is both a compensation, as typically argued in the literature, and an insurance device.[7] In the next two sections I evaluate this logic empirically: the third section studies limits to the centralization of interpersonal redistribution, and the fourth focuses on the political origins of interregional redistribution and its connection with the issue of mobility within the Union.

ECONOMIC GEOGRAPHY AND THE LIMITS
TO INTERPERSONAL REDISTRIBUTION

As analyzed in detail in Chapter 3, the institutional design of the European Union fits closely the profile of a political union with centrifugal representation. Put simply, no major alteration of the status quo in the area of fiscal redistribution occurs without the unanimous consent of its constituent members. According to the theoretical argument developed above, given these institutional conditions, an uneven economic geography would render proposals towards the centralization of interpersonal redistribution politically unfeasible. To assess these claims, this section proceeds as follows: first, I

---

[7] In line with this logic, a rich literature has documented the design of the EU budget as the product of a long series of intergovernmental bargains between the constituent members of the Union (Carruba 1997; Lange 1993; Mattila 2004; Moravcsik 1998; Pollack 2003; Rodden 2002; Weber 1999).

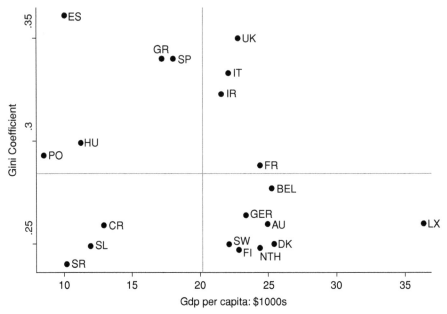

FIGURE 4.5. The Geography of Income Inequality in the European Union

provide evidence on the economic geography of the union; second, I develop a qualitative overview of the evolution of social policy in the European Union; and finally, I present empirical evidence on the actual mechanisms linking economic geography and institutional choices by analyzing the preferences of citizens, political parties, and governments on the centralization of redistribution.

The Economic Geography of the Union

In Chapter 3, I identified two dimensions of economic geography as particularly relevant: the geography of income inequality and the geography of labor market risk, in turn, driven by levels of regional economic specialization and the scope of cross-regional mobility.

To gain a concrete sense of the distributive tensions emerging from the geography of income inequality, Figure 4.5 plots levels of GDP per capita in 2001 against a standardized measure of income inequality, the Gini coefficient for disposable income inequality around 2000/2001 as calculated by the Luxembourg Income Study (LIS).[8]

---

[8] Note that, because of data limitations, I can only include twenty of the twenty-seven members of the Union. The countries included are Austria (AU), Belgium (BEL), Czech Republic (CR), Denmark (DK), Estonia (ES), Finland (FI), France (FR), Germany (GER), Greece (GR), Hungary

On the assumption that existing levels of disposable income inequality capture, even if partially, domestic preferences for levels of fiscal redistribution (*t* in the model), Figure 4.5 conveys the picture of a very heterogeneous union. Moreover, European countries (i.e., regions in the Union) not only differ in their preferences about redistribution, but also in their levels of economic resources (*y* in the model). In fact, using the average levels of income inequality and resources as cutting points, the variation along these two dimensions can be broken into four subgroups. Spain, Greece, Estonia, and, to a lesser extent, Hungary and Poland, are countries that are both relatively poorer and more unequal. In turn, Slovenia, the Czech Republic, and Slovakia, while being among the poorest members of the EU(25), show very moderate levels of income inequality. In contrast, the Benelux countries, together with Germany, Austria, and Scandinavia are relatively richer and fairly egalitarian societies. Finally, France, Ireland, Italy, and the United Kingdom, while still well off in terms of resources, show much higher levels of income disparities.

Given these specific patterns of inequality, the adoption of a hypothetical centralized redistributive policy would imply: (1) a transfer of resources, inherent to the transfers between individuals, from relatively wealthier to relatively poorer countries; (2) a necessary reduction in the levels of redistribution enjoyed by lower income citizens of the richer and more egalitarian countries (most notably, Scandinavia); and (3) an unwelcome disruption of the systems of redistribution at work in relatively poorer societies. In political terms, these effects work to facilitate the formation of several coalitions of interests opposing any change towards a more centralized redistributive system.

As long as political contentions within the EU remain dominated by country (as opposed to income or class divisions), the incumbents of relatively richer countries have incentives to block any additional transfer of resources to poorer countries. In fact, they face heavy electoral constraints. Upper income citizens of wealthier countries are the likely net payers of any integrated system. Their first preference is fiscal independence. In turn, poor citizens of rich countries have no incentives to share their transfers with poorer citizens of poorer countries. On the contrary, they have incentives to coalesce with their wealthier fellow nationals to prevent any loss of resources from which they benefit the most. Indeed, these incentives will be stronger the more generous and egalitarian the domestic welfare state. The well documented distrust of Scandinavian citizens towards the expansion of EU institutions' powers is consistent with this line of reasoning (Brinegar, Jolly and Kitschelt 2004).[9] Finally, it is not straightforward that poorer nations would automatically endorse a centralized

---

(HU), Ireland (IR), Italy (IT), Luxembourg (LX), Netherlands (NTH), Poland (PO), Slovak Republic (SR), Slovenia (SL), Spain (SP), Sweden (SW), and United Kingdom (UK).

[9] Lower income citizens of a wealthier state would support the centralization of redistributive policy only if the levels of generosity they benefit from are extended to the overall union. However, the budgetary effects that such policy would immediately gather the opposition of wealthier and less egalitarian societies, thereby rendering it politically unfeasible.

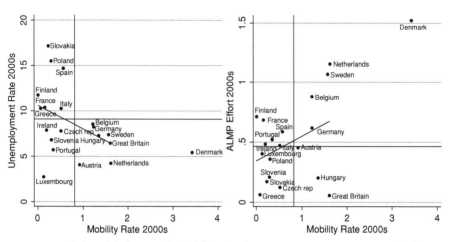

FIGURE 4.6. Labor Markets and Mobility in the European Union (*Source:* Author's elaboration. See Appendix for variable definitions and data sources.)

fiscal policy in the EU. Figure 4.5 shows how poor countries such as Slovenia or the Czech Republic are also fairly egalitarian. A majority of citizens in these countries may fear that changes imposed to their social security system by a centralized decision maker will be the source of increasing inequalities, despite the potential transfer of significant resources from other areas of the Union. In sum, the distributive tensions associated with the geography of income inequality in the European Union define a constellation of preferences in which, for very diverse reasons, not even the poorest citizens within the poorer states have incentives to mobilize politically in support of a more centralized redistributive policy.

The constraints upon a centralized system of interpersonal redistribution would only grow stronger should an uneven geography of risk overlap with an uneven geography of income inequality. Social policy systems combine, often indistinctly, redistributive and insurance components in their design. Some aspects of the latter, most centrally unemployment and old-age insurance, tie directly with the workings of labor markets (Iversen, 2005; Snower and De la Dehesa 1997). Thus, as elaborated in detail in Chapter 2, regional differences in the incidence of labor market risks and the organization of labor markets also shape preferences about the institutional organization of systems of interpersonal redistribution. Figure 4.6 displays the extent to which European countries vary in the organization of their labor markets by combining three relevant indicators: the unemployment rate, as a measure of realized labor market risk; the mobility rate, that is, the percentage of the domestic population that relocated relative to the country's total population, as a proxy for the scope of cross-regional population externalities; and the expenditure share in active labor market policies, as a proxy for the government's intervention in the organization of "local" labor markets.

Risk-wise, Europe is also quite a heterogeneous union. Countries vary largely in their approaches to the organization and regulation of labor markets, as reflected by the significant differences in effort on active labor market policies. These policies are meant to facilitate the retraining of workers in less demanded occupations, thus enhancing geographical mobility between regions. According to the data displayed in the right half of Figure 4.6, there is indeed a positive relationship between the effort governments put into active labor market policies and the level of geographical mobility within countries in the Union.[10] As governments facilitate transition between jobs, people become more mobile geographically and the level of risk associated with specific occupations declines; and, since different economic activities tend to concentrate territorially (Krugman 1991), so does the risk concentration in particular areas of the country. In contrast, a weaker policy commitment to facilitate work transitions limits peoples' ability to move, and contributes to a higher realization of labor market risk. The left panel in Figure 4.6 displays evidence bearing on this link: there is a negative and significant relationship between the level of interregional mobility and the incidence of unemployment across European nations.

Given this background, a common system of unemployment insurance would necessarily distort the workings of a significant group of countries. The combination of very generous unemployment benefits with active labor market policies and fairly unregulated hiring decisions at work in some Scandinavian economies would be either fiscally unfeasible or highly distortive in most continental labor markets. Likewise, a move toward less generous and less extensive benefits would alter the complementarities at work in many European countries between social and labor market policies (Hall and Soskice 2001; Kenworthy 2008; Pontusson 2005). Arguably then, such a move would be frontally opposed by national governments should it ever become the path proposed to reform existing social security models. As a result, in light of the predictions of the model, I expect these patterns to exacerbate the distributive tensions associated with the geography of income inequality discussed previously.

Social Policy in the European Union: An Overview

Is it the case that the economic geography of the Union constrains the development of a centralized system of interpersonal redistribution? The history of the European Union is rich in attempts to add a social dimension to the integration project. Though vaguely mentioned in the founding treaties (art. 117 to 128), in the *Social Charter* of the Council of Europe as well as in the 1974 *Community Social Action Programme* (Cram 1997; Hantrais 1995), social policy, much like many other realms, gained political salience only when the European

---

[10] Data for Figure 4.6 correspond to the early 2000s. The fitted lines represent the relationship excluding the case of Denmark.

Commission tried to expand its sphere of influence during the negotiations of the Single European Act (1987). Jacques Delors, believing that any attempt to give new depth to the Common market without introducing a social dimension would be doomed to failure, became a strong advocate of a social dimension to the Union. In general, the Commission pursued the expansion of its powers by seeking a reduction in the number of issues to be decided by unanimity at the Council.[11] Accordingly, the Commission argued, decisions should be more flexible in those areas of social affairs of particular importance for market integration and performance. In this environment, the Single European Act yielded two initiatives: the Community Charter of the Fundamental Social Rights of Workers (not binding), introducing a certain degree of equalization of workers' rights to prevent social dumping, and an Action Programme, where the Commission considered specific measures to achieve such equalization. In a typical example of the sort of dynamics associated with a divergent geography of labor markets, the UK considered the latter initiative an unacceptable intervention on market mechanisms and blocked it (Rhodes 1997; Room 1991; Springer 1992). The Maastricht Treaty marks the next step in the attempt to approach, however remotely, a European social policy. Again, it did so by introducing specific changes to expand the number of social policy issues to be decided by qualified majority. In addition, the Treaty incorporated an Agreement on Social Policy and the provision of Protocol 14 (Social Protocol) towards its implementation. In light of previous historical experience, these provisions bounded all members except the UK. In terms of actual policy content, these measures opened the door to increasing the role of social partners (unions and employers' associations) in the negotiation, agreement, and implementation of EU social policies. As such, they constituted a mild attempt to throw the seeds of a European corporatist system.

Subsequent efforts to incorporate the UK into the Social Protocol, and the Social Protocol into the Amsterdam Treaty, brought out again the constraints that geography of risk and inequality imposed upon attempts to develop a common labor market framework, however loosely (Cram 1997; Rhodes 1997). Ultimately, the UK, who had opted out in Maastricht, only accepted the full incorporation of the Social Protocol into the Amsterdam Treaty after Blair's government secured the unanimity requirement for issues about "protection of workers in the event of termination of their employment contract and representation and collective defense of workers' and employers' interests, where many other delegations would have preferred a qualified majority decision making procedure" (Petite 1998: 15). In other words, the UK signed the Amsterdam Treaty only after sheltering politically its model of decentralized collective bargaining and unemployment protection (Soskice 1990: 36–61), thus limiting the feasibility of a common social policy agenda.

[11] For instance, amendments to articles 118a and 118b of the founding treaties (1957) were introduced so that health and safety of worker matters were to be decided by qualified majority. In addition, articles 100a (regulations on the rights and interests of people) and 130a (strengthening economic and social cohesion) were also changed to introduce qualified majority voting.

Supporters of a stronger social Europe had to wait until the Lisbon Summit (2000) to restate their case, launching a new approach: the open method of coordination (OMC).[12] Essentially, the OMC implies the setting of common policy purposes while leaving the choice of actual policies to national governments. This approach recognizes that "under the principle of subsidiarity, social policy remains the responsibility of the Member States. It was agreed that each Member State should implement a national two-year action plan for combating poverty and social exclusion, setting specific targets. [....] The OMC involves using a management by objectives approach, whereby EU institutions draw up guidelines and monitor their implementation" (Atkinson 2002: 628).

The policy format of such an attempt to integrate social policy in the European Union remains undefined.[13] This ambiguity aside, one major conclusion stands out (Scharpf 1998, 2002; Seabright 1993): the only EU social policy that is likely to be feasible in the future would be a regulation such that a set of common standards is agreed upon by the EU executive powers and the member states are left with the freedom to choose the ways and means to achieve it. And even this approach is bound to meet considerable resistance. In a political context in which regional leaders are mainly obliged towards their local constituencies, disagreements about the nature and scope of such a move appear far too large given Europe's economic geography. This scenario is unlikely to change in the context of a Union enlarged to twenty-seven members.

Assessing the Mechanisms: Economic Geography and Institutional Preferences in the EU

In an effort to validate the mechanisms posited in the theoretical model, I turn now to analyze the extent to which Europe's economic geography accounts for disagreements about the design of fiscal institutions. I present several analyses of how macrolevel indicators of countries' politico-economic conditions shape the preferences of citizens, political organizations, and governments. The goal throughout is to evaluate the connection between countries' relative positions

---

[12] The OMC was originally established in the Maastricht Treaty for the coordination of economic policies, and expanded in the Amsterdam Treaty to labor market policies. Then, during the Lisbon Summit, the Council agreed to start using it to approach social-policy issues. Detailed characterizations of the use of the OMC in the realm of social policy can be found in Scharpf (2002); and Vandenbroucke (2002).

[13] Scharpf has suggested that a combination of framework directives and the OMC could meet the task (2002). The first tool would allow the Commission to punish those states failing to meet the agreed standards; the latter would allow countries to retain autonomy even if agreeing to a set of common measures and standards on the basis of which to be evaluated. In this way, "member states would retain considerable discretion in shaping the substantive and procedural content framework directives to suit specific local conditions and preferences. Yet if they should abuse this discretion in the political judgment of their peers in the Council, more centralized sanctions and enforcement procedures would still be available as a 'fleet in being.'" (Scharpf 2002: 34). In contrast, Vandenbroucke (2002) considers this combination of framework directives and the OMC potentially counterproductive as it is likely to foster distributive political contentions among member states.

in the Union's economic geography and the preferences of political actors. I pay particular attention to the left of the political spectrum as the source of any potential demand for a centralized system of redistribution.

The study of the impact of economic geography on citizens' preferences builds on a combination of individual and country level data capturing different political and economic aspects of EU member states.[14] The dependent variable in the analysis is an ordinal measure of support for the integration of welfare systems in the European Union. The question reads as follows:

Today, each European Union Member State is responsible for its own social welfare system. To what extent would you be in favor or opposed to the harmonization of social welfare systems within the European Union?

The survey records four possible answers to this question:

(1) Strongly in favor;
(2) Somewhat in favor;
(3) Somewhat opposed; and
(4) Strongly opposed.

I evaluate the probability that individual respondents choose one of these four categories as a function of both individual and country level variables capturing specific aspects of the economic geography of the Union. The specification of the model is:

$$WH = \beta_1 Inq + \beta_2 Gdpc + \beta_3 Inq^* Gdpc + \beta_i \phi + \chi_i \theta + \varepsilon \qquad (1)$$

where WH captures attitudes towards welfare harmonization at the EU level as defined above, Inq and $Gdpc$ stand, respectively, for the level of income inequality and GDP per capita in each of the members of the Union, and $Inq^* Gdpc$ stands for the interaction between the two. In turn, $\beta_i \phi$ and $\chi_i \theta$ capture a set of country (ϕ) and individual level controls (θ). I estimate equation (1) via maximum likelihood in the context of a mixed model (with individuals and countries) in which the link function is specified to be an ordinal logit, thus accounting for the nature of the dependent variable.

The country level controls include the following two variables: a measure of the net budgetary balance per capita of each country in the EU, to capture the relative position of each country as a net recipient (contributor) in the system of interregional redistribution in the Union (a topic to which I return in the next section), an indicator of Union members' effort in active labor market policies; and countries' average unemployment rates between 2000 and 2005. These variables control for the heterogeneity in labor market conditions associated with the uneven geography of risk, a factor known to shape social policy preferences (Cusack, Iversen and Rehm 2006). As individual controls,

---

[14] I obtained the individual level data from the ICPSR Study 20321: Eurobarometer 65.1, *The Future of Europe*, February-March 2006. I provide a detailed account of the definition and sources of the variables used in this section in Appendix B.

I also include all the available standard variables in the literature on preference formation: age, gender, education, ideology (as captured by a question asking respondents to place themselves in a left-right scale), and a variable asking whether respondents reside in rural or urban areas. Unfortunately, the data set does not include a direct measure of respondents' individual income. The data set does include, however, a variable capturing respondents' occupations which allows me to identify whether they are working (α in the model) or receiving income support from the welfare state ($1 - \alpha$ in the model). Taking advantage of this variable, I run the statistical analysis twice, once for the full population and once isolating the preferences of those whose income depends upon national welfare systems. A detailed presentation of the statistical results appears in table format in Appendix B (Table B.1).

The analysis yields very interesting results.[15] In line with the argument of this study, the models reveal a strong and statistically significant effect of macrolevel income and labor-market conditions on individual preferences for the centralization of welfare policy at the EU level. In other words, there is a direct link between the Union's economic geography and citizens' preferences for the centralization of interpersonal redistribution. The link operates through three channels.

Consider first the two variables measuring differences in the structure of labor markets among member states. The results reported in Table B.1 suggest that as the incidence of unemployment increases so does the average support for the harmonization of social welfare systems among the citizens of any given country. By implication, as member states diverge in their labor market performance, the disagreement about the desirability of centralizing interpersonal redistribution increases. In addition, the empirical models also support the claim that regional economic specialization limits the feasibility of a common European social policy. Recall that, as a proxy for cross-regional differences in economic specialization and the organization of labor markets, I included a measure of national government's budgetary effort to support active labor market policies. To be sure, the higher the effort in active labor market policies in a particular country, the lower the support for the harmonization of welfare systems in the EU. For instance, keeping all individual characteristics constant, the average citizen of a country that is moderately rich and unequal and puts very little effort in the activation of labor markets has a twenty percent chance of showing "strong support" for such an institutional change. If his/her government spent about 1% of GDP on active labor market policies, the probability that same citizen offered the same answer would decline by ten percentage points. These results are consistent with a recent literature that links varieties of capitalism and welfare regimes with individual preferences for European integration. While focused on a broader issue, the central intuition is very similar: individual attitudes toward integration are conditioned by the organization of labor markets and welfare states across countries (Brinegar and Jolly 2005;

---

[15] The individual level control variables display the anticipated results.

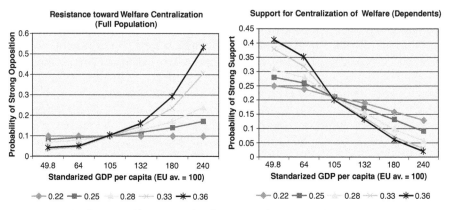

FIGURE 4.7. Preferences About Social Policy Centralization in the European Union

Brinegar et al. 2004; Marks and Steenberger 2004). Consistently, preferences for social policy integration reflect differences in the level of unemployment and the effort countries devote to the activation of labor markets.

Given the geography of risk presented previously, there is little room for agreement within the European citizenry on a common European welfare state. The potential externalities between this hypothetical system and an array of pretty heterogeneous labor markets reduce the political room for institutional changes that demand national units delegating redistributive policy to Brussels. Taken together, these results trace a direct connection between the geography of labor markets and individual institutional preferences that is consistent with the notion that a heterogeneous geography of labor markets constrains the centralization of interpersonal redistribution.

The second channel through which economic geography shapes individual preferences is the interplay between the member states' levels of aggregate income (w in the analytical model) and income inequality (w_i's spread). The findings convey that the geography of income inequality has a very substantial impact on citizen's attitudes toward a hypothetical centralized welfare system in the European Union. As the estimates of a generalized mixed level ordinal logit model are not interpretable directly, Figure 4.7 presents two sets of predicted probabilities for citizens' positions. The panel on the left displays, for the full population, the probability of showing "strong opposition" conditional on the countries' levels of GDP per capita (x axis) and income inequality (different series). In contrast, the panel on the right is limited to the dependent population only, citizens whose main source of income is welfare state transfers, and displays the probability of showing "strong support" for the transformation of national welfare systems into a common European welfare state.

Consider first the results based on the full population. Citizens in poor countries are much less likely to oppose centralization of redistribution regardless of the level of inequality. As countries become wealthier though, citizens' preferences diverge as a function of countries' levels of inequality. *Ceteris paribus*, as inequality within rich countries increases, so does the opposition to the harmonization of welfare systems in the EU. This result offers direct support for the theory presented in Chapter 2.

Note, however, that this is just a picture of the average patterns taking place in each of the countries. Combining the individual and country level estimates, one can also explore more precisely some of the predictions emerging from the model of preference formation presented in Chapter 2 by focusing on specific groups. The panel on the right of Figure 4.7 undertakes this task by examining how the geography of income inequality shapes the preferences of welfare state dependents throughout the union. In line with the argument's predictions, the results suggest a powerful income effect at work. Dependents in poor countries are much more likely to support social policy centralization than dependents in rich countries. Dependents that reside in countries below the average income in the Union show a chance of 25% or higher to express "strong support" for centralization. In the very poor members of the Union, this likelihood rises above 40%. In contrast, this magnitude declines as countries become wealthier, converging toward zero at the highest levels of income per capita. Clearly, income dependents in rich countries do not want to share the tax base from which they derive benefits with dependents from other members of the Union. Interestingly, this desire to protect the "domestic" tax base grows stronger the more unequal the society in which the dependents operate, as reflected by the vertical differences between the inequality series. Overall, the institutional preferences of dependents vary significantly as a function of their relative position within Europe's geography of income.

Regretfully, the limitations in the data prevent a similar analysis of the preferences of high-income people. The estimated effect of education seems to suggest that more-educated people tend to be more supportive of integration. Indirectly, this would indicate that high-income people throughout the Union are *more* supportive of centralizing redistribution than low-income people. Recent contributions to the study of the determinants of support for European integration suggest that this would be too rushed an inference though. While admittedly predicting support for the process of integration as a whole, and not for integration in a particular policy area, these analyses suggest that the preferences of high-income voters are as conditional on macroeconomic factors as those of welfare dependents (Brinegar, Jolly and Kitschelt 2004; Brinegar and Jolly 2005; Ray 2004). Ray (2004: 56–57) reports results that suggest that high-income people in countries with high social spending are less concerned than dependents about social policy being implemented at the Union level. In his own words, "respondents in nations with higher social protection spending are more likely to fear the loss of benefits, but this effect weakens for higher income groups" (p. 53). Consistent with the model, tax payers in countries with large welfare states may see social policy integration as an opportunity to restrain redistributive efforts.[16] The fears of high-income people towards

---

[16] According to the model they will endorse this view when inequality at the regional level is higher than inequality in the overall union. The implicit assumption is that the demand for redistribution will be larger in the former than in the latter.

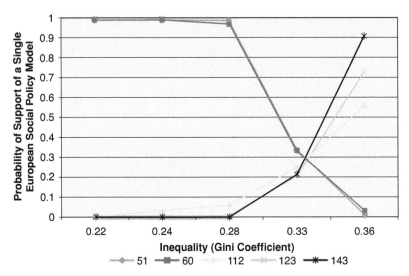

FIGURE 4.8. Attitudes Toward Welfare Centralization Among European Social Democratic Parties and Labor Unions

integration tend to increase, however, when one considers the geography of economic specialization as well. Brinegar and Jolly (2005) provide solid evidence that national politico-economic factors mediate the views of high income citizens on the process of integration. Specifically, their results indicate that "support for European integration decreases much faster among respondents in social democratic welfare states than in residual welfare states as education increases" (p. 174). The reason, arguably, lies in the fact that "high-skilled workers in social democratic states have more to fear than high-skilled workers elsewhere because their relatively more generous welfare states permit investment in specific skills and high economic openness" (p. 175). To summarize, the geographies of income and economic specialization condition the preferences of both low and high-income citizens in ways consistent with the model's predictions.

Interestingly, the dividing impact associated with economic geography also operates at the level of social and political organizations. Figure 4.8 reports the findings of an additional set of statistical analyses of a dataset of about forty European left-wing political parties and labor unions.[17] The dependent variable reads as follows: "Is a single European social model to be aimed

---

[17] The data come from a study by the Friedrich Ebert Foundation on the "European Social and Economic Model." See Busemeyer, et al. (2006). The survey was conducted during 2004/2005 on leading personalities from trade unions, ministries, political parties, and employer organizations, in the following European countries: Austria, the Czech Republic, Denmark, Finland, France, Germany, Great Britain, Greece, Hungary, Ireland, Italy, the Netherlands, Poland, Portugal, and the Slovak Republic. I thank the authors of this study for giving me access to the survey of political and social organizations on which this study is based.

at?". I have recoded the answer to be either 1 (yes) or 0 (no) and limited the sample to left-wing political organizations, that is, parties that proclaim to have a social democratic platform (or more radical redistributive proposals) and labor unions. Given the nature of the dependent variable, and the fact that all variables are measured at the country level, I report results based on a standard logit model.[18] To capture the impact of the geography of inequality I include the same interaction between the spread of the distribution of income (Gini coefficient) and the level of income per capita (GDP pc) that I used to model citizens' preferences. I also keep as control variables the same country level determinants: the budgetary effort in active labor market policies, the unemployment rate, and the net EU budgetary balance of the countries in which each of these organizations operate. As before, I include the full set of statistical results in Appendix B (see Table B.2). Figure 4.8 reports the predicted probability that left leaning social and political organizations in Europe offer their support to the notion that a single European social model ought to be pursued. The x axis displays different levels of inequality, whereas the different series, ranging from 51 to 143, capture each country's distance to the average level of GDP per capita (EU = 100).

There is a considerable amount of variation in the position adopted by these organizations, variation that appears systematically associated with Europe's geography of inequality. The analysis presents a divided European left. Consistent with the position of dependents identified above, organizations that operate in relatively wealthier and egalitarian contexts show virtually no support for a hypothetical common European social policy. Much like one of their key constituencies, they do not want to share their tax base with potential beneficiaries of redistribution elsewhere. They see in Europe a source of potential dismantlement of their very generous and comprehensive welfare systems. In contrast, the left parties of poor and egalitarian European countries see social policy integration as an attractive source of resources, one that might help them sustain their social security systems.

Figure 4.8 brings up one other additional pattern: there seems to be an inequality threshold beyond which the political positions of European left leaning organizations switch. The critical point is situated around a Gini coefficient of about .33. Given relatively higher levels of income inequality, leftist organizations in rich countries tend to support a common European social policy model, while the same type of political organizations in relatively poorer nations appear highly skeptical of its benefits. The left of relatively poor and unequal countries, such as Poland, seems to perceive Europe as a constraint to the development of social redistributive platforms, whereas the left in relatively rich and unequal countries, such as Spain, sees the pursuit of a European social dimension as a feasible alternative to tackle social issues (such as immigration and its implications) that have long transcended nation-state boundaries. Obviously, the reasons behind these policy positions are complex and respond to

---

[18] Nevertheless, as a robustness check, I also include a set of probit results in Appendix B.

multiple strategic considerations that are tied to domestic political competition and fall well beyond the scope of this chapter. Despite these limitations, though, the main point remains: Europe's economic geography introduces a considerable amount of variation in the institutional preferences of organizations that a priori share a common pro-redistributive ideology.

While the evidence presented so far on the preferences of organizations is limited to trade unions and social democratic parties, a heterogeneous economic geography generates similar effects on employers. In a series of analyses of the responses by unions and employers' organizations to the attempts by the Commission and the European Court of Justice to promote economic liberalization through regulation, Höpner and Schäfer (2010a, 2010b) find that unions and employers tend to cluster more around "production and distribution cultures" (2010a: 27) than around ideological positions over the political control of economic activities. In other words, employers' associations display preferences that reflect the specificity of their local economy and not an alleged cross-national class interest. By implication, the more heterogeneous the economic geography of the Union, the more difficult it is for employers to converge in a unionwide strategy. The contentions over the Service Directive offer an illustrative case.

An attempt to reinterpret the scope of economic liberalization within the Union, the Service Directive was an effort to fully liberalize the service provision market in Europe. Its key principle, that of "country of origin," was stated in article 16 of the original proposal:

Member States shall ensure that providers are subject only to the national provisions of their Member State of origin which fall within the coordinated field. [...] The Member State of origin shall be responsible for supervising the provider and the services provided by him, including services provided by him in another Member State.

If applied, this clause would imply not only a higher exposure to competition in coordinated economies but also an effective deregulation of key areas of economic activity, both private and public. In practical terms, this would imply for instance, that a Lithuanian private hospital could potentially open a branch in Spain with no supervision by local authorities, and paying Lithuanian wages. While this would have created a scenario in which continental employers could have benefited from hiring labor at a much lower cost, reactions to the proposal ranged from skepticism to outright opposition throughout continental (Austria, Germany, France) and Scandinavian economies (Höpner and Schäfer 2010b). France's big business organization, MEDEF, challenged the directive as a potential source of social dumping (MEDEF 2005). In contrast, British and East European employers' associations were supportive of the directive. This example illustrates how the diversity of production systems within Europe's economic geography shapes not only the preferences of workers and unions, but also those of employers and their representative organizations.

Overall, the results reported in Figure 4.7 and 4.8 reinforce the claim, central to the argument in this book, that a disperse geography of income inequality constrains the feasibility of a common system of interpersonal redistribution through its effect on citizens' preferences and the exacerbation of distributive trade-offs among the Union's political elites.

Given this mapping of preferences it should come as no surprise that, in the context of the constitution-making process, an overwhelming majority of member states rejected the possibility of expanding the role of EU institutions in the realm of interpersonal redistribution. Indeed, according to data from the Domestic Structures and European Integration Project (DOSEI), nineteen of the twenty-six cabinets involved during 2003/04 in the drafting of the constitutional project opted to preserve the status quo regarding the role of EU institutions in social policy.[19] The DOSEI data classify country positions in several aspects of the constitution-making process, applying a scale of 1 to 3 to the question of what the role of the EU in a particular policy domain ought to be. A score of 1 implies that a particular country thinks the EU should have less power. A score of 2 implies compliance with the status quo. Finally, a score of 3 means that the representatives of that country support the allocation of more power to the EU. In the following paragraphs I focus on the area of social policy but the DOSEI data also offer information about two other relevant aspects of member states' institutional preferences: whether a country prefers decisions to be made by unanimity or majority voting within the Council, and whether countries prefer to exclude the European Parliament from the legislative process or colegislate with it. Realistically, all three bits of information are relevant to establish the extent to which a country agrees to delegate power to the EU in a particular policy area. Supporting a larger role of the EU without giving up the unanimity requirement and/or allowing the European Parliament to engage in the legislative process comes dangerously close to cheap talk. Thus, to analyze countries' preferences during the constitution-making process, I make use of the following variable:

> Preferences on EU Role in Social Policy
> = Policy Preference*Decision Rule*Role of Parliament

This calculation yields an index that ranges between 1 and 12, where 1 represents extreme levels of opposition towards a larger role of the EU and 12 characterizes a national government that is willing to increase the EU's role in social policy, to give up the unanimity requirement, and to strengthen the EU Parliament as the Union's decision making arena. Admittedly, this operationalization does make aspects of representation part of the dependent

---

[19] These data were generously provided by Thomas König. The DOSEI data document factor positions in the EU constitution building process. Data are from the Fall 2003, after the European Convention has drafted its proposal for an European Constitution and shortly before the Intergovernmental Conference has been discussing this draft proposal. The dataset includes the official governmental positions of the twenty-five EU member states, plus the position of the Spanish government after the governmental change in March 2004, as well as the official positions of the European Commission and the European Parliament. For a detailed description of the project and the sources, see König (2005).

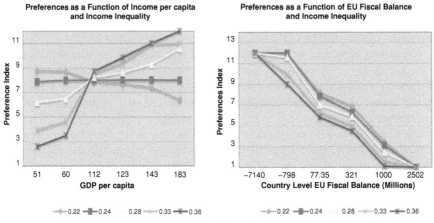

FIGURE 4.9. EU's Role in Social Policy as a Function of the Geography of Inequality

variable. After all, decision rules and the role of Parliament are key determinants of the balance of power between the member states and the "federal" government. It should be remembered however that these are policy specific issues and not attributes of the political system. The continuum centrifugal-centripetal concerns the balance of power between people and territories as a way of organizing the political will *across* policy issues. Hence, I treat all three dimensions above as part of the choice to centralize redistribution.[20]

To conclude this section on the limits to interpersonal redistribution in the European Union, I develop a model of preferences over the EU's role in social policy as a function of the geography of inequality and the same set of country level aggregate controls as in the previous section. As before, I report the full set of results in the Appendix B (Table B.3). The left panel of Figure 4.9 displays the predicted value of the index of preferences over the EU's role in social policy as a function of different combinations of the two dimensions of the geography of income inequality; the countries' level of GDP per capita (x axis) and income inequality (different series). The first thing to note is that, overall, the level of support for a stronger role of the EU in the realm of social policy is very mild. Recall that even the highest value in the dependent variable, 12, only represents a willingness to forego unanimity, share decisions with the Parliament, and support a rather indeterminate increase in authority in this realm for the European Commission. So, even though the notion of "assigning more power to the EU" does not necessarily imply the full centralization of European social policy, only a minority of incumbents supported it. This is consistent with what one might expect given Europe's economic geography. The natural follow up question, though, is to identify which specific countries

---

[20] Should the latter occur, and the decision rules be altered, it would obviously feed back into representation, an issue discussed in detail in Chapter 3. Nonetheless, this contingency falls out of the realm of interest in this section.

are in favor of a stronger role of the EU is social policy, and determine if their positions bear any link to the patterns of Europe's geography of inequality. A more careful scrutiny of the left panel in Figure 4.9 offers interesting insights on this issue, insights that combine expectable results with rather counterintuitive ones.

Among the countries supporting a stronger role of the EU in the development of social policy two subgroups emerge: countries that are both relatively poor and equal, and countries that are relatively wealthier and more unequal. Similarly, among the countries that during the constitutional process opposed any alteration of the status quo or even wanted to limit any possible future EU social policy initiative, one can also distinguish two subgroups: countries that are relatively wealthier and more equal, and countries that are relatively poorer and more unequal.

The behavior of relatively equal countries matches intuition perfectly: in the absence of stark distributive conflicts within the nation, poorer countries will see the extension of the EU's social policy as a venue to extract more resources even if, partially, at the expense of sharing policy. Likewise, the behavior of rich and equal countries also fits the predictions of the model, and is perfectly consistent with earlier results. The same countries in which dependents and left-leaning parties oppose social policy expansion in EU are the countries that during the constitution-making process showed less than tepid support for a rather minor delegation of power to Brussels. In line with the model's predictions, the poor among the rich do not want to share their tax base with the rest of the poor in the Union. Accordingly, the parties mobilizing them do not pursue that route, and the governments, traditionally controlled by Social Democracy in rich and equal countries (Iversen and Soskice 2006), oppose alterations of the status quo during the constitution-making process.

The behavior of relatively unequal countries, on the other hand, seems puzzling. Why do poor and unequal countries object to an expansion in European social policy? And, similarly, why would rich and unequal countries see it favorably? Admittedly, there may be many reasons beyond economic geography that bear some influence on these choices, but I would argue that these positions become less of a mystery if, in line with the argument, one considers the interplay between interpersonal and interregional redistribution in the EU. To that effect, the right panel of Figure 4.9 presents a slightly different model of EU leaders' preferences over social policy. The variables of interest here are income inequality and, instead of just the average income in society, the net balance in EU structural funds perceived during the period before the Constitutional Convention. This variable provides a direct measure of the levels of inter-regional redistribution, that is, inter-country redistribution within the EU, (T in the model). Interestingly enough, and notwithstanding some exceptions (like Spain after the election of Zapatero as head of the government), there emerges a strong negative relationship between being a net recipient of EU transfers and the resilience to advance a common system of interpersonal redistribution in the Union. This unwillingness to pursue such a course of action is particularly strong the more unequal the distribution within recipient countries is.

Taken together, the results presented in both panels of Figure 4.9 suggest that the elites of poor and unequal European countries are happy with a scenario in which they extract as many resources as possible from the wealthier partners of the Union (via interregional transfers) but remain committed to transfer as little control over the design of their social policy as possible. While admittedly at odds with a simplistic view of the "poor" as those always willing to centralize social policy, this behavior offers strong support to the theoretical expectations emerging from the model. Poorer regions are happy to sustain decentralized redistributive systems as long as they extract interregional transfers from other areas of the union.

In contrast, at the other end of the spectrum, net contributors have an interest in preventing the misuse of these funds by unrestrained incumbents in poorer countries. Given the transfers in place, they have an incentive to influence as much as possible how they are put to use. In line with the argument in Chapter 2, given a sufficiently skewed distribution, tax payers in wealthier regions have an interest to implicitly transfer part of the tax burden to their counterparts in poorer areas via a more integrated system. And to be sure, the data suggest that large EU contributors, especially those with skewed income distributions, are indeed more prone to enhance constraints on national social politics via Brussels.

MOBILITY AND INTERREGIONAL REDISTRIBUTION IN THE EUROPEAN UNION

The results in the previous section highlight the close connection between actors' preferences for the centralization of interpersonal redistribution and countries' relative positions in the system of interregional transfers. Countries' stance on interpersonal redistribution (t) reflects to a large extent their relative status in the system of interregional redistribution (T) and their level of income inequality. In this section, I turn to the question of the determinants of interregional redistribution amidst a very heterogeneous economic geography.

In exploring what drives the European Union to design and implement a complex web of programs geared towards bridging the economic gap among its regions, the literature has traditionally put most emphasis on the logic of compensation.[21] Potential losers in a wider Union demand compensation to accept expansion. In turn, potential winners accept these side payments as a way to grease the bolts of enlargement. As long as the net benefits of broadening markets exceed the cost of these side payments, these compensation payments are a worthy investment.

---

[21] Along these lines, the Common Agricultural Policy and the Structural Actions are theorized as side payments without which further market or political integration would not be feasible (Moravcsik 1998). See fn. 7 for a detailed set of references.

Without neglecting at all the importance of compensatory motives, the argument in this book highlights a different set of motives to pursue interregional transfers. The emphasis is not so much on compensation, but on a broader strategy to minimize disruption within a Union increasing in internal complexity. I put significant weight on mobility: constituent units face a trade-off between the interregional income transfers implicit to centralization and their capacity to maintain their preferred policy choice to cope with their specific labor market risks. This trade-off will be all the more intense the larger the levels of mobility (or the prospect thereof) between regions. Interregional transfers, I argue, facilitate a mutually beneficial exchange: poor regions obtain additional resources whereas wealthier specialized regions protect themselves against undesired inflows of low-skilled workers and dependents. In so doing, interregional transfers are both a compensation to weaker members of the Union and an insurance mechanism that helps protect the more advanced, specialized ones. Is there any evidence in support of such logic during the process of European integration?

The free circulation of workers has been a central concern throughout the process of integration, a concern that grows stronger as the economic heterogeneity of the Union increases. In an innovative analysis Schneider (2009: 85–103) shows that the likelihood that current members require restrictions on the movement of workers from new entrants increases when current members and candidates share high levels of industry employment, significant unemployment, and a large contingent of foreign population. The demand for restrictions is even stronger in current members with relatively lower levels of GDP per capita. As far as low-skill competition is concerned, poorer members have more to fear from similarly poor (or poorer) new entrants. Indeed, temporary restrictions on workers' movement applied to new entrants in both the Mediterranean and East European enlargements, and were closely linked to issues of interregional redistribution.

The case of Spanish negotiations to enter the European Economic Community provides an illustrative example. Several aspects of this process help illuminate the link between mobility and interregional transfers. The first one concerns the nature of the costs for current members. In line with the argument, a large proportion of the costs in current members' economies derive from specialized sectors. During the negotiation period (1978–1985), core members of the European Economic Community expressed serious concerns about the impact of the incorporation of the two democracies, Spain and Portugal. The concerns affected first and foremost the circulation of agricultural products, and its impact on producers. The large size of agricultural and fishing employment sectors in Portugal and Spain posed a looming threat on similar sectors in France and Ireland. Second, there were significant worries about a large inflow of workers. These reflected concerns, notably by traditional destinies of Spanish low-skilled labor (such as Germany, Luxembourg, or France), about the inability of current members' labor markets to properly incorporate an unwelcome surge in labor supply. Finally, Ireland and Greece were worried that new entrants would absorb a significant share of the interregional transfers they were currently benefiting from.

Naturally, core members of the Union were happy to incorporate two large new markets into the European economic space, but they wanted to do it on their own terms: maximizing the market space for their own products by reducing industry tariffs, and limiting the effect on their producers by containing as long as possible the free circulation of agricultural products and workers from the Iberian peninsula. In this context, Spain's bargaining position was weak, and the final agreement, reached as late as 1985, reflected much more the aspirations of current members than those of the newcomers. Analysts of this process generally recognize that *"the behavior of EC member states mirrored that of members of a select club who, when faced with newcomers, seek to protect their position by transferring any cost onto new members"* (Closa and Heywood: 2004, p.21). Current members combined two strategies. First, restrictions on mobility and circulation of products were notorious. Free movement of workers and agricultural products would not take effect until 1994; in parallel, the Spanish executive gained a similar period to remove industrial duties, allow foreign banks to enter the new economic space, and remove state monopolies. The process was bitter for Portugal and Spain, as many domestic sectors needed structural reform before acquiring full status within the common economic space. Second, current members agreed to finance a series of programs designed to overcome the structural differences between new and current members (Torreblanca 1998). These efforts were not just a side payment. They were also a purposeful effort to bolster local economic activity and limit the scope of population outflows towards wealthier areas of the Union. Economically, these programs created a stimulus in the short run and contributed to the economic convergence of backwards regions. The rationale behind both initiatives was the creation of new sources of employment in the poorest areas of the new members. By bolstering the demand of labor locally, interregional transfers helped absorb the domestic supply of labor, thereby limiting migration towards more advanced regions in the Union.

The dual role of interregional transfers as compensation and insurance becomes apparent when analyzing disputes among current members about where and how best to use these funds. Current recipients demand compensation for the broadening the economic union, and therefore demand additional resources so that the arrival of new members does not lead them to a relative loss of resources. In contrast, net contributors want to cap overall costs and, more importantly, also want the flow of interregional transfers to be redirected toward the new members, if possible at the expense of current recipients. The purpose of interregional transfers, in their view, is to help new members bridge the development gap during the transition period. Interestingly, there is a close link between mobility restrictions and the expected impact of expenditures toward infrastructural convergence. Restrictions on mobility buy time to reduce the modernization gap. The transition period operates as a buffer to protect core members while interregional transfers work to reduce the population flows expected at the time of full incorporation to the Union. In the case of Spain, the free circulation of workers was brought forward two years, from 1994 to 1992, in the context of the negotiations about the monetary union, and coincided in time with a large increase in interregional transfers.

As Schneider has recently unveiled (Schneider 2009), this diversity of goals and interests creates an important distributive conflict between current and future beneficiaries of transfers on the one hand, and between net contributors and current beneficiaries on the other. The budgetary conflict during the Mediterranean enlargement was solved by increasing the overall budget of the Union so as to prevent a zero-sum distributive conflict between Ireland and Greece, and Portugal and Spain. Ireland and Greece were able to extract significant compensation for their acceptance of Spain and Portugal. The latter, in turn, received significant funds to pursue their structural adjustments and facilitate a smoother economic integration once the restrictions in place during the transitory period expired.

An insider to the Union since 1986, Spain gained bargaining leverage in subsequent rounds of negotiations about interregional transfers, in particular during the process leading to the European monetary union (Maastricht) the treaty became feasible only when the concerns of Southern European economies as to how the regulations under discussion were going to affect their economies were compensated (Lange 1993; Scharpf 1997b). In practical terms, this implied a large increase in the participation of Spain, Greece, Italy and Ireland in the benefits of the interregional redistributive programs (Structural Funds).

Late developing economies had regularly used currency devaluations as a strategy to boost competitiveness. By joining the European Monetary System (EMS), modeled after the German Bundesbank, these economies committed not to make use of this tool any longer, thereby renouncing their monetary policy autonomy. In exchange, Germany and France, direct beneficiaries of the EMS, accepted to "pay" these countries with the creation of the Cohesion Fund, meant to overcome the potentially negative consequences of adopting a tighter monetary regime, and to bridge, along with other components of the Structural and Cohesion policies, the economic gap between different members of the Union. In short, interregional redistribution creates incentives for poorer members of the Union to accept regulations and economic policies not always befitting the short terms needs of their domestic economies. Again, both the logic of compensation and the logic of insurance apply here.

To put it in terms of the book's argument, Maastricht was approved because wealthy European nations, Germany in particular, agreed to pay to reduce the gap in terms of economic structures between Southern European countries and the rest of the Union. Despite being a net contributor, Germany's support for the Spanish proposal at the Edinburgh Summit was critical to reach an agreement on the Cohesion Fund and the monetary union more generally. The latter, in Kohl's view, could not function in the absence of a stronger and more integrated Europe. Bridging the gap between North and South was critical in this regard. Germany supported the Cohesion Fund even in the context of the economic consequences of Reunification and with a looming economic recession. The economic and financial stability of the Union required additional resources to be transferred to Ireland and the Mediterranean rim, both as compensation for necessary adjustments and as stimulus that helped contain unemployment, support structural reforms toward meeting the EMU criteria, and contain undesired disruptions within the common market. The EMU required economically feasible partners, or else, as recently witnessed, financial and budgetary disruptions could prove too taxing for wealthier partners themselves (Eichengreen 2007).

The dual nature of interregional transfers, compensatory and insurance, emerged again in the way the European Union approached the enlargement to the East. With the collapse of the Berlin wall, the geopolitical situation of Europe changed. The same concerns that motivated EU insiders to incorporate the South in the Mediterranean enlargement applied now to the East. Hardly anyone disputed that, in the medium run, the Union would be better off if these younger democracies consolidated politically and modernized economically. Germany, the biggest contributor to the EU budget, while clearly in favor of pursuing the process and expanding its area of economic influence was concerned about two things. Together with Austria, Luxembourg, and other advanced democracies from central Europe, they were worried about the scale of the migration of workers from the East and the potential disruptions this could cause to their economies. In addition, and in stark contrast with the Mediterranean enlargement, they were also concerned about the overall budget size of the Union. This time Germany could not afford to foot the bill for an increase of resources that would ameliorate the distributive conflict between current and future recipients of interregional transfers. As Schneider's (2009) analysis reveals, the menu of strategies was constrained by these budgetary limitations. Germany aimed for a combination of two measures: restriction on the mobility of workers and a redirection of interregional transfers from the South to the East. Naturally, Spain, the biggest recipient of interregional transfers, along with other South European members, objected to the proposal and demanded measures that would not worsen drastically its status as a net beneficiary within the Union.[22]

In an illustrative twist during the negotiations, Aznar famously threatened to block the restriction on workers' movements if his demands were ignored. For obvious geographical and cultural reasons, this was a much more important issue for Germany, Austria, or Luxembourg than for South European democracies. What Aznar sold domestically as a courageous defense of national interests the rest of Europe perceived as an outrageous blackmail (Rodrigo and Torreblanca 2001).[23] The deadlock was finally overcome through an agreement that

---

[22] On Spain's fears about a reorientation of structural funds towards the East, see Barbe (1999).
[23] As an example of the perceptions generated by this and other similar moves by Aznar's European strategies, see "The Ugly European," Die Zeit, September 14, 2000.

highlights the role of interregional transfers as an insurance mechanism: restrictions on labor movement, and with them on access to public insurance systems, will apply until 2011; at the same time, the new members would have gradual access to structural funds during the period 2004–2007 whereas current recipients would see their access reduced in a similar gradual fashion during the same period. Thereafter, the share of transfers toward new members increases significantly, allowing the Commission to redirect transfers to these new members before the restrictions on mobility are finally lifted. Mobility restrictions and interregional transfers operate jointly as mechanisms aimed at reducing negative economic externalities: the former apply while the latter measures are implemented and help activate local economies in backward areas, thereby limiting the labor outflow from those areas.

The targeting of specific migrant minorities, such as Roma, within the programs funded via structural funds illustrates the logic further. The Roma provide an interesting case in that they are very mobile and particularly hard to integrate socially and economically. Hence, if the notion of interregional transfers as a tool to limit undesired population movements bears any truth, it should be the case that efforts towards the social and economic integration of these minorities in their countries of origin absorb an increasing share of resources, particularly in those countries where groups such as the Roma are especially sizable. The evidence on the use of structural funds in countries like Hungary or Romania lends support to this conjecture. Indeed, the structural funds agenda for the period 2007–2013 places particular emphasis on programs targeting the social and economic incorporation of Roma. The ESF shall "reinforce the social inclusion of disadvantaged people with a view to their sustainable integration in employment" (ESF Regulation 1081/2006). In practical terms, this implies a significantly higher proportion of activities that target Roma, and an attendant increase in the amount of resources devoted to them with respect to the period 2000–2006. This is primarily due to the fact that the largest Roma minorities are concentrated in countries such as Hungary or Romania that have only recently joined the Union. The interesting fact lies in the reallocation of effort towards minorities that are potentially very mobile around the Union. Though data remain partial, one indicator is illustrative enough: in Hungary and Romania, Roma minorities constitute the explicit goal of more than one half of the initiatives sponsored by the structural funds (EU Roma Report 2010, p.52).[24] The activities funded focus on the promotion of education, vocational training, employment, access to social services, and community development. All these activities work to bolster economic progress and social networks in underdeveloped areas, reducing the need for its inhabitants to seek welfare or work opportunities elsewhere.

This overview of the politics behind major decisions concerning interregional transfers suggests that an important motive behind these efforts

---

[24] For a detailed breakdown of the different initiatives and the budgetary effort allocated to them, see *EU Roma Report*, 2010, pp. 103–111.

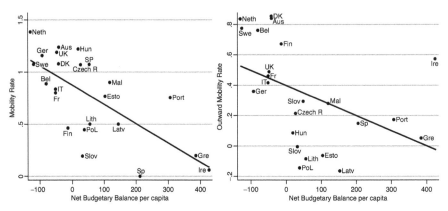

FIGURE 4.10. Interregional Redistribution and Mobility in the EU: 1990–2003.

concerned the limitation of negative economic externalities within an increasingly heterogeneous Union. Throughout the Union's history, measures to bridge the economic gap between poor and rich regions, and thereby limit (among other things) undesired population flows, have been adopted prior to granting full mobility rights to workers and dependents from newly incorporated areas. As a result, to the extent that they succeed in limiting mobility from areas receiving the funds to areas providing the funds, there should be a clear negative relationship between the amount of resources received by a particular member state and the level of mobility out of that same state.

Figure 4.10 presents evidence on the scope of the insurance role I attribute to the Common Agricultural Policy and the Structural and Cohesion Funds. The data build on a statistical analysis of the determinants of two mobility rates: the internal mobility rate, the share of the population that moved geographically within the country; and the outward mobility rate, the share of the population that moved to other EU countries.[25]

Clearly, over the period 1990–2003, interregional redistribution in the Union has been very effective in reducing the levels of population mobility in the Union. It is worth recalling that interregional transfers are targeted to regions in need within recipient countries. The left panel shows the relationship between redistribution and the internal mobility rate, that is to say, population movements from one region to another within the recipient nation. In turn, the right panel shows the relationship between the former and the levels of

[25] Mobility data from EUROSTAT (see Appendix B). Net budgetary balance per capita is defined as the difference between what countries contribute and what countries receive from the European Union, weighted by population size. The relationship reported in Figure 4.10 is controlled for the level of economic growth, the level of inequality, the share of retired population and the unemployment rate in the countries being compared. An annual panel data analysis for the period 1990–2003 yields substantively similar conclusions about the relationship between horizontal redistribution and mobility in the European Union.

outward mobility, that is, the proportion of people that move to a different country altogether. The picture conveyed by this analysis is pretty conclusive: through interregional transfers aimed to foster economic convergence, net payers have managed to reduce substantially the mobility rate within net recipient countries (left panel). Similarly, by targeting resources to backwards regions, net contributors have succeeded in deactivating potential migration movements by transient dependents from net recipient areas to contributing areas outside their nations (right panel). In sum, these findings provide evidence that interregional transfers have limited the potential disruptions associated with market integration. The efforts by net contributors to prevent potential negative externalities from the relatively poorer members of the Union appear moderately successful in light of these results. This success has allowed them to sustain their commitment to decentralized forms of interpersonal redistribution.

THEORETICAL IMPLICATIONS

This chapter has analyzed the determinants of the EU's fiscal structure as the outcome of the interplay between a very heterogeneous economic geography and the need to cope with the externalities emerging from economic integration. In addressing why the EU combines virtually no system of interpersonal redistribution through taxes and transfers with a limited, yet highly significant in relative budgetary terms, system of interregional redistribution, this chapter has shown that the answer to the first element of this question lies in the combination of a very disperse geography of income inequality and labor market risk with a highly centrifugal system of political representation. In an effort that provides broader support to the microfoundations of the argument in this book, I have relied on survey data to show how economic geography shapes the institutional preferences of both individuals and organized political actors (unions and parties) in ways that are consistent with the analytical premises of the book. Subsequently, I have also shown, relying on the DOSEI dataset, how the unanimity requirement to pass any major change in the Union translates this diversity of preferences into an institutional gridlock when it comes to the possibility of pursuing the integration of interpersonal redistribution. As implied by the argument, the centrifugal nature of the decision making process facilitates the extent to which territorial inequalities constrain the feasibility of larger redistributive efforts.

Yet a decentralized system of interpersonal redistribution requires, according to this book's argument, cross-regional externalities to be under control. As I have shown theoretically and will prove empirically in subsequent chapters, large levels of mobility put pressure to centralize. Therefore, when a diverse economic geography and a centrifugal system of representation create strong pressures to keep interpersonal redistribution decentralized, there are political incentives to try to keep cross-regional externalities as low as possible. The analysis of interregional transfers in the EU in this chapter supports this logic. Interregional redistribution is a tool to contain potential negative externalities from economic integration, mobility in particular. Overall, the study of the nuts and bolts behind the EU's fiscal structure offers considerable support to the central claims in this study. In the conclusion, I shall briefly discuss the implications of the analysis for the understanding of the current Euro crisis.

5

North America's Divide

Distributive Tensions, Risk Sharing, and the Centralization of Public Insurance in Federations

Unemployment insurance emerged in North America as a response to the economic crisis that shattered the social, economic, and political world at the end of the 1920s. The Great Depression yielded very different responses in the two North American federations. While Canada developed a centralized system of unemployment insurance in 1941, in the United States the Social Security Act (1935) included provisions leaving the ultimate design and implementation of unemployment insurance in the hands of the states (Webber and Wildavsky 1986: 453–464). These differing approaches are particularly intriguing because the two unions confronted the Depression from very similar positions, economically and politically. Economically, both federations were hit similarly by the Depression. Politically, they confronted the challenge from very similar starting positions as in both cases subnational governments enjoyed veto power over proposals to centralize unemployment insurance.

Hence, the different responses by Canada in 1941 and the United States in 1935 constitute a very useful test case to evaluate this book's argument. I chose to focus on unemployment insurance policy for two reasons. First, it is central to coping with labor market issues and, secondly, the interplay between cross-regional externalities and regional economic specialization is bound to be particularly visible in this realm. The contrast between Canada and the United States allows me to explore how much leverage my argument has to account for differences in the level of public insurance program centralization when the organization of political representation is comparably centrifugal at the onset of the process. In addition, the analysis provides two additional data points on the scale ranging from extremely centrifugal to extremely centripetal political unions, thereby contributing to the broader comparative agenda of this volume.

In theoretical terms, the very existence of two different outcomes poses a puzzle for single factor explanations based on either the existence of institutional veto points or the need to pool resources to face a structural economic shock. The American approach appears consistent with the former, as has been shown by a large number of contributions that explain why the United States is a welfare laggard.[1] But the Canadian experience points to the existence of other factors that may lead the units of a federation to alter institutional design and renounce, through an amendment, their constitutional veto capacity on a national program for unemployment insurance. The history of the emergence of the Unemployment Insurance Act (1940) is the history of a failure, the ultimate failure to preserve the welfare provisions established under the British North America Act (1867), in particular the Act's resort to local and provincial relief and charities as the optimal layer to deal with a problem, unemployment, that was viewed as an individual issue. The unemployed were so because of "some fault of their own" and, hence, society should apply the criteria of "less eligibility," which implies caring just for those obviously unable to fend for themselves (e.g., war injured). Such a view was shared by liberals and conservatives during the 1920s and early 30s and was generally abandoned by the late 30s. Given the magnitude of the Depression, one could see the Canadian response as a natural one: such a shock must necessarily lead to pooling resources. But then why did the United States take a different route?

According to the model developed in this book, given the institutional similarities between the two federations, what determines the institutional design of social security is the scope of risk sharing between regions. More precisely, the theoretical model points to four potential keys to understanding the divergent paths between Canada and the United States: income inequality between regions, the size of the dependent population by region $(1 - \alpha)$, the extent to which the level of dependents' mobility homogenizes this ratio across regions, and the incidence of risk associated with specialized economic activities (δ).

Similarly uneven in both countries, the geography of income hardly explains the institutional divide in response to the Depression. Indeed, in terms of income, wealthier Canadian provinces had incentives to prevent a centralized system of unemployment insurance. Yet they did not. In turn, some of the poorest American states worked, successfully, to prevent a national program that, in pure income terms would benefit them. The key must lie elsewhere, namely, in the different balance between the scope of interregional economic externalities (primarily the level of dependents' mobility) and the extent to which specific regional economies shape the geography of preferences with regard to public insurance systems. The remainder of this chapter develops this claim in detail.

In light of the argument in this book, there are two possible alternatives. The first one would be to argue that the two systems of representation were actually quite different by virtue of the fact that Canada has a parliamentary system and has a more centralized party system. The second alternative would contend

---

[1] See Noble (1997); and Quadagno (1994). Incidentally, the consideration of the United States as a welfare laggard must be treated with caution. This label is only applicable to the second half of the twentieth century. Lindert (2004) offers estimates of the extent of redistributive social spending for 1910 and 1930, concluding that Continental Europe does not outperform the United States in the first half of the twentieth century. See also Skocpol (1992).

that the Depression's impact on the economic geography of both unions was different, thereby generating a different pattern of demands. I begin this chapter by rejecting these two alternatives.

The first section marshals empirical evidence to show that the systems of representation yielded comparable levels of effective power for provincial leaders, and that the impact of the Depression on these unions' economic geography was indeed quite similar. On these grounds, the rest of the chapter proceeds in three analytical steps. First, I analyze the key mechanisms in the argument: the differences in the interplay between regional economic specialization, and the mobility patterns in the aftermath of the Depression. Second, I show how these differences shape key political actors' (most prominently employers' and subnational elites') preferences regarding the convenience of launching a centralized program of unemployment insurance. Finally, I trace the political process linking these preferences to the actual decision on centralizing unemployment insurance. The chapter closes by drawing out the main theoretical implications of the analysis.

THE STATUS QUO AND THE DISTRIBUTIVE CONSEQUENCES OF THE GREAT DEPRESSION

During the first three decades of the twentieth century Canadian and American social welfare systems shared a common approach to the issue of unemployment, including a similar underlying philosophy and some failed attempts to launch public insurance systems earlier in the century. Both countries proceeded in the footsteps of the British Poor Laws. With some remarkable exceptions, the worse off were left to be taken care of by charity, either organized by the local administration or directly dispensed by private philanthropic organizations. The ruling approach to indigents was that they did not constitute a public policy issue. Those who were laid off were expected to fend for themselves and search for whatever jobs were available. Only those lacking any possible opportunity (because of illness or age) were considered the target of the relief provided normally by locally organized voluntary associations and only exceptionally (civil war pensions) by the federal government (Skocpol 1992). In general, during the first fifteen years of the century public authorities were not directly concerned with social issues. State/provincial and federal governments refrained from direct intervention and only in exceptional circumstances did they launch one-off programs of emergency assistance.

Demobilization after World War I changed the landscape. In Canada, the issue of how to cope with the income needs of a large contingent of citizens during their transition from war to work, and the influence of Beveridge's ideas, increased the prospect of an insurance-based approach to the problem of unemployment. To cope with demobilization in Canada the Employment Service was established, collecting for the first time systematic information about the labor force and reallocating workers throughout the country. Moreover, Department of Labor officials recommended the adoption of an unemployment insurance system. In 1919 the Canadian Royal Commission on Industrial Relations recommended a national insurance scheme to deal with the temporarily unemployed (McIntosh and Boychuk 2001: 81–82). The context changed rapidly half way through the decade when a slight economic recovery put the issue aside in the political agenda. In addition, at this point the liberals were in coalition with the Progressive Party, an organization, created to defend the interests of farmers, who had little interest in developing any form of encompassing unemployment insurance at the federal level. Their key policy aimed to secure, via immigration and resettlement, a large enough contingent of unskilled workers for agricultural tasks, a legacy, I argue, that directly shaped the patterns of interprovincial migration in Canada.

The link between demobilization and early discussions about unemployment insurance is also very clear in the case of the United States. As in Canada, discussions about Unemployment Insurance date back as far as 1916, when Congress voted to draft legislation on the matter. The proposal did not go forward. During the 1920s and early 30s the conventional approach to unemployment relief remained unchallenged at the federal level. As the depth and duration of the Depression extended, the Senate Committee on Education and Labor held hearings "on the national problem of unemployment" (McGowan 1999: 3). In 1931 and 1934 Senator Robert Wagner introduced proposals for a joint federal-states Unemployment Insurance system. Although the bills were not even voted on, the 1934 proposal became a very important precedent of the institutional design ultimately adopted for unemployment insurance in the United States.

The institutional evolution on both sides of the border reflects an enduring legacy of political fragmentation in the approach to public policy issues. In the United States the use of local poor relief was heavily linked to organizational features of patronage democracy (Orloff 1988). In Canada, as Pal puts it, "the British North America Act had little to say about those activities that now comprise the welfare state [...]." In addition, as elaborated in Chapter 3, both in Canada and the United States at the time, political representation follows a decentralized form of federalism (Chhibber and Kollman 2004; Finegold and Skocpol 1995). This brings us back to party system organization, already introduced in Chapter 3.

The institutional fragmentation of the welfare system was a direct correlate of the presence of a decentralized party system. The Liberal Party in Canada is generally thought to be a stronger and more centralized political machine. Arguably, this would reflect Canada's parliamentary system, whereas the United States has a presidential one. Following this line of argument, it would be logical to conclude that the eventual centralization of unemployment insurance in Canada simply follows from the fact that the parliamentary system created a more centralized party structure, which in turn prevailed over provincial differences about the policy. While this contention might be a good characterization of the post-1945 situation, it misrepresents the political situation of the two North American federations at the onset of the Depression.

The reality in the Liberal Party during the 1920s and 30s was a very different one. Whitaker depicts an internally fragmented and conflictive organization in the 20s, held together by local barons, each at the head of patronage networks. Even in the 30s, the party did not hold a particularly tight grip on its provincial leaders. For example, Michael Hepburn, the Premier of Ontario, maintained a high level of autonomy and was fairly hostile to the idea of a centralized group of party leaders dictating policy from Ottawa. Indeed, as we shall see, at first he was not enthusiastic about the idea of the national unemployment insurance program championed by Canada's liberal premier, King, as part of the solution to the Depression. M. Hepburn, Ontario's liberal premier, held his veto until the fiscal pressure associated with the social consequences of the Depression and entering the war altered his own preferences on the matter. Similar dynamics are at work in other provinces, such as New Brunswick, where Premier Dysart had developed his own policy agenda to move people "from the dole to the payroll," and was wary of constraints from above on provincial autonomy.[2] In addition, Quebec liberals were themselves shaped by the nature of political competition within their province, and the need to compete against the Union Nationale regarding the protection of Quebec's autonomy. Altogether, it seems very implausible that the centralization of unemployment insurance in the 40s results from the influence of a relatively more centralized party organization. To describe the liberals as a centralized party in the context of a parliamentary system in the 30s would be an erroneous transposition of postwar dynamics onto the past.

Furthermore, party fragmentation was reinforced in both countries by well established systems of judicial review protecting the constitutional allocation of power to different territorial realms. Regarding unemployment, this institutional setup implied that the Constitution granted subnational governments effective veto power over any proposal to alter the distribution of power across territories. In the case of Canada, provinces need to agree to a formal reform of the British North America Act. In the case of the United States, state rights were also protected by the Supreme Court. In addition, U.S. Southern representatives enjoyed a privileged position in both the House and the Senate. The lack of political rights for the majority of the labor force generated an effective single party dominance of the Democratic Party (Alston and Ferrie 1999; Key 1949; Kousser 1974). This, in turn, gained them seniority in both houses. And, with seniority came the capacity to determine the agenda in the relevant committees, which implied a huge power to shape any legislation under consideration. Overall, politically and judicially, regional elites in both countries have the institutional capacity to prevent the federal government from launching any program potentially disruptive of their specific political economy.

---

[2] These policies included a reduction in the provincial relief effort and a budgetary increase in public works to counteract the endemic lack of labor demand caused by the Depression. Source: Allison Dysart. Biography. New Brunswick Legislative Library. See also Struthers (1983).

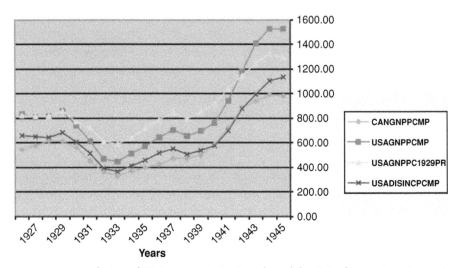

FIGURE 5.1. Evolution of GNP per capita in Canada and the United States (1926–1945)

If the status quo in terms of the preexisting policy and effective veto power of subnational units were similarly biased toward states and provinces, why did the paths of these two systems diverge between the late 1930s and early 40s? Does the answer perhaps lie in the different impact of the Great Depression as an exogenous shock to each of these political economies?

This does not appear to be the case. Canada and the United States were hit similarly by the sequence of economic downturns that reached its peak during the late 1920s and early 30s. Briefly mentioned, these were four: an ongoing process of deruralization that created a massive surplus in the Canadian and American labor forces, the European monetary crisis (1930–1931), an insufficient and late reaction in terms of macroeconomic policy, and, finally and most visibly, the worldwide collapse of financial and stock markets. Together these four factors provoked a long lasting reduction in wealth and consumption, which, in turn, affected expectations about the recovery, making the Depression longer (Temin 1976: 62–96, 138–179). The social consequences of the Depression were dramatic on both sides of the border (Epstein 1936).

Figures 5.1 and 5.2 display the magnitude as well as the timing of the Depression through two indicators: the GNP per capita[3], and the percentage of the total civilian labor force that is "not working and seeking a job."[4]

---

[3] These are the Gross National Product per capita at market prices, the Gross National Product at 1929 prices and the Disposable Income per capita at market prices. Source: see previous footnote). Canada: Historical Statistics and represent Gross National Product at Market Prices.

[4] Sources: Canada: Historical Statistics. United States: The unemployment rate is defined as one minus the proportion of the civilian labor force that is actually employed (Historical Statistics of the United States. Colonial Times to 1957, US Department of Commerce, Bureau of the Census, 1961, pp. 68–69).

North America's Divide

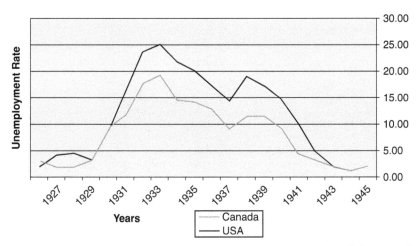

FIGURE 5.2. Evolution of the Unemployment Rate in Canada and the United States (1926–1945)

Issues of comparability aside, the trend shown by these indicators is similar in both countries. The peak in the unemployment rate is 1931, with 19.32% of the civilian labor force in Canada[5] and around 24% in the United States. Likewise, the GNP per capita hit the floor during the period 1930–1931 in both nations. Talking about the United States, Achembaum (1986: 16–17) offers the following picture of the Depression's implications:

[...] this time the extent, intensity, and duration of the upheaval were unprecedented. Between October 1929 and June 1932, the common stock price index dropped from 260 to 90. The nation's real GNP, which had risen 22 percent between 1923 and 1929, fell 30.4 percent over the next four years. Nearly 5,000 banks, with deposits exceeding $3.2 billion, became insolvent; 90,000 businesses failed. The gross income realized by farmers was cut nearly in half [...] More than one thousand local governments defaulted on their bonds [...] Breadlines formed [...] Bankrupt firms could not honor their pensions obligations to superannuated workers. [...] Misery was a threat to everyone.

The picture looked no better in Canada (Struthers 1983: 44–104). The Royal Commission on Dominion-Provincial Relations put it blatantly when stating that "the livelihood for hundreds of thousands of citizens seemed to be entirely dependent upon public charity" (1940: 162). Along with its widespread scope, the Depression also had a geographical dimension. Figure 5.3 illuminates this dimension by mapping the distribution of states and provinces along three variables: the level of regional income per capita at the beginning of the crisis

---

[5] Guest (1997: 83) offers estimates that put Canada closer to the US: "At the bottom of the Depression in 1933 nearly one quarter of the labor force was out of work and seeking jobs and an estimated 15 percent of the population was in receipt of relief."

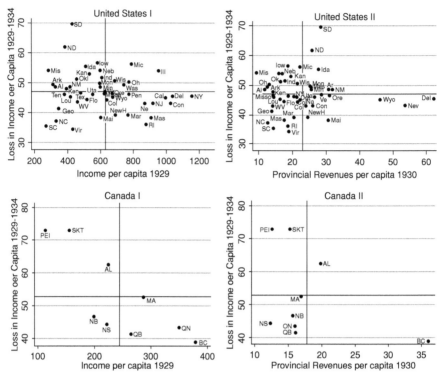

FIGURE 5.3. The Geography of the Depression in the United States and Canada

(1929); the drop in personal income per capita between then and the Depression's peak (1934–35); and subnational governments' level of financial capacity, as captured by state/provincial revenues per capita in 1930.

Amidst a context of economic decay (after all, the "lucky" provinces/states saw drops of 30–40% in their levels of income per capita), it seems undeniable that the depression hit some regions much harder than others. Those states/provinces whose economies were of an agrarian basis were especially damaged by the fall in consumption and attendant drop in agricultural prices.[6] In Canada these were the western prairieprovinces, Alberta and Saskatchewan most prominently.

As Figure 5.3 displays these two provinces not only were among the poorest in terms of income per capita in 1929 but also took the worst hit, together with Prince Edward Island, losing between 60% and 70% of their income five years into the Depression. In the United States, the upper left quadrant (i.e., those with income levels below average and income losses above average) is populated by the American Midwest and southern states, where a lot of planters were unable to keep their labor force. In addition to the fact that these states had very

---

[6] Guest (1997: 83–135) reports, for instance, a fall in the price of wheat from $1.60 in 1929 to 38 cents in 1931.

few resources at their disposal (their revenues per capita were scant at best), charitable institutions had very little, if any, presence in rural and agricultural dependent areas (Patterson 1986). As a result, during these years chronic, long-term poverty became particularly acute in the South (Alston and Ferrie 1999: 49–50). Generally, it was the case in both countries that those with the worst problems had the least resources with which to respond. The situation was particularly extreme given the states' and provinces' very low fiscal capacity. While the average provincial income per capita in Canada was around $240, the average provincial revenue per capita was $18. Similarly, while the average state income per capita was above $600, the average state revenue per capita was just above $20. The right hand side of Figure 6.3 also suggests that this scarcity was quasi-uniform throughout Canada (with the relative exception of British Columbia) and slightly more heterogeneous in the United States. Faced with such a worsening of social conditions the existing welfare institutions were politically and financially powerless.

These patterns fostered distributive tensions within and between the two countries, and demand for adjustment of existing fiscal and social security institutions. Bankrupted provinces and states pleaded Ottawa and Washington for help. Others, for different reasons to be explored below, were wary of too much federal intervention. In the United States the case for centralizing unemployment insurance to cope with these tensions failed. In Canada, it succeeded. In the rest of this chapter I argue that the key difference between the two experiences lies in the interplay between economic geography and the mobility patterns of dependents and unskilled workers. This interplay works differently in Canada and the United States because of the way large masses of unskilled workers were incorporated into labor intensive agricultural sectors during the two decades preceding the Depression. In this sense they were largely exogenous with respect to contentions over the scope and organization of public insurance systems.

THE BALANCE BETWEEN ECONOMIC GEOGRAPHY AND MOBILITY
IN THE AFTERMATH OF THE DEPRESSION

To understand why mobility patterns vary between Canada and the United States, it is helpful to revisit the way both countries dealt with the demand for unskilled labor in the preceding decades, and how this in turn shaped internal migration patterns. To a large extent, migration patterns in Canada reflect changes in demand for low-skilled workers along the East-West axis. Between the early 1910s and early 20s, the unskilled workers migration pattern transformed Canada, and settling the ever increasing contingents of workers became a dominant policy priority. The recovery following the economic depression of 1907 was largely driven by the boost in agricultural production in the West. By 1909, the number of immigrants into Canada was about 110,000; by 1914, the number had reached 400,000 (DMPI 1974). After the sharp break imposed by World War I, immigration rose again between 1918 and the recession of

TABLE 5.1. *Intercensus Net Migration Ratios, by Province, Canada 1901–1921*

Provinces	1901–1911	1911–1921
PEI	−13.6	−16.4
Nova Scotia	−0.6	−7.6
New Brunswick	−3.8	−7.3
Quebec	4.3	−4
Ontario	9.3	2.3
Manitoba	41.2	5.1
Saskatchewan	125.6	15.1
Alberta	123.8	20.9
British Columbia	69.4	14.8

Ottawa: Government Publication, 1969. p. 138.

the early 20s. Clearly, not all of these immigrants were unskilled men in search of labor. Many of them arrived into Canada escaping political, religious, or racial persecution, not just hunger. But enough were unskilled to shape the patterns of internal migration within the union. Table 5.1 displays the interprovincial migration rates in Canada between 1901 and 1921. There is a clear population shift from the Maritimes towards the rural West, most notably, Saskatchewan and Alberta.

In this context, the 1921 elections yielded a coalition between King's liberals and the Progressive Party, an organization created to promote the interests of farmers. As the economic recovery ensued during the post-WWI years, Western farmers found themselves in need of labor. The Progressive Party led the government to pursue a two-fold policy on the issue: relocate the unemployed to work on farms (the "*back to the land*" strategy), and facilitate the immigration of unskilled workers to be incorporated both into farming and natural resource extraction industries.

These measures only added to the migration trends reported in Table 5.1. Due to the harsh Canadian Winter and the nature of these industries, unskilled workers' reliance on the West for their economic fortunes created a huge group of seasonal, highly mobile, workers. Depending upon the time of the year, they would be hired in different provinces across the country to perform tasks that demanded nothing but physical effort. In good times, the seasonal nature of employment nurtured a cross-regional flow of workers; in bad times, as we shall see below, potential workers turn into a wave of dependents seeking relief. This will have important political consequences during the process leading to Canada's Unemployment Insurance Act of 1940.

The reality was quite different in the United States, as race shaped the nature of the interplay between economic geography and mobility. During the late nineteenth and early twentieth centuries, racism shaped the "unfinished democracy" (Quadagno 1994) at work in the southern states. The Ku Klux

Klan was spreading into the plantation areas and many black families found it rational to migrate to urban areas either in the North or in the West (Steckel 1983). According to historical census data, the proportion of blacks born in their state of residence fell from 83% in 1910 to 75% in 1930. In the context of the Great Migration, concerns about an adequate supply of labor grew among planters. According to Alston and Ferrie (1999: 17), "some planters chose a new course – turning to honesty, fair dealing and a host of nonwage aspects of their relationship with their workers as additional margins for competition." Over time a system of mutual obligations emerged and consolidated. "By the early twentieth century planters had come to act as intermediaries between their workers and much of the outside world. Planters exercised control over the credit extended to their workers, but they were also willing to stand good for their workers' debts with local merchants. [. . .] Planters reported significant outlays for the payment of doctor's bills, the establishment and maintenance of schools and churches, and various unspecified forms of entertainment. And planters commonly paid legal fines incurred by workers and served as parole sponsors for their workers." (Alston and Ferrie 1999: 20). In return, workers, especially tenants and croppers, "were expected not only to work hard in the fields but to display deference toward their landlords" (ibid: 25). Such basic exchange underlies what economic historians conventionally refer to as *Southern Paternalism*.

Its logic was compelling. Tenants and croppers gained protection and side benefits for their families. From the planters' point of view an adequate supply of low-cost labor was guaranteed. The longer the duration of the exchange the bigger the levels of mutual dependency and hence the larger the opportunity cost of moving away for croppers and tenants. Put differently, paternalism reduced mobility and hence maintained the specificity of the planters' system of production and social dominance. In fact, the proportion of blacks born in their state of residence did remain constant between the 1930 and 1940 censuses, as reflected in Table 5.3. Planters, in turn, had incentives to keep "looking after" their tenants as well as to prevent any external input potentially disruptive of this particular relationship.

This brief historical overview shows how, after WWI, Canada and the United States took opposite paths on the issue of immigration. While the United States increasingly made a more selective policy, Canadian borders were open to large amounts of unskilled labor, let in to work primarily in farming and extractive industries. From the beginning these immigrants were a very mobile sector of the Canadian labor force in that their familial and cultural ties did not belong to any particular province. When the Depression affected both countries, transients were a Canadian peculiarity, a mass of seasonal workers moving between jobs and the quest for welfare, operating as a multiplier of the social consequences of the Depression across territories. In contrast, by the late 1920s the Great Migration was over in the United States, and Southern Paternalism had emerged as a politico-economic model tying down workers to secure steady levels of labor supply. Accordingly, cross-regional mobility

TABLE 5.2. *Interstate Mobility in the United States*

	USA Census Data: Born in State of Residence		
	All Races	Black	White
1870	76.8	81	76
1880	77.9	84	76.8
1890	78.5	84.5	77.5
1900	79	84.2	78.2
1910	78	83.2	77.2
1920	77.4	80	77.1
1930	76.2	75.4	76.2
1940	77.1	75.9	77.3
1950	73.5	69.8	74

of dependents was a more significant social and political factor in the post-Depression years in Canada than in the United States.

By moving both eastward and westward, transients passed the effects of all these adverse shocks to the more industrialized Canadian provinces. For instance, according to Struthers (1983: 44–71), transients from the West constituted 40% of the total demand for relief in the city of Toronto. As mentioned earlier, Vancouver suffered a similar shock by receiving over 10,000 people in need of support by the end of 1930. Estimated at over 100,000, transients worked to homogenize risk profiles across Canadian provinces. The social composition of this floating population was fairly homogeneous: male, unskilled, and in search of either manual labor or public relief. To put these numbers in context, transients amount to 3% of Ontario's total population in 1931. More importantly, between 1931 and 1941, Alberta and Saskatchewan suffered a net immigration loss of, respectively, 41,841 and 157,545 people, amounting to 5% and 18% of their populations at the outset of the Depression. During the same period, Ontario and British Columbia experienced a net immigration gain of, respectively, 77,484 and 82,498 people.[7] These population moves made the incidence of the Depression much more balanced territorially. No evidence of similar patterns is to be found in the United States during the Depression years.

Tables 5.2 and 5.3 and Figure 5.4 bring to bear more systematic evidence on this point. A comparison between Tables 5.1 and 5.3 reveals the changes in the nature of migration flows caused by the Depression. During the period 1911–1921, the rural West was a preferred destination, a magnet for unskilled rural workers that drive the net migration rate up in places like Manitoba or Saskatchewan. In contrast, during the post-Depression decade the agricultural

---

[7] Source: Statistics Canada. Historical Statistics (online version).

TABLE 5.3. *Intercensus Net Migration Ratios, by Province, Canada 1921–1941*

Provinces	1921–1931	1931–1941	1931–1941 (absolute numbers)
PEI	−11.1	−4.61	−2672
Nova Scotia	−14.5	2.34	7848
New Brunswick	−11.5	−3.99	−10177
Quebec	0.9	−0.11	−1991
Ontario	5.1	3.22	77484
Manitoba	−1.7	−10.40	−48478
Saskatchewan	−0.7	−27.45	−157545
Alberta	3.8	−8.77	−41841
British Columbia	18.7	16.14	82498

Ottawa: Government Publication, 1969. p. 138.

provinces of the West became a major source of migrants. Interprovincial migration brought about large population changes across Canadian provinces, with areas worst hit by the Depression losing population in favor of Ontario and British Columbia. In turn, the contrast between Tables 5.2 and 5.3 reveals that no such process is observable in the United States.

According to census data, the proportion of people born in their state of residence actually did increase between 1930 and 1940 throughout the United States. More specifically, Figure 5.4 shows that migration in and out of the South actually dropped during the Depression years, picking up rapidly only after WWII. As Rosenbloom and Sundstrom (2004: 11) put it, "familiar tales

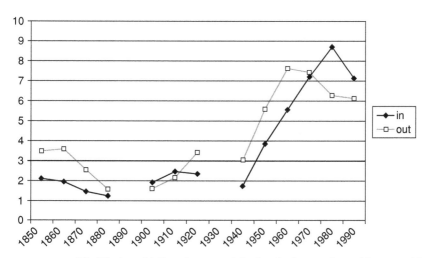

FIGURE 5.4. The Timing of Migration out of the South. *Source:* Rosenbloom and Sundstrom (2004)

about the Okie migration notwithstanding, interstate migration rates were low during the Depression."

In terms of the model, mobility brings provinces much closer in their value of $(\alpha/1 - \alpha)$ thereby homogenizing the demand for welfare and insurance across territories. Moreover, these patterns of interprovincial mobility also contributed to a reduction in the gap between provinces in the value of δ. Being mobile across provinces between seasons, transients and their associated risks became a shared sector of the labor force.

Put shortly, transients did contribute to the increase of levels of risk sharing between provinces. Meanwhile, despite the Dust Bowl exodus immortalized by John Steinbeck, no such group of seasonally mobile rural workers/dependents emerged in the United States as Southern Paternalism worked successfully to limit the interstate mobility of agricultural workers. Although there were different degrees of specialization among the provinces, and some Premiers (like Alberta's) developed their own attempts to cope with regional labor markets, in Canada there was nothing like the Southern American states in terms of specificity of production or the peculiar internal equilibrium of their system of labor, social, and political relations. In brief, even in the context of the Depression, the labor market specificities of the American states (including not only the South, but also some Northern and Midwestern states) reduced levels of risk sharing between subnational units. In terms of the model, interstate differences in the value of δ were higher in the United States than in Canada. In line with the argument of this book, in Canada I would expect a political process in which the scope of externalities and their fiscal consequences undermines the resistance towards unemployment insurance centralization. By contrast, I expect the interplay between economic geography and mobility in the United States to nurture political pressures to preserve a more decentralized insurance system. In the next section, I explore whether these expectations bear any relationship with the political processes in the two North American federations.

THE POLITICAL PROCESS: A COMPARATIVE OVERVIEW

As economic conditions worsened and governments muddled through recurrent downturns, unemployment became central to the political agenda. In Canada, it conditioned the electoral outcomes of the competition between the liberals (1921–1930; 1935–1941) and the conservatives (1930–1935) and the dynamics of the dominion-provincial relations. In the United States as well, it shaped the relationships between the states and the federal government. In this section, I analyze how the different balances between economic geography and mobility in Canada and the United States shaped key social and political actors' preferences, ultimately explaining the very different responses to the problem of unemployment in the two North-American federations. I proceed in two steps: first I analyze the initial responses by employers and subnational governments in Canada and the United States. These, I argue, reflect the heterogeneity of preferences in the early post-Depression years and shape the initial responses of the federal governments in Ottawa and Washington DC. Thereafter, I study comparatively how King's liberal government managed to overcome the initial resistance while Roosevelt's government struggled to include in the Social Security Act provisions much more respectful of states' autonomy.

Preference Heterogeneity and Initial Responses

Canadian Prime Minister Bennett's conservative government took office shortly after the 1929 financial crash on Wall Street. At the time, there was much contention about passing the buck. As the provinces and the municipalities were overloaded, Ottawa tried to keep its financial and administrative involvement to a minimum and hence insisted that, constitutionally, taking care of the unemployed was their task. Ottawa remained committed to this view and succeeded until the second half of the 1930s.[8] Yet demand for relief was increasing across the country, as was demand for a national, noncontributory, unemployment insurance system. Such demands fueled as much support as opposition and motivated the mobilization of important institutional, social, and political actors.

In 1932 Bennett was presented with a petition in support of a national, noncontributory insurance system endorsed by 94,169 people. Behind the petition were, among others: several members of the parliamentary left, most prominently A. Hasleep and his Cooperative Commonwealth Federation; the Worker's Unity League, a fairly radical trade union responsible for significant industrial action and mobilization during the first half of the 1930s; and veterans, who felt entitled to better treatment in terms of relief and opportunity in compensation for their war service. Veterans were indeed very active at the local, provincial, and national levels, and supported actively the demand for social security throughout post-Depression Canada (Campbell 2000). Many overstretched municipalities also supported the initiative. Even certain sectors of the industrial and financial elite supported the introduction of an insurance scheme, though for very different reasons. In 1932, the *Financial Times* complained that "workers, unlike corporations, did not have the good sense to build reserves against distress in the event of future unemployment" (Finkel 1979: 85). The potential fiscal effects of such hazardous behavior would justify new government regulations to administer and control workers' exposure to risk.

This view was far from universally shared amongst employers though. Large manufacturing companies, represented by the Canadian Manufacturing Association, were opposed to the idea. Worries stemmed from the cost of the state assuming the development of this program, and, interestingly, from the potential disfunctionality of implementing the same plan in companies with many

---

[8] This summary draws on historical accounts by Guest (1997); Pal (1988); and Struthers (1983). The latter provides the richest historical account of the unemployment problem in Canada between 1914 and 1941.

different needs (Finkel 1979: 87–88). Finally, employers in seasonal industries were concerned about the medium term implication of insurance programs from the standpoint of labor supply.

In sum, during the early years of Bennett's government the political landscape included both important labor organization mobilization and divisions among employers about the pertinence of a national insurance program. In this context, the transients issue was gaining in social and political importance. According to Whitton's estimates (1933; cfr. Struthers 1983) there were up to 100,000 seasonal workers in the West on whom unemployment was (and would continue to be) especially concentrated. This large subset of seasonal dependent population, not being settled residents, highlighted the issue of which layer of government should take care of them. Municipalities and provinces looked at Ottawa and demanded a response to the added relief burden of the transients.

Bennett's initial response was rather traditionalist; aligning with employers (important among his supporters), he opposed a new insurance system. He insisted on a sharp divide between relief and insurance, putting aside the latter on the grounds that it would require a constitutional reform of the British North America Act (BNA). He agreed to increase funds to cover the cost of transients' relief until July 1933. At the same time he adopted a strict policy of "provincial self-reliance" in dominion-provincial financial relations, constraining the provinces' capacity to take debt to $1 million per year. Finally, he expanded the "back to the land" strategy by launching the National Defense Relief Camps, a system of concentration camps for "single, unskilled men and recent immigrants" in which these would work for the government in exchange for meals, shelter, and money received as relief. The explicit goal was to expel the specter of socialism by drawing transients out of the cities.

At the same time, the central government's lack of initiative prompted regional leaders to develop their own alternatives. The most interesting example in this regard was the success of the Social Credit Movement. A predominantly rural province devoted to farming, Alberta rested on a highly specialized economy. Farmers and political elites alike traditionally felt that the national policies designed in Toronto and Ottawa undermined their provincial economy. A platform mixing religious fundamentalism, antiindustrialism, a universal basic income of $25, and the cancellation of all farmers' debt emerged in 1932 and seized the provincial premiership in 1935. W. Aberhart's party would be reelected in 1940 and stay in power in Alberta until 1968 (Barr 1974; Calderola 1979; Finkel 1989). The Social Credit Movement was notorious for its close defense of Alberta's farming sector and constitutes the most prominent example of a highly specialized region acting to protect its autonomy during the political process leading up to the Unemployment Insurance Act.

The post-Depression landscape in the United States shares some features of the Canadian experience, but it offers important differences as well. As in Canada, significant developments in unemployment policy took place at the industry and state levels prior to the Depression. Likewise, a number of radical political proposals also emerged in the United States, raising the level of awareness among political elites about the need to provide timely alternatives in terms of relief and insurance. Among these proposals were Long's plan for a flat universal pension to be given to anyone over sixty or Tawsend's plan to issue a sales tax to pay $200 per month to every American Citizen except convicted felons (Berkowitz 1991: 1–39); or, later on in the process, the Lundeen Bill, submitted to (and defeated in) Congress by Representative Lundeen from Minnesota in 1934 and 1935. The bill provided "for the payment of unemployment compensation out of the funds of the national government to all unemployed persons over the age of eighteen years for as long as they were out of work through no fault of their own" (Douglas 1936: 74).

These and much less radical proposals met two sources of resistance: a virtually universal opposition from business to the comprehensive development of social insurance, and a very heterogeneous set of positions at the state level on how to respond to the problem of unemployment. Both the level of business opposition to social insurance initiatives and the heterogeneity in the stated positions by subnational governments were more intense in the United States than in Canada. After an extensive review of the position of business on the development of social insurance policies in the United States, Hacker and Pierson (2002) concluded that business interests systematically resisted the development of social insurance programs throughout the country.

However widespread, the intensity of resistance was not homogeneous across states. In line with the expectations derived from the model, business is especially hostile to the centralization of social insurance in those states with lower levels of development and asset specific, labor intensive, industries. In these cases, concerns for the income implications of the program reinforce concerns about federal intrusion on the workings of the local economy. In a thorough account of the position of American states on the development of social insurance in the years immediately preceding the New Deal, Patterson (1969) shows how the most adamant hostility came from leaders like Eugene Talmadge, the openly racist and reactionary governor of Georgia. Typically, the rejection of the federal government's proposal took the form of a strong advocacy of states' rights. At the 1935 Governors' Conference he stated, "Any regulation of business – any of it – we object to it. We Governors object to them taking our sovereign rights; we object to them coming into the states to setup activities that we know are states' rights" (cfr. Patterson 1969: 237). Other Republicans raised similar concerns.

Partisanship exacerbated these criticisms, but it did not eliminate tensions within the Democratic Party. Indeed, several Democratic states (Montana, West Virginia) oscillated between skepticism and frontal opposition to Roosevelt's approach to the issue of unemployment. Even as late as 1936, when the Social Security Act had already passed and Roosevelt was a dominant political figure, Montana's Democratic Governor, Elmer Holt, expressed the following concern: "It does seem to me that some departments of the Administration are catering too much to the 'Red' element."[9]

---

[9] Letter from Elmer Holt from September 11, 1936, as quoted in Patterson (1969: 154).

At the other extreme, a number of progressive leaders launched initiatives well before the federal government proposed the Social Security Act. McNutt in Indiana managed to pass a gross state income tax to fix his impoverished state's finances. More importantly, Wisconsin pioneered the development of unemployment insurance programs thanks to the efforts of La Follete's Progressive Party (Nelson 1969). The Wisconsin Plan consisted of a system of unemployment reserves. Each company would be taxed to build up reserves, to be tapped in case some of its workers fell into unemployment. In this plan employers have an incentive to maximize employment levels and reduce the amount of tax they would have to pay. This system, tailored to the needs of Wisconsin's productive structure, did not travel to other states (Amenta et al. 1987). Ohio, for instance, considered a proposal, ultimately defeated due in large part to the objections of business, to introduce "taxes on both employers and employees and the establishment of a state funded pooled insurance fund" (Amenta et al. 1987: 146).

This heterogeneity across states reflects differences in the level of economic development and geography of economic specialization and undermines the feasibility of a centralized solution in the United States. The drop in crossstate mobility patterns during the post-Depression years did not help alter the situation. At the same time, the objections of business organizations remained strong and influential. Even in those states, such as Wisconsin, Indiana, or Minnesota, where regional elites were able to launch new relief and insurance programs, they could only do so after local business associations had shaped these initiatives so as to minimize their share of the burden. Despite these pioneering efforts though, by 1934–1935 unemployment insurance was a privilege available only to a minority of the American labor force.[10] At the same time, the Depression had just reached its peak: the unemployment rate was 25%. Much like in Canada, the situation required a proportional policy response from the federal government (Skocpol and Ikenberry 1983: 87–148; Weir 1988: 149–199).

Divergent Approaches to Unemployment Insurance: The Political Processes

Canada: Preference Homogenization and the Overcoming of Resistance. Initial responses to the problem of unemployment in Canada soon proved insufficient. If anything, the relief camp strategy backfired, facilitating the mobilization of a large contingent of unskilled workers. By 1934 the failure of this strategy to guarantee prosperity and the achievements of Roosevelt's policies made Bennett change his approach in a twofold way. He proposed to progressively abandon relief and substitute it with a program of public works able to generate

---

[10] For instance, according to Department of Labor of the State of New York estimates, "in 1934 trade union plans covered about 100,000 workers; joint unions-management plans covered about 65,000 and voluntary company plans covered another 70,000" (McGowan 1999: 5).

employment while at the same introducing an unemployment insurance system for the bad times to come. Both programs were part of a strategy to overcome the resistance expected from the provinces against Ottawa's withdrawal from unemployment relief. The strategy, again, backfired as it actually alienated provinces and eliminated the possibility of any such agreement. The proximity of the elections led Bennett to present his own "New Deal" in a series of radio speeches to the nation outlining a number of initiatives to overcome the country's social and economic crisis. These included a national minimum wage, working-hours legislation, a more progressive tax system and, among other things, a contributory old age pension and health and unemployment insurance.

The liberals highlighted that most of these initiatives would require a reallocation of political capacities from the provinces to Ottawa but did not oppose the Employment and Social Insurance Act, passed in March 1935. Inspired by the 1911 British System, the proposal for unemployment insurance had stricter benefits, in accordance with the 'less eligibility' doctrine, and very limited coverage (the agricultural sector was excluded, dealt with only through relief). Moreover, the government would only cover one fifth of the total cost of the program and neither sickness nor transitional benefits were considered. In general, federal involvement would remain at a minimum in that Unemployment Insurance would be neither financed nor administered by the dominion. Bennett's proposal, remarkably attached to the status quo, was never implemented. The Supreme Court (1936) and the British Privy Council in London (1937) declared it *ultra vires*, restating the need to amend the BNA if Ottawa was to develop any unemployment insurance program.

In addition to this major political backlash, the transients issue reemerged forcefully with strikes in the relief camps of British Columbia, the organization of the On to Ottawa Trek and the Regina riots. Social unrest kept increasing while financial relations between the provinces and the dominion were broken (the four Western provinces owed Ottawa $117 million). Not surprisingly, in the 1935 elections Bennett was defeated by a large margin and, with him, "the idea that the care of the unemployed was a local responsibility" (Struthers 1983: 137). The Liberals, led by Mackenzie King, regained office.

King's moves were cautious and continuist at first. The approval of the Unemployment Insurance Act (1941) required a major constitutional amendment that spanned from 1936, the year the provisions of the Bennett's New Deal (1935) regarding unemployment were declared unconstitutional by the Supreme Court of Canada, and 1940, the year the Federal Government and provinces agreed to reform the British North America Act so that the former could, among other things, take full control of the emerging national program of unemployment insurance. Indeed, King became tighter on public finances, demanding from provinces a balanced budget and aiming at a progressive reduction in the federal share of relief expenditures (mainly via a program of progressive decrease in grants in aid to the provinces). However, he also pursued new avenues by appointing a National Employment Commission (NEC) to study alternative courses of action on unemployment. The NEC recommended closing relief concentration camps and replacing them with a land settlement program (1936).[11] It also proposed an employment service to enhance coordination among employers and employees, an ambitious public housing program to both create employment and lessen shortages in the housing supply, as well as a National Volunteer Conservation System along the lines of the one developed by Roosevelt in the United States. Of these only the land settlement program was implemented. In addition, after Bennett's constitutional fiasco, King sounded out the provinces regarding the amendment of the Constitution, necessary to develop a centralized unemployment insurance program. To this end he appointed, in August 1937, the Rowell-Siros Commission on Dominion-Provincial Financial Relations. At this point six provinces, including British Columbia, agreed to transfer the capacity to deal with unemployment to the federal government. New Brunswick decided to wait for the conclusions of the Commission before making a decision. Quebec and Ontario,[12] provinces with average to high income per capita and relatively less hit by the Depression, wary of the fiscal and political implications of a common program, claimed concerns about provincial autonomy and refused the amendment. Incidentally, both provinces are bound to be net contributors in any national insurance system. Finally, Alberta's Premier (Aberhart), whose earlier attempt to develop a system of social credit specifically tailored to the type of production dominant in the province had been overruled by Ottawa, rejected any constitutional amendment unless he could see the specific legislation first. As a unanimous agreement on constitutional reform was not within reach, King decided to postpone the issue until the Rowell and Siros report was published. However, exogenous circumstances altered King's plans, accelerating events and providing a clear illustration of the mechanisms behind the process of homogenization of preferences that took place among Canadian elites between the end of 1937 and the approval of the Unemployment Insurance Act in 1941.

By the end of 1937 a heavy drought increased the magnitude of the Depression in the West, creating yet another conflict between British Columbia (BC) and Ottawa about the costs of coping with transients. Relatively wealthier than any other province, BC was a natural point of destination for the transients. Municipal Relief Office estimates indicate that during 1930 Vancouver's

---

[11] Conditions under the new program were much better than in Bennett's concentration camps. Now workers would get a proper salary, "a $5 monthly stipend to both the farmer and person he hired plus a $2.50 deferred bonus for each month worked to be received during the winter months" (Struthers 1983: 159–160) and the program would be much broader in coverage (targeting the estimated 100,000 transients, it ended up taking care of 37,000 homeless men and 5,000 women, which were excluded from Bennett's camps). For a short period of time, this strategy solved the transients issue and contained the cost of relief expenditures to the provinces. However, British Columbia and Ontario refused to take part in it, limiting its positive effects.

[12] Despite belonging to the same party, Liberal Premier Hepburn of Ontario was deeply hostile to King and not particularly in favor the Unemployment Insurance Act at this stage. Premier Dysart of New Brunswick was similarly opposed.

population increased by 5% due to the arrival of 10,000 seasonal unemployed begging for care. With its capital dubbed the "mecca of the unemployed," BC's financial capacity was strained. In this context, King insisted on a balanced budget approach, with proposals to freeze grants in aid to the previous year's level, to limit up to 30% Ottawa's share of total relief costs, and to set a maximum level of relief to be provided by the provinces. The proposal exacerbated tensions with the provinces as well as within King's own government. In response, the BC premier successfully forced Ottawa to pay for the relief expenditures generated by these nonresident workers by closing the camps six weeks earlier and cutting off relief for these workers. Transients had become, again, the most visible symbol of the shared, nonlocal, nature of the unemployment problem.

In December 1937 the NEC issued another report calling for a policy shift toward a national approach combining assistance and insurance. In response to these demands, King's government put aside the balanced budget issue and agreed to spend $40 million on unemployment relief expenditures. However, no Unemployment Insurance Act was proposed as the Rowell-Siros report was not yet concluded.

Concerns about the fiscal implications of relief, directly associated with the magnitude of the flow of transients, and its potential implications for Canada's macroeconomic stability, altered the position of Canadian employers. What earlier in the process was a divided group became, by early 1938, an active support for the centralization of social insurance in Canada. Expressions of concern and support for the initiative were especially strong in those provinces, like British Columbia, suffering the social consequences of the Depression with greater intensity. A.E. Grauer, president of BC Power Corporation, and one of the leading figures in BC's business community, conveys the new perspective of employers forcefully (Finkel 1979: 83):

Since the Great War, the Great Depression has been the chief stimulus to labour legislation and social insurance. The note sounded has not been so much the idea of social justice, as political and economic financial expediency. For instance, the shorter working week was favored in unexpected quarters not because it would give the workers more leisure and possibilities for a fuller life but because it would spread work; and the current singling of unemployment insurance for governmental attention in many countries is dictated by the appalling costs of direct relief and hope that unemployment insurance benefits will give some protection to public treasuries in future depressions and will, by sustaining purchasing power, tend to mitigate these depressions ...

Along similar lines, the Chamber of Commerce became a major force in support of a centralized system of unemployment insurance:

The people of all the provinces will have an opportunity of passing on this social security legislation through their representatives in the federal parliament and we cannot see the necessity for hesitancy on the part of the provincial governments at the present time. The unfortunate fetish of provincial 'rights' is ever with us but it is high time we learned that progress can best be kept on the march by the centralization of government consistent with 'individual' not 'provincial' freedom. [Finkel 1979: 96]

And on the East, employers organizations in Ontario and Quebec offer similar positions. R. Dandurand, a leading French Canadian Businessman, states:

When I think of them and of the inevitably slow process of reabsorbing into industry those who are now unemployed, I feel more and more concerned that if our capitalist system is to survive we shall have to establish a contributory unemployment system to tide our people over periods of economic depression.

Similarly, the Montreal Board of Trade argues in Keynesian terms:

Taxation for the purpose of social services transfers purchasing power from the richer to the poorer classes, raises the standard of living of the poor, increases their demand for commodities and thereby tends towards industrial stability and prosperity. Furthermore, in a period of economic depression, heavier government expenditures, whether paid by taxes or by loans, are justified and necessary in order to fill the gap resulting from the fear and inactivity which paralyze private enterprise. [Finkel 1979: 139]

This series of quotations illustrates how the position of employers shifts over time as a result of the scope of cross-provincial economic externalities, largely motivated by the mobility of unskilled dependents across provinces. The fiscal impact of skyrocketing relief expenditures threatened all provinces alike, not just the ones particularly hurt by the Depression, and rendered the need to establish preventive mechanisms, such as unemployment insurance, a national priority for employers.

Finally, the beginning of the Second World War only added to these concerns by creating yet another source of cross-regional externalities, ultimately pushing the Canadian government to seek constitutional reform even before the publication of the Rowell Siros Report. Concerns about the future demobilization and socioeconomic integration of veterans, already salient after WWI, rendered unemployment an even greater national problem (Campeau 2005). Taken together, all these factors gradually erased hesitations among the provinces that either doubted or openly opposed the amendment. Unemployment itself contributed to the replacement of M. Duplessis, Quebec's conservative premier, by A. Godbout, a liberal who quickly switched positions in line with the majority of labor unions and employers' organizations in Quebec. In turn, the level of economic externalities and the War undermined Ontario's earlier concerns for its fiscal position within the union. Finally, Alberta's premier, according to Struthers (1983), faced strong pressures as he became, on the basis of Alberta's specific regional economy, the only opponent to an amendment viewed as a national need for the difficult days ahead. Along these lines, the Rowell-Siros Report came at last to back up all the economic arguments in favor of Unemployment Insurance, namely: administrative efficiency, interprovincial equity, and especially the fact that all provinces were affected by the problem, i.e., unemployment "was no longer seen as the result of local conditions." In July 1940 the Unemployment Insurance Act was approved.

A fully centralized program was finally at work. It was heavily based upon Bennett's legislation, with three important qualifications (Dingledine 1981).

First, benefits were no longer at a flat rate, but graded according to previous earnings. Second, a bigger effort was made in terms of coverage (75% of the labor force), eligibility (the qualifying period drops from forty to thirty weeks) and duration. Nonetheless, seasonal agriculture, forestry and fishing workers remained excluded, treated only under assistance policies still guided by the "less eligibility" principle and with no national minimum. Following the Rowell-Siros Report, the full cost of the latter was finally assumed by Ottawa. The report, however, did suggest a centralization of taxation and the design of an inter-provincial system of revenue sharing so that the average provincial cost of relief would be equalized in the end.

The United States: The Continuity of State Autonomy. Roosevelt approached the issue of insurance under very different circumstances, determined by a much more heterogeneous set of state actors and the absence of large levels of mobility from 1929 onward. Therefore, he was cautions in his strategy. His efforts on unemployment and old age relief allowed him some time to carefully design longer term measures to handle the various dimensions of "economic instability." In his own words, "the federal government, of course, does have to prevent anyone from starving, but the federal government should not be called upon to exercise the duty until all other agencies fail. The primary duty is that of the locality, the city, county, town. If they should fail and cannot raise enough to meet the needs the next responsibility is on the states and they have to do all they can. If it is still proven that they cannot do any more and the funds are still insufficient, it is the duty of the federal government to step in" (*New York Times*, May 23, 1933; cfrd. Singleton 2000: 108). The latter was indeed the case. Roosevelt's action on this matter was much quicker and less reluctant than that of his Canadian counterparts. Right after taking office he introduced the Federal Relief Emergency Act, "appropriating $500 million to the States" (Singleton 2000: 102–110). In so doing he responded "to the plight of the unemployed and to the non inconsiderable protests of state and local welfare officials, whose agencies were overwhelmed financially by the proportion of the need produced by the crisis" (Orloff 1988: 69). At the same time, however, Roosevelt was well aware of the political objections of many state governors and businessmen against any attempt to impose from above a national program of social insurance.

By 1934 the social consequences of the Depression were most pressing, but, as analyzed previously, so were pressures against excessive federal intervention by businesses and a significant number of states. To balance these two opposing forces, Roosevelt appointed the Committee on Economic Security to study, among other social security issues, the problem of unemployment. The history of America's response to unemployment runs from this point, the Committee's report, through to the final approval of the Social Security Act. The contentious drafting process and numerous inputs at different points along the way help to explain why in the end, facing as "national" a problem as Canada, it is the states, and not the federal government, that retain full political control of unemployment insurance.

The remainder of this section builds on materials produced by direct participants in the process: E. Witte's[13] *The Development of the Social Security Act* (1962), Arthur Altmeyer's[14] *The Formative Years of Social Security* (1968), and Paul H. Douglas'[15] *Social Security in the United States, An Analysis and Appraisal of the Federal Social Security Act* (1936).

In analyzing this material, I first focus on the discussions within Committee on Economic Security (CES). Specifically, I present the different alternatives as to the institutional design of unemployment insurance and discuss the reasons underlying the final choice. Second, I analyze the political influences on the redrafting of the Social Security Act titles devoted to unemployment insurance during its legislative process. This includes inputs from both the House of Representatives and the Senate as well as the Conference Committee to reconcile disagreements between cameras. Finally, I present a succinct summary of the final outcome.

Douglas (1936: 28–69) and Witte (1962: 111–143) concur that there were basically three alternative institutional designs on the table of the Committee on Economic Security. These were: 1) a national system in which the federal government would collect contributions from workers and employers and make transfers directly to the unemployed; 2) what Witte calls a "subsidy plan," a system in which "in essence, [...] the amount of revenues collected through the federal tax from employers in each state [would] be returned to that state to be used for unemployment compensation purposes, subject to the state's compliance with standards to be prescribed by the federal government" (Witte 1962: 115); and finally, 3) a tax offset system along the lines of the Wagner-Lewis Bill (1934), which proposed a payroll tax upon employers equal to 5% of what they pay in wages. If a state passed a law and met the federal standards, "then the contributions paid by employers under such an act would be credited as an offset against the federal tax" (Douglas 1936: 23). Otherwise, states are free to choose any system or institutional design for their provision of unemployment insurance. While the project did not pass through Congress in 1934, the provisions of the Social Security Act follow in the footsteps of the Wagner-Lewis Bill.

---

[13] Executive Director of the Committee on Economic Security (1934–1935). This book is based on a diary kept by the author during the entire process.

[14] Second Assistance Secretary of the Department of Labor and Head of the Technical Board of the Committee on Economic Security.

[15] Professor of Economics at the University of Chicago. He served throughout the years as external assessor as well as discussion leader in the National Conference on Economic Security, a convention held in Washington (1934) where initial discussions on the different types of institutional designs to be implemented were held. Thereafter, he served as close collaborator of Bryce Stewart, Head of the Committee's Area of Study on Unemployment Insurance and former Director of the Employment Service (1919) in Canada.

Despite this outcome, the proposal to adopt a national system of unemployment did not lack either support (the trade unions among others) or an articulate defense (Douglas 1934: 215–216). On the grounds of administrative efficiency, distributive equity, and cost effectiveness, Bryce Stewart and his supporters advocated treating a "national problem" with a "national solution," following a route similar to the one the Canadian provinces would take in 1940 (Stewart 1930). Indeed, a recommendation for a national system was officially made on October 1, 1934 as part of the first report presented by the Unit of Study on Unemployment to the CES board:

if constitutional, a nationally administered system of unemployment insurance is to be preferred to a state system, but the Committee should be satisfied that the nationally administered system is constitutional before commitments in favor of such a system are made to the public.

The paragraph also reflects how supporters of the tax offset system along the lines of the Wagener-Lewis Bill centered their strategy around the issue of the unemployment insurance system's constitutionality. By that I refer to the need to respect state rights while developing policy on matters, like social security, in which the constitution does not guarantee the federal government an exclusive political capacity. Indeed, the Wagner-Lewis Bill was itself inspired by the Federal Inheritance Tax Act. That legislation was the response of President Coolidge's administration to the attempt by Florida to expand its tax base through the elimination of inheritance taxes. The federal government introduced an inheritance tax with the provision that "80 % of the sums thus collected would be returned to those states which had state inheritance tax laws. If a state did not have such a law, however, the federal government retained all the amounts paid in from the states residents" (Douglas 1936: 22). Florida presented a case for state autonomy before the Supreme Court and lost it. Aware of this precedent, supporters of the tax offset system were closer to Roosevelt's views. In the same Declaration of Policy (June 8, 1934) where he announced the appointment of the CES, he indicated that "he favored a plan providing for a maximum of cooperation between the states and the federal government, leaving to the states a portion of the cost of management and to the federal government the responsibility of investing, maintaining and safeguarding the funds constituting the necessary insurance reserves."

While Roosevelt's administration was concerned with social insurance potentially being turned down by the Supreme Court (Douglas 1936: 33), this fear did not stop him in the case of old-age insurance. Thus, I would argue, what really resonates behind his words are the strictly political concerns about potential opposition from the Southern states to anything disrupting their specific system of labor relations. Roosevelt effectively encouraged the CES to factor in any issue that could jeopardize the passing of the Social Security Act (Berkowitz 1991; Noble 1997). Francis Perkins, labor secretary, and Witte took this encouragement as a mandate, and made every effort to prevent the final CES report from recommending a national unemployment insurance system.

In addition, early supporters of unemployment insurance at the state level worried about a national program. They saw it is a political risk in that it would eliminate provisions tailored specifically toward state labor markets and impose dysfunctional policy designs. Witte himself, a member of the Commons' School instrumental in the development of the Wisconsin model of unemployment insurance (Nelson 1969, 119–169), held this position, as did Wagner from New York (Altmeyer 1968: 18–24; Orloff 1988: 69–75). Combined with Roosevelt's recommendations, these reservations shaped deliberations within the CES. On 9 November 1934 a motion according to which "all the thought of an exclusively federal system be abandoned" (Witte 1962: 118) received approval. By November 14 Roosevelt announced that unemployment insurance would be a "federal-state undertaking." In other words, there would be no national unemployment insurance system in the United States. Roosevelt's administration had factored into its planning the heterogeneity of preferences across states and the likelihood of meeting legal objections on the constitutionality of such an initiative. Theretofore, the question had been narrowed down to a choice between a "subsidy plan" and a tax offset system. After several rounds of consultation between the CES and the Advisory Committee of the Department of Labor (initially in favor of the subsidy plan by nine to seven votes), it was decided to draft the unemployment insurance provisions along the lines of the Wagner-Lewis Bill, not only because it guaranteed each state the possibility of pursuing its own strategy, but also for reasons of constitutional pragmatism. According to Douglas (1936: 48), "the one major argument that came to be urged for the offset plan as opposed to the tax remission system was that, if the latter were later to be declared unconstitutional, the whole system of unemployment insurance would necessarily collapse, whereas, even if the tax offset method were finally rejected by the Supreme Court, the states would in the meantime have passed acts that would continue."

On August 18, 1935 Roosevelt signed the Social Security Act, with the following provisions on unemployment insurance:

1. Unemployment insurance is a joint effort between the federal government and the states, and takes the form of a tax offset system in which the participation of the states is voluntary.
2. The federal government levies a payroll tax on employment that would be equal to 1% of total payroll in 1936, 2% in 1937 and finally equal to 3% from 1938 onward. This tax is deposited in a federal unemployment trust fund under the control of the Secretary of the Treasury. 90% of the revenues are devoted to transfers to the states that effectively develop their own unemployment insurance system. The remaining 10% is devoted to cover administrative costs.
3. States are free to choose the specific institutional form of their unemployment insurance system (plant reserves, industry reserves, etc.).

They are also free to adopt any scale of benefits they wish. Furthermore, they have full control on waiting periods and duration of benefits.
4. State's unemployment insurance systems must, nonetheless, conform to a number of standards established in the law, most of which come directly from the Wagner-Lewis Bill. These are:
   4.1 The payment of benefits must be made through the public employment offices of the state or in any other form "approved by the Social Security Board."
   4.2 No state system can disqualify a recipient if he refuses to take up a job vacant due to any kind of labor dispute.
   4.3 The same applies to the unemployed who refuse work, which pays "substantially less" than the ongoing wage rate and/or has "substantially worse working conditions" attached to it. The specific meaning of "substantially less" and "substantially worse" is left to be decided by the states within a range (or zone of tolerance) established by the Social Security Board.
   4.4 The same applies if the worker refuses to sign a "yellow-dog" contract. A yellow dog contract is one that requires the worker to join the company union and/or refrain from joining "bona fide labor organizations" (Douglas 1936: 137).
5. Finally, the Social Security Act excludes from the unemployment insurance system a number of specific occupational categories and businesses. These are: agriculture (including croppers and tenants), domestic service, shipping, public employees (federal, state and local), nonprofit organizations and the self-employed. In fact, every firm with seven or less workers is exempted from paying the federal payroll tax.

Interestingly enough, there is a significant distance between these and the provisions of the original bill as drafted by the Committee on Economic Security. A very illustrative political process took place in the interim, where conflicts about the details concentrated the bulk of political contention, thus shedding light on the ultimate causes behind the selection of a decentralized unemployment insurance system. These conflicts were to take place in the Ways and Means Committee of the House of Representatives as well as in the Finance Committee in the Senate. Table 5.4 presents the diachronic sequence of the legislative process by comparing its four main stages: the original draft, the changes introduced in the House, those introduced in the Senate, and, finally, the agreements reached in the Conference Committee.[16] The comparison is structured around four aspects of the law: the revenues to pay the unemployment funds, the institutional design of the state systems, the program's

---

[16] The Conference Committee is a joint Committee where conferees from both cameras meet in order to reach a consensus on those specific points of the legislation where the decisions of the House and Senate have previously differed.

coverage, and the provisions for the administration of the system. Two aspects are particularly noteworthy: the LaFollette amendment in the Senate and the evolution of provisions on coverage.

The original version of the bill granted states freedom to design their unemployment insurance provision. However, reforms introduced in the House limited the number of designs the unemployment insurance program could take on grounds of accounting efficiency. This meant, among other things, that states were no longer permitted to adopt or maintain systems of industry or plant reserves. Should this provision have passed, the Wisconsin system would have had to be reformed. As one of the pioneers of unemployment insurance in the United States, Wisconsin fought to protect the system they thought best served their economy. Senator Robert La Follette Jr., junior senator from Wisconsin and member of the Progressive Party, successfully introduced an amendment to restore the original provision. Paradoxically, to protect the early developments in unemployment insurance, he facilitated the task of those who wanted to ensure as late and weak a policy as possible. Southern states were also successful in limiting federal control over implementation logistics. They succeeded in abolishing the requirement of meeting the Federal Standards of Personnel and organizing payments only via public employment offices (see the Administration section in Table 5.4).

The introduction of specific provisions excluding agricultural workers from the unemployment insurance system highlights even more clearly the weight of the South as the political engine beneath the process. Alston and Ferrie (1999: 49–75) argue that Roosevelt and the CES were aware of this and managed to anticipate potential objections when they decided 1) to exclude firms with less than four workers and 2) reclassify croppers and tenants as agricultural workers. They thought both measures would be enough to keep the system of labor relations in the South unaffected by the new unemployment insurance system. Southern democrats wanted more guarantees (Brinkley 1984; Whatley 1983: 905–930) wanted more guarantees though, hence the specific changes introduced both in the House and the Senate, on the threshold of exclusion and, more directly, on the occupational categories left out of the program. After these changes, the Social Security Act constituted no threat.[17]

The key for Southern Paternalism to work was the mutual dependency between planters and tenants/croppers. So when, in the context of the Depression, several federal relief and insurance programs (including unemployment

---

[17] An even more straightforward example is offered by the changes in old-age insurance legislation. Southern Democrats managed to erase from the Social Security Act any paragraph that potentially could lead to the inclusion of "negroes" in the program. So, for instance, they erased from the Act a special old age insurance program recommended by the CES. They also eliminated a general requirement in the law according to which "assistance could not be denied to any US citizen." However, during the post WWII period, old age social security was much faster than unemployment insurance in abandoning these restrictions. For instance, the inclusion of agricultural and domestic workers did not occur until 1976. For a systematic analysis of the racial effects of unemployment insurance, see King (1995, 2007); and Lieberman (1998).

TABLE 5.4. *The Legislative Process of the American Social Security Act*

USA: Legislative Evolution of the Provisions for Unemployment Insurance in the Social Security Act (1935), Titles III and IX.

	Original Bill	House of Representatives (Ways and Means Committee)	Senate (Finance Committee)	Conference Committee
Revenues (Federal Payroll Taxes)	The rate of the federal payroll tax is related to previous years level of production[1]. The normal level is thought to be 3%.	The rate is to be established following an annual scal, 1935: 1%; 1936: 2%; 1937: 3%. It ceases to be related to previous years' levels of production.	Remains.	Remains.
Institutional Design	Freedom to adopt any type of unemployment insurance system.[2]	The options a limited on grounds of accounting efficiency. States are no longer permitted to adopt systems of industry or plant reserves[3]. Plant reserves were also said to be too inegalitarian.	La Follette amendment passes. Previous freedom is restored.	The Senate position prevails, states are fully free to choose their system of unemployment insurance.
Coverage	Wide Coverage, no specific exclusions beyond public agencies. Only those firms with less than 4 workers are exempted from the federal payroll tax.	Specific occupations (mainly agricultural workers, including croppers and tenants) are excluded.	Remains. The threshold of exemption is set back to 4 workers.	Compromise: The threshold for a firm to be exempted from the federal payroll tax is 8 workers.
Administration	Federal Standards of Personnel are required to all States systems. Benefits are to be paid only by the Public Employment offices of the States.	Abolishment of Federal Standards of Personnel. Remains.	Remains. The requirement of paying only via Public Employment offices is eliminated.	Compromise: Benefits will be paid in any form "approved by the Social Security Board". A minimum control is established.

[1] If the index of production of the Federal Reserve Board was by September 1935 less than 84% if its 1923–1925 average, the payroll rate would be 1%. If the Index was between 84 and 95% the rate would be 2%. If the Index was above 95% of the 1923–1925 average, the rate would be 3%.

[2] In the case of the states willing to go for an industry or plant systems, it was provided that they should contribute 1% of their payroll to a pooled state fund in order to generate a reserve for other industries.

[3] Note that under these conditions the existing Wisconsin system would be doomed to change or disappear.

Sources: Data collected from Douglas (1936); Witte (1962); and Altmeyer (1968).

insurance) were under consideration, planters faced the following dilemma: "How could it accept the government assistance that so many plantation owners desperately needed to sustain their labor force until prosperity's return without allowing the government to replace them as the benefactors of their workers?" (Alston and Ferrie 1999: 49). Direct federal provision of relief, FERA, (Williams 1939) and insurance in favor of croppers and tenants would have undermined their dependence upon planters and, eventually, led to the ultimate crisis of paternalism. Hence, the trade-off between federal welfare and the protection of a specific labor market. And, hence, the final choice of the Southern elites was to press for the preservation of "state rights" in the management of welfare provision as well as, more specifically, for the successful exclusion of their workers from any type of insurance program, including old age and unemployment. Given the institutional position of Southern representatives in the House and the Senate, "agricultural labor and domestic services were excluded [from unemployment insurance] as a matter of course" (Witte 1962: 132).

Other states joined the South in defense of regional specific interests, even if of a different kind. Such is the case, again, of the pioneers of unemployment insurance in Wisconsin for instance, as proved by La Follette's intervention during the legislative process in defense of states' freedom to tailor unemployment insurance programs to the specific needs of regional economies. Overall, differential risk profiles across states played a crucial role in shaping the American response to the Depression.

THEORETICAL IMPLICATIONS

In conclusion, and to put it in terms of the analytical model, the American response includes an increase, through tax offsets, in transfers to regional governments (T in my analytical model) so that each state can design at will its own system of unemployment insurance (that is to say, the decentralized t). This creates a hybrid system (H) where regions receive resources from the central government and then locally control the provision of public insurance. In turn, Canadian political elites opted for a fully centralized system (C).

The comparative historical analysis of the emergence of unemployment insurance in Canada and the United States offers a good deal of empirical support to the argument developed in this book. Canada adopted a centralized system in 1941 because the scope of the interprovincial externalities was strong enough to overcome provincial concerns. The income base of wealthier provinces, such as Ontario and British Columbia, was effectively undermined already by the inflow of dependents, whereas the ability to resist of those relatively poorer members with alternative designs tailored to their provincial needs, such as Alberta, was undermined by their overwhelming income needs. The Canadian experience illustrates how, as suggested by the model, large scale interregional externalities can overcome the fragmenting effects of an uneven economic geography, even under conditions of centrifugal representation.

The balance between regional specificities and interstate externalities was reversed in the United States. Regional economic specificities were much stronger, particularly in the race-based political economy of the South. Whereas mobility data suggest that interstate economic externalities, while present in the United States, were not as pressing as in Canada. Under these circumstances, the fragmenting effects of the geography of labor market risk constrained the development of a centralized system of unemployment insurance. And thus, consistent with the model, the United States launched a system that combined moderate levels of interregional redistribution via a tax offset system with the protection of a decentralized provision of unemployment insurance. In sum, given a system of representation that privileges regions, the balance between interregional economic externalities, the geography of inequality, and labor market risks drives the design and organization of fiscal structures.

The centrality of interterritorial mobility to understanding the structure of incentives underlying different institutional designs is reinforced by the evolution over time of American social policy. When, as a consequence of WWII, the Western American states demanded more labor supply, the Southern states managed to pass the Bracero program (1942–1964), a policy that arranged the immigration of temporary Mexican laborers for that purpose. They thereby succeeded once again in preventing an external influence to undermine the dependence of their croppers and tenants (Alston and Ferrie 1999: 99–119).

Over the years, Southern paternalism would disappear because of technical change and mechanization. Only then did African Americans become more mobile, entering the national political economy and gaining civil and political rights. Indeed, the rate of African Americans born in their state of residence started to decline again between 1940 and 1950, dropping from 76% to 68%. Focusing specifically on the South, Quadagno (1994) reports that while in 1940 77% of African Americans lived in the South, by 1970 only 53% still did. As a result, "the presence of black migrants in northern cities moved racial inequality from the periphery to the center of national politics" (p. 25). Again mobility increased risk sharing, eventually contributing to a major step forward in the development of the American welfare state, Lyndon Johnson's War on Poverty and the Equal Opportunity Act (1964). Only then, "the barriers to equality of opportunity the New Deal had created" were challenged (p. 31).

Finally, the findings of this chapter relate to earlier scholarship and the controversies motivating this book in a number of ways. Contrary to the dominant notion that federalism and decentralization are necessarily inegalitarian, this chapter has shown how similarly decentralized political systems can vary in the organization of their fiscal structures, as well as in the scope of their efforts to prevent the spread of inequality (Lindert 2004; Obinger, Leibfried and Castles 2005). In addition, it supports a theory as to why these variations occur. The argument brings insights from the literatures on economic geography (Krugman 1991; Venables 2001, 2007) and factor mobility (Cai and Treisman 2005; Wildasin 1991, 1995) to the literature on endogenous fiscal institutions (Alesina and Spolaore 2003; Beramendi 2007; Bolton and Roland 1997; Persson and Tabellini 1996a, 1996b; Wibbels 2005a). In doing so, this chapter identifies risk sharing between regions as a key factor, separate from income, shaping the political economy of fiscal institutions. More specifically, it highlights the mobility of dependents as a particularly relevant factor behind cross-regional externalities, accounting for the design of public insurance programs. Herein lies an important key to understanding why some federations have more centralized welfare states than others, and ultimately why some political unions redistribute more than others. In making this case, this study moves beyond the voluminous literature on mobility as a constraint to redistribution (Peterson 1995) in federations and places mobility and its interplay with the geography of labor market risk at the center of an endogenous theory of institutional design.

6

Germany's Reunification

Distributive Tensions and Fiscal Structures under Centripetal Representation

An important argument in this book is that the organization of political representation in complex unions conditions the relationship between the distribution of preferences in a particular federation and the actual design of fiscal structures. In the previous chapter, I analyzed how U.S. Southern senators were able to maximize their local interests during the elaboration of the Social Security Act. They managed to do so because of their pivotal position in the Senate, in turn guaranteed by a direct and persistent link between elected officials and represented constituencies.

This chapter examines a contrasting case, in which a radical transformation of the geography of inequality has not resulted in institutional reforms conducive to the protection of particularistic interests: the evolution of Germany's fiscal structure after Reunification. This process meant the incorporation into the union of five new länder and over twenty-million citizens significantly poorer than the western länder. Yet the German fiscal structure displays a remarkable continuity of preexisting arrangements, large levels of transfers from the West to the East, and an absence of any real move toward larger levels of fiscal decentralization despite a large increase in levels of interregional income disparities. Hence the puzzle: if economic geography drives the selection of fiscal institutions, what accounts for the absence of a major reconfiguration of preexisting arrangements? What has muted the transmission of larger levels of regional income disparities into larger levels of fiscal decentralization?

The answer to these questions combines two distinctive elements: first, the specifics of the institutional design of the German federation, and its effects on both the incentives and ability of regional incumbents to pursue "local" special interests; second, the nature of Reunification as a shock, and its implications on levels of risk sharing among länder.

In developing this answer, the chapter is structured as follows. To begin, I present an overview of Germany's fiscal structure and institutional design before 1989. I then analyze the exacerbation of distributive tensions associated with the incorporating into the union five Eastern and significantly poorer members (Brandenburg, Mecklenburg-Vorpommern, Saxony, Saxony-Anhalt, and Thuringia), amounting to about twenty-two million citizens. Third, I describe the multiple efforts to incorporate the East into systems of both interpersonal and interregional redistribution during the period 1990–1994. Fourth, in so doing I analyze the relationship of preferences, political constraints, and political incentives during the incorporation process. And finally, in section five, I analyze how these preferences evolve over time after 1995, fostering new distributive conflicts over the design of both interpersonal and interregional redistribution. Again, the way these conflicts resolve illustrates well the interplay between economic geography and political representation in conflicts over the design of fiscal structures. I close the chapter by drawing out the core theoretical implications of the analysis.

GERMANY'S FISCAL STRUCTURE BEFORE REUNIFICATION: THE EXISTING INSTITUTIONAL DESIGN

Scholars of federalism often cite Germany as the case that best illustrates the compatibility of a federalist structure of government and a generous and comprehensive welfare state (Obinger, Leibfried and Castles 2005). Indeed, by comparative standards, the German welfare state compares well to those of many centralized countries. By 1985, for instance, the German fiscal system managed to reduce the level of household income inequality from a Gini coefficient of 0.40 (pretaxes and transfers) to a Gini coefficient of 0.26 (disposable income). By 1990, reflecting data of the period immediately preceding the Reunification, the same numbers were 0.41 and 0.25 respectively. The level of fiscal effort these figures imply is much closer to Scandinavia than it is to other advanced industrial federations such as Canada or Australia, let alone the United States (Beramendi and Cusack 2009).

This apparent compatibility between federalism and the pursuit of solidarism has deep historical roots. In an excellent historical overview of the relationship between federalism and social policy in Germany, Manow (2005) shows how some of the central aspects of Germany's fiscal structure reflect compromises between the central government and the länder in a number of historical junctures. Four aspects of Manow's account are relevant here. First, social policy serves, from the very early existence of the union under Bismarck, as a tool to expand the power of the central government relative to the states. The compromise between the two produced a system of overlapping jurisdictions across policy domains, state boundaries, and different stages of the policy process. Second, this political expansion in new policy domains requires revenues for which the central government's share is clearly insufficient. Bismarck tried to fund social policy through taxation, but failed due to the opposition of the states. As a result, social insurance contributions become the primary source of revenue for social policy (Mares 2003).

Third, the socialization of risks in the interwar period propelled the coverage expansion and the centralization of social policy during the Weimar years.

Common risks required common solutions. The Weimar constitution facilitated this process by limiting the veto capacity of the länder in the Reichsrat (the council of länder respresentatives). Whereas in the Imperial Constitution (1871) the Reichsrat had an absolute legislative veto, the Weimar Constitution limited it to a suspending veto that could be overruled by a qualified majority of the lower chamber (Reichstag). Consistent with the predictions of this book's argument, this shift toward a more centripetal system of representation translated quickly into changes in the fiscal structure. The tax reform of 1920 made taxation an exclusive responsibility of the central government, thus increasing its revenue autonomy. The states "could regulate their tax affairs autonomously only insofar and only as long as the central government abstained from enacting nationwide standards (Article 8 of the Weimar Constitution)" (Manow 2005: 236). Similarly, the central government assumed full control of the design and implementation of unemployment insurance in 1927 and even pursued the centralization of social assistance policies. This expansion and centralization of social policy was purposefully designed to prevent "a federalist fragmentation of living conditions" (Manow 2005: 238).

Fourth, the focus of political conflict was less on the scope of interpersonal redistribution and more on the allocation of its cost across the different levels of government. The central government used its new constitutional position to shift costs downward, thus triggering a political conflict over the distribution of resources among the different levels of government that added to Weimar's political instability and ultimate failure (Hefeker 2001).

This quick overview provides the background shaping the design of Germany's fiscal structure before 1990. Many of the Weimar's lessons carried over to the design of the Federal Republic's fiscal constitution. Concerns about the link between regional inequalities and political stability led the designers of the German Constitution to establish a requirement for uniformity of living conditions within the federation as the driving principle of the overall institutional design (Scharpf 1999). In its original format the requirement reads as follows (GG 1949: #72.2. #106.3):

[...] 72.2.. – In the field of concurrent legislative power the federation has legislation if and insofar as the establishment of equal living conditions or the preservation of legal and economic unity necessitates, in the interest of the state at large, a federal regulation.

[...] 106.3.2. – The coverage requirements of the Federation and of the States (Länder) are coordinated in such a way that a fair balance is struck, any overburdening of tax payers precluded and uniformity of living conditions in the federal territory ensured.

To meet these requirements, Germany's post-WWII fiscal structure combined three distinctive features. The first one, directly inherited from Weimar and reinstated by Adenauer in the years immediately following the approval of the new constitution (1949), was the development of a series of centralized, occupation and insurance based, uniform policies in the realm of interpersonal redistribution (t). Pensions and unemployment benefits are earning based, closely tied to previous contributions, as these two programs are primarily funded through earmarked contributions by employers and employees. Old Age Insurance is administered by the Ministry of Labor and Social Policy and a dedicated agency, the Federal German Pension Insurance. Likewise, Unemployment Insurance is run by the Ministry of Labor and the Federal Employment Agency, with local agencies helping out with job placement and benefit administration. The important point to remember, though, is that for any given industry, the contribution rates and benefit entitlements for unemployment and old age insurance are nationally uniform. In turn, other income support programs (such as family related benefits, sickness insurance, survivor benefits, or housing benefits) are funded through taxes and administered jointly by the central and state governments. The second feature concerns low income support policies (non contributory social assistance). These policies are funded and managed by local authorities, on the basis of resources transferred from the federal and state governments.[1]

This equal treatment of individuals across unequal territories, and the fact that a significant share of the social policy effort is either fully funded and administered or implemented by subnational governments, raises once again the problem of resource allocation across different territories. Herein lies the third feature of Germany's fiscal constitution: the main locus of contention is not so much the nature of social policy, but the distribution of resources across territories and levels of government (T). In what follows I characterize how Germany's fiscal constitution dealt with this issue prior to the Reunification in 1990.

The system of allocation of resources among territories is divided into two branches: the Trennsystem and the Verbundsystem. The former represents 30% of the total tax revenues in Germany and it includes all taxes whose revenues are exclusively run by one territorial level. The left half of Table 6.1 describes the Trennsystem by way of listing the tax items exclusively in the hands of each level of government. The right half of Table 6.1 illustrates the distribution of the different taxes within the Verbundsystem across different levels of government. Note though that the fact that the Verbundsystem is uniform across regions does not imply that the länder lack political input in its design. They have input via its legislative capacity in the Bundesrat (Leonardy 1996: 73–85; Spahn 1993: 89–97, Spahn and Franz 2002).

The guidelines of the Verbundsystem were established in the reform of the financial constitution, *Finanzverfassungsreform* of 1969. The Verbundsystem itself is organized around two dimensions: *Primärer Finanzausgleich*, vertical distribution of revenues among the Bund, länder, and municipalities; and *Sekundärer Finanzausgleich*, or horizontal adjustments between richer and poorer länder (also called Länderfinanzausgleich). The term Finanzausgleich (from now onward FA), as normally used, refers to this second dimension

---

[1] For a more detailed characterization of Germany's social security and income support programs, see Flockton (1999); and Mathias (2003).

TABLE 6.1. *The Allocation of Tax Sources by Level of Government*

Trennsystem (30% of total fiscal revenues)			Verbundsystem (70% of total fiscal revenues)			
Bund	Municipalities	Länder	Joint Tax	Bund-share	Land-share	Local-share
Insurance tax	Business tax	Personal wealth tax	*Personal Income Tax*	42.5%	42.5%	15%
Bills of exchange tax	Real property tax A	Motor vehicle tax				
Domestic tax	Real property tax B	Beer tax	*Corporate Income Tax*	50%	50%	0
Investment tax	Licensing tax	Real property tax				
Stock exchange tax	Entertainment tax	Property transfer tax	*Value Added Tax*	65%	35%	0
Transaction tax	Hunting and fishing tax	Betting and Lotery tax				
Custom duties	Dog tax	Fire protection tax				
Mineral oil tax	Municipal beverage tax					
Coffee tax						
Tea tax						
Sugar tax						
Salt tax						
Spirits tax						
Sparkling wine tax						
Light fixture tax						
Tobacco tax						

139

TABLE 6.2. *Interregional Redistribution before Reunification, 1979–1989*

Land	1979–1982	1983–1989
Baden-Württemberg	−1516.25	−1621.86
Bavaria	277.33	44.67
Bremen	203.00	439.33
Hamburg	−500.25	−172.40
Hesse	−362.50	−1120.20
Lower Saxony	972.50	1174.00
North Rhine-Westfalia	0.00	25.83
Rhineland-Palatinate	275.67	354.25
Saarland	259.25	332.00
Schleswig-Hosltein	393.75	550.80

Author's calculation on data from Finanzbericht 1991: 112–113.
Figures in millions DM.

of the Verbundsystem, and constitutes the key mechanisms for interregional redistribution (T) within Germany's fiscal structure. Table 6.2 provides a picture of how each of the western länder stood in the system of interregional redistribution (FA) in the years before the Reunification.[2]

Predictably, the key practical issue is the identification of the financial strength of each of the länder. Two indicators serve this purpose: a measurement of fiscal capacity and a measurement of fiscal need, also called compensation measurement, which is weighted according to the number of inhabitants. The calculus of the former has been the object of an ongoing political conflict which included a challenge of the overall system before the Constitutional Court by North Rhine Westphalia. Before the 1987 reform, the index of fiscal capacity was calculated by adding a land's share of the VAT, the local corporations tax and the (federal) personal and corporate income taxes. As a result of conflicts regarding what ought to be included in and excluded from the calculation, especially during the period 1983–1987, a number of items were added to the list. These included land sales, fire protection, taxes on natural resources and extraction, and, last but not least, the effect of the local taxes in each land.[3]

Once these two indicators have been calculated, the pie is shared. The need to guarantee a balance between richer and poorer länder does not imply full financial equalization among them. The FA works as a two stage process

---

[2] Note, however, that these financial adjustments are not the only tool for fiscal equalization: additional vertical financial transfers (Ergängzungszuweisungen), special grants in aid for economic investment (Finanzhilfe) and structural funds created in 1988 in order to compensate for the exclusion from the FA system of a number of growing social burdens are also meant to have equalization effects.

[3] Länder transfer money to the local councils up to a certain level. The more these collect in revenue, the less the regional government needs to transfer to them and, therefore, the greater their fiscal capacity.

(Biehl and Ungar 1991: 39–65). First, those länder whose fiscal capacity is below the mean receive a compensatory transfer from the richer länder to raise their capacity to that level. For those länder whose fiscal capacity is between 92% of the mean fiscal capacity and the mean itself, a transfer is made for the value of 36.5 % (37.5% since the 1987 reform) of the difference between their level and the mean. Länder whose fiscal capacity lies between 100% and 102% of the mean neither receive transfers nor contribute to FA. Only those länder with a fiscal capacity above 102% have to provide funds for horizontal equalization: if their fiscal capacity is between 102% and 110% of the mean, they contribute 70% of the difference. The contribution to FA is 100% of the difference in relation to the mean only if the fiscal capacity of the land is greater than 110% of the mean fiscal capacity.

In a second step, the system aims at increasing the fiscal capacity of all länder with a low fiscal capacity up to 95% of the mean. Here, the indicator of fiscal capacity as derived from the first stage is compared with the indicator of expenditure needs. Those länder whose fiscal capacity is higher than their expenditure needs finance further contributions in favor of the weaker ones. However, this equalizing principle has a limit, the so-called Hansestadt Klausel[4]: after the second stage is implemented, no contributor land can end up with its fiscal capacity reduced below the mean (before the 1987 reform this limit was 95% of the mean itself). Should this be the case, it would receive an extra payment to raise its levels to the mean.

The history of Germany's fiscal structure before 1990 reveals a system that is stable in its basic parameters but rife with contestation over its implementation and performance, contestation often triggered by a changing economic geography due to structural transformations. The latter changed the relative positions of the länder, thus opening the door to a series of conflicts about the need and direction of potential reform. During the 1970s and 80s, deindustrialization hit those länder whose economic structures were more heavily based on manufacturing industries, namely Bremen, Saarland, North Rhine Westphalia and Lower Saxony, harder. The major consequence was the emergence of a North-South divide among the länder that made the former demand more resources with which to face the burdens derived from the new structural conditions. This income effect (differential in the value of w^r in the model) led them to request more redistribution of capacities from their partners in the federation. This is even more the case because, consistent with the model, the structural economic transformations, by way of highlighting the differences in economic and labor market structures, led the federation to transfer a larger share of the responsibility of several welfare state programs to the länder.[5] In Benz's words, "efforts to modernize the welfare state and to adapt its structures, procedures

---

[4] It refers to the city-states Hamburg and Bremen.
[5] As Degg has put it, "the task of managing the industrial adjustment in Germany is falling increasingly to subnational political and economic actors" (Degg 1996: 28). See also Anderson (1992).

and policies to the challenges of socioeconomic change have led to new tensions between governments.[6] The federal government tends to react more selectively to political demands and to favor activities that promise to foster the national economy; the länder and local governments have become the representatives of the losers in the process of structural change" (Benz 1989: 205). Under these conditions, the design of interterritorial redistribution could not remain unchallenged. As a result of the structural economic transformations, the länder split into two groups, with clearly divergent institutional agendas, "those who have sufficiently strong economic resources to pursue autonomous policy answers and those who do not" (Degg 1996: 31–33). The former demand more fiscal autonomy; the latter, an increase in the levels of solidarity.

A careful consideration of three specific episodes which occurred between 1983 and 1989 helps illustrate the nature of these conflicts. The first one regards the inclusion/exclusion of oil extraction duties (Förderaufgabe) in the FA formula. By 1983, Lower Saxony was the major recipient of FA (1.5 DM billions, 32% of total volume) at the same time that "it was raising an income of 2 DM billions per financial year from a licensing fee for the granting of oil extraction rights" (Exler 1991: 83–105). At the time, the fee was not technically considered a tax. Meanwhile Baden-Württemberg was the main contributor to the system (2 DM billion, 55% of the total volume) and North Rhine Westphalia, fully affected by deindustrialization and its socio-economic effects and for decades a net contributor, did not receive any net transfer from FA. A major conflict within German cooperative arrangements started when North Rhine Westphalia (and five other länder including Baden Württemberg)[7] denounced the system before the Constitutional Court, demanding, among other things, the inclusion of oil duties in the FA system. The FA was amended in 1987 along these lines, following a June 1986 ruling of the Constitutional Court.

A second major issue concerned the city-states problem. The problem here stemmed from the negative impact that high levels of urban concentration have on the ratio, as defined by the FA legislation, between fiscal capacities and expenditure needs. On the understanding that large cities have greater expenditure needs per capita, Bremen and Hamburg receive a population weight in their expenditure needs of 135% as opposed to the 100% applied elsewhere (Exler 1991: 85). While both cities considered this weighting insufficient, the rest of the länder saw it as excessive, including a case against it in their denouncement

---

[6] The consequences of European integration for the distribution of powers within the federation overlapped with this process, contributing to a rising tension between the Bund and the länder. Indeed, it was remarkable how the länder could combine fierce arguments among them regarding FA with a united position in favor of their presence at the EU level in all the arenas where their interests were at stake (Borkenhagen 1990: 36–44; Jeffery 1995: 253–266; Jeffery and Yates 1993: 58–82; Sturm and Jeffery 1993: 164–177).

[7] As Bulmer (1991: 118) puts it, "the court case was brought by a mixture of contributing and recipient Länder sharing the conviction that the system was unfair."

to the Constitutional Court. The 1987 amendment was, in this case, favorable to the two northern city-states (Biehl and Ungar 1991: 39–65). The point to note here is that the differential, in terms of the population structure, between länder was underpinning this conflict about the design of interterritorial redistribution in Germany during the 1980s.

The Albrecht Initiative (derived from the Conference of Northern Länder, Norddeutschland Konferenz) provides the final example. The then prime minister of Lower Saxony, with the support of the other northern länder, asked the federal government to share social welfare costs with the länder across the federation. Obviously, länder with larger dependent populations were also net recipients of FA. The conflict here did not emerge from the need to cope with the extra costs derived from deindustrialization, but from the funding mechanism proposed, in that "it would have led to a significant redistribution of resources from South to North with the federation acting as intermediary" (Exler 1991: 86–88). In reaction to this proposal, the Conference of Southern Länder (Süddeutschland Konferenz) presented an ultimately successful alternative, the Strukturhilfegesetz. This law limited the role to be taken by the Federation to 2.5 billion annually, as opposed to the 10 billion proposed by the Conference of Northern Länder. Underpinning this process is the classic conflict between rich regions supporting decentralization and poorer ones in favor of centralization. This becomes evident when taking a closer look at the proposal by the Conference of Northern Länder regarding the funding of the Structural Aid. The resources necessary would have been raised in two steps: first, by increasing taxes on oil consumption and, more importantly, by shifting the distribution of the turnover tax revenue so that the Federation would have increased its share from 65% to 70%. If implemented, such a proposal would have implied a clear step in the direction of fiscal centralization (Renzsch 1989: 333–345; 1991: 269–279).

Overall, the 1980s have shown how the different regions' preferences have responded to changes in their dependent populations and in their relative position within the overall economic structure, thus triggering tensions within the system. The fundamental features of the system, however, remained stable. This is largely so thanks to a set of federal institutions designed to foster cooperation and consensus across levels of government. Within this institutional framework, the länder have the capacity to influence, via the Bundesrat, the shape and scope of interterritorial redistribution transfers (FA). But in exercising such an influence, regional incumbents in Germany must compromise across territorial and party lines, which in turn limits severely their ability to devote themselves exclusively to the protection of local interests. In line with the models' predictions, Germany's centripetal system of representation muted the potentially destabilizing effects of the changes in economic geography associated with the process of deindustrialization in the late 1970s and 1980s. At the turn of the decade, though, Germany's fiscal structure was to confront a more sudden and radical transformation to its economic

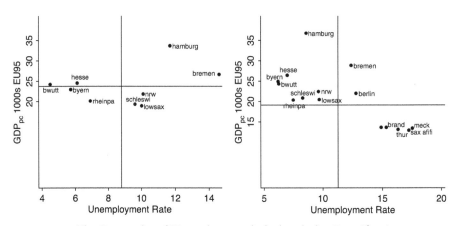

FIGURE 6.1. The Geography of Unemployment before and after Reunification

geography and, as a result, a much more probing test of the design of its fiscal structure.

THE IMPACT OF REUNIFICATION ON GERMANY'S ECONOMIC GEOGRAPHY

Triggered by processes exogenous to the existing fiscal structure of the Federal Republic (see Chapter 3), the political reunification of the East and the West involved a major alteration of Germany's economic geography and political landscape. It implied both a sudden increase in regional disparities and a huge financial burden on western länder and the Federation. In economic terms, one simple data point goes a long way in capturing the scope of the economic gap between the old and new members of the federation: "in 1991 the GNP per capital in the new Eastern Länder was 30% of that of the Western länder" (Renzsch 1998: 127). Accordingly, the GDP per capita of the newly unified Germany in 1991 was approximately 85% of that of the old Germany (Renzsch 1995: 167–195). As a result of this incorporation, in political terms, a poorer government was in charge of meeting a steep increase in the demand for services and income transfers.

A process like Reunification produced a set of economic and political events that relate directly to the parameters of the analytical model in this book. Figures 6.1 and 6.2 tap a bit more closely into these effects. Figure 6.1 plots the level of state GDP per capita against the state's unemployment rate, again before and after October 1990. In turn, Figure 6.2 presents four panels capturing the geography of income and income redistribution in Germany at two specific moments: 1989, immediately before Reunification took place; and 1994, the first year for which I had access to household income data comparable to those of 1989 (LIS data). The panels relate the länders' GDP per capita (expressed in constant euros from 1995) to their levels of market and disposable income

Germany's Reunification

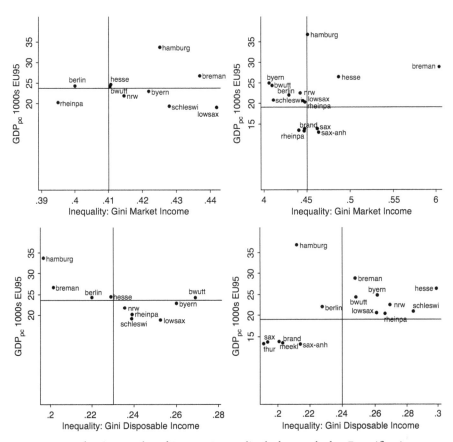

FIGURE 6.2. The Geography of Income Inequality before and after Reunification

inequality in both years.[8] A number of aspects of Figures 6.1 and 6.2 are worth noting.

Germany's level of gross state product (GSP) per capita was significantly lower in 1993–1994 than it was in 1989, as reflected by the decrease over time in the horizontal line depicting, in both figures, the länders' average GDP per capita. The incorporation of the eastern länder contributed to a reduction of the amount of resources per inhabitant available to the union. This development relates in turn to a second aspect of the process captured by Figure 6.1: an extreme gap in terms of the ability of different regional economies to generate employment. Even as late as 1993, four years after the programs of economic recovery for the East had begun, the East alone constituted a major factor skewing the geography of unemployment. The range of variation among the

---

[8] Figures represent Gini coefficients for household market and disposable income per equivalent adult. These calculations were performed by the author on the basis of LIS data (1989, 1994; full sample). The equivalent scale used is the standard square root of the number of members of the household.

western states was about 9%. The range for unified Germany was about 14%. More importantly, the spatial concentration of unemployment also changed: the lack of work was particularly intense in those states with the lowest levels of GDP per capita, that is to say, in those states with the smallest tax bases to finance income transfers in favor of large contingents of dependent population. This strong correlation between low income per capita and high unemployment did not exist in 1989. In turn, the combination of changes in both the spatial concentration of unemployment and aggregate levels of income across territories is bound to reshape the geography of the incidence of inequality across territories.

Overall, Reunification implied an increase in the distance between regions in terms of income, the size of their dependent populations (α), and the incidence of or risks associated with economic specialization (δ). The new members of the union have a dysfunctional economic structure, with very different guiding principles to allocate goods and services. The merging of a social market economy in the West and a state driven economy in the East produced a more heterogeneous economic geography.

In addition, the merging of two economic areas with such divergent performances opens the door for people to seek either better wages or better benefits. As a result, the risk of a massive inflow from East to West, either of dependents or working age citizens, was a primary concern for policy makers from the very early stages of the process (Streeck 2009; Wiesenthal 2003). According to this book's argument, these concerns demand an effort by the federation to bring the eastern länder to terms with the union, thus insuring the western against potential negative externalities.

To be sure, Reunification added intense pressure to the system of interregional redistribution. To convey the magnitude of this new pressure, Table 6.3 shows how the system of interregional redistribution (FA) would look had the newcomers been automatically included into the system without adjustment (Peffekoven 1990: 348).[9] If the logic of the Reunification had been applied to the FA system without any kind of adjustment, the total amount of transfers would have risen from 3,468 DM billion, with positive effects for five western länder, to 20,998 DM billion with negative effects for all the western länder except Hamburg and Bremen, and a positive balance for East Germany of 20,716 DM billion. Bavaria, for instance, instead of paying 12 DM billion a year would have paid 3,475 DM billion. These numbers convey the extent to which the economic geography of the new Germany altered the relative position of preexisting union members concerning interregional transfers.

Finally, Figure 6.2 also indicates that Reunification brought along an increase in the levels of market income inequality. Two distinctive groups emerge: one anchored around the former average level of market income inequality in the West (.41–.42), with a fairly spread out distribution in terms

---

[9] The data in Table 6.3 are necessarily a simulation because, as we shall see, the incorporation of the new länder did not take place until 1995.

TABLE 6.3. *Interregional Redistribution in Germany with and without Eastern Länder*

1990	NRW	BAY	BW	NDS	HE	RP	SH	SAA	HH	HB	DDR	TOTAL
FA without Integration of Eastern Länder	−18	−12	−1433	1619	−2005	319	579	329	4	618	0	3468
FA with Integration of Eastern Länder	−5803	−3475	−4733	−767	−3960	−820	−234	−83	−853	282	20716	20998
Financial Conseq.	−5785	−3733	−3300	−2386	−1955	−1139	−813	−412	−857	−336	20716	
Financial Conseq. in DM per inhabitant	−343	−338	−350	−332	−351	−312	−317	−390	−534	−507	+1256	

Source: Peffekoven.1990,348.
Figures in millions DM.

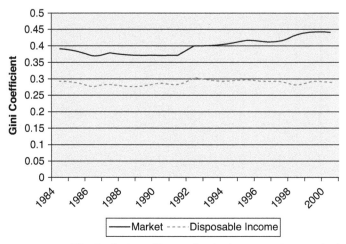

FIGURE 6.3. The Evolution of Inequality in Germany. *Source:* Author's calculations on the basis of LIS surveys (see fn.129 for details).

of wealth, and a second one anchored at a higher average level of inequality (.45) with much lower and homogeneous wealth. As a result, the average level of market income inequality across all länder went up by 3% (the average Gini increases from about 0.40 to about 0.44).[10] This is hardly surprising. The incorporation of a large share of dependent population, even if heavily concentrated in particular regions is bound to increase levels of pretax, pretransfer inequality. If anything, the differences should be larger.[11]

What is more surprising is how the German economic geography in 1994 changes when one compares the figures for market and disposable income inequality. The same group of Eastern länder that, in terms of market income, concentrated around levels of inequality of 0.44–0.46 anchors around Ginis of 0.22–0.26 when one considers the impact of taxes and transfers. In a nutshell, what these numbers suggest is that the system of interpersonal redistribution at work in Germany is generating an enormous transfer of resources from the relatively well off tax payers, mostly located in the West, to a large contingent of dependents, heavily concentrated in the East. The effort is of such a scale that it brings the levels of disposable income inequality among Eastern Länder to about one-half (!) its market income value. Accordingly, as reflected in Figure 6.3, despite the rise in economic disparities associated with Reunification, the

---

[10] These patterns are consistent with other analyses of the distributive implications of Reunification (Grabka, Schwarze and Wagner 1999; Schwarze 1996).

[11] That they are not is largely a function of the fact that the calculations in Figure 6.2 are performed on the basis of the entire population. This implies that a huge contingent of retirees in both the East and the West have a level of market income set to zero, thus muting the distributional gap between the two regions. The advantage of this procedure, though, is that it captures the full size of the dependent population and not just the share directly related to the labor market.

overall levels of posttax, posttransfer inequality in the new Germany changed relatively little between 1989 and 1994 (and thereafter).

What this level of redistribution represents is that the new dependents were fully incorporated into the existing system of interpersonal redistribution, thus increasing exponentially the financial burden on the shoulders of western citizen's and elites. To these efforts, as we shall see, additional transfers in the form of interregional redistribution followed. A redistributive effort of such nature in the context of a federal polity in which relatively wealthier territories ought to be able to voice their concerns and maneuver to protect their relative position is intriguing. According to the argument developed in Chapter 2, the modification of economic geography triggered by Reunification should exacerbate the distributive conflicts between the different territories and fuel contestation of existing fiscal arrangements. And yet, the latter did not happen. Why? The model hints at the fears associated with massive population flows and national party elites' political incentives as key to addressing these questions.

THE INITIAL YEARS (1990–1994): THE POLITICAL AND ECONOMIC INCORPORATION OF THE EAST

Reunification brought along important political consequences as well. The incorporation of five significantly poorer members impacted the political incentives of federal and state elites. While the system of representation did not formally change, politicians' incentives did as a large pool of new voters suddenly became available for the articulation of political coalitions. Paying particular attention to the issue of the political representation of the poor, Jusko (2006) offers estimates of the magnitude of some of these effects:

> prior to Reunification, low income citizens were fairly evenly distributed across the German länder. With Reunification, low income citizens are now overrepresented in the East. [...] In the post reunification allocation a low income voting block could secure as many as nine SMD seats, all but one in the former East German länder. (pp. 10–11)

In addition to these effects on the composition of the lower chamber (Bundestag), the incorporation of five new members to the union also had the potential to significantly alter the political alliances in the upper chamber (*Bundesrat*).

At the time of reunification, the formula to allocate seats by land was as follows (Gunlicks 2003; Lees 2005): länder with up to two million people, three seats; länder with between two and six million inhabitants, four seats; finally, länder with six million inhabitants or more, five seats in the upper chamber. According to these rules, the new eastern länder would receive nineteen out of a total of sixty-five seats in the upper chamber, about a third. Given that as many as 53% of all the law passed in the German federal system require the approval of the upper chamber, that delegates are representatives of regional governments and that they must vote *as a block*, the political incorporation of eastern länder into the Bundesrat brought them a great deal of political leverage at the federal level. In the context of the centripetal system of representation described in Chapter 4, the courting of Eastern voters and control of regional governments in the new states became a top political priority for both the CDU (Christian Democratic Union) and the SPD (Social Democratic Party).

The political and economic consequences of Reunification generated a web of economic and political incentives over two issues: what will be the pace and scope of the effort to integrate the new länder, and who is going to meet the cost of such efforts. In what follows I address how the different actors approached these two issues and the extent to which their preferences and political strategies bear any linkages with the theoretical mechanisms identified earlier.

In political terms, the early measures after Reunification reflected Kohl's concerns for political survival. The federal government saw the East as a critical source of political support, one that could not be neglected if a stable majority at the federal level was to be achieved. The SPD experience in 1990 proved these fears right. Because of voicing its opposition to transfers early on in the process, the SPD suffered a crashing defeat. As a result, both parties realized that they could only win national leadership by depoliticizing the East-West Divide. The political alienation of the East and the rise of "regional" specific interest parties was to be prevented at all costs. In addition, Kohl was driven by short term electoral concerns:

only a high pace unification would guarantee the governing Christian-Democratic liberal coalition government the opportunity to time the all German elections sufficiently early to take advantage of the initial popular enthusiasm and optimism before its cost and frictions could surface and lead to disenchantment. (Wiesenthal 2003: 39)

Concerned with its electoral fortune in the short term, the incumbent coalition decided to speed up the East's economic integration.

The political fears of the major national parties had their economic correlate in business and labor organizations. Both shared two concerns: the potential creation of a low-wage area that would put downward pressures on wages in the West (labor), unravel the system of industrial relations, and reduce the market share of western firms (business)[12]; and, especially, the risk "that East Germans would migrate to the West in massive numbers had their former country been turned into a low-wage enclave of the unified German economy" (Streeck 2009: 225). Finally, trade unions and business organizations were also concerned with the risk of political radicalization should the East be allowed to undergo a more draconian transition to capitalism.

This set of preferences reflect the workings of two important elements of the analytical model: employers and western wage earners (high income people in high income regions) are supportive of redistribution towards the East to limit the negative externalities associated with excessive internal migrations

---

[12] Most critically, neither unions nor business organizations in the west had any interest in seeing eastern counterparts emerge. For a more detailed account of the position of the main labor and business organizations during the process, see Ritter (2006); and Streeck (2009).

and the creation of an isolated, low-wage economic area. In turn, the centripetal nature of political institutions (both the Parliament and the Senate), renders the East a pivotal electoral region, further motivating the incorporation effort. These two factors limited the political disintegrating effect that the new economic geography could have caused on preexisting fiscal arrangements.

Market Integration and Redistribution: Early Steps on Interpersonal and Interregional Redistribution

Two measures characterize the so called "Big Bang" approach to German unity (OECD 1991; Schmidt 1992): the creation of a monetary union overnight (Wiesenthal 1995, 1996) and the subsequent push toward equalization of wages throughout the new Germany (Czada 1995, 1999, 2004; Sinn 2002). The effects associated with these two measures are well known to students of Germany's political economy. The monetary union increased dramatically the consumption capacity of Eastern Germans overnight, thus contributing a great deal to ease the transition to a market economy, but at the same time created regional labor markets in which the gap between labor costs (real wages) and labor productivity became insurmountable. With Eastern productivity levels at about 30% of those in the West, the East was de facto deindustrialized (Witte and Wagner 1995; Uhlig 2006) and, as a result, at risk of depopulation. The prospect that the thin layer of young, high-skill labor would flee the East in search of better opportunities in the West led to an agreement among employers, the restructuring agency (Treuhandanstalt), and western trade unions to progressively equate Eastern wage rates to Western level. Full harmonization was to be reached by 1996.

Of questionable success in retaining younger and better educated workers in Germany,[13] this measure added to the gap between labor costs and productivity in the East, thus worsening the unemployment problem, and more generally, the prospects of activating the labor markets of the new members of the union. In sum, the urge to equalize wages and consumption capacity between East and West fired back in the form of a reinforced process of deindustrialization.

This reality check shifted the focus in the political agenda from the launching of a market economy in the East to the extension of the social insurance and redistributive system as well. The incorporation of the East was not limited to currency. It applied as well to the labor relations system and the systems of interpersonal and interregional redistribution. As markets failed to launch, the demand for social protection increased, and so did the size of the effort toward the East.

In terms of interpersonal redistribution, the deindustrialization of the East triggered a massive social policy effort, primarily concentrated in four areas:

---

[13] According to Mathias (2003); and Sahner (1999), the average population loss among East German districts between 1991 and 1997 was 4.6%, with an overrepresentation of young and well-educated people.

TABLE 6.4. *Incorporating the East: A Multidimensional Effort (*)*

1991–1998	1991	1992	1993	1994	1995	1996	1997	1998
Transfers from the Federal Budget	75	88	114	114	135	138	131	139
German Unity Fund	31	24	36.5	36	–	–	–	–
EU	4	5	5	6	7	7	7	7
Unemployment Insurance	25	38	38	28	23	26	26	28
Pension Scheme	–	5	9	12	17	19	18	18
Transfers from Western Länder/Gemeinden	5	5	10	14	10	11	11	11
TOTAL	140	165	212.5	210	192	201	193	203

* Figures in DM billion.
Source: Antwort der Parlamentarishen Staatssekretärin (Hendriks, 03/28/2006) & Nebaümer (1996, p. 580).

early retirement policy/pensions, unemployment insurance, social assistance, and subsidized public employment programs. The unsuccessful attempt to pursue wage equalization and the new structure of political incentives demanded a fast pace in the process of extending Western social insurance and welfare systems toward the East. In fulfillment of provisions established in the Unification treaties, and with start-up financial resources channeled through the German Unity Fund, unemployment insurance was extended as early as July 1990, whereas social assistance and public insurance pensions were open to Eastern citizens as early as 1991 and 1992 respectively (Flockton 1999: 33–51). Table 6.4 provides a systematic overview of the incorporation effort.

Concerning direct interregional transfers, early efforts were dominated by the German Unity Fund. The German Unity Fund was created in 1990. Much like richer countries in the European Union, Western länder were willing to transfer resources interregionally to insure themselves against massive immigration of dependents. The German Unity Fund consisted of an extra budgetary provision of 115 DM billion (that actually increased to over 140 DM billion, as reflected in Table 6.3). Out of this amount, 15% was dedicated to federal spending in the new länder and 85% was allocated to direct transfers to them according to the number of inhabitants. These 140 DM billion were raised via borrowing on credit markets and were to be paid in five years jointly by the Bund and the western länder (20 DM billion initially by the Bund and 47.5 DM billion by both the federation and Western länder as debt services for five years).

The flip-side of this effort, though, was the effective exclusion of the new länder from the formal system of interregional redistribution (FA) for a period of five years, until the end of 1995. Furthermore, their inclusion in the Verbundsystem was subject to a number of important exceptions (Biehl and Ungar 1991: 39–65). The share of VAT was the most important one. As of 1990, Eastern länder would receive the equivalent of 55% of the share of the VAT received by their Western counterparts. This proportion would increase yearly until reaching 70% of the Western länder by 1994.

Given the nature of the initial reaction, it soon became clear that the German Unity Fund and the partial integration of Eastern länder in the Verbundsystem were insufficient from a fiscal point of view. Additional changes were necessary to increase the financial capacity of the Eastern länder. They were fully integrated in the VAT revenue allocation. The 15% share of the German Unity Fund to be spent by the federal government was delivered to the Eastern länder (Renzsch 1998: 127–146). And, funds for several additional work and investment programs were established (Upswing East Program, worth 24 DM billion), upgrading the effort to cope with the shock affecting the former Federal Republic. Incidentally, by December 1991 the Bund raised income tax by 6.5 points and VAT from 14% to 15%, while at the same time increasing the länder share from 35% to 37%.[14] These developments consolidated the pattern of transfers from the Bund to the Eastern länder displayed in Table 6.4.

Political Preferences and the Costs of Reunification: Interpersonal and Interregional Redistribution and the Solidarity Pact

Shortly after Reunification the economic context had changed: by early 1992, the need to keep the deficit under control returned to the political agenda, shaping the negotiations over the Solidarity Pact. The Solidarity Pact, publicly presented on March 16, 1993, was a government initiative to get all major sectors, levels of government, and social actors to share the skyrocketing costs of Reunification. With an eye on the electoral horizon of 1994, Kohl's chief concern was how to keep the deficit under control without sacrificing transfers to the East (Sally and Webber 1994). The allocation of Reunification's cost dominated the negotiations between the federal government, the state governments, and the main political parties. Actors' preferences during this process concerned both interpersonal and interregional redistribution. Table 6.5 summarizes the preferences and goals of the main actors involved in the process.

Given the complexity of actors' preferences over two dimensions, the final outcome was uncertain. Ultimately, to understand the outcome it is necessary to revisit the central role of the Bundesrat and its interplay with the negotiations over the allocation of the cost of Reunification.

The rich länder were concerned about their relative contribution from the very beginning of the process. Given the rules of seat allocation in the Bundesrat described above, since 1989 any coalition among the Bund, the Eastern länder, the financially weak Western länder and the affluent ones, was a possibility.

---

[14] This particular decision shows how regional preferences can overcome partisan loyalties within the federation. When the SPD threatened to use its majority in the Bundesrat to block the proposal of an increase in the länder share of VAT, Brandenburg departed from the party decision and supported the Bund's proposal (Gunlicks 1994: 81–99; Lehmbruch 1996: 169–204; Renzsch 1994: 116–138).

TABLE 6.5. *The Effort to Incorporate the East: Map of Preferences (*)*

	Economic Incorporation and Interpersonal Redistribution	Interregional Redistribution
Federal Government (CDU-FDP)	– Sustain Transfers to the East – Wage Moderation – Limit Wage Convergence between East and West, linking salaries to productivity.	– Shift as much of the cost as possible to previous net recipients in the west (mostly under SPD control).
Federal Opposition (SPD)	– Sustain Welfare Provision – Pursue industrial recovery in the East – Sustain wage convergence – Increase taxes to high income earners	– Shift to the federal government as much of the cost as possible – Protect the financial capacity of current recipients
Trade Unions	– Similar to SPD	– Interest in sustaining transfers to prevent the East from developing its own organizational structure
Business Organizations	– Minimize the cost of contributions by banks and insurance companies	– Concerned about the efficiency implications of the effort, not about the effort itself
Eastern Lander	– Interested in maximizing support in terms of both industrial recovery programs and social security	– Eastern States länder pursue the maximization of resources at their disposal
Western Rich Lander (net contributors)	Concerned with the negative externalities of a low-wage economy in the East, these regions are supportive of the incorporation effort at first. Yet, in concert with their pre-unification concerns, they are wary of large increases in their net contributions and, in line with their position since the 1980s, maintain an aspiration for more fiscal autonomy and less redistribution.	
Western Poor Lander (former net recipients)*	Controlled in large part by the SPD, they endorse the incorporation effort but are worried about their relative position within the system. They do not want to be net losers of the incorporation.	

* The division of the Länder among these three groups was clear from the beginning of the process. *Cornerstones*, a joint report of the Länder Ministerpräsidenten in July 1990, lacked coherence due to the need to incorporate everyone's preferences. Pleas to reform FA in favor of higher levels of fiscal autonomy were made at the same time that more care to eliminate structural differences between Eastern and Western Länder was demanded. Indeed, the proposed demands for more fiscal autonomy would have meant, if implemented, a radical step in the direction of full fiscal decentralization: "It would have established a far more subsidiaristic federal system. It would have tended to reverse the established commitment to inter-Länder solidarity and uniformity of living conditions to allow for much greater inter-Länder diversity and differentiation than hitherto" (Jeffery 1995: 259).
Sources: Lehmbruch (1990, 1996); Renzsch (1994); Sally and Webber (1994); Streeck (2009).

Germany's Reunification

However, some coalitions were more likely than others. As G. Lehmbruch (1996: 188–189) has pointed out, an alliance between the Bund, Eastern länder and the poor Western ones at the expense of those other regions demanding more fiscal autonomy was a possible outcome facilitated by the combination of the distribution of seats and the regional patterns of inequality in the new Germany. Bavaria, Baden-Württemberg, and North-Rhine Westphalia were very much aware of this possibility and so was Lower Saxony (a net recipient of FA before Reunification).

The four directly connected the consequences of the new economic geography with an ultimately successful change in institutional design. Early on in the process, they sought to preserve their relative positions within the existing general arrangements. To prevent the possibility of becoming a minority when it comes to making distributive decisions, they conditioned their support for integration of the Easter länder to a modification of article 51 of the German Constitution (GG) (Thaysen 1994: 12–13). The new article should establish that those länder with a population of seven millions or more (i.e., the larger länder) would have six votes in the Bundesrat. Assembling them all together would count for more than one third of the total votes (twenty four out of sixty eight after October 1990), which is to say that they assured themselves a capacity to veto any legislative reform of the territorial design of redistribution opposed to their interests.[15] Albeit not very obvious at first sight, this change in the Constitution can be taken as a direct consequence of the increases in regional differences in terms of dependent population and risk specificity (δ) generated by Reunification on the German structure of inequality.

As a result, when the negotiations over the Solidarity Pact unfolded, the Bundesrat's allocation of seats reflected this change, facilitating a stronger institutional position for contributing länder vis-à-vis the federal government. In addition to the distribution of seats by länder, between 1990 and 1993 the partisan profile of the upper chamber also changed. From 1991, the SPD controlled a majority of the vote in the senate, gaining leverage as a major partner in the negotiation of the Solidarity Pact.

Given these political and institutional conditions, Kohl and the CDU were in a weak bargaining position. As Sally and Webber (1994) have noted they were primarily concerned with reaching an agreement that helped them share the burden and the political blame of the escalating costs of Reunification. This conditioned the outcomes in terms of the continuing effort in interpersonal redistribution and, especially, in the strategy to reform interregional redistribution within a broader package of revenue raising measures.

Interpersonal Redistribution

In terms of economic integration and interpersonal redistribution, Kohl accepted as policy most of the proposals from trade unions and the SPD.

---

[15] For an analysis of the centrality of the Bundesrat in fiscal and legislative power-sharing in the context of Germany's cooperative federalism, see Adelberger (1999); and Scharpf (1997a, 2007).

He failed to obtain a formal commitment to wage moderation. He could not formally undo the policy of wage convergence between East and West, thus failing to link wages and productivity. And, he committed to not engage in welfare retrenchment policies as a way to contain the growing deficit. In doing so he sided with Eastern members of the CDU against his own finance minister, Theo Weigel, and his government coalition partners, the Liberal Party (FDP).[16] As a result, indirect transfers to the East via public insurance programs kept growing strong. The effort was particularly visible in the areas of pensions, unemployment insurance, public employment policies, and social assistance.

The integration of Eastern pensioners was a major challenge for several reasons (Hegelich 2004): for one, current Eastern pensioners lacked previous contributions to be entitled to Western-like payments; second, the large levels of unemployment also implied a lack of revenue into the system for the future. The mechanical implementation of Western criteria to the East would have produced an unsustainable gap in terms of benefits between Eastern and Western pensioners. Amidst a long list of legislative reforms, two provisions were especially important to correct the lack of earlier contributions and boost entitlements in the East. First, the legislative framework extending the Western pension system to the new länder recognized the years of service of workers in Eastern Germany. And, second, it also recognized as contributory years those spent by women in the East providing for their children. Because of the "right to work" in the GDR and the recognition of womens' household work, these provisions implied that the majority of Eastern pensioners could show longer work histories than their Western counterparts. Needless to say, the implementation of this system required not only large start up funds but also a constant flow of transfers to fund the new pool of entitled recipients. The figures reported in Table 6.4 are reflective of these efforts. As a result, despite the fact that their salaries remain significantly lower, the gap between Eastern and Western pensions was not just closed, but actually overcome in a remarkable redistributive overturn. According to data from the German Parliament reported by Hegelich (2004: 90), the average pension in the old länder was 1438 DM. In contrast, the average pension in the new länder that same year was 1610 DM.[17] By 2000, Hegelich reports, "the average level of pensions (men and women) in the new länder was still 113% of the level of the old länder" (p. 89). Clearly old age citizens and the newly retired stand out, in financial terms, among those benefiting from Reunification.

Concerning unemployment, the failure of the many initiatives, such as the Treuhandanstalt (Czada 1994), to generate a quick jump start of the Eastern

---

[16] For details, see Sally and Webber (1994: 36).
[17] If this figure is broken out by gender, the impact of the decision to recognize the years of household work in the East becomes apparent: while the average pension for men was almost identical in the new Germany (1827 DM in the West versus 1864 DM in the East), the average pension for women in the East was, as of 1998, 25 % larger than in the West (1176 DM in the old länder vs. 1457 DM in the new länder).

Germany's Reunification

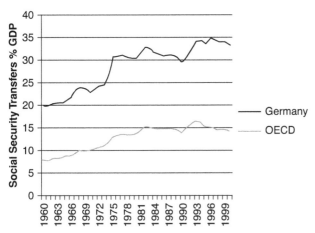

FIGURE 6.4. The Evolution of Social Security Transfers in Germany. *Source:* OECD Social Expenditure Statistics (2001).

economy exacerbated dependency on public transfers. Put shortly, a huge gap emerged between the East and the West, with people entering the labor force in the former region facing rather bleak prospects. As Mathias (2003: 35–65) depicts:

[...] the East-West divide could not be more obvious. By 1998, [...] all East German local government districts apart from the Eichfeld, a small strip of Thuringia along the borders to Bavaria and Hesse, showed unemployment rates of at least 125 percent of the federal average. By contrast, none of the West German local government districts were in that category, and only about one-fifth showed rates around the federal average [...] Between December 1991 and June 1998, unemployment in the eastern Länder rose by 57 per cent as the number of industrial jobs declined by 65 per cent. The service sector, despite going through a massive expansion, was clearly unable to absorb that much labor. Indeed, between 1991 and 1996, employment in the service sector rose only by two per cent [...]. (p. 55)

In light of these developments, it seems hardly surprising that the amount of transfers to the East in the form of unemployment insurance was nearly double that spent on pensions during the 1991–1998 period. The sheer magnitude of this effort also implies that active labor market policies became hard to fund and implement. As a result, passive income transfers became a dominant feature of post unification labor market policies. Consistent with the political incentives underpinning the social and political incorporation of the East, and despite growing criticisms in the West, the federal government continued to provide very generous unemployment benefits throughout Kohl's incumbency. Indeed, the new social needs emerging from Reunification singled out the trend of Germany's social policy efforts relative to other industrial democracies. For instance, Figure 6.4 shows how Germany's social security transfers as a percentage of GDP peaked during the period 1990–1994 at a much faster pace than the rest of the OECD. Only toward the end of what would be his last term, the introduction of a number of marginal reforms to contain the costs of both pensions and unemployment insurance were successfully exploited by the opposition as a conservative attack on social rights, facilitating the victory of the Red-Green coalition (Kitschelt 2004).

Given the concentration of welfare recipients in the East, public insurance transfers to individuals account for a significant share of the overall financial effort to incorporate the East. For instance, in 1995 social security outlays in the East amounted to about 20% of the overall effort. These resources, together with additional funds to allow state and local governments the provision of additional policies, funded a "warm shower of resources" (Kitschelt 2004) designed to facilitate in social and political terms the economic integration of the new members of the union.

The last dimension of the incorporation effort involves social assistance (Sozialhilfe) and public employment policies. The former encompasses a variety of programs and services provided by local authorities to look after individuals who have exhausted their rights to unemployment compensation, lack minimum pension contributions or otherwise need basic care in their daily lives. The latter implies an effort to reduce the scope of the unemployment problem through an increase in the number of jobs available in the public sector, often via small infrastructure and reconstruction programs. What distinguishes these two programs from public pensions or unemployment insurance is that local authorities are much more involved in their organization, implementation, and most importantly, their funding (Mathias 2003). Because local authorities diverge largely in the size of their tax base, this design is the source of significant inequalities in service provision and public employment offerings, as well as a source of dependency for local authorities, who need the financial support of regional governments to undertake their efforts. Given the social consequences of Reunification and the failure to launch a functional capitalist economy in the East, such dependencies became particularly acute in the new länder. On the one hand, both social assistance and public employment became necessary tools to cope with the transition process: the former to cope with dependents, the latter to contain unemployment and the population outflow. On the other hand, neither local governments nor the new länder were capable of sustaining these efforts. This required an additional transfer of resources from the federal government and the western länder. A large share of the transfers from the federal budget and the western länder reported in Table 6.4 helped cope with this problem.

In sum, Reunification demanded a massive effort from Germany's fiscal system. Indeed, it is hard to find a historical precedent for the sheer magnitude of the economic effort toward the incorporation of eastern länder into the federation. To give yet another point of reference, the overall incorporation effort in 1994 amounted to 7% of Germany's GDP that year. And, the cumulative effort throughout the period of interest amounted to about 46% of Germany's GDP in 1994, almost half of Germany's economy. Its noble goals aside, this massive transfer of resources spanning multiple policy instruments was no free lunch. Rather, it demanded a massive fiscal effort by the federal government and western citizens and länder, thus exacerbating conflicts over interregional redistribution. This is the issue I turn to next.

Cost Allocation and Interregional Redistribution

In terms of interregional redistribution the federal government tried to use Reunification to rebalance its position vis-à-vis the länder. The ultimate goal was to increase the federal government's share of tax revenues and to shift a good portion of the cost of unification to previous net receivers, that is, financially weak länder mostly controlled by the SPD. Given the involvement of the federal government in the social and economic incorporation of the East, it was only natural to seek a stronger role in the revenue system. To achieve this goal, however, Theo Weigel, minister of finance, needed to break the party ranks in the Bundesrat, controlled by the SPD. Indeed, the issue of interregional transfers had caused breaches in intraparty discipline before, as shown by Brandenburg's on the VAT allocation (see footnote 14).

Accordingly, his basic strategy consisted of trying to exploit the differences between the three groups of länder in Table 6.5 and forge a coalition comprising the Bund, the financially strong western länder and eastern länder against the financially weak western länder (Renzsch 1994: 123–137). To this end, Weigel proposed the following (Lehmbruch 1996: 187): "in return for a higher federal share (plus 5%) of the turnover tax yields, the Eastern Länder were promised extra federal grants in aid mounting to an annual 32 DM Bill, while financially strong Western Länder were attracted by a long-term reduction in the horizontal transfers to their less wealthy neighbors".

However attractive in terms of cash flow in the short term, Weigel's proposal was perceived by the financially strong western länder (including Bavaria) and his own party, the CSU, as an attempt to rebalance the distribution of power in favor of the federation, a process which in turn could potentially lead to an increase in their share of the Reunification's fiscal cost (Gunlicks 1994: 81–99; Katzenstein 1987; Sally and Webber 1994).

This generated a unified response by the länder. Bavaria (CSU) and North Rhine Westphalia (SPD) provided the initial documents for a common alternative position, seeking to protect the position of the länder relative to the federal government within existing fiscal arrangements. Saarland (SPD) and Saxony (CDU) represented the interests of lower income länder, while Brandenburg played a key role as a bridge between the SPD-ruled western länder and the five CDU-ruled eastern ones (Renzsch 1994: 116–138). Their common proposal succeeded over Weigel's, and, eventually, became the Solidarity Pact. Ultimately, under conditions of uncertainty about the future of the system of interregional redistribution, all länder found it more rational to preserve their relative institutional position within the fiscal system rather than accept exchanging political capacity for short-term income transfers.

Two reasons account for the success of this alternative proposal. First, it is incremental. Second, from the standpoint of the revenue capacity of the länder (and in stark contrast with Weigel's proposal), it is Pareto optimal in that, if implemented, it would leave no Land worse than the federal proposal (Renzsch 1998). The alliance among länder across party lines, orchestrated by Oskar Lafontaine (SPD) and Kurt Biedenkopf (CDU), successfully prevented the federal government from shifting the cost of Reunification to lower levels of government. As a result, the would be losers under Weigel's proposal need not exercise their veto in the Bundesrat. The unanimous endorsement of the alternative to Weigel's proposal led to the approval by *consensus* of the CDU (Christian Democracy), the SPD (Social Democracy) and the FDP (Liberals) of the Solidarity Pact.

The main provisions of the agreement to allocate the costs of Reunification are as follows (Lehmbruch 1996; Renzsch 1998: 127–146): 1) Full inclusion of the eastern länder in FA as of January 1, 1996; and 2) adoption of a set of measurements to prevent heavy financial consequences to be met by western länder. These include:

a) Extra federal grants in aid up to 36 DM billion to balance the German Unity Fund;
b) An agreement by the federation (Bund) to assist eastern länder with extra payments of 20.6 DM billion a year for a period of ten years;
c) Concessions to the financially weak western länder of 1.34 DM billions a year for a period of ten years, as well as a reduction in their share of the debt service of the German Unity Fund;
d) The Bund takes the service of the debt generated by the Treuhandstalt, the ruinous entity in charge of privatizing public firms in East Germany;
e) It was agreed that points a) to d), above, were to be financed mainly by selective spending cuts and by a small solidarity "surtax" (up to 5.5%) on income and corporations from 1996 onward;
f) And, last but not least, it was decided to further decentralize VAT: the länder share of VAT turnover would rise from 37% to 44%.

Overall, the final agreement implies an increase of resources to all länder funded primarily by marginal increases in income taxes, indirect taxes, and, over time, growing social security contributions (Streeck 2009; Wiesenthal 2003). Reunification triggered an increase of both interpersonal and interregional redistribution born primarily on the shoulder of western tax payers and consumers.

The Incorporation Effort: Quantitative Evidence

The size of the redistributive effort toward the East through the combined effect of interpersonal and interregional redistribution is unprecedented and appears consistent with the logic developed in the theoretical argument of the book. The political incentives of federal elites, given the system of representation

TABLE 6.6. *The Allocation of Interregional Transfers in Germany, 1991–1994*

	Interregional Transfers per capita	
Mobility	107.1***	111.75***
	(32.7)	(33.065)
GDP Per Capita	–	−9.87
		(15.41)
East	734.26**	596.09
	(363.7)	(395)
Copartisanship	−161.39*	−163.67*
	(95.00)	(95.64)
East*Copartisanship	292.43*	299.95*
	(175.02)	(170.85)
Intercept	−14.25	202.33
	(66.83)	(340)
N	55	55
Adjusted R squared	0.93	0.93

Standard errors in parentheses.
Key: * $p < .10$, ** $p < .05$, *** $p < .01$

and the fears about massive population displacements out of a low-wage, low-productivity area, drove the preferences and choices of key social and political actors. In this section, I delve into these linkages through a quantitative analysis of the determinants of the regional fiscal flows (defined as total transfers per capita received by each region).[18]

More specifically, one should observe that, given the centripetal system of political representation at work in Germany, efforts ought to be concentrated on those regions in need where the national government has larger political stakes. Thus, one would expect that in the early years after Reunification, those eastern länder controlled by the CDU were the biggest beneficiaries of the transfer of resources. In addition, one would also expect that those länder with the highest rates of outward mobility are the ones attracting a larger share of the redistributive effort, reflecting an attempt by the federal government to stop the bleeding from those areas particularly hurt by the economic transformation. In an effort to evaluate these expectations, Table 6.6 reports the results of a time series cross-sectional analysis of the determinants of the level of transfers per capita received by the German länder between 1991 and 1994. The transfers per capita are modeled as a function of five variables: the outward mobility rate, that is, the share of the total land's population that emigrated to another land during the past year; the land's GDP per capita (expressed in 1995 euros); an interaction term between a dummy variable, valuing 1 if the land was part of the former GDR and 0 otherwise; and an indicator of copartisanship that

---
[18] These data include transfers via public insurance (interpersonal) and interregional (FA) fiscal programs. For a description of sources see Appendix C.

takes the value of 1 if both the regional and federal government are controlled by the same party (or coalition) and 0 otherwise.[19]

The results support the claim that federal authorities will concentrate their efforts in those regions of the union with the highest levels of emigration to other parts of the country. They also show that Kohl's government saw the East as a critical area to secure its political survival, concentrating efforts especially in those regions where the CDU managed to secure the regional government early on in the process. The latter effect is captured by the significant differential in resources accrued by those eastern länder controlled by the CDU.[20] Overall, the picture emerging from these results is one of a government pouring resources into the East to stop the population outflow and to secure its own political survival.

To summarize, the analysis of early responses to Reunification paints a picture in which federal elites engage in a massive increase of both interpersonal and interregional redistribution towards the East. Political incentives associated with centripetal representative institutions and economic incentives associated with the risk of under-sided mobility patterns drove actors' initial strategies in ways that lend support to the core argument in this book. In turn, the massive transfers towards the East channeled the distributive tensions emerging from the new economic geography to the revenue side. The conflict was not about the need or even the size of the effort at first, but about who was going to meet the cost. Early on in the process, the net contributors to the FA in the West managed to reallocate seats in the Bundesrat to protect themselves from excessive extraction in the future. At the same time, when the federal government tried to build a coalition of net contributors and eastern länder at the expense of those previously benefitting from the system, the efforts backfired. The latter managed to exploit their role as colegislators in the Bundesrat to protect their relative fiscal position vis-à-vis the Bund. The federal government and western tax payers (consumers) met the bulk of the unification effort. The agreements reached in the Solidarity Pact appeased the distributive tensions within the union, though not for long.

BEYOND NATIONAL UNITY: CENTRIPETALISM AND DISTRIBUTIVE CONFLICTS AFTER REUNIFICATION (1995-2005)

The previous section has focused on the early response of Germany's fiscal system to the challenges of Reunification. Taking advantage of the sudden transformation of Germany's economic geography, I have been able to identify how the centripetal nature of political institutions and the concerns about negative

---

[19] The estimates reported include panel corrected standard errors with a Prais-Winsten correction for serial autocorrelation.
[20] Note that the effects are directly interpretable only because the two terms in the interaction model are dummy variables. Also, I am reasoning on the premise that, given the small number of observations, a 10% significance level is an acceptable threshold while interpreting the results.

Germany's Reunification

TABLE 6.7. *The Redistributive Impact of the FA System*

	1996			2000		
	Before	After	% Change	Before	After	% Change
NW	79253	76128	−3.94	88071	85871	−2.5
Bavaria	53876	50925	−5.48	62219	58470	−6.03
BW	46432	43911	−5.43	54453	50581	−7.11
Lower Sa	30379	31292	3.01	33793	34906	3.29
Hesse	29122	25883	−11.12	35254	29901	−15.18
Rhine Pal	15824	16056	1.47	17002	17782	4.59
Schl-Hols	11201	11217	0.14	11932	12291	3.01
Saarland	4017	4251	5.83	4402	4731	7.47
Hamburg	10099	9618	−4.76	12178	11079	−9.02
Bremen	2917	3552	21.77	2990	3862	29.16
West Germany	283391	272831	−3.73	322294	309474	−3.98
Saxony	15890	17855	12.37	17344	19672	13.42
Sax-Anh	9447	10688	13.14	10247	11654	13.73
TH	8629	9757	13.07	9444	10764	13.98
BB	8907	9942	11.62	10163	11426	12.42
MV	6260	7116	13.67	6879	7862	14.29
East Germany	49133	55357	12.67	54077	61378	13.5
Berlin	13787	18123	31.45	14381	19902	38.39
Total Germany	346311	346311	0	390752	390752	0

Sources: Bundesfinanzministerium (Mill. DM).

externalities potentially emerging from the consolidation of a vastly underdeveloped regional economy drove federal and regional elites to accept a massive redistributive effort. As a corollary, this section closes the chapter by taking a succinct look at the dynamics that followed. Clearly, from this point forward, distributive tensions are no longer exogenous. Yet, a careful overview of the conflicts that emerged, and how they were resolved, sheds additional light on the interplay between economic geography and political representation in modern Germany, ultimately providing additional leverage to empirically evaluate the logic posited in this book.

Table 6.7 illustrates the redistributive implications of the arrangements resulting from the Solidarity Pact by looking at the financial power of the länder before and after FA applies in 1996 and 2000. Table 6.7 conveys a picture in which three large western länder (Bavaria, Buden-Württemberg, and especially Hesse) meet most of the costs, and suggests that the scope of this redistributive effort remained fairly stable during the second half of the 1990s.

Interestingly, the persistence of the effort runs parallel to a transformation of the structure of economic and political incentives at work during the early period post-Reunification.

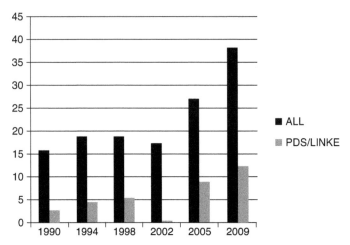

FIGURE 6.5. The Growing Leverage of Smaller Parties in the Federal Parliament. *Source:* Statistisches Bundesamt Deutschland

Economically, the strategy to uplift capitalism in the East as a way to secure employment opportunities and prevent mobility was of limited success. The East did emerge after all as a low-productivity, subsidy-dependent, low-employment area, where lack of opportunity drove people away. With the possible exception of Thuringia, the outmigration rate in all other eastern länder trends upwards. In three cases (Mecklenburg-Pomerannia, Saxony-Anhalt, and Brandemburg), the outmigration rate at the end of the period (2000–2002) is actually higher than the outmigration rate observed during the 1990–1992 period (Heiland 2004; Statistische Bundesamt, several years). The initial strategy to bring the East up to standard at a fast pace proved to be far too optimistic. Market incentives in the West were far too strong, and the economic reconstruction of the East far too slow, to prevent people (particularly young skilled workers) from migrating (Parikh and Van Leuvensteijn 2002). These developments fed back into the political motives underpinning efforts toward the East. As passive transfers, rather than active measures, constitute the bulk of the effort by regional governments in the East as well, the incentive to add resources for ultimately failed initiatives (such as local public employment programs) becomes less and less obvious for tax payers and political parties in the West.

These concerns had their immediate political correlate as the much feared East-West divide in terms of party systems and competition unfolded through the 1990s. Table 6.8 provides an overview of the regional elections results in unified Germany since 1990. Figure 6.5 displays the increasing share of Parliamentary seats other than the CDU/CSU and the SPD. Together, they convey several changes in the structure of political incentives in the new Germany.

Table 6.8 portrays significant transformations in Germany's patterns of political support. During the second half of the 1990s, the CDU becomes

TABLE 6.8. *Partisan Composition of Regional Parliaments since 1990*

State	Election Year	SPD	CDU	FDP	Greens	PDS/Linke/(Other)	Total Seats	Coalition
WEST								
Baden-Wuerttemberg	1988	42	66	7	10		125	CDU/SPD
	1992	46	64	8	13		146	CDU/SPD
	1996	39	69	14	19		155	CDU/FDP-DVP
	2001	45	63	10	10		128	CDU/FDP
	2006	38	69	15	17		139	CDU/FPD
Bavaria	1990	58	127	7	12		204	CSU
	1994	70	120		12		204	CSU
	1998	67	123		14		204	CSU
	2003	41	124		15		180	CSU
Bremen	1987	25	25	10	10		100	SPD
	1991	32	32	10	11		100	SPD/FDP/Greens
	1995	38	37		14		100	SPD/CDU
	1999	41	42		10		100	SPD/CDU
	2003	34	29	1	12		83	SPD/Greens
	2007	32	23	5	14	7	83	SPD/Greens
Hamburg	1987	55	49	8	8		120	SPD/FDP
	1991	61	44	7	9		121	SPD/Greens
	1993	58	36		19		121	SPD
	1997	54	46		21		121	SPD/Greens
	2001	46	33	6	11	25 (Schill)	121	CDU/Schill (center-right)
	2004	41	63		17		121	CDU
	2008	45	56		12	8	121	CDU/Greens (probably)
Hesse	1987	44	47	9	10		110	CDU/FDP
	1991	46	46	8	10		110	SPD/Greens
	1995	44	45	8	13		110	SPD/Greens
	1999	46	50	6	8		110	CDU/FDP
	2003	33	56	9	12		110	CDU
	2008	42	42	11	9	6	110	
Lower-Saxony	1990	71	67	9	8		155	SPD/Greens
	1994	81	67		13		161	SPD
	1998	83	62		12		157	SPD
	2003	63	91	15	14		183	CDU/FDP
	2008	47	68	13	12	11	152	CDU/FDP

(*continued*)

TABLE 6.8 *(continued)*

State	Election Year	SPD	CDU	FDP	Greens	PDS/ Linke/ (Other)	Total Seats	Coalition
North Rhine-Westphalia	1990	123	90	14	12		239	SPD
	1995	108	89		24		221	SPD/Greens
	2000	102	88	24	17		231	SPD/Greens
	2005	74	89	12	12		187	CDU/FDP
Rhineland-Palatinate	1987	40	48	7	5		100	CDU/FDP
	1991	47	40	7	7		101	SPD/FDP
	1996	43	41	10	7		101	SPD/FDP
	2001	49	38	8	6		101	SPD/FDP
	2006	53	38	10			101	SPD
Saarland	1990	30	18	3			51	SPD
	1994	27	21		3		51	SPD
	1999	25	26				51	CDU
	2004	18	27	3	3		51	CDU
Schleswig-Holstein	1988	46	27			1	74	SPD
	1992	45	32	5		1	89	SPD
	1996	33	30	4	6	2	75	SPD/Greens
	2000	41	33	7	5	3	89	SPD/Greens
	2005	29	30	4	4	2	69	CDU/SPD
EAST								
Thuringia	1990	21	44	9		9	89	CDU/FDP
	1994	29	42			17	88	CDU/SPD
	1999	18	49			21	88	CDU
	2003	15	45			28	88	CDU
Brandenburg	1990	36	27	6		13	88	SPD/FDP
	1994	52	18			18	88	SPD
	1999	37	25			22	89	SPD/CDU
	2004	33	20			29	88	SPD/CDU
Mecklenburg-Western Pommerania	1990	21	29	4		12	66	CDU/FDP
	1994	23	30			18	71	CDU/SPD
	1998	27	24			20	71	SPD/PDS
	2002	33	25			13	71	SPD/PDS
	2006	23	22	7		13	71	SPD/CDU
Berlin	1990	76	101	18	23	23	241	SPD/ (Greens-AL (from 91) CDU/SPD)
	1995	55	87		30	34	206	CDU/SPD
	1999	42	76		18	33	169	CDU/SPD
	2001	44	35	15	14	33	141	SPD/Greens (from 2002) SPD/PDS)
	2006	53	37	13	23	23	149	SPD/PDS

TABLE 6.8 *(continued)*

State	Election Year	SPD	CDU	FDP	Greens	PDS/ Linke/ (Other)	Total Seats	Coalition
Saxony	1990	32	92	9		17	160	CDU
	1994	22	77			21	120	CDU
	1999	14	76			30	120	CDU
	2004	13	55	7	6	31	124	CDU/FDP
Saxony-Anhalt	1990	27	48	14		12	106	CDU/FDP
	1994	36	37		5	21	99	SPD/Greens (Minority-Gov)
	1998	47	28			25	116	SPD
	2002	25	48	17		25	115	CDU/FDP
	2006	24	40	7		26	97	CDU/SPD

* The Seats written under CDU in Bavaria is actually CSU and the Greens in Hamburg is the GAL (Green Alternative List).
Sources: Statistisches Bundesamt Deutschland; http://www2.politik.uni-halle.de/schnapp//Forschung/Landesregierungen/; Election.de

somewhat underrepresented in the East, especially in relation to the earlier period (1990–1995). The CDU controlled, either by itself or in coalition with the FDP, a majority of regional governments in the East. Between 1990 and 1994, Brandenburg was the only exception to this pattern. After 1994, the scenario changed quite significantly. The progressive ascendant of the PDS as a major post-GDR party, capable of holding the SPD at bay in the East, altered the coalition map throughout the region. Thuringia and Berlin see the CDU sharing its power with the SPD as early as 1994. In the case of Mecklenburg-Pommerania, an SPD-PDS coalition was in office between 1998 and 2006.

In parallel the regional elections reveal a consolidation (over time) of the Greens and the Liberals in the West. While relatively distant in policy dimensions such as environmental regulation or the degree of implication of state institutions in the economy, they target a common constituency. Increasingly, both draw their support from the well-educated, well-off Western urban strata, while at the same time they have very little electoral support in the East. They are the quintessential organizations for the net payers of the Reunification efforts.

These changes in regional electoral arenas have their correlate at the federal level. Figure 6.5 illustrates the share of seats in the German Parliament (Bundestag) held by parties other than the CDU/CSU-SPD. More specifically, it also illustrates how the consolidation of the PDS in the East grants it, with the exception of the 2002 election, an increasing presence at the national level.[21]

---

[21] The spike for the PDS in the 2005 and 2009 elections needs clarification. I should highlight that the post-1995 period encompasses two subperiods: a first period, between 1995 and 2002,

The rise of the PDS in the East, and the consolidation of the Liberals and the Green Party at roughly similar levels of support translate to higher levels of political fragmentation that consolidate precisely the East-West cleavage that Western political elites were so keen to prevent.

Unsurprisingly, as the contours of an East-West divide become sharper, an increasing number of leaders of Western länder became less constrained by the notion that massive transfers towards the East were a necessary sacrifice in extraordinary times. As a result, the nature and cost of efforts toward the social and economic integration of the East became the focus of renewed political contentions over the organization of Germany's fiscal structure. These conflicts affected the design of interpersonal and interregional redistribution alike and reflect neatly the interplay between economic geography and representation in the aftermath of Reunification. Ziblatt (2002) offers an excellent analysis of these conflicts in the context of the political revival of "competitive federalism" in the German federation (Gunlicks 2005).

In terms of public insurance and interregional redistribution, the most revealing conflict in this period concerns the attempt by the CSU government of Bavaria to pursue the decentralization of unemployment insurance. As illustrated in an earlier section of this chapter, a great deal of transfers to the East operated indirectly, that is, via the territorial incidence of public insurance policies designed to cope with individual labor market circumstances. The high rate of unemployment in the East implied large transfers out of Western paying states. Hence the question by the Bavarian minister of social affairs, as reported by Ziblatt (2002: 637–638): "Why should a hard-working construction worker in Bavaria have to pay for the problems of unemployment in Mecklenburg-Western Pomerania?"

This question provides an excellent illustration of this book's proposed logic behind elites' behavior. CSU's Edmund Stoiber, a regional leader in a relatively wealthy region (who is relatively less concerned with national elections than the rest of his party) launches, through his minister of social affairs, a political appeal for low income voters within his region in a clear attempt to mobilize the "poor among the rich" against the existing centralized system of public insurance. The argument is logically appealing to tax payers and employers within Bavaria, as they would hope to see their share of taxes and social security contributions reduced in a decentralized regime. However compelling for Bavarian tax payers and employers though, the proposal had a very short

---

where the East-West divide is starkest; and a second period in which welfare retrenchment at the federal level (Hartz IV and pension reform most notably) causes a split in the SPD, the formation of a new political force (WASG), and ultimately the merger between the PDS and the WASG into Die Linke in 2007. Arguably, this latest development helps rebridge the East-West divide. In line with the argument, given centripetal representation, a fraction of the "poor among the poor" and a fraction of the "poor among the rich" join forces along class lines under the same organizational umbrella. The implications of these recent events for contentions over Germany's fiscal structure remain to be seen and fall out of the scope of this chapter.

political life span for reasons that, again, lend strong support to the argument of this book. To put it shortly, the structure of incentives emerging from centripetal representation constrained the proposal's support even within the CSU/CDU itself. As Ziblatt's (2002) tracing of the process reveals, the proposal met the resistance not only of the SPD representatives, but also of those party officials representing the CSU at the federal level. Those members of the party with the task of representing Bavaria at the national level could hardly bear the thought of defending a proposal that virtually everyone else in the party and the country would regard as selfish, parochial populism. Accordingly, Ziblatt (2002) reports, "it can be argued that the formal institutional constraint in the Bundesrat resulted in the loss of enthusiasm by the Bavarian Minister President for this most radical component of the competitive federalism agenda" (639). In line with the predictions of the model in Chapter 2 (hypothesis 2), centripetal representation constrained rather directly Bavaria's attempt to decentralize unemployment insurance in the late 1990s.

Concerning interregional redistribution, FA was perceived again as a purely distributive conflict between regions, and, just as before Reunification, the net payers moved on to challenge the status quo (Renzsch 2001). I have shown above how the incorporation effort during 1991–1995 increased the level of interregional redistribution. In turn, Table 6.7 indicates how such levels remain fairly stable over time. However, the transformation of the economic and political context triggered new political initiatives to trim the scope of interregional redistribution during the late 1990s. A bipartisan group of net contributors (SPD: North Rhine Westfalia, Hesse; CDU: Bavaria, Baden-Wuerttemberg) proposed a reform along three lines: 1) increasing tax autonomy by the länder; 2) reducing the contribution to the fiscal equalization system (FA); and 3) reducing the level of overlapping jurisdictions and joint tasks, that is, increasing the political and tax autonomy of the länder. Despite the CSU's efforts to reach an agreement with their (CDU-ruled) Eastern counterparts, the latter refused to endorse a common proposal out of fear of "election time recriminations from the PDS that the Eastern CDU government has "sold out" Eastern interests to the rich Bavarians." (Ziblatt 2002: 644). The distributive incentives of net winners, a majority in the Bundesrat, and their electoral constraints, motivated by the regionalization of party competition during the 1990s, ultimately derailed the proposal. Again, in a centripetal system of representation, the CSU finds it unfeasible to overcome the resistance of those states benefiting from the status quo.

Aware of the political limitations imposed by the centripetal nature of German federal institutions, Western net payers adopted a different strategy and challenged the system before the German constitutional court (Scharpf 2007). In 1997 the three biggest financiers of the FA, Bavaria (CSU), Baden-Württemberg (CDU) and Hesse (SPD), filed a suit against the existing system at the constitutional court of Germany. Their grounds were that, under the procedures and percentage points set for equalization, some of the net recipients were actually better off in the end than some of the net contributors

(Finanzministerium, Baden-Württemberg). In September of 1999, the German constitutional court ruled in their favor and demanded new scales for the FA system.[22] The decision stated that the existing Finanzausgleichgesetz (fiscal compensation law, in the following equalization law FAG) could be used until the end of 2004 on the condition that the legislature would introduce the required changes through a Maßstäbegesetz (scaling law) by January 1 of 2003. Otherwise, the old FAG would be deemed unconstitutional. In addition, the Parliament would have to pass a longer term reform on the basis of the new scaling law by December 31, 2004. Moreover, the constitutional court also ruled that, "horizontal fiscal compensation should lessen the differences in financial power between the Länder, not eliminate them." In other words, and this is critical from the standpoint of net contributors, the FA system should not alter länder ranking in terms of their relative financial power. Furthermore, the decision also stated that additional federal payments should only be given in cases where one land is left incommensurately under the financial power average and this cannot be rectified through the regular mechanisms of the system, a word of warning explicitly included for the new German länder. Finally, the legislature was to reform the weighting system based on the länder population.

Upon the court's mandate, the federal government and the states set out to negotiate along the guidelines established by the ruling. By June 2001 no agreement had been reached. Schroeder decided to intervene and facilitate an agreement by, once again, transferring the cost of reform to the federal government (Gunlicks 2001). Two measures were key to securing the reform: first, the federal government guaranteed the continuation of subsidies toward the East in the form of a new Solidarity Pact, becoming effective in 2005 after the expiration of the one negotiated in 1993; second, from 1 January 2005 onwards the federal government would assume the reduction in the payments made by the richer länder. These arrangements will last until the end of 2019, when it is expected that special aid to the East and the additional "solidarity" income tax will both cease to apply (Finanzministerium, Bayern).

More specifically, the main implications of this reform are as follows:

1) As part of the new Solidarity Pact, the federation and the states agreed that the former would cover the lingering costs of the German Unity Fund. To this effect, though, the federation would keep 1.323 billion euros on a yearly basis until 2019 out of the states VAT contingent. Of the remaining amount, all länder continue to receive the same amount of VAT revenue per inhabitant for at least 75% of the VAT revenue. The remaining share is distributed according to the financial power of the länder. As a result, those länder below the average financial capacity receive compensation to close the gap.[23]

---

[22] See Bundesverfassungsgericht, 2 BvF 2/98 of November 11, 1999, sec 1–347.

[23] Those states with revenues up to 97% of the mean receive transfers such that that 95% of the gap is closed. Those states with revenues above 97% of the mean receive transfers such that

2) To appease those who challenged the system in the first place, and to ensure that the FA system does not alter the ranking in terms of financial capacity, the reform introduced several provisions to limit the amount of interregional redistribution. First, to improve the consequences of the new compensation mechanism for the rich länder and provide a higher incentive to increase tax revenues, rich states are allowed to set aside for themselves 12% of their revenue surplus, that is, 12% of the amount of revenues collected above the average (Finanzministerium Niedersachsen). Second, the reform adjusted the compensation brackets.[24] Finally, to limit the payments of the donor states, the average compensation payments from the net contributors to the system are limited to 72.5% of their surplus revenues. As an example of the implications of these limitations, relative to the status quo, Bavaria saves about 200 million euros on a yearly basis due to the new laws (Finanzministerium Bayern).
3) Significant adjustments also took place through the revised computation of each land's financial capacity. Contrary to the previous system, 64% of the revenues coming from municipal taxes in a land are now included. The federation wanted 100% of municipal taxes included but gave up this demand in the bargain. Paradoxically, due to the new accounting of municipal taxes the richer länder will pay even more because they tend to include the wealthier municipalities (Finanzministerium Niedersachsen).
4) Finally, to meet the Constitutional Court's request, the reform introduced a dispersion weight intended to benefit those areas with sparse and heavily spread-out populations (Mecklenburg-Western Pomerania 1.05, Brandenburg 1.03, Saxony-Anhalt 1.02). Meanwhile, the three city-states (Bremen, Berlin, and Hamburg) retained a weight of 1.35 (Finanzministerium Baden-Württemberg).

In conclusion, it took a decade after Reunification and a Constitutional Court ruling to create the conditions for a reform that aimed at containing excessive redistribution from wealthier to poorer länder. However, note that these agreements, do not imply a reduction in the amount of redistribution towards the East. They simply entail a shift of part of the cost from net contributing länder to the federal government. On the whole, though, and despite the changing

---

between 95% and 60% of the remaining gap is covered. The transfers received decrease with the amount of revenue generated by each state (Finanzministerium Baden-Württemberg). For the year 2007, these transfers amounted to 10% of the länders' share of the VAT.

[24] Those länder below 80% of the average financial capacity will be compensated such that 75% of the gap is covered. If the revenues they collect fall between 80% and 93% below the mean, they will be compensated according to a scale between 75% and 70%. The scale decreases continuously to 44% of the gap for those länder between 93% and 100% of the average. In turn, länder above the mean from 100% to 107% will pay from 44% to 70% of their surpluses, again in a scale of continuous increase. Those above the mean from 107% to 120% will pay from 70% to 75% of their surpluses. No land will can be requested to pay more than 75% of its surplus (Finanzministerium Baden-Württemberg).

political climate and the adjustments introduced during the second half of the period, the FA system remains a major source of redistribution between territories in Germany, and the levels to redistribution towards Eastern länder have not declined. Indeed, they are unlikely to do so as the reform of the fiscal equalization system remains stalled by insurmountable distributive conflicts in the context of long lasting efforts towards federalism reform.[25]

The Aftermath of Reunification: Quantitative Evidence

Table 6.9 replicates earlier analyses of the developments of interregional transfers per capita for the period 1995–2002. The contrast between these results and those for the earlier period reveals interesting differences.

In this section I have highlighted two major differences between the post-1995 period and the earlier years. First, political and economic elites realized over time that the initial strategy to jumpstart capitalism in the East and stop the population flow is not working. As a result, federal elites should no longer target their transfers towards those areas that are more likely to expel population. In Table 6.9, the lack of association between mobility and transfers in the post-1995 period is consistent with this development. Mobility is no longer a predictor of the magnitude of interregional transfers per capita. After the initial phase, in which a conscious effort to stop undesired migration patterns from East to West took place, interregional transfers are no longer responsive to mobility patterns.

Second, the failure to relaunch capitalism in a short period of time had its political correlate in the ultimate failure to prevent the emergence of an East-West divide in the patterns of party competition. Given the new partisan geography, one should observe a weaker correlation between the size of transfers received and a particular party (or coalition) controlling both the federal government and the länder.

The results reported in Table 6.9 are consistent with this expectation. While, according to the estimates reported, Eastern länder continue to be privileged beneficiaries of interregional redistribution, they no longer receive an additional premium associated with the copartisanship between their regional incumbents and the federal ones. Transfers forge coalitions to deliver votes, as successfully experienced by the CDU during the early period postunification (see Table 6.6). Consistent with the qualitative evidence provided in this section, changes in the partisan composition of regional and federal legislatures altered the federal government's incentives when targeting recipients.

---

[25] These recent efforts, initiated first by the Red-Green Coalition in 2003, and resumed, after their initial failure, by the Grand Coalition after 2005, are still ongoing. For details of these negotiations, and the unlikely prospects of a consensus-based reform of fiscal federalism in Germany, see Gunlicks (2005, 2007); Moore, Jacoby and Gunlicks (2008); and Scharpf (2007).

TABLE 6.9. *The Allocation of Interregional Transfers in Germany, 1995–2002*

	Interregional Transfers per capita	
Mobility	−6.18	−5.02
	(8.05)	(8.0)
GDP Per Capita	−	−6.2*
		(3.4)
East	268.22***	205.66***
	(102)	(107.5)
Copartisanship	−15.9	−13.6
	(20)	(19.8)
East*Copartisanship	11.22	8.03
	(33.1)	(32.6)
Intercept	28.7	171.5**
	(22)	(80)
N	128	128
Adjusted R squared	.12	.14

Standard errors in parentheses.
Key: * $p < .10$, ** $p < .05$, *** $p < .01$

THEORETICAL IMPLICATIONS

This analysis of the response of Germany's fiscal structure to the challenge of Reunification yields one clear conclusion. The sudden increase in geographical disparities in income and labor market risk did not result in a process of decentralization and a reduction in levels of interregional transfers, as one would predict on the basis of income distribution approaches (like Bolton and Roland's median voter approach, 1997). Rather, it triggered first a massive redistributive effort on both the interpersonal and interregional dimensions. As a result of this effort, the natural increase in inequality of pre-tax and transfers income associated with Reunification did not translate to an increase in levels of disposable income inequality.

Over time, however, distributive tensions reemerged and a major East-West divide renewed political contentions over the design of interpersonal and interregional redistribution. In line with this book's argument, this chapter has shown that both the initial effort and the outcome of more recent contentions reflect the impact of two factors: the need to cope with the risk (and subsequent reality) of a significant and undesired migration from East to West; and the combination of political incentives created by the new economic geography and the political capacities granted by the centripetal nature of the system of representation. Challenges by net payers from the West, such as Bavaria, met two ultimately critical stumbling blocks: net winners in the East have no incentive to accept any proposal toward increasing fiscal autonomy, and they have the political capacity to veto them. Eastern voters remain an essential constituency in federal elections, and their regional leaders an essential voting block in the Bundesrat. Overall, the combined role of cross-regional economic externalities and the system of representation overcame the disintegrating effect of a radical transformation in the patterns of economic geography, thus securing the continuation of very large levels of redistribution among territories.

7

Endogenous Decentralization and Welfare Resilience
Spain, 1978–2007

The analysis of the German experience in Chapter 6 illustrated how centripetal representation works to contain the decentralizing push emerging from post-Unification economic geography. This chapter analyzes the interplay between economic geography and political representation in a rather different context, the process of fiscal and political decentralization that has taken place in Spain since the early 1980s. The chapter serves two purposes, one theoretical and one empirical. Theoretically, the chapter contributes to the study of how status quo conditions, in terms of political representation, shape subsequent political processes where distributive tensions emerge endogenously. By focusing on a case in which the original arrangements were purposefully centripetal, it offers a contrast to that of the European Union, and helps cover the range of possible initial conditions.

Empirically, this chapter addresses the puzzle of the coexistence over time of two processes that, according to the preeminent theoretical views, one would expect to be at odds: the expansion of the welfare state; *and* a fast paced process of political and, partially, fiscal decentralization. The key to this joint development lies in the resilience of core components of the interpersonal redistribution system (mostly on the expenditure side) when virtually all other policies, including healthcare, education, and, more recently important aspects of the revenue collection system have been decentralized. In this chapter I show that it is the interplay between the system of representation, asymmetric fiscal arrangements embedded in the original constitutional contract, and economic geography that explain this puzzle.

An uneven economic geography, coupled with a centralized fiscal structure, generates largely uneven patterns of costs and benefits allocation across regions. On this basis, a centripetal system of representation privileges politically the winners in the status quo, who are able to resist a proposal to fully decentralize interpersonal redistribution in Spain. Hence, the resilience over time of the centralized nature of interpersonal taxes and transfers.

Consistently, the observable modifications of fiscal federalism in Spain reflect specific historical moments in which national parties are unable to form a solid majority of their own, and need the political support of those net payers in favor of a rebalancing of the system (primarily Catalonian and/or Basque nationalist parties). The demand for change stemmed from the distributive consequences associated both with the centralized system in place and with the asymmetric nature of the original fiscal contract, which allowed the Basque Country and Navarra to have largely independent fiscal systems outside of the fiscal system at work in the rest of the country (the so-called common system). However, the partial modification of fiscal federal arrangements was only feasible when the national parties representing the beneficiaries of the existing fiscal structure needed to compromise to secure a sufficient majority in Parliament.

This process reflects, in part, an endogenous transformation over time of certain aspects of the system of representation itself, most notably the nature of partisan political competition at national and regional levels. The intensification of demands at the regional level creates a centrifugal spiral in terms of competition that forces national parties to adjust their position and partially accept adjustments to the fiscal structure.

Yet these dynamics have found a limit in the organization of social security. Even during periods of national minority government, attempts to question the centralized nature of social security have, so far, been aborted from the start. This was the case during the discussion of the *Plan Ibarretxe* Plan as well as during the drafting and approval of the new *Estatuto de Catalunya* (Constitution of Catalonia). In both instances, internal resistance within the Socialist party (PSOE) toward further concessions to demands from Catalonia and the Basque Country, and fear that the national opposition party would benefit from becoming the last line of defense of Spain's social security system, successfully preempted any move towards the decentralization of social security. Given the system of representation in place, the electoral consequences in those regions currently benefiting from the system were too high to seriously pursue such a move.

In the following sections I will, first, provide a detailed characterization of the original constitutional contract and its asymmetries (both in political and fiscal terms) and provide an overview of the evolution of Spain's fiscal structure during democracy. Second, I discuss the interplay between Spain's economic geography and the status quo in terms of fiscal structures, thereby providing an analysis of the distributive implications of the current system. The third and fourth sections analyze the political conflicts emerging from such tensions and how they are resolved, involving both adjustments to interregional transfers and attempts to decentralize social security. Finally, the closing section brings together the main theoretical implications of the chapter.

THE ORIGINAL CONTRACT AND THE EVOLUTION OF SPAIN'S
FISCAL STRUCTURE[1]

The evolution of Spain's fiscal structure is largely dependent upon the specific arrangements that emerged during the transition to democracy. These arrangements reflect a complex historical compromise between two opposing forces: Francoist elites and the military, who were particularly concerned with the preservation of Spain as a unified nation under a centralized state; and those mobilizing for a decentralized state capable of integrating the demands of nationalist movements in Catalonia, the Basque Country, and to a lesser extent, Galicia.[2] The strategy to balance these two forces combined the asymmetric treatment of regions, particularly those with a tradition of autonomy and nationalist mobilization, with an intentionally lagged process of decentralization. The latter was to unfold under conditions of centripetal representation, built around a strongly malapportioned proportional representation system for the lower house.[3] Four relevant aspects follow directly from this original contract: 1) asymmetry of access and openness about how political powers were to be distributed; 2) electoral asymmetry and centripetal representation; 3) absence of institutionalized cooperation; and 4) a centralized fiscal structure as the status quo (except for Navarra and the Basque Country).

Asymmetry of Access and Openness in the Distribution of Political Capacities

Perhaps the most important characteristic of the way the Spanish Constitution of 1978 organized the territorial distribution of power is the fact that the final text did not reflect any coherent model of state. Actors at the time were much more focused on what they did *not* want to be reflected in the constitution than on anything else. The very notion of the *Estado de las Autonomias* (EA, a Spain made up of autonomous regions) is not even recorded in the constitutional text. The Spanish Constitution, like most others, was an incomplete contract with lacunae to be closed by normal politics (Dixit 1996). But in this case, the degree of incompleteness was remarkably high by comparative standards.

Rather than stating clearly who does what, the Spanish Constitution lists those subjects and fields on which the state had exclusive jurisdiction (art. 149) and those subjects and fields on which regions (Autonomous Communities, henceforth referred to as ACs) "were entitled to assume exclusive jurisdiction"

---

[1] This section builds on and, in part, reproduces materials originally published in Beramendi et al. (2004).
[2] For a historical analysis of this process, see De la Granja, Beramendi and Anguera (2001); and Moreno (1997).
[3] Aja (1999); and Bañón and Agranoff (1998) offer good overviews of the formal institutional aspects of the EA.

TABLE 7.1. *The Limits of the Federalization Process*

State Exclusive Domains/ Jurisdictions (art. 149.1CE).	AC Potential Exclusive Domains/Jurisdictions (art.148CE)	*State- AC (potentially)* Overlapping Domains and Jurisdictions (art. 148, 149.1)
Guidelines for the general economic activity Public Order and Safety Defense and Armed Forces General Public Finance Fiscal and Monetary Policy, Justice International Relations, including representation before the European Union Statehood and Immigration Policy Credit, Banking and Insurance Regulation Foreign Trade Transports and Communications Unemployment and Pension Benefits Authorisation to call for a referendum	Institutional Organization (Executive, Parliament, Ombudsman) Industry Handcraft Commerce Urbanism Tourism Agriculture, Farming, Cattle Raising and Stock Breeding Social Assistance and Social Services Inner Fisheries (Rivers, Lakes) Means of Transport (railway, roads) whose limits are within the AC Culture, Language and Research Policies Museums and Libraries related to the AC	SHARED JURISDICTIONS[4]: Commercial Law Penitentiary Law Intellectual and Industrial Property Labour Law Other Social Security Policies CONCURRENT JURISDICTIONS[5]: Administrative Law Health Education Environment Protection and Regulation Municipalities and Regulation of Local Entities Mass Media Building Saving Societies

(art. 148). Note here that it does not say that the political capabilities and jurisdictions listed in the article are in fact allocated to the AC. Table 7.1 presents a summary of both articles, which set up the limits of an otherwise open process.

Within this framework, several specific features are relevant to understanding the dynamics of decentralization in Spain. First, the pace at which different regions (AC) can access these competencies is very asymmetric. By asymmetry of access I refer to the existence of two alternative ways to draw up an AC's Constitution (its *Estatuto*) and, thus, set initial levels of decentralization.

---

[4] Shared Jurisdiction: the Spanish Parliament legislates and the AC implements the legislation in those domains.
[5] Concurrent Jurisdiction: the State legislates the basic guidelines in the domain, establishing what is to be considered basic nation-wide. Under such guidelines, the AC are entitled both to legislate and implement their own legislation. As we shall see in coming sections, how to define what "basic" means is a highly contested political issue.

Article 143CE of the Spanish Constitution presents the standard procedure: provinces are the unit of references for the process. For an AC constitution to be passed, it must to be approved by two-thirds of the local electorate, whose population represents the majority in each province or island involved. The initial level of power for each AC shall be adopted within the limits presented in Table 7.1. Once the constitution is passed, the initial level of power will not be susceptible to any expansion for five years (art. 148.2CE). In relation to this procedure, the second method of access (art.151CE) is exceptional because, after introducing a few additional requirements, it allows faster and more far-reaching initial access to powers. And, even more importantly, it removes the five-year limit on the possibility of acquiring control over further domains and jurisdictions. The rationale underlying this distinction is rooted in the political need to allow those regions with strong and fairly mobilized national identities to avoid the constraints applicable to the rest of the country. In fact, the final dispositions of the constitutional text state clearly that those territories enjoying full access to autonomy in the past could proceed along the lines of this second access method.

But real politics could not be kept so simple. At the very early stages of the process, the Union of the Democratic Center (UCD) launched an attempt to distinguish between two levels of autonomy: the maximum level constitutionally recognized (autonomy for Catalonia and the Basque Country[6]), and the minimum level for the rest of the country. In this proposal, the approval process for the constitutions of regions in the second group was to be the same as for any other ordinary law, with no further institutional protection. Political pressures and mobilizations in Galicia (the third region with a formally approved constitution during the II Republic) and Andalucia frustrated the UCD's attempt. In the end, all Estatutos (AC constitutions) had the same level of national constitutional protection, but very different levels of content. The Basque Country, Catalonia, Galicia, and Andalucia achieved much higher levels of autonomy than the rest of the regions, with the exception of the Canary Islands and the Comunitat Valenciana after they joined the high-autonomy group in late 1982. As we shall see below, the consequences of this gap were far reaching for both the political dynamics of the system and the evolution of fiscal arrangements.

---

[6] The constant presence of a violent terrorist organization claiming independence in the Basque Country must be regarded as a major and special source of asymmetry. Violence has altered the structure of the bargaining process and modified the relative position that one major actor, the Basque Nationalist Party (PNV), would have had otherwise. In fact, the evolution of both the political profile and the strategies of this party illustrate my case clearly. Because of violence, the PNV's position is that of a gatekeeper, with one foot in each world. It generates both costs and constraints (impossible full acceptance of the Constitution, risk of being blamed from both sides), but also further bargaining resources (monopoly in the management of any possible solution, in the relations with Madrid, in the relations with the social network of ETA) which have allowed the Basque Country to achieve and maintain the highest levels of political autonomy (Corcuera 1991: 70–125).

The second feature relevant to understanding the dynamics of decentralization in Spain is the lack of a precise definition of the initial level of power to be adopted by each AC. Consistent with the asymmetry of access to different levels of power, the actual content of each constitution was open subject to political contention. They were not fixed a priori (art. 148.3 CE). In addition, the system contemplates some "catching-up" mechanisms, allowing the revision and expansion of the levels of decentralization initially achieved. So, for instance, the state has the capacity through specific procedures to decentralize those domains that, being under its jurisdiction, happen to be susceptible to delegation (art. 150.2). Moreover, every AC has the possibility to expand its level of power five years after the approval of the Estatuto (art. 148.2). But the Spanish Constitution also includes some clauses that could well allow the state to slow down, or even undo, part of the decentralization process on behalf of the general interest. Everything was left to further political bargaining; hence the importance of the organization of political representation.

Electoral Asymmetry and Centripetal Representation

The Spanish electoral system is one of proportional representation, built upon the D'Hondt Law. It was originally designed both to overrepresent rural provinces (with lower levels of population density and a higher likelihood to opt for conservative forces) and to ensure the generation and stabilization of a two-party political system at the national level (Montero 1998: 53–80). Electoral asymmetry refers to the differences in electoral success of political forces representing exclusively regional interests. In other words, it depicts the differences (in terms of presence and political capacity) between nationalist parties in the national political institutions. Table 7.2 maps these differences by presenting a summary of the distribution of parliamentary seats between 1977 and 2008.

In both respects it must be regarded as successful, according to the very simple evidence presented in Table 7.2. For instance, the communists (PCE/IU) have never been able to obtain any representation in 34 out of the 52 provinces of Spain, in spite of being a fairly stable political force in the national Parliament. Also, the examples of the CDS (Centro Democrático y Social) and the notorious failure of the PRD (Partido Reformista Democrático) help support this case.[7] But this electoral system has allowed for those nationalist parties with a high presence in their regions, the PNV (Basque Nationalist Party) and CiU (Nationalist Party of Catalonia), and later on CC (Coalición Canaria), to have an almost constant and growing presence in the Parliament of Madrid. This differential in terms of social and political presence has conditioned the formation and evolution of Spanish federalism from its very early stages. During the

---

[7] The founding of the PRD was an attempt to construct from Catalonia a reformist, countrywide party. The CDS was a party created by Adolfo Suarez after the collapse of the UCD, the center-right party heading Spain.

TABLE 7.2. *General Elections: Distribution of Seats in the Spanish Central Parliament – Lower Chamber (Total Number: 350)*

	1977	1979	1982	1986	1989	1993	1996
PCE/IU	12	23	4	7	17	18	21
CiU	2	8	12	18	18	17	16
PNV/EA	2	7	8	6	7	6	6
EE	1	1	1	2	2	–	–
BNG	0	0	0	0	0	0	2
UV	0	0	0	1	2	1	1
ERC	1	1	1	0	2	1	1
UPC/AIC/C	0	1	0	1	1	4	4
PA	0	5	0	0	2	0	0
CDS	–	–	2	19	14	–	–
UPN	0	1	0	0	0	0	0
PAR	–	1	0	1	1	1	0
UCD	165	168	12	–	–	–	–
PSOE	103	121	202	184	175	159	141
AP-CD-CP-P	16	9	106	105	106	141	156

Source: Ministerio del Interior (Secretary for Home Affairs), official publications of electoral results.

periods 1993–96 and 1996–2000 the political capacity of certain nationalisms has increased remarkably. Due to a combination of several factors, which we will discuss later, region-based nationalist parties have become a key factor in achieving a stable government when neither the socialist nor the conservative party has an absolute majority. As Linz and Montero (1999) have pointed out, PNV, CC, and CiU share the double condition of having strong coalition potential in the central parliament and holding office in their regions.

Absence of Institutionalized Cosovereignty: Regions Do Not Formally Participate in the Production of National Legislation

Traditional and well-established definitions of federalism present it as a mix of self-rule and shared rule (Elazar 1987). At this point we may safely argue that after twenty years of permanent decentralization, Spain qualifies as "federal" in all respects related to the first dimension. But it can also be argued that, in terms of shared rule, Spain does not qualify as federalist at all. Shared rule implies a systematic, coordinated, and institutionalized means for making all those decisions affecting both realms of power in such a way that both nationwide and regionally bounded interests are represented and protected. Yet unlike Germany or Canada, to cite just two examples, there is no institution performing such a function in the Spanish political system. There is a fairly limited number of arenas for cooperation. The Fiscal and Financial Policy Council, and the regular meetings of all national and regional ministers for specific policy areas (Colomer 1998: 49–55).[8] There is also a Senate. And even though, oddly enough, the Spanish Constitution presents it as "the Chamber for territorial representation" (art. 69.1), neither the way it is elected nor the array of its functions are those of a federal second chamber. The vast majority of its members are elected at the same time as the members of the national parliament. And, more importantly, on the same territorial basis – the province (CE art. 69.2 to 69.4). Each province is allocated four seats, totaling 208 of the 256 seats. The remaining seats are appointed by the different AC regional parliaments. Each AC must appoint one senator by default plus one more per million inhabitants within its boundaries (art. 69.5). They make up the balance of seats, between 44 and 48 depending on the year. As a result of this election method, the Senate's composition resembles that of the national parliament. This in turn makes its real institutional influence very small, and its capacity as a forum in which to represent territorial interests nonexistent. In cases of disagreement, the Lower House always prevails (CE art. 90.2).

The absence of institutionalized cooperation brings about two major consequences.[9] First, the Constitutional Court remains the final and last instance to resolve contentions about the distribution of policy domains, jurisdictions and duties (Aja 2003: 148–158). Second, actors engage in an endless process of negotiations, in which mutual pressures and exchanges share just one feature: bilateralism. And this is, in turn, intimately linked to the last pillar of the original contract, fiscal asymmetry.

Fiscal Asymmetry and the Status Quo

Finally, fiscal asymmetry refers to the constitutional facilitation and further political development of a two-fold system of fiscal federalism in Spain. Two regimes are at work: the general or common one, applied to 15 out of 17 AC;

---

[8] León and Ferrin (2009) document the existence of twenty-five field specific intergovernmental conferences. Their assessment suggests a very uneven role for these institutions, and a high degree of partisan interferences by conservatives (PP) and socialists (PSOE).

[9] Some minor devices to promote cooperation and coordination among the different levels of government have been launched. Among all of the devices, two deserve attention: the *Conferencias Sectoriales* (Sector Conferences) and the *Acuerdos de Cooperación entre el Estado y las Comunidades Autónomas* (Cooperation Agreements between the States and the AC). The former are basically policy-specific realms to exchange information and carry out consultative functions (Cruz Villalón 1990; STC 76/1983). The latter have been established as a joint effort in specific fields or projects (such as public works or joint programs; see Aja 2003:221; Albertí Rovira 1996: 616–636) and channel a considerable amount of resources. Given the relative increase in the use of these two arrangements, there has been substantial discussion and conflict about their scope and nature. It has forced the Constitutional Court to explicitly rule out the possibility that either of these two mechanisms may mean any change or constraint in the policy domains allocated to the AC. In spite of the fact that they provide arenas for interaction among the different layers of power, neither can be considered an alternative form of institutionalized cooperation.

Spain, 1978–2007

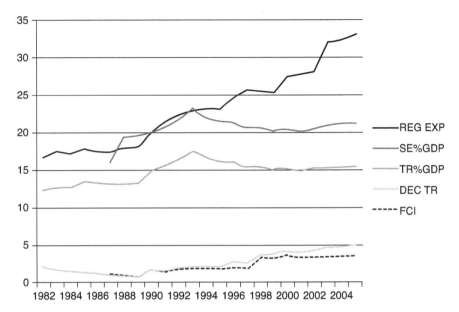

FIGURE 7.1. Evolution of Spain's Fiscal Structure

and the special one, applied only in the Basque Country and Navarra (Aja 1999: 172–198; Monasterio et al. 1995). These two AC collect their own income, corporate, and VAT taxes, transferring after a fixed quota to the central state administration. The rest of the ACs' revenues are apportioned by the central state. Of the total revenues received by these regions, State transfers represent more than 95%.[10] The remaining comes from the very limited number of taxes that AC and local councils are entitled to impose. As a result of the dual character of the institutions ruling fiscal federalism in Spain, only Navarra and the Basque Country enjoy the necessary conditions to be fiscally accountable and responsive. As for the other fifteen (including Galicia, Catalonia, and Andalucia) the institutional design adopted generated a gap, growing over time, between their capacity to spend and their capacity to collect revenues. These are the political and institutional conditions that shape the evolution of Spain's fiscal structure.

ECONOMIC GEOGRAPHY AND DISTRIBUTIVE IMPLICATIONS OF FISCAL STRUCTURES

Figure 7.1 presents a number of indicators on the evolution of Spanish fiscal structure: REG EXP captures the share of regional expenditure over total

---

[10] For more detailed information about the structure of fiscal revenues in Spain see Valle (1996: 2–26). On page 18, he analyzes the structure of fiscal revenues. The AC percentage is 1.72 %, whereas local councils' is 2.76 %.

expenditure by all levels of government in Spain (national, regional, and local).[11] The second series (SE%GDP) displays the evolution of total social expenditure as a percentage of GDP. Next, I present the same indicator but focusing only on welfare state transfers and excluding health and active labor market programs (TR%GDP). The next indicator (DCE TR) measures the proportion of welfare state transfers that are actually decentralized. Finally, I include a measure of the proportion of all interregional transfers that has a clear redistributive purpose (the Fondo de Compensacion Interterritorial, or FCI).

This figure brings out a number of interesting patterns. Clearly, there has been a fast-paced process of decentralization on the expenditure side, primarily due to the steady transfer of powers to regional governments in areas such as infrastructural development, education, and more recently, the decentralization of health expenditures to all AC. Interestingly, this process has taken place along with a significant increase in levels of social policy effort. This increase has the same trend for services (mostly health) and for welfare transfers, and was concentrated between the period immediately following the general strike of 1988 and the economic recession in 1993. From the mid-1990s onward, income transfers have essentially remained stable until 2004–2005, whereas the effort in public services increases slightly during the early 2000s. Overall, these data reveal that decentralization and social policy expansion can coexist perfectly over sustained periods of time. The data also reveal two other interesting features of Spain's fiscal structures. Notably, the decentralization of public expenditures has hardly affected income transfers. At the end of the period of scrutiny, barely 4 to 5% of all income transfers are controlled by regional authorities. This percentage corresponds mostly to a plethora of social assistance and minimum income schemes put forward by regional governments since the late 1990s (Moreno 2007; Nogera and Ubasart 2003). These policy initiatives notwithstanding, the bulk of transfers in the Spanish welfare state remain under control of the central government. Finally, as the process of decentralization unfolds the amount of interregional transfers also grows. As regions assume control over infrastructure, education, and health, the government transfers more and more resources to enable them to meet the costs of providing such services. As the size of these transfers grows, so does the demand for resource redistribution between regions. Interestingly, the share of total transfers specifically and purposefully devoted to interregional redistribution (FCI) accounts for a very small proportion of interregional transfers. This small share is potentially deceiving though. Recall that this book defines

---

[11] The sources for the different series are as follows: REG EXP, data provided by the Ministry of Finace; data on total social expenditure as a percentage of GDP (SE%GDP) and income transfers as a percentage of GDP (TR%GDP) come from the OECD Social Expenditure Database (2009); likewise, the index of decentralization of welfare transfers (DEC TR) is computed as the ratio between the budgetary importance of decentralized transfers to the value of total welfare transfers on the basis of the OECD social expenditure database. Finally, the share of the FCI relative to total interregional transfers makes use of the BADESPE database (Institute for Fiscal Studies, Ministry of Finance).

interregional redistribution as transfers of resources from rich to poor regions that allow the latter to exercise political discretion on the transfers received. In addition to these relatively small tranfers, the Spanish system contains a number of programs that commit interregional redistribution of resources to the provision of certain services by regional governments, most notably education and healthcare. The more services provided by the region, the higher its budgetary needs. Accordingly, there are a number of programs in place to bridge the gap between resources and needs across all ACs.[12]

The combined effect of service provision decentralization, the increase in transfers to regions, and the centralized nature of income transfers generates very high levels of redistribution across territories in Spain. The fiscal flows of public expenditure in general, and social security in particular, generate significant redistributive effects across regions. These flows shape Spain's geography of income inequality and nurture distributive tensions between those parties and regions benefiting from the status quo and those parties and regions that feel unduly exploited by an excessively centralized fiscal structure. Figures 7.2 and 7.3 and Table 7.3 examine more closely the nature of these effects and the main patterns in Spain's geography of inequality. Figure 7.2 displays, for different periods of time, the relationship between GDP per capita and the net regional balance in terms of all policies by the central public administration. Figure 7.3 displays a similar analysis but focusing more narrowly on the territorial incidence of contributory social security. Finally, Figure 7.4 exploits a series of household budget surveys[13] to compute the level of inequality by region and over time between 1984 and 2000.[14]

Throughout the period 1991–2005 there is a very strong and negative correlation between regional GDP per capita and the net balance obtained by each of the regions. This applies both to the overall central public administration activity (Figure 7.2) and to the flows of contributory social security (Figure 7.3). Though the relative positions of specific AC changes within each period,

---

[12] These include the *Fondo de Garantia*, created for the period 1997–2000 to ensure that all ACs could meet the demand for public services; and the *Fondo de Suficiencia*, a fund that covers the gap between ACs' budgetary needs and the resources obtained (either through their own taxation or other funds). These additional transfers are conditional, that is, tied to the provision of specific services on behalf of the central government until 2001, and unconditional after 2001, when most regions assume control of health policy and the resources to cope with it. Because these are levelling funds, they are automatically reduced if, for instance, fiscal autonomy increases and regions collect more revenues through their own taxes. The definition of budgetary needs, and therefore of the leveling needs, was very comprehensive and included all policy domains. Since 2009, the levelling of needs applies only to education, health, and social services.

[13] Througout this section the indicator of inequality used is the Gini coefficient for household income per equivalent adult at the regional level. These figures are calculated by the author on the basis of the income surveys available at the Luxembourg Income Study.

[14] The lines in Figures 7.2 through 7.4 correspond to the average values of the variables displayed in the x and y axis.

reflecting, among other things, differences in the time when control over different policy areas was assumed, the negative association between regional income and net balances shows remarkable stability over time. Most cases are concentrated in the top-left and bottom-right quadrants. Over time the internal composition of these two quadrants remains fairly constant as well. Among the core beneficiaries of the system are Galicia, Asturias, Andalucia, Extremadura, and Castilla La Mancha. In contrast, the funds flowing into these regions originate primarily from Madrid, Catalonia, and Illes Baleares. The Basque Country and Navarra are also net contributors but, because of their special arrangements, their net contribution is smaller than it would be if they were part of the common system. This is reflected by the fact that both regions are actually net recipients of total fiscal flows despite having a GDP per capita comparable to that of Madrid, Baleares, or Catalonia. In addition, and despite being part of the common social security system, the Basque Country has also managed to maintain a position of relative privilege with respect to the social security system. Though in this case it is a net contributor, its actual balance is consistently much closer to the average than that of Catalonia, Madrid, or Baleares.

Not surprisingly, the redistributive nature of fiscal flows translates directly into the geography of inequality. Table 7.3 conveys this point forcefully: the gap in terms of income inequality between regions is much smaller than the gap in

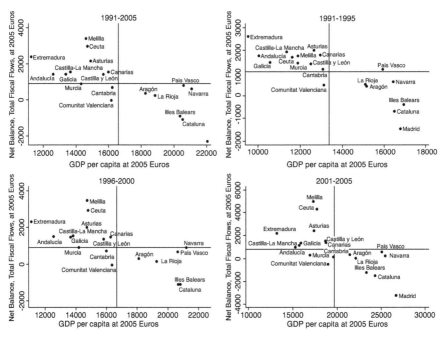

FIGURE 7.2. Net Balance in Total Fiscal Flows (1991–2005) (*Source:* Uriel and Barberán 2007)

Spain, 1978–2007

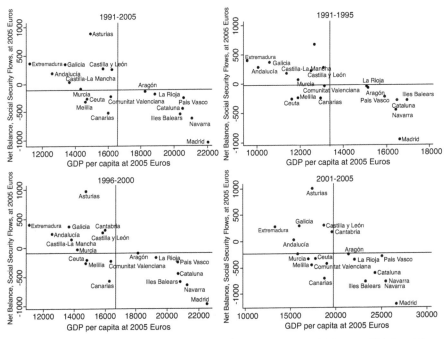

FIGURE 7.3. Net Balance in Social Security Flows (1991–2005) (*Source:* Uriel and Barberán 2007)

terms of income per capita. While the coefficient of variation in regional GDP per capita remains at .20, the same indicator for the incidence of inequality is much lower (.07). Also, between 1984 and 2000 there is a reduction in cross-regional differences in GDP per capita.

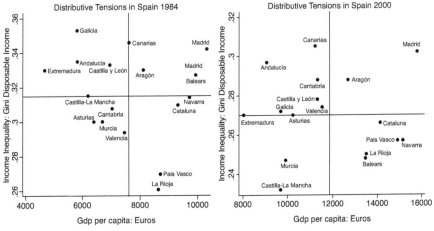

FIGURE 7.4. Income per capita and Inequality across Regions in Spain

TABLE 7.3. *The Geography of Income and Inequality in Spain: An Overview*

	Average Regional GDP pc	Gini	CV* Regional GDP pc	CV* Regional Gini
1984	7607	.31	.21	0.08
1990	9655	.30	.20	0.07
2000	11856	.27	.19	0.07

* CV stands for coefficient of variation.

Over the same period of time there is also a reduction in the level of income inequality in Spain. In 1984, the average Gini coefficient of household disposable income per equivalent adult is 0.31; in 2000, it drops to 0.27. Accordingly, the spread between regions becomes slightly narrower in 2000. Nonetheless, there are clearly three groups of regions within Spain's economic geography in 1984: a group of regions that are highly unequal and relatively poor (these include most prominently Galicia, Andalucia, Extremadura, and both Castilla la Mancha and Castilla-Leon); a group of wealthier and relatively more equal regions (the Basque Country and Catalonia); and finally, a group of wealthier and relatively unequal regions (Madrid and Baleares).

Over time, the composition of the groups sees some changes, ultimately reflecting the very consequences of fiscal policy and decentralization between 1984 and 2000. Clearly, transfers toward poorer regions bring the level of inequality in the first group down, in particular in regions like Galicia and Extremadura. In relative terms, inequality also declines among the net contributors (Catalonia and, especially, Baleares, now joining the group of rich and relatively equal regions). In turn, Madrid remains as the prominent rich and highly unequal region of Spain. Overall, however, there is still a contrast between a group of poor and relatively more unequal regions (Andalucia being the most prominent example) and a group of rich and relatively more equal regions (the Basque Country and Catalonia being the most prominent examples). The former also happens to be the bigger beneficiaries of net flows in the Spanish fiscal structure, while the latter (in particular Catalonia, Baleares, and Madrid), are the main contributors to the common pool (see Figures 7.2 and 7.3).

According to the model of preference formation developed in Chapter 2, the first group should support the status quo, as they receive large benefits through both interpersonal (social security) and interregional redistribution. In contrast, I would expect the second group to reduce the share of their tax base devoted to distributive conflicts beyond their regional borders. Hence, I would expect the main political parties in Catalonia, Baleares, and the Basque country to push for more fiscal autonomy and the decentralization of public insurance systems, raising the flag of fairness and efficiency. And I would expect the main parties in Galicia, Andalucia, Extremadura, and

Castilla-la-Mancha to push for protection of the status quo, championing solidarity and equality. To be sure, political contentions over the fiscal structure in Spain reflect this logic. In the next section, I explore how these contentions have evolved over time, and the conditions under which those demanding change have managed to achieve partial reforms to the system. I pay particular attention to two policy areas: the timing and pace of the regionalization of the income tax, as part of broader changes in Spain's fiscal arrangements; and the fate of the case to decentralize social security.

ENDOGENOUS DECENTRALIZATION AND CHANGES TO THE STATUS QUO: THE PARTIAL ACHIEVEMENT OF FISCAL AUTONOMY AND THE RESILIENCE OF SOCIAL SECURITY

In addition to the distributive tensions between a group of wealthier and relatively more equal regions (Catalonia, the Basque Country) and a group of poorer and relatively more unequal regions (Andalucia, Extremadura, Galicia), the Spanish process of decentralization reflects a fundamental tension between those seeking the reduction of asymmetries across policy realms (including revenue generation and allocation) and those seeking to maintain them. The Basque Country and Catalonia are not only richer and more equal. They are also regions where a different national identity has been mobilized by parties that have long enjoyed a dominant position in the regions' political spectrum, the PNV in the Basque Country and CiU in Catalonia. Moreover, these parties are influential players in the national parliament. The presence of national identity as a second dimension introduces a centrifugal element that counterbalances an otherwise centripetal institutional design and contributes to shaping the dynamics of political and fiscal decentralization in Spain. In the case of the Basque Country and Catalonia, national identity reinforces the distributive incentives to seek a more decentralized fiscal structure. At first, national parties resist these pressures. Over time however, the political influence of these forces changes with important consequences for the evolution of Spain's fiscal structure. By way of background, a brief overview of the dynamics of decentralization in Spain follows.

After the initial steps of Spain's federalization process, the first big inflection point came with the launching of the *I Acuerdos Autonómicos* (First Autonomous Agreements), signed by both the PSOE and UCD in 1981. This was the very first attempt to control the emerging dynamics of the system, since at the early stages of Spanish democracy no avoidable instability could be afforded. The failed coup d' état in February 1981 provides us with a good indicator of the complexity of the environment at the time. The objectives pursued by the Socialists and the UCD government are easily traceable through the contents of the Agreements (MAP-1982): clarification and generalization of the number and institutional design of all of the ACs in the process of being formed; adoption of a common position regarding the fiscal arrangements to be implemented; and, last but certainly not least, the creation of a law aimed at harmonizing the decentralization process, the LOAPA (*Ley Organica de Armonizacion del Proceso Autonómico*). This law was the first major event in the tension between harmonization and asymmetries. It created a conflict about the real meaning of the process of decentralization. As an answer to this conflict, the Constitutional Court formulated two far-reaching qualifications of the notion of autonomy. In its ruling 37/1981, the Court legitimated differences in the way citizens are treated by the different realms of power. Civil rights are regarded as the only field in which absolute equality must be guaranteed. Subsequently in its ruling 73/1983, it overrode most of the LOAPA and established that the *Estatutos de Autonomia* (AC Constitutions, henceforth referred to as EA) enjoyed a constitutional status well above ordinary legislation. Autonomy was constitutionally protected thereafter (Aja 1999: 65).

The First Autonomous Agreements had further consequences. They ended the first phase of federalization, and autonomy became embodied in the newly elected institutions. Following the elections on May 8, 1983, thirteen new regions (ACs) were finally on stage. The decade 1983–1993 was marked by a process of expansion and consolidation of the Estado de las Autonomias, mainly driven by the three consecutive governments of Felipe Gonzalez who benefited from an absolute majority in Parliament (see PSOE in Table 7.2).

Most of the intense transfer of power activity during this period involves the construction of regional political institutions and administration, as well as the shifting of some elementary services formerly provided by the central government to the regions. After 1986, the process slows down significantly. In the particular case of the Basque Country this is very much related to the issue of violence. For the rest of the ACs it just indicates an intensification of institutional conflict between several levels of government. As a result, the Constitutional Court had to assume the key political role of resolving many of the open aspects of Spanish federalism during these years. Levels of tension about who had the right to do what rose rapidly during the mid-1980s. The strong parliamentary majority of the socialists during this period facilitated bringing issues to the Constitutional Court, if bilateral exchange failed. If the disagreement was about legislation approved by either level of government and the other disagreed, the expected outcome was an appeal questioning the constitutionality of the law. Conflicts involved some of the most important policy fields, such as education, environment, and health. Not surprisingly, the high number of conflicts between 1983 and 1991 introduced significant delays in the development of programs in these fields and, in turn, in the overall pace of the decentralization process.

At the end of the period socialists (PSOE) and conservatives (PP) shared the view that the level of instability generated by several unresolved issues, the increasing demands for further decentralization in those AC (art. 143 CE) that were gaining autonomy at a slower pace, and the practice of bilateral exchanges demanded some sort of coordinated reaction by the two country-wide parties. As a result, the Second Autonomous Agreements (*II Acuerdos Autonómicos*) were adopted.

TABLE 7.4. *The Structure of ACs' Revenues, 1986–2002*

	1986	1991	1996	2001	2002
Revenues transferred by the Central Government[15]	80.9	78.4	72.28	70.02	47.18
Ceded taxes*[16]	11.40	14.13	10.65	19.80	48.81
Income tax	–	–	–	7.19	16.25
Participation VAT					14.48
Special taxes[17]					7.70
Others				12.60	10.39
Regional share of income tax (15%)	–	–	8.81	5.84	
Regional own taxes	0.66	1.08	1.30	1.05	0.92
Other fees and small taxes	6.01	4.5	5.7	2.5	2.2

* The taxes originally ceded to ACs in the common system are those with the least revenue generating capacity, including, for instance, inheritance and donation taxes, wealth taxes, and gambling taxes.
Source: Bosch and Durán 2005; Durán 2007.

Retrospectively, these pacts can also be seen as a temporary commitment by the two parties not to use issues concerning the institutional design of the country as opposition tools. The major effects of this agreement were twofold. On the one hand, they meant a great step forward in the overall levels of decentralization. The reform of the *Estatutos de Autonomía* allowed ACs with slower access to autonomy (art. 143 CE) to potentially receive most of the transfers enjoyed by those that achieved autonomy earlier and faster (e.g., the Basque Country, Catalonia, Galicia, and Andalusia). By 1994, the process was almost concluded except for the transfer of power over health and education policy. Somewhat paradoxically, the center-rooted parties provided, in the early 1990s, an average increase in levels of decentralization. But implicit in this expansion was the pursuit of horizontal equalization of power, which is to say, a potential decline in the levels of political asymmetry.

Throughout this period, the levels of regional fiscal autonomy are kept to a minimum. As decentralization unfolds, regions see their capacity to spend increased, but not their capacity to collect their own revenues. Table 7.4 summarizes the main revenue sources for ACs over time. Clearly, until the mid 1990s, regions have no say or direct access to the revenues raised through the main tax instruments, including the VAT and income tax. Their ability to perform policy depends largely on the transfers they receive from the central government.

---

[15] These include: funds to pay for services provided by the AC on behalf of the government as well as indirect solidarity mechanisms (Bosch and Durán 2005).
[16] The taxes originally ceded to the ACs in the common system are those with the least revenue generating capacity, including, for instance, inheritance and donation taxes, wealth taxes, gambling taxes.
[17] These include taxes on the production of carbohydrates, alcohol, and tabacco.

As a result, excluding the Basque Country and Navarra, the fiscal arrangements at work transfer large amounts of income and resources towards the less developed regions of Spain, as depicted in Figures 7.2 and 7.3. Quite unsurprisingly, the nationalist parties in relatively wealthier regions demand political protection of asymmetries and economic protection of their tax bases. Due to its harmonizing character, the Second Autonomous Agreements, contrary to their original goals, resulted in further polarization.

The Partial Achievement of Fiscal Autonomy

Interestingly, Table 7.4 captures a number of changes over time in the composition of regional revenues, giving a measure of the relative success of some ACs in pursuing fiscal autonomy. In 1996, regions are allowed to keep 15% of the income tax collected within their boundaries. By 2001, in addition, they had the freedom to adjust some of the parameters of the income tax for another 15% of income. And by 2002, the regional component of the income tax accounts for over 16% of regional revenues, whereas the share of direct transfers from the central government has dropped to 47%. Finally, the very recent reform of December 2009 implies additional steps in this direction, as it increases the share of ceded taxes to the ACs, and reduces the scope of direct intergovernmental transfers. These figures capture a process of fiscal decentralization whose political underpinnings date back to 1993.

The 1993 general elections results opened a new stage in the development of fiscal decentralization in Spain. The elections of 1993 and 1996 yielded minority governments (see Table 7.2). Neither the socialists (PSOE) in 1993 nor the conservatives (PP) in 1996 achieved enough seats to rule on their own. This prompted significant changes in the scenario of relations between central and nationalist state governments. Catalan (CiU) and/or Basque nationalists' (PNV) support was now a precondition for a stable executive in Madrid.

As a result, the case against higher levels of harmonization was now much stronger politically. Higher bilateral pressures and demands for fiscal autonomy fared better after two terms (1986–1989 and 1989–1993) in which nationalist demands were constrained by unified Socialist Party majority governments. The evolution of Spanish fiscal federal arrangements captures this process. Table 7.5 describes in detail these reforms to the territorial allocation of different Income Tax sources along with the key changes in the surrounding political conditions. Counterfactually, it is hard to think of any of those reforms being implemented under the political conditions prior to 1993.[18]

The key stages in Table 7.5 illuminate the changing interplay between demands for higher levels of fiscal autonomy (and therefore a reduction in the scope of redistribution) and the nature of the system of representation. The changes in 1993 and 1997 are directly explained by the loss of a sufficient

---

[18] Ruiz-Huerta and López Laborda (1996: 582–614) present an excellent review of the major issues associated with the implementation of these reforms.

TABLE 7.5. *The Income Tax and the Evolution of Fiscal Decentralization (1993–2009)*

Period	Political Context	Main Changes to Income Tax in Connection with Regional Financing
1993–1996	Socialist Minority Government Support by Catalan Nationalists needed in Madrid	ACs keep a 15% share of the income tax paid by their residents. Note, though, that ACs *do not* have the capacity to legislate about the income tax in their territories.
1996–2000	Conservative Minority Government Support by Catalan and Basque nationalists needed in Madrid	*1997–2001 System* – For the first time, there are two income tax tariffs, the national one that applies to 85% of income, and the regional one, that applies to 15% of income in the region. The AC tariff must have the same number of brackets as the national one. Also, ACs can manipulate the tax deductions applicable to this 15%. – In addition, ACs continue to keep 15% of the overall income tax paid by their residents. – Importantly, Andalucia, Extremadura, and Castilla-la-Mancha opt out of the new system and continue to operate under the pre-1997 framework.
2000–2002	Conservative Majority Government Exacerbation of tension between Basque Parties (PNV) and Catalan (CIU, ERC) Nationalist Parties and the Conservative Government. Attempt to harmonize and close the system through bi-partisan agreement: – Full Decentralization of Health Policy – Need to increase regional financial Autonomy – Increase in the overall contribution to the system of regional financing by the central government	*2002 Reform* The number of ceded taxes increases (VAT, 35%; Special taxes, 40%). The share of the income tax on which the ACs' tariffs apply increases to 33%. Increase in the number of deductions available to ACs in their share (including deductions for first residence) Increase of regulatory freedom in other ceded taxes such as inheritance and donation taxes, wealth taxes, gambling taxes.*

(*continued*)

TABLE 7.5 (continued)

Period	Political Context	Main Changes to Income Tax in Connection with Regional Financing
2004–2009	Minority Socialist Government Coalition government in Catalonia between Catalan Socialists and left-wing nationalist parties Support needed by Catalan nationalist parties (on the left (ERC) and occasionally on the right (CiU)) and other minority forces in parliament. 2008- General Election in 2008. Again, Socialist Minority Government in need of support by different groups to pass legislation.	*The new Constitution of Catalonia (June 2006):* – The share of the income tax claimed by Catalonia increases to 50%. – The share of the VAT and Special Taxes raises up to 58%. – Establishes a legal limit to the effects on Catalonia of the equalization system: Catalonia shall not lose its relative position in terms of GDP per capita because of redistribution towards other regions (see Table 7.6). – It sets a minimum level of investment by the national government in Catalonia proportional to Catalonia's GDP share within Spain. *December 2009 Reform:* Essentially, a generalization of the system built in the June 2006 Constitution of Catalonia: a) ACs' share of VAT limited to 50% b) ACs' share of Special taxes to 58% c) ACs' share of income tax kept at 50% The equalization of financial capacity between regions for the purposes of public service provision is limited to three policy fields: health, education, and social services. Everything else is excluded from the calculation of regions' expenditure needs.

* See Cabré-Durán (2007: 113) for details.
Sources: Bosch and Durán (2005); Durán (2007); León-Alfonso (2007); and Maldonado and Gomez-Sala (2003).

majority in Madrid. In 1993, the centripetal mechanisms originally devised during the transition fail to deliver for the first time. The PSOE falls short of 16 seats to reach a sufficient majority and engages in negotiations with Catalan nationalists. Two themes dominated Felipe Gonzalez's speech requesting Parliament's support: reopening the process of legislative implementation of the constitutions of Catalonia and the Basque Country, and pursuing fiscal coresponsibility between levels of government.[19] While the concessions approved in October 1993 were not all that radical, they shaped future interactions (Bosch and Durán 2005). Allowing ACs to retain 15% of the payments made by their residents set the precedent that the territorial organization of the income tax was negotiable.

The elections of 1996 yielded another minority government, this time led by the conservative party (PP) and with a larger margin to fill through agreements with Catalan (CiU) and Basque nationalists (PNV). Interestingly, the same party that accused the PSOE of rendering Spain for sale during the previous term proved much more receptive towards the nationalists' demands for fiscal autonomy in 1996–1997. For the first time, ACs of the so-called "common regime" had the option to assume legislative capacity on the income tax, as detailed in Table 7.5. CiU also extracted additional funds to cover the expenditure needs generated by the decentralized provision of health care, which Catalonia had had since 1981. In addition, the PNV extracted a number of important concessions. In particular, they obtained additional funding for vocational training policies and support for a renewal of the Cupo and the Concierto (the Basque Country and Navarra's special fiscal arrangements) in the context of which the Basque government's fiscal autonomy increased significantly.[20]

The political agreements in 1993 and 1996 reflect the logic behind the interplay between economic geography and political representation: the distributive consequences of existing fiscal structures (Figures 7.2. and 7.3) bolster the demands for fiscal autonomy by net contributors on both interregional transfers and Social Security. In turn, these demands translate into actual changes in the fiscal structure only when national parties fail to obtain a majority in

---

[19] *Source:* Spanish Parliament, Diario de Sesiones. To explain the privileged position of nationalist parties in the period 1993 to 1996, one must understand that their electoral success is a necessary, though not sufficient, condition given the fact that the sum of the votes of the PSOE and IU would be enough to support a stable government (see Table 7.2). The enormous difference between the socialists and the communists regarding the European Union process and the guidelines of economic policy must be brought into the picture in order to understand why the CiU nationalists were able to achieve a much higher political capacity to impose their preferences. At the same time, however, the feasibility of alternative coalitions limited de facto the demands by Catalan nationalists. For further references see Linz and Montero (1999); and Maravall (1999: 154–197).

[20] In particular, they gained full control over: income tax (with freedom to deviate up to 20% from the tariffs set by the central government), special taxes (tobacco and alcohol once the state monopoly ceased to exist), environmental regulations, and the issuing of academic degrees. See Ley 38/97 de Modificacion del Concierto Economico Vasco.

the national Parliament, that is, when the political levers originally devised in 1978 fail to contain the electoral dominance of nationalist parties in Catalonia and the Basque Country.

The interplay between economic geography and fiscal structures also emerges through the behavior of those regions benefiting from the status quo. After the 1997 agreement of a regional financing system until 2001, Andalusia, Extremadura, and Castilla-la-Mancha decided to opt out of the new system, rejecting the increase in fiscal autonomy offered by the reform, and staying under the umbrella of the previous system. According to the analyses above (Figures 7.2 and 7.3), all three regions, key electoral strongholds for the Socialist Party, clearly benefited from a more integrated and highly redistributive fiscal structure. Given that they had the option, it is hardly surprising that they chose not to accept higher levels of fiscal autonomy. On the other hand, among those regions controlled by the conservatives (PP), two groups emerge: those that endorse the reform as they benefit from it (e.g., Madrid or Valencia); and those whose concerns were ironed out by the fact that the central government targeted additional resources so that they also enjoyed more resources at their disposal than under the previous system(e.g., Galicia or Castilla-Leon).[21]

The reform of 2001 presents a puzzle. Given that the conservative party (PP) enjoys an absolute majority from March 2000 and before 1996 never supported fiscal decentralization, what accounts for its support for higher levels of autonomy in 2001–2002? To address this question it is important to revisit the tension between harmonization and asymmetry at the core of the politics of decentralization in Spain (Beramendi and Maiz 2004; León-Alfonso 2007). During the years of minority government, nationalist parties pursued an agenda that went beyond the design of fiscal structures and advocated a more encompassing constitutional reform.

Indeed, in July 1998 the PNV (Basque Country), CiU (Catalonia), and the BNG (Galicia) committed to create a working partnership to pursue a rather indeterminate "con-federal" solution to what they perceived as a lack of articulation of the multiple national identities within the Spanish State.[22] Leaving aside the vagueness of their statements, these three parties agreed upon a set of *minima* for the constitutional reform: 1) explicit acknowledgment of the plurinational character of Spain, with the only subjects of sovereignty being their three historical ACs and Castilla (a term referring to the rest of Spain); 2) the transformation of the Senate into a perfectly asymmetrical territorial chamber; 3) the establishment in Galicia and Catalonia of the special fiscal regime currently enjoyed by the Basque Country and Navarra; 4) the reform of the Constitutional Court so that they can take part in the appointment of its members and have some representation on it; 5) the achievement of full

---

[21] León (2009) offers a detailed analysis of how different national governments use this strategy to smooth out resistance to change among those benefiting from the status quo.
[22] The contents and principles of these proposals can be found in the background documents of the Barcelona, Gasteiz, and Santiago meetings.

external representation before the European Union; and finally 6) the decentralization of the Social Security system. These positions provoked two different responses. The socialists (PSOE) seek to reform the Spanish Constitution along a federalist path[23] and the conservatives (PP) seek to defend it as it is.

In March 2000 the PP won the national election by a margin that allowed it to rule on its own. Meanwhile, the reactivation of terrorism after the 1998–1999 truce and growing disagreements with the PNV as to how to pursue peace in the Basque Country, exacerbated debates about both the EA and the path towards its reform. As a result, positions became more extreme. While the Basque nationalists (PNV and Eusko Alkartasuna) openly advocated a radically new institutional framework that would situate the Basque Country outside the EA framework, albeit still "associated" with the Crown, the PP declared the Constitution untouchable and warned against any discourse proposing its reform, regardless of its content. After 2000, such discourse became the axis of a neo-centrist approach to institutional reform.[24] As a reaction to the neo-centralist approach, the demand for a reform of the Constitution of Catalonia (henceforth referred to as CoC) grew stronger and more radical, triggering a process of competition within Catalonia as to who could best champion its interests. In fact, both the Catalan right-wing nationalists (CiU) and the Catalan socialists (PSC-PSOE) put forward proposals that advocate direct representation at the EU, adoption of a fiscal regime similar to the one in the Basque Country and Navarra, and recognition of Catalonia as a nation within a plurinational state.[25] In brief, due to a neo-centralist twist of the PP in the last legislative term, disagreements regarding the EA have became more bitter and visible.

This is the canvas on which political negotiations regarding regional financing after the 1997–2001 period began. The goal of Aznar's government was to reach an agreement that would "close" the system, thereby reducing the levels of asymmetry between the ACs in the "common system." The reform was

---

[23] The full contents of the socialist proposal are available in their document *La Estructura del Estado. Politica Autonomica y Municipal del PSOE* (The Structure of the State. Regional and Local Policy), 1998. The PSOE proposal shares very little with the nationalist proposals. The only foreseeable points of agreement may concern the representation of ACs in the European Union. But even that is dubious, given their fundamental disagreement as to who should be the major collective actors. For the nationalists, not all ACs should be entitled to such a representative capacity. For the socialists, there is no question that the existing seventeen AC must have representation. Moreover, their proposals show further and clearer differences on more specific aspects: equality, as opposed to asymmetry, should guide a general reform of fiscal federalism in Spain; cooperation and intergovernmental coordination are the principles needed for a stable development of the system; and finally, the reform of the Senate should be as symmetrical as possible.

[24] In this framework, the federalist solution proposed by the PSOE was considered a dangerous game that objectively facilitated the ultimate goals of those aiming to destroy the EA.

[25] A comparative analysis of these proposals was published by El Pais (March 2006, p. 30). The full version of the proposal by the Catalan socialists is contained in the document *Bases per a l'elaboracio de l'Estatut Catalunya*.

also influenced by the ACs' sharp increase in budgetary needs, as closing the system implied transferring health policy to ten of the seventeen ACs that had not yet assumed this responsibility.[26] This transfer had huge budgetary implications (Urbanos and Utrilla 2001), and required an increase in the amount of revenues under regional governments' control. This situation triggered the reform of 2001, and a significant increase in levels of regional fiscal autonomy vis-à-vis the central government. Indeed, as captured by Table 7.3, the level of AC dependence on direct transfers from the central government drops from 70% in 2001 to 47% in 2002.

Interestingly, the reform was unanimously accepted by the representatives of all ACs, including all the socialist strongholds that had opted out of the 1997 system. There are two reasons for this unanimity. First, the reform increases both the levels of fiscal autonomy and the total revenues available to all ACs. To secure the agreement, the central government transferred enough funds to ensure that no region was financially worse off in the new system (León 2009: 73–74). This, in turn, created strong financial incentives for socialists ACs to support the system and, as a result, caused much intraparty debate.

The bargaining process leading up to the 2001 reform reflects the second factor undermining the centripetal nature of the system of representation. As decentralization unfolds, so does the balance of power between political elites at different levels of government (Amat, Jurado and León 2010; León-Alfonso 2007). Over time, decentralization alters party organizations by undermining the effective power of national leaders: the electoral center of gravity shifts. Regional elites become more salient, and their electoral needs more pressing, thereby altering the workings of the system of representation and limiting the ability of national elites to establish policy positions.[27] Indeed, by 2001, the ability of socialist party national leaders to impose a particular policy position upon their regional counterparts had declined significantly.

Rather than trying to block the reform as part of their opposition strategy, national leaders of the Socialist Party became part of the lobbying effort to maximize the resources obtained by those regions entering the new system.[28] Zapatero, the socialist leader at the time, became a coordinator among regional executives in an effort to maximize the amount of compensation received in exchange for their joining the new system and accepting the decentralization of health policy.

Once again, the passing of the reform required the transfer of additional resources to the regional financing system so that all participants in the "common system" improved their fiscal capacity relative to the previous cycle.

---

[26] These AC are: Asturias, Aragon, Baleares, Cantabria, Castilla y Leon, Castilla-La Mancha, Extremadura, La Rioja, Madrid, and Murcia.

[27] For empirical evidence on these transformations and their implications for political competition in the case of Spain see Bartomeous (2003); Heller (2002); and Van Houten (2009).

[28] Jordi Sevilla, PSOE representative during the bargaining process, was particularly focused on "compensation" to those Andalucia, Extremadura, and Castill-La Mancha for the losses they incurred by opting out of the 1997 reform (El Pais, 05/06/2001).

For instance, Andalusia received enough resources to increase its annual budget by 10% from 2001 to 2002.[29]

The results of the Catalan elections in fall 2003 and the national elections in March 2004 produce yet another change in the political conditions surrounding conflicts over fiscal structures reform. For the first time since the democratic transition, CiU loses its majority in Catalonia. A coalition government between the Catalan socialists (PSC-PSOE) and the left-wing nationalist party *Esquerra Republicana de Cataluny* (ERC) arrives in office. Shortly thereafter, the PP lose the national election, and Zapatero leads a minority government supported in Parliament by, among others, a number of left-wing nationalist organizations (ERC, BNG).

From 2004 onward, the two factors undermining the centripetal nature of the system of representation reinforce each other: a minority government in Madrid, and a decentralized branch of a national party competing against nationalist forces to champion Catalan interests in Barcelona. The door was wide open for a new push in the pursuit of fiscal autonomy. "España Plural," the socialist leitmotif against the monolithic conception of the state relished by Aznar, reached power and reopened the process to accommodate nationalism politically and, once again, reform fiscal arrangements economically.

Pasqual Maragall, president of the government of Catalonia, and his allies quickly launched the process to draft a new CoC, which included several provisions further increasing Catalonia's fiscal autonomy (as detailed in Table 7.5). In addition, this CoC affirmed the identity of Catalonia as a nation and included a wide ranging expansion of its political and judicial autonomy. Zapatero stated, to his later regret, that he would accept whatever draft was approved by the Catalan Parliament. Unsurprisingly, the conservative party (PP), yet again, beat to quarters in defense of national unity. The draft was endorsed by 90% of the Catalan Parliament and incorporated many demands of the nationalist parties. Contrary to Zapatero's earlier promise, the national Parliament intervened to ensure that this new draft fitted within the constraints of the national constitution. The process evinced the differences between the Catalan (PSC) and the national (PSOE) socialists. Table 7.6 contrasts the original language of the draft approved by the Parliament of Catalonia with the text finally approved by the Parliament in Madrid.

Reaching an agreement on these modifications as well as on the specific terms listed in Table 7.5 was far from straightforward. Moreover, the fact that these discussions were intertwined with disagreements about the denomination of Catalonia as a nation and the architecture of judicial power did not make things easier. Catalan socialists (PSC-PSOE) were trapped between the demands of their coalition partners in Barcelona, in particular the left-wing nationalist party (ERC), and the constraints imposed by the socialist party in Madrid. In the end, the PSOE decided to change partners in Madrid and secure the passing

---

[29] *Source: El Pais*, October 9, 2001.

TABLE 7.6. *The Legislative Production of the New Constitution of Catalonia*

Version Approved by the Parliament of Catalonia (September 30, 2005)	Version after Negotiations with the PSOE in the National Parliament (June 2006)
Art. 202.3: bilateralism as a core principle guiding the legislation on regional financing for Catalonia Art. 202.4: "According to the principles of proximity and subsidiarity, what this Estatuto establishes prevails in case of a legislative conflict with the [Spanish] State" Art. 207: Limits the sources of contribution from Catalonia to the state finances Art. 209: Contributions to solidarity will ensure similar levels of resources provided that regions make a similar level of "fiscal effort" Art 210: Long list of conditions determining Catalonia's contribution to Spain's revenue system. Of them, two are particularly important: 210.2.b. Equity criteria should reflect relative population; and efficiency criteria should reflect regional income per capital and relative fiscal effort.	Art. 202.3: direct mention of bilateralism is eliminated Art. 202.4: the original article is eliminated and replaced with the following: "In agreement with art. 138.2 of the Spanish Constitution, the funding for the Generalitat must not entail discriminatory effects against Catalonia relative to other ACs. This principle must respect fully the criteria of solidarity enumerated in art. 208 of this Estatuto" Art. 207, 209, 210 are eliminated and replaced by a new draft of art. 208. This draft leaves the specifics of the financing system to further negotiation (see Table 7.4 for details) and eliminates references to relative fiscal effort. However, it introduces three important provisions: 1. The Catalan contribution to the common system will be re-evaluated every five years 2. Population, population density, immigration, and the size of cities are explicit criteria for calculating expenditure needs 3. The State will ensure that implementation of the mechanisms of equalization ("nivelación") will not alter, under any circumstances, the relative position of Catalonia in terms of income per capita before equalization takes place.*

* This provision is directly inspired by the German Constitutional Court's 1999 ruling about the FA system.

of the newly drafted CoC through an agreement with the right-wing nationalist party (CiU), adding to tensions within the local party and with their coalition partners (ERC).

Despite being trimmed, the new CoC implied a major step forward in Catalonia's pursuit of higher levels of fiscal and political autonomy. A rich and

TABLE 7.7. *The ACs Before the Reform of Regional Financing in Spain (2008–2009)*

	Net Recipient	Net Contributor
Socialist incumbent (PSOE/PSC)	Andalusia, Extremadura, Asturias, Aragon, Castilla-La Mancha	Catalonia, Baleares
Conservative incumbent (PP)	Galicia, Castilla-Leon	Madrid, Valenciana

relatively more equal region was able, once more, to introduce marginal corrections to an otherwise hyper-redistributive system. This was only possible because of: the Catalan socialists' need to compete with nationalist parties within the region, the reduced clout of the PSOE at the national level, and the latter's need for parliamentary support to secure a stable executive. The preferences derived from an uneven economic geography and changes in an originally centripetal party system jointly account for this change in Spain's fiscal structure.

The new CoC included provisions for yet another round of revising the regional financing system, to be completed by the end of 2009. In the interim, Zapatero had been reelected as head of yet another minority government in 2008, and faced a bargain in which territorial interests, as determined by economic geography, cut once again across party lines. The prospect of the generalization of the system agreed as part of the new CoC split ACs into four groups defined by party loyalty and their relative positions in Spain's economic geography. Table 7.7 identifies the different sub-groups.

The ACs in the top left quadrant are concerned about the reduction in overall levels of redistribution that would follow the generalization of the Catalan model. The Catalan government, under the close scrutiny of nationalist parties, is deeply committed to retain what had been so hard to achieve, and issued a clear warning that they would not accept less. The conservative net recipients oppose the generalization of the Catalan model on partisan and distributive grounds. Finally, Madrid and Valencia have every financial incentive to accept the reform, given their relative position in the system (see Figures 7.2 and 7.4) but their partisan identity suggests otherwise. In the end, their distributional interests prevailed and these two regions refrained from opposing the reform openly, thereby weakening the political position of the PP against the reform. In turn, the fundamental dilemma for the government was how to reconcile the distributive interests of Catalonia and Baleares on the one hand, and the rest of the socialist regions on the other.[30]

Being a minority government in Madrid, Zapatero was trapped by the interests of the Catalan socialist incumbent, who was himself under pressure by the

---

[30] A detailed analysis of this dilemma with plenty of evidence on the positions of different ACs is avaiable at the 2009 *Informe sobre la Democracia en España*, Fundacion Alternativas, Madrid.

nationalist opposition (CiU). Therefore, the core model of the CoC was ultimately retained in Law 3/2009, Regional Financing for ACs. The scope of ceded taxes is only marginally adjusted, as described in Table 7.4. More importantly, the new model limited the scope of redistribution within the system. Interregional redistribution of resources was limited to core policy programs (health, education, and social services) rather than extending to overall expenditure needs, as before. This would ensure that the system of regional financing did not alter the relative position of Catalonia in terms of income per capita, as requested by art. 208 of the CoC.[31] In turn, agreement of the potential net losers of the reform (top left quadrant in Table 7.7) was secured through the central government's commitment to cover the gap in redistributive effort created by the limitation of equalization to health, education, and social services.[32] Put simply, the central government assumes the cost of limiting net contributors' redistributive burden. This required, once again, increasing the amount of resources in the system so that no one is worse-off in absolute terms (hence, for instance, the passive support of the Galician regional government in the form of abstention, and the endorsement of the reform by all socialist regions).

The Resilience of Social Security

Spain's fiscal structure history since the early 1990s is one of progressive reduction of a highly redistributive system. Analysis of the distributive consequences of Spain's fiscal structure (Figures 7.2) revealed two mechanisms: the collection and allocation of revenues across governments, and social security (Figure 7.3). The bulk of the third section has analyzed the political process of adjusting the regional financing system. Curiously, in the midst of major reforms of the revenue allocation system, Social Security remains entirely a national program. The reason is simple. Even when national parties faced the most complicated negotiations to form a stable government, they consistently refused to compromise on social security.

In 1993 the socialists failed to reach an agreement with the Basque nationalists (PNV). The latter's demand to collect and manage social security revenues met flat refusal by the socialists (PSOE): "the management of Social Security is what guarantees solidarity among territories."[33] In 1996, the conservatives (PP), despite their eagerness to rule, did not compromise on social security either. The PNV demanded the transfer of the capacity to manage a subset of social security contributions (the Fondo de Garantia Salarial, for instance).

---

[31] This article has been recently striken down by the Constitutional Court in its ruling on the Constitution of Catalonia that partially accepts some of the objections raised by the conservative party (PP) after its approval in 2006. Art. 208 is the only important aspect of the new regional financing system that was invalidated by the Court. The rest of the system approved in Organic Law 3/2009 remains in place.

[32] Technically, this is done through transforming the existing Fondo de Suficiencia into the new Fondo de Suficiencia Global.

[33] *Source: El Pais* November 15, 1993.

Again, they met a categorical denial by the conservatives: "If this is the price of the agreement, there will be no agreement."[34] The PP did not want to set a precendent on this matter at the same time that it was engaging with trade unions to ressume nationwide social pacts, and, more importantly, it did not want to open a political battle about the breach of the key redistributive mechanisms in the system. The electoral consequences in those regions benefiting from it would have been devastating.

The trade unions voice their concerns about the fate of social security in the context of negotiations for the new CoC (2004–2005). They feared that decentralizing the management of social security (art.165) would undermine the redistributive effects of the program. Miquel Iceta, the speaker of the Catalan Socialist Party (PSC) responded to these concerns directly: "The proposal for a new Estatuto [...] does not break the common pool principle because that is not only againt the [national] Constitution but also contrary to our socialist ideas. [...] The proposal concerns only the management of social security services in Catalonia. [...] This is something already contemplated in the Estatuto of 1979."[35] Along similar lines, Zapatero insisted that "the common pool and the unitary character of Social Security are going to remain in place because they are part of the socialist identity and a key mechanism of social and territorial cohesion in Spain."[36] The decentralization of social security was never a real issue during negotiation of the new CoC.

Finally, the recent ruling of the Constitutional Court striking down parts of the CoC has alienated Zapatero's government from all Catalan nationalist parties, themselves engaged in a race of demands with an eye toward the upcoming regional elections. The new frontier is Catalonia's adoption of the Cupo System at work in the Basque Country. In this context, CiU has removed its parliamentary support for the 2011 budget, thereby increasing the barganining power of Basque nationalists. Without their support, there is no budget, and the government will be put in an impossible position. Interestingly, the central government has refused to decentralize social security even under these extreme circumstances. They have only agreed to decentralize active labor market policies, a long-standing demand of Basque nationalists, but not any of the passive labor market policies that consitute the core of social security.[37]

What explains this resilience, given the ability of the Basque and Catalan parties to push for increasing levels of fiscal autonomy on the revenue side? First, the interplay between the territorial distribution of Social Security beneficiaries and, secondly, the centripetal nature of the electoral system creates incentives to preserve a centralized social security system. Welfare recipients,

---

[34] *Source: El Pais* April 19, 1996.
[35] Miquel Iceta: "El Estatuto y la Caja Unica de la Seguridad Social," *Expansion*, October 27, 2005. "Caja Unica" refers to the principle that all social security contributions form a common Spain-wide pool, out of which transfers to recipients are drawn.
[36] *Source: El Pais* October 19, 2005.
[37] *Source:* Spanish Parliament. Diario de Sesiones September 24, 2010. *El Pais* September 24, 2010.

especially pensioners, are an important constituency, and direct welfare transfers (such as pensions) are an important tool to build coalitions of political support (Esping-Andersen 1985). Proportional representation in national elections ensures that benefits targeted to pensioners distributed across multiple regions yield high political returns. Hence, the tendency by national party leaders to resort to Social Security as a political weapon during electoral cycles, in Spain and elsewhere (Orriols 2009). Put shortly, given centripetal electoral rules, national incumbents have no incentive to give up an effective electoral tool. Moreover, given that regions benefiting from a centralized social security, almost by definition, tend to have a stronger concentration of pensioners in their voting age population, and to the extent that these regions are necessary to win a majority of seats in Parliament (as it is the case in Spain[38]), the consideration of any proposal to decentralize social security brings about considerable political costs.

Furthermore, the leaders of benefiting regions also know that losing the implicit transfers from social security would limit the resources available to them and, therefore, jeopardize their electoral survival. Unlike regional financing, a decentralization of Social Security would be a net loss that could not be compensated by additional resouces put forward by the central government (Figure 7.3). As a result, any suggestion that could remotely lead to breaking the common pool and limiting its redistributive impact meets the fiercest resistance by all other regional leaders of the party.[39] Aware of these electoral and organizational risks, national leaders have every incentive not to give in to demands to question the centralized and unitary nature of Social Security in Spain.

THEORETICAL IMPLICATIONS

This chapter has analyzed the link between economic geography and decentralization in a system with a centralized fiscal structure and a centripetal representation system at the status quo. The study identifies two engines of change. First, the distributive consequences of existing fiscal arrangements fuel preferences for higher levels of fiscal autonomy in net-contributing regions, particularly those in which distributional and identity grievances are jointly mobilized by succesful nationalist parties. Second, the presence of dominant nationalist parties alters the structure of political competition in several regions, most notably Catalonia, and introduces a centrifugal element in the political system that, over time, counterbalances the centripetal nature of the electoral system.

---

[38] For evidence on the electoral behavior of social security beneficiaries see Gonzalez (2004).

[39] In the case of the socialist party, for instance, this would only exacerbate past tensions between the socialist leaders in Andalucia and Extremadura and their Catalan counterparts over the architecture of redistribution in Spain. See for instance Rodriguez-Ibarra's fierce opposition in the PSOE Executive Committee to the regional financing proposals in the Constitution of Catalonia, which he considered an undue attack on solidarity between regions (*El Pais* January 11, 2006).

The balance of power between national and regional elites becomes more centrifugal for two reasons. Since 1993, it is increasingly common that the national government needs agreements with nationalist parties to secure stable rule. In addition, as decentralization unfolds, regional party elites within national parties become more autonomous, and less prone to abide by top-down instructions from the center. This is particularly the case when regional branches of national parties compete with nationalist parties for office.

Taken together, these alterations in the balance of power between national and regional elites open the window for a series of reforms of the regional financing system that include the partial decentralization of the income tax. These reforms are part of a process of correcting the redistributive effects of the existing system. Insofar as there is a special system at work for the Basque Country and Navarra, and a "common system" for the rest, the system will be unstable by design. Each reform will only nurture conditions for further fiscal autonomy demands by the net contributors within the common system (León 2009). For all its implications on the revenue side, though, this centrifugal push has proved, so far, unable to overcome the incentives to preserve the centralized and unitary nature of social security. The territorial distribution of welfare dependents, in combination with a proportional representation system at the national level, remains a strong constraint on national party elites. Accordingly, they have refused to decentralize Social Security even when they were in dire political need of support by nationalist parties.

Overall, the Spanish experience adds to previous chapters in showing that demands for fiscal autonomy emerge directly from the interplay between economic geography and exisiting fiscal structures, and that these demands are successful only when an originally centripetal system changes as a result of the centrifugal push by nationalist parties on patterns of political competition. These findings lend additional support to the central claim of this book, that the origin and evolution of fiscal structures reflects the interplay between economic geography and the system of representation (hypothesis 2).

8

The Legacy of History

So far, my analysis has focused on specific examples in which the interplay between economic geography and political representation has influenced the design of fiscal structures. Through these cases I have identified the consequences of the interaction between mobility and economic geography in two systems of representation where regions had veto power over change (Canada, the United States). Symmetrically, I have illustrated the importance of the representative structures. Representation mediates the consequences of exogenous changes in the geography of inequality (Reunification vs. Great Depression), and shapes the political dynamics in unions where distributive conflicts emerge endogenously (EU vs. Spain).

I selected these cases with the aim of identifying viable scenarios approximating the requirements of a "counterfactual." In some instances, natural experiments such as the Great Depression or Germany's Reunification, provided relatively straightforward examples. Others, such as the EU or Spain, were less so. Throughout, the quest for counterfactual conditions remains somewhat quixotic and one needs to dig deeper to identify some exogenous determinants of either economic geography or the structure of political representation.

These challenges aside, the analyses in the previous chapters have provided adequate evidence on the causal mechanisms that drive the relationship between economic geography, political representation, and fiscal structures. The results are generally consistent with the central contentions of this book.

Yet the ability to draw inferences about non-observable cases on the basis of these historical examples is limited. There will always be uncertainty about the extent the conclusions can be applied to other realities, as it is impossible to fully meet the counterfactual conditions for inference. To reduce these doubts, this chapter aims to assess econometrically the book's core ideas, to evaluate whether the findings that emerge from the analysis of specific unions can be applied to other cases.

There are a number of reasons why the consistency between the results of the detailed study of individual examples and the statistical scrutiny of a *relatively larger* number of observations is valuable. One reason is that observable data at a particular time are the result of medium to long-term processes, such as those studied earlier in this book. The observable relationships between any phenomena–in this case economic geography and the structure of political representation–are the legacy of history. This means that they are short-term manifestations of the long-term interplay between these two variables of interest.

To the extent that the examples analyzed represent the dominant empirical regularities within the universe of interest, the different empirical approaches to the relationship between economic geography, political representation, and fiscal structures ought to yield broadly consistent findings. Should this be the case, the central claims in this book can be more widely generalized, even if only within the small number of unions for which there is available data.

As the observable data is historical, scholars must work with small, non-random segments of a longer term, evolving relationship between institutions, geography, and outcomes. Two major implications follow: the first concerns causality, the second concerns data availability and the strategy behind the organization of the chapter.

Regarding causality, let me briefly return to the more extensive discussion in Chapter 3. The generation process behind the available data makes causal identification a challenging task. I will make use of an instrumental variable approach to minimize the problems associated with the fact that fiscal structures, inequality, and representation are endogenous over time. However, the use of instrumental variables is a source of growing skepticism in that their proposed solution appears optimal in theory but is rarely, if ever, to be found in the real world. With the exception of some structural geographic features, the proposed instruments seldom meet restriction assumptions. This is because they consist of variables that are part of the same long-term process, and these are bound to be correlated in some form or another.

In light of these concerns, this chapter makes a limited yet crucial contribution to the overall project. Rather than being the ultimate proof of a particular causal effect, I see the analyses below as a correlational validation of a set of expectations about the nature of the association between economic geography, representation, and redistribution. In other words, if the central claim of the argument remains firm and the case study findings broadly apply, the examination of any medium to large subset of political unions ought to yield a particular set of systematic patterns. Assessing this condition is the ultimate goal of this chapter.

In this endeavor, a common trade-off between data quality and the spatial and temporal scope of the study is faced. As we shall see below, this trade-off is particularly acute when the necessary data involves both the nature and organization of fiscal structures and the distribution of income. To overcome these limitations the following sections combine two sets of analyses. The first maximizes data quality, thus sacrificing geographical scope. The second set does the reverse.

The former will focus on countries covered by the Luxembourg Income Study and the OECD between 1980 and the early 2000s (the specific dates are determined by the availability of household surveys, used to analyze the geography of inequality within political unions). This ensures comparable data on the geography of inequality. The latter focuses on a larger sample combining much more heterogeneous data sources. This allows an exploration of the extent to which the expected patterns of association hold beyond the reduced ranks of advanced industrial societies.

The chapter is organized around the core theoretical claims of the book. First, I focus on the relationship between economic geography, and in particular the geography of income inequality, and the (de)centralization of interpersonal redistribution. This first half of the chapter evaluates two claims: 1) that mobility brings down interregional differences in economic geography (here proxied by the level of inequality within regions), as stated in hypothesis 1 and 2 that the impact of economic geography on the decentralization of interpersonal redistribution is mediated by the system of representation, as stated in hypotheses 2a and 2b. The opening section addresses these hypotheses on the basis of a reduced sample of OECD countries with comparable household income surveys. The second section replicates the analysis for a broader sample including developing countries. Thereafter, the third section addresses implications for the argument in terms of the association between interregional and overall income inequality in society. The expectation that emerges from the argument is that such an association ought to be stronger in centrifugal political systems (hypothesis 2c). Finally, the fourth section focuses on the determinants of interregional redistribution in political unions (hypotheses 3a and 3b).

ECONOMIC GEOGRAPHY AND INTERPERSONAL REDISTRIBUTION: POLITICAL CONTINGENCIES

At the core of this book is the notion that economic geography and mobility shape preferences over fiscal structures. These in turn are filtered through the system of political representation to produce observable fiscal configurations. This argument implies a particular causal hierarchy in the relationship between economic geography, preferences, and institutional choices, supported by the analyses of previous chapters. In this section, I restate the key elements of this causal hierarchy and introduce a methodological strategy to approach it in the context of a larger number of observations.

Inequality, Geography, and Preferences

According to the analytical approach in Chapter 2, the extent to which regions hold different preferences relates directly to economic geography, and in

The Legacy of History

particular to the geography of income inequality. An uneven geography of inequality implies that different territories face different distributive tensions and risk profiles.

Thus, to validate the argument, one should observe systematic relationships among the different dimensions of economic geography. In particular, the geography of income inequality is assumed to primarily reflect income and risk differences between regions on the one hand, and the presence of cross-regional economic externalities on the other. As a single proxy for the geography of income inequality, I use the differences in levels of inequality between regions (also referred to as the territorial structure of inequality). To substantiate this premise, the first relationship on which the argument builds is:

$$f(ineq_{it}^{ir}) = \alpha + \beta_1 gdp_{it}^{ir} + \beta_2 unemp_{it}^{ir} + \beta_3 tradeop_{it} + \beta_4 mobility + \varepsilon$$
(8.1)

Where $ineq_{it}^{ir}$ is a measure of the geographical differences in the incidence of income inequality in a particular country at a particular point in time (superscript ir stands for interregional). This measure works as a proxy for the geography of income inequality. In turn, the geography of inequality is modeled as a function of interregional differences in GDP per capita (gdp_{it}^{ir}) and unemployment ($unemp_{it}^{ir}$), captured in both cases through the coefficient of variation among regional rates. These two indicators capture those dimensions of the geography of inequality that arguably drive preferences toward a more fragmented system of interpersonal redistribution. The former captures differences in terms of income whereas the latter captures differences in the incidence of labor market risks. In turn, trade openness ($tradeop_{it}$) and mobility speak to the scope of interregional social and economic externalities by capturing, respectively, the impact of external shocks and the extent of citizens' (particularly labor's) flow across territories (Cameron 1978; Garrett and Rodden 2003; Rodrik 1998). The estimation of the impact of the latter offers an (admittedly partial) test of the hypothesis that mobility reduces interregional differences in the incidence of inequality, thus working facilitating the centralization of interpersonal redistribution (hypothesis 1).

Is the geography of inequality related to the factors identified in the theoretical model developed in Chapter 2? And do these factors operate in the specific direction hypothesized by the argument? In addressing these questions, Table 8.1 reports three different estimations of equation (8.1), including OLS (robust) and Panel Corrected Standard Errors (with and without correcting for autocorrelation).[1]

The results are generally consistent with the logic developed in the preference formation model. While income and labor market risk differences increase cross-regional differences in terms of inequality, more exposure to external shocks and larger levels of mobility increase the levels of risk sharing between

---

[1] For definitions and sources of variables, see Appendix D.

TABLE 8.1. *Dimensions of the Geography of Income Inequality, 1980–2000*

	OLS Robust	Pcse	Pcse (ar1)
	β (s.e)	β (s.e)	β (s.e)
Interregional Differences in Growth	2.59*** (.81)	2.59*** (.81)	1.44 (1.2)
Interregional Differences in the Incidence of Unemployment	.312** (.12)	.312** (.12)	.17 (.20)
Trade Openness	−.0025*** (.0006)	−.0025*** (.0006)	−.0024*** (.0008)
Mobility	−.0058* (.003)	−.0058* (.003)	−.0009 (.0008)
Intercept	1.07*** (.10)	1.07*** (.10)	1.23*** (.131)
N	60	60	60
F/Wald Chi	11.39	346.28	141.34
R-squared	.47	.62	.76

Key: * p < .10, ** p < .05, *** p < .01

regions, and reduce the differences in the shape of the income distribution between regions, thereby reducing incentives to pursue or sustain separate tax rates.[2] These results offer direct support for the hypothesis that mobility reduces interregional differences in economic geography, working to facilitate the centralization of interpersonal redistribution (hypothesis 1). The next hurdle is to assess how these inequalities, as proxy for heterogeneity of preferences between regions, are reflected in different choices about territorial fragmentation of the system of interpersonal redistribution.

Inequality, Representation, and Fiscal Structures

Concerning the translation of preferences into outcomes, the central claim throughout this book is that the way contending preferences for fiscal structures actually translate into observable levels of interpersonal redistribution is contingent on the balance of power between the center and the subnational

---

[2] It should be noted, however, that the variable capturing exposure to external shocks (trade openness) is the only one that shows consistent effects across the different specifications. Once a potential process of serial correlation is taken into account, the effects of all other determinants are reduced by half and cease to be significant, although they consistently show the right sign. As a result, trade openness appears to be the only robust "good instrument" in equation (8.1). In contrast, the proxy indicators for income and risks differences are good instruments, yet not robust to autocorrelation. Finally, mobility is a weak instrument throughout the different specifications.

The Legacy of History

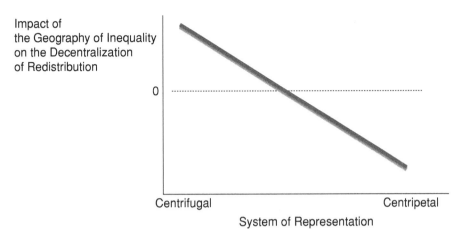

FIGURE 8.1. Economic Geography and Interpersonal Redistribution: Political Contingencies

units across different political unions. This brings us back to political representation, to the continuum between centrifugal and centripetal representation structures.

Figure 8.1 restates hypotheses 2a and 2b graphically. *Ceteris paribus*, an uneven geography of inequality will be associated with a more decentralized system of interpersonal redistribution *under conditions of centrifugal political representation*. That is, when the balance of power privileges the political position of the constituent members of the union. In turn, the impact of the geography of inequality on the levels of decentralization of redistribution is muted under conditions of centripetal representation, that is, when the balance of power privileges the political position of the national actors, including the central government.

At the extreme, in highly centripetal political unions, the relationship reverses: a more uneven economic geography is associated with a more centralized system of interpersonal redistribution. The in-depth comparison between the experiences of the European Union, the United States in the 1930s, Germany during Reunification, and Spain provides strong evidence in support of this contention. To further evaluate this theoretical claim though, I proceed to estimate the following set of empirical relationships:

$$f(IPR) = \alpha + \hat{ineq}_{it}^{ir} + bp_{it} + (\hat{ineq}_{it}^{ir} * bp_{it}) + \theta_{it} + \varepsilon \qquad (8.2)$$

where *IPR* represents the level of decentralization of interpersonal redistribution in a particular country at a particular point in time, bp_{it} defines the balance of power between the center and the units, and θ_{it} depicts a set of controls, to be detailed below, that are meant to capture alternative explanations for the decentralization of fiscal policy.

Note that $\widehat{ineq}_{it}^{ir}$ is instrumented by the variables determining the territorial structure of inequality (8.1) in an effort to ensure that its impact on *IPR* is exogenous (independent of) the effect of *IPR* on the geography of inequality itself. To the extent that the independent variables included in (8.1) do not have a direct effect on *IPR* other than the one they have through their impact on $\widehat{ineq}_{it}^{ir}$, the results will not be affected by an endogeneity problem.[3] Because the restriction assumptions are highly contestable, and because the use of a weak instrument might artificially create relationships that are not very robust otherwise, for both equations I report several specifications with different sets of instruments. In addition, these specifications also vary in their approach to two issues that could potentially bias the results, namely the potential impact of serial correlation and the potentially confounding effect of unobserved unit-specific effects. In an effort to deal with these multiple sources of concern, I estimate each of the two specifications of the conditional relationship between the geography of income inequality and the balance of power between the center and the regions in three different ways. A brief description follows.

First, I report an OLS estimation with panel corrected standard errors with a common (ar1) serial correlation correction (a version that applies the Prais-Winsten first differences correction to panel data. In Table 8.3 I label this model as PCSE, AR1. Second, I report an application of the standard two-stage instrumental variable approach for panel data created by Baltagi (Baltagi 2008). I refer to the Baltagi estimation as TSIV in Table 8.2. Finally, I report estimates from a panel regression with vector decomposition following the procedure developed by Plümper and Troeger (2007). This model is referred to in Table 8.2 as FEVD. This procedure is particularly helpful to control for the presence of unobserved unit effects when, as is the case in these models, some of the control variables are time invariant. I should note that all three sets of results are instrumental variables approaches, that is to say, they try to contain the effects of endogeneity by using the values of $\widehat{ineq}_{it}^{ir}$, as predicted by (8.1). The difference between them lies in the set of instruments being included. While the OLS with panel corrected standard errors and the vector decomposition approaches restrict the list of instruments to those included in the opening section, the Baltagi approach takes as instruments all the exogenous variables in the system.[4]

---

[3] There is a problem of endogeneity when "the values of our explanatory variable are sometimes the consequence, rather than the cause, of our dependent variable" (King, Keohane, and Verba 1994: 185; Manski 1995). More technically, endogeneity refers to the fact that an independent variable is potentially a choice variable, correlated with unobservables in the error term. In the real world this distinction is often subtle and complicated. Indeed, the specialized literature seems to have taken a different path by establishing the conditions under which an independent variable x can be considered strictly exogenous in relation to y. These are mainly two: weak exogeneity and absence of Granger causality. For a discussion on these issues see Greene (2000). Additional statistical tests indicate that, whereas trade openness is a "good" instrument (that is, strong effect on $\widehat{ineq}_{it}^{ir}$ yet unrelated to the error term of (6.2)), mobility qualifies only as a weak instrument.

[4] Note that the estimation of (8.2) using a standard one-way OLS approach supports the argument's predictions strongly. These results are available upon request.

The Legacy of History　　213

TABLE 8.2. *Decentralization of Interpersonal Redistribution in Advanced Democracies, 1980–2000*

	Inequality Interacted with Representation			Inequality Interacted with Heterogeneity in the Structure of Political Competition		
	PCSE (ar1)	TSIV	FEVD	PCSE (ar1)	TSIV	FEVD
Geography of Inequality (predicted)	13.6*** (2.06)	6.35** (3.0)	1.74*** (.6)	.772 (.87)	2.32 (1.95)	−3.14*** (.66)
Representation	23.66*** (4.29)	13.6** (5.6)	3.06*** (.73)			
Heterogeneity				−9.41*** (3.14)	−6.38*** (2.38)	−10.9*** (1.5)
Geography of Inequality * Representation	−21.01*** (3.59)	−11.6** (4.5)	−2.6*** (.65)			
Inequality * Heterogeneity				7.52*** (2.55)	5.11*** (1.90)	8.9*** (1.23)
Country size (log)	.8*** (.23)	.684* (.36)	.69*** (.003)	.564*** (.15)	.38 (.32)	.75*** (.05)
Ethnic Fractionalization	9.46*** (1.04)	12.07*** (2.8)	11.8*** (.035)	13.9*** (.81)	11.56*** (2.38)	12.11*** (.39)
Total Taxation	.19*** (.05)	.065 (.048)	.066*** (.015)	.126*** (.04)	.040 (.048)	.042*** (.013)
Income Growth	.09 (.106)	.076 (.078)	.075*** (.014)	.04 (.05)	.013 (.085)	.040 (.042)
Intercept	−34.6*** (4.56)	−20.3*** (6.32)	−14.68*** (.041)	−14.35*** (3.9)	−10.12** (4.5)	−8.63 (1.21)
R-squared	.81	.78	.98	.78	.72	.98
N	69	69	69	69	69	69

Key: * p < .10, ** p < .05, *** p < .01

A word on measurement of the key variables of interest is in order. I measure the decentralization of interpersonal redistribution (IPR_D) as follows:

$$IPR_D = (100 - \text{Percentage of direct transfers to households} \\ \text{by consolidated central government}) * \\ (\text{Proportion of total regional revenues collected} \\ \text{by second - tier regions themselves})$$

The first term of the indicator measures the amount of total direct transfers to households performed by governments other than the central one. It is well known, though, that the fact that a particular level of government makes a

TABLE 8.3. *Determinants of Interregional Inequalities in Political Unions Around the World: Dimensions of the Geography of Income Inequality, 1980–2000*

	OLS Robust	Pcse	Pcse (ar1)
	β (s.e)	β (s.e)	β (s.e)
Mobility	−.138*** (.065)	−.138*** (.044)	−.070*** (.026)
Oil Dependence	−.44 (.30)	−.44* (.23)	.053 (.056)
Regional Distribution of Ethnic Groups	−.21 (.42)	−.21 (.30)	−.87 (.67)
Intercept	2.11*** (.29)	2.11*** (.28)	1.69*** (.38)
N	243	243	243
R-squared	.34	.34	

Key: * $p < .10$, ** $p < .05$, *** $p < .01$

transfer does not necessarily mean that it has full political control over that transfer (Rodden 2004). To correct for this possible source of noise, I proceed on the assumption that fiscal autonomy is a good proxy for political autonomy and weight this first term by an indicator of fiscal autonomy (proportion of total regional revenues collected by regions themselves). This approach is preferable to existing alternatives (e.g., regional share of social expenditures as a percentage of total social expenditures) in that interregional transfers are effectively excluded from the calculations.[5] Hence, this indicator of fiscal decentralization is less blurred by measurement error around the real fiscal and political autonomy of the regions.

The set of predictors includes the instrumented measure of the geography of income inequality (8.1) in interaction with a measure of the balance of power between the center and the regions. To capture the latter, I use two approaches. The first one captures representation (R) through the role of subnational units in the formation of national will, and is defined by

$$BP_{\mathrm{I}} = R = \frac{PC}{n} \quad (8.3)$$

where PC (*party centralization*) is Riker's index of party centralization (share of subnational incumbents that belong to the same political party in power at the federal level) and n is the number of levels of power with directly elected politicians represented at the national level. If subnational representatives are directly elected by their local constituencies, n takes the value of 2, because a stronger link to the local constituency of local candidates weakens party

---

[5] The empirical estimations are robust to the use of either indicator of fiscal decentralization.

centralization. Otherwise, n takes the value of 1. Overall, representation can range between 0 and 1.

In turn, the second approach captures the extent to which the structure of political competition varies across the subnational units of any given multitiered system. The intuition behind this measure of heterogeneity of political competition across subnational units (HPC) is that the larger the distance between the center and the units in terms of the effective number of parties, the higher the gap in patterns of political competition. The measure is computed as follows:

$$BP_2 = HPC = \frac{1}{r}\sum_{1}^{r}\left(|ENP_r - ENP_n|\right) \tag{8.4}$$

where ENP_r represents the effective number of parties in region/subnational unit r, and ENP_n defines the effective number of parties at the union level.[6] The models reported in Table 8.2 include estimates in which $ineq_{it}^{ir}$ is interacted with both indicators of the balance of power between the center and the units, thereby providing additional robustness checks.

Note that these two indicators relate directly to the parameters capturing the importance of national elections and their implications for intraparty relationships across territories, as specified in the theoretical model (Φ). While this is a multidimensional phenomenon in itself, and as a result each individual indicator is necessarily partial, I proceed on the assumption that the different institutional aspects of representation are correlated with one another, thus operating similarly in the continuum between centrifugal and centripetal representation. For instance, a directly elected senate with strong legislative powers increases the importance of regional politics relative to a case in which such an institution does not exist. Likewise, a strongly malapportioned lower house that facilitates the formation of local strongholds would reduce the party discipline of (at least some) local leaders, thus lowering the value of Φ in the model. In support of this premise, the correlation between the two indicators of the balance of power between the regions and the center at use in this chapter is −0.65. Clearly they are not identical, as they capture different aspects of the political process, but they do covary in ways consistent with the claim that the different dimensions of political representation affect the balance of power in similar ways.[7]

The models in this section and throughout this chapter also control for several alternative logics accounting for the decentralization of fiscal structures. The literature so far has paid particular attention to three distinctive lines of reasoning: decentralization as a *functional* response to the growth of

---

[6] Descriptive statistics on these two measures in a number of advanced federations are included in Appendix D.
[7] Note that the negative sign of the correlation coefficient reflects the fact that R and HPC are scaled differently. While large values of R imply a more centripetal system, large values of HPC imply a more centrifugal system of representation.

government, decentralization as a response in terms of *specialization* to growing international exposure, and finally decentralization as a response to the *demands* by social and political groups mobilized around cleavages other than those of interest in this book (most prominently religious, cultural, and identity driven political mobilization).

The *functional* logic posits that as government size grows there are efficiency gains associated with decentralization. Based on standard welfare economics assumptions the intuition behind this logic is that delegation across levels of government will allow the public sector to meet an ever growing stream of demands (Oates 1991; Persson and Tabellini 2003). To evaluate and control for these effects, the models include two variables: total taxation as a percentage of GDP and a measure of GDP growth.[8]

The *specialization* logic suggests that in an increasingly integrated economy, regional differences exacerbate and economic actors will benefit from specializing to compete. As regional economies specialize, fiscal structures must respond to increasingly diverse circumstances by decentralizing (Alesina and Spolaore 2003; Kessing, Konrad and Kotsogiannis 2007; Stegarescu 2009). To control for the potential effects of this process, I proxy international exposure by country size. The latter is well known to correlate negatively with exposure, as larger domestic markets reduce the need for economic integration (for empirical support on this, see Alesina and Wacziarg 1998).

Finally, to control for alternative sources of social and political demand for larger levels of political autonomy across the board, I control for ethnic fractionalization. The choice of this particular control follows from the well-established link between the existence of multiple cultural, linguistic and/or religious identities and the use of decentralized political arrangements to accommodate them (Linz 1997; Stepan 2001). Put briefly, decentralized/federal polities are more likely to emerge in ethnically, linguistically, and/or culturally fragmented social contexts. The expected direction of the relation is clear. Notwithstanding the inherent limitations of any measurement of fractionalization, the higher its values the higher the expected levels of decentralization.

I turn now to the findings displayed in Table 8.2. I center the discussion around the mechanism highlighted by the theoretical argument, the interaction between the geography of inequality and the system of representation.[9]

---

[8] I use a measure of GDP growth rather than a measure of income per capita because OECD countries show relatively similar levels of economic development relative to the rest of the growth. Growth rates vary more, potentially triggering the logic associated with functional explanations of decentralization.

[9] The control variables show the anticipated effects. In line with the functional logic, total taxation shows a positive and significant impact on the decentralization of interpersonal redistribution. In contrast, the indicator of national income growth adds nothing to the explanation of levels of fiscal decentralization in the OECD. The findings are also consistent with the specialization and demand logics discussed above (Panizza 1999). Both ethnic fractionalization and country size are positive and significantly associated with higher levels of fiscal decentralization across the different specifications.

The Legacy of History

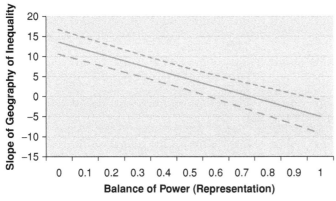

FIGURE 8.2. Conditional Effect of the Geography of Inequality I

For an accurate interpretation of the conditional effect of the geography of inequality, I calculate the conditional coefficients and standard errors on the basis of the TSIV(2) specifications. Figure 8.2 presents the conditional coefficients and standard errors for the interactions between inequality and representation. Figure 8.3 performs a similar exercise for the interaction between inequality and the levels of heterogeneity in patterns of political competition across subnational units.

In both cases, the argument that the effect of inequality on decentralization of interpersonal redistribution is contingent on the specific architecture of power at work in different political unions receives considerable empirical support. These findings complement the evidence obtained via the detailed in depth analysis of particular historical experiences, thereby providing a more general empirical validation of the argument.

The results suggest that inequality is positively associated with decentralization of interpersonal redistribution in those cases in which parties are hardly centralized at the national level and/or subnational representatives at the

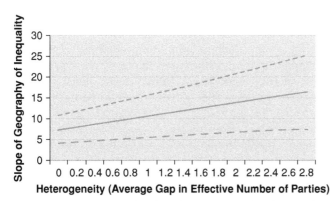

FIGURE 8.3. Conditional Effect of the Geography of Inequality II

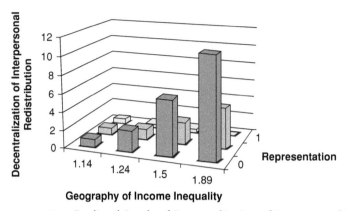

FIGURE 8.4. Predicted Levels of Decentralization of Interpersonal Redistribution as a Function of the Geography of Income Inequality and Representation

national level are directly elected. In contrast, as the balance of power between local and national elites becomes more equilibrated (e.g., federations with an integrated party system), interregional differences in the incidence of inequality map less and less onto the actual fiscal design of institutions. Finally, in heavily centralized contexts, higher inequalities are associated with more, rather than less, centralization of the fiscal system. This is consistent with the hypothesis that the winners under the status quo constitute a powerful veto coalition with strong incentives to block any reform proposal that jeopardizes their relative position (the dynamics of Spanish decentralization provide a good historical example of the workings of this process).

Likewise, Figure 8.3 shows very clearly how inequality carries a much stronger effect on decentralization in those multitiered systems in which the structure of political competition is heavily fragmented. The more idiosyncratic the political competition in different units, the less able subnational incumbents are to weigh into their strategies the preferences of the national party. As a result, fragmentation of political incentives enhances the institutional consequences of changes in the territorial patterns of inequality.

To illustrate the magnitude of the effects, Figure 8.4 presents the predicted values of decentralization of interpersonal redistribution under different levels of representation and inequality. These values are calculated on the basis of the TSIV(2) version of the equations reported in Table 8.2. In countries where representation (i.e., integration between regional and national parties) is low, an increase in the ratio between the Gini coefficient of the richest region and the Gini coefficient of the poorest region, from 1.24 to 1.84, increases the level of decentralization of interpersonal redistribution from 2.4% to 11.25%. In contrast, as representation becomes more centripetal, the impact of the geography of income inequality on the levels of decentralization is progressively muted, to effectively disappear in those unions with very centripetal representative institutions. So, at very high values in the scale of political representation, even

The Legacy of History

the highest levels geographical disparities in the incidence of income inequality bear no impact on levels of decentralization of redistribution.

In conclusion, the hypothesis that the effects of inequality on the decentralization of interpersonal redistribution are contingent on the way different political institutions shape the balance of power between the center and the regions receives a good deal of empirical support. These findings, however, are based on a small subset of advanced industrial societies. If the relationships identified hold only in a small subgroup of rich democracies, and not across political unions around the world, the argument would not be necessarily wrong but the realm of its validity would be much narrower. In other words, this sampling restriction could potentially cast doubts on the scope of the argument and findings in this book.

BEYOND THE OECD: ECONOMIC GEOGRAPHY AND INTERPERSONAL REDISTRIBUTION IN POLITICAL UNIONS AROUND THE WORLD

To alleviate these concerns, I replicate the analysis on a different sample, one including nineteen political unions from both the developed and the developing world during the period 1978–2001.[10] To the extent that the data allow, I follow the approach presented in equations (8.1) and (8.2). There are important differences concerning measurement issues that condition the analysis throughout: while I operationalize the dependent variable (IPR) in the same way as before, I rely now on IMF data as opposed to the better quality OECD ones. In addition, in the absence of household income surveys that are representative at the subnational level, comparable, and accessible, I cannot measure the incidence of inequality across regions, much less calculate the ration between most and the least unequal region. As an alternative, I rely on a more limited measure. For every union included in the analysis, I proxy the geography of income inequality with the p90/p10 ratio of its members' GDP per capita.

Determinants of Interregional Inequalities

Because of the nature of the data and the sample of countries under consideration, I introduce important modifications in the first equation. The geography of income inequality is modeled as a function of the levels of interindustry labor mobility, the country's level of oil dependence, and the distribution of the ethnic population across regions. The rationale behind the selection of these variables follows from established findings in economic geography.

---

[10] The countries included in the analysis are: Argentina (11), Australia (22), Austria (20), Belgium (3), Brazil (2), Canada (20), Czechoslovakia (3), Germany (17), India (20), Malaysia (5), Mexico (20), Pakistan (2), Russia (2), South Africa (5), Spain (19), Switzerland (9), United States (19), Venezuela (2), and Yugoslavia (12). In parentheses I report the number of years for which I actually have valid observations for all the variables included in the analysis. The panel is obviously unbalanced.

For reasons related to the agglomeration of production (Krugman 1991), industrial production tends to cluster in particular regions within any given union. As a result, in line with the previous estimates of (8.1), the larger the pattern of interindustry labor mobility, the larger the scope of cross-regional externalities within the labor force, and other things being equal, the more homogenous the wage structures across industrial regions. By implication, large levels of interindustry labor mobility serve as a proxy for interregional mobility in that they work to even the geography of inequality among subnational units.[11] As in the previous section, this provides an indirect test for the connection between mobility and preferences for the centralization of interpersonal redistribution posited in hypothesis 1.

Cross-regional differences in production also relate to the importance of oil dependency. Those unions with a lower dependency on oil imports are likely to have more heterogeneous regional economic structures, leading to larger interregional income differences (Wibbels and Goldberg 2010). In addition, a recent line of research has established that the territorial distribution of different ethnic groups is endogenous to physical geography (Michaelopoulos 2008). As a result, one would expect unions with larger levels of regional ethnic concentration to have a more uneven geography of income inequality. The results are presented in Table 8.3.

The results offer a mixed picture on the instruments selected. The expectations concerning the concentration of ethnic groups do not receive any empirical support. In turn, the notion that oil dependency is negatively correlated with interregional income disparities is only consistent with some of the results reported and lacks robustness across the different specifications. In contrast, the proxy for interregional mobility is negatively and consistently associated with interregional income differences. This association provides additional empirical grounds for the hypothesis that mobility drives the centralization of interpersonal redistribution indirectly through its effect on the geography of income inequality (hypothesis 1).[12]

---

[11] The measure of interindustry labor mobility comes from Zhou (2009) and is defined as the elasticity of labor to interindustry wage differentials. The rationale behind the measure is defined as follows by Zhou (2009): "The advantage of elasticity measure over either the real labor movement or the variation of interindustry wage differentials is that it takes into account both employment shifts in the labor market and the factor price (i.e., wages) changes that purport to incentivize the employment shifts. In other words, it looks at the sensitivity of rational labor owners to the observable wage differentials across industries [...]. Ideally, higher degrees of the sensitivity of labor to factor price differentials would mean higher levels of ILM, and vice versa for lower degrees of sensitivity. Therefore, empirically we should be able to distinguish economies that have higher labor mobility from economies that have lower labor mobility by finding higher degrees of labor-wage sensitivity in the former and lower degrees of labor-wage sensitivity in the latter set of economies."

[12] These findings are robust to the inclusion in equation (8.1) of all the other instruments used to predict, in equation (8.2), the centralization of interpersonal redistribution (reported in Table 8.4).

Inequality, Representation, and Fiscal Structures in a Broader Sample

In this section I use the predicted level of interregional differences as an explanatory variable of the decentralization of interpersonal redistribution, following the specification detailed in equation (8.2). Because of the nature of the data, a number of control variables differ. First, to the extent that democracy is a prerequisite for the sort of political contentions analyzed in this book to unfold (Dahl 1983), in particular the ability of voters and parties to pursue their preferred level of decentralization, it is important to control for the nature of the political regime. This is particularly the case in a sample that combines old and established democracies with young and often unsettled ones. Accordingly, I introduce as a control the standard polity index (polity IV). Second, since differences in the levels of economic development are much larger now, I introduce a control for cross-national differences in the levels of GDP per capita. Finally, I can only make use of one of the two balance of power indicators described above. While I manage to compute the same measure of representation used in the previous section (as defined in equation (8.3)), I am not able to compute the measure of heterogeneity of party competition for all the unions included in the analysis. Finally, in terms of the econometric approach, I follow the same procedure as in the previous section. Thus, I instrument inequality first as described above and afterwards I estimate the same three models as in equation (8.2): an OLS model with panel corrected standard errors and serial correlation of order one (PCSE, AR1), the Baltagi two-stage instrumental variables model (TSIV), and the panel regression with vector decomposition (FEVD) that allows discrimination between unit's fixed effects and time invariant covariates. The results are presented in Table 8.4. Again, I limit the discussion to those variables tapping the key causal link in the argument.[13]

The results show unequivocally that the conditional relationship between the two posited in the theoretical argument, and empirically identified in the context of advanced democracies, also applies to political unions in the developing world.

The conditionality of the impact of interregional differences in income inequality on representation, displayed in Figure 8.5, shows a remarkable similarity with Figure 8.3. The relationship is virtually identical: an uneven economic geography fosters a fragmented system of interpersonal redistribution only when the system of representation allows local elites to voice and effectively pursue their agendas in the national arena. Otherwise, the impact

---

[13] All the control variables with the exception of country size show the anticipated effects. Note though that ethnic fractionalization is the only robust one across all specifications. The expectations, first outlined by Wallis and Oates (1988), on the relationship between decentralization and economic development using a sample of developed and developing nations seem to hold in two out of three of the specifications: economic growth fosters decentralization. Finally, total taxation displays the anticipated effects, supportive of the notion that unions collecting larger revenues decentralize their fiscal structure to become more functional.

TABLE 8.4. *Decentralization of Interpersonal Redistribution in Political Unions Around the World, 1978–2001*

	PCSE (AR1)	TSIV(2)	FEVD
Inequality (predicted)	8.49**	4.38**	5.84***
	(4.03)	(2.15)	(1.7)
Representation	33.9**	10.35*	24.80***
	(16.5)	(6.08)	(7.08)
Inequality* Representation	−16.45**	−3.27**	−12.39***
	(7.7)	(1.7)	(3.09)
Country Size	.96	1.01	−1.13***
	(.76)	(1.33)	(.09)
Economic Development	.823***	.178	.135
	(.214)	(.20)	(.118)
Ethno-linguistic Fractionalization	8.45**	13.17**	14.37***
	(4.05)	(6.6)	(.46)
Total Taxation	1.25	−.057	.70**
	(.89)	(.67)	(.33)
Democracy (Polity)	−.40**	.058	−.98***
	(.16)	(.125)	(.024)
Intercept	−18.23**	−10.05	18.56***
	(10.1)	(15.22)	(.986)
R-squared	0.347	0.15	.95
N	243	218	221

Key: * $p < .10$, ** $p < .05$, *** $p < .01$

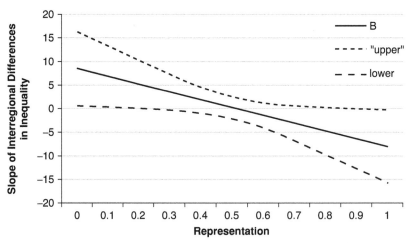

FIGURE 8.5. The Conditional Effect of Income Geography on the Decentralization of Redistribution

The Legacy of History

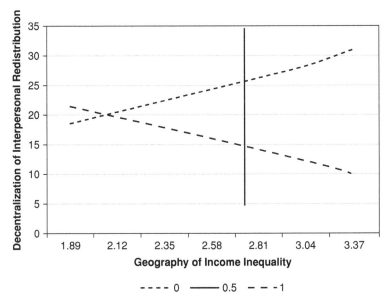

FIGURE 8.6. Income Geography and Representation as Determinants of the Level of Decentralization of Redistribution in Political Unions Worldwide (predicted values)

of economic geography on the design of fiscal structures is either muted or, in highly centripetal systems of representation, reversed.

Moreover, the substantive impact of the interaction between the geography of inequality and representation is of similar magnitude. Figure 8.6 presents the predicted level of decentralization of interpersonal redistribution on the basis of the two-stage instrumental variables estimations (TSIV). Each of the series reported captures how countries situated in different positions of the representation scale (0–1) respond to changes in the spread of the geography of income inequality. The thick vertical line indicates the point after which the predicted changes meet the threshold of statistical significance. By way of an example, an increase in the ratio between the wealthiest and the poorest region from 2.7 to 3.3, leads to a 20% *increase in the level of decentralization* under centrifugal representation (R=0). In contrast, under centripetal representation (R=1), the same alteration in the geography of income inequality provokes a *centralizing* impact of similar magnitude. These findings are not only consistent with those obtained in a subsample of wealthier democracies but also with the insights emerging from the in-depth study of the EU and Germany, two unions at the extremes of the representation scale.

FISCAL STRUCTURES AND THE REPRODUCTION OF INEQUALITY

Both the argument in this book and the findings reported so far bear direct implications for understanding the impact of decentralized fiscal structures on inequality. The process implied by this book is not one in which decentralized fiscal structures create exogenously new inequalities. Rather, the often observed association between high income inequality and decentralized systems of interpersonal redistribution reflects a different causal dynamic, one in which the geography of inequality creates the conditions for its own sustainability through the very process of selection of fiscal structures. The decentralization of interpersonal redistribution does not operate as a mechanism that generates a particular outcome exogenously, but rather as a mechanism that, once selected and established, sustains and reinforces the same patterns of inequality that facilitated its emergence in the first place.

Arguably, if this "reproduction" effect of decentralization holds, the same set of political and institutional conditions that mute the link between the territorial patterns of inequality and the decentralization of public insurance systems should mediate the relationship between the territorial patterns of income inequality and the overall levels of interpersonal inequality. In other words, the relationship between interregional and interpersonal inequalities should be a function of the same political process that drives the selection of the transmission mechanism, that is, decentralization itself. Hence, the last hypothesis on the interplay between economic geography and representation (hypothesis 2.c): the association between interregional inequality and overall income inequality in the union should be the strongest in unions with centrifugal systems of representation. In what follows, I evaluate this claim by contrasting two models of the determinants of interpersonal income inequality in the OECD.

The dependent variable is the series of Gini coefficients for disposable income inequality provided by the Luxembourg Income Study (LIS). The particular indicator used here captures the distribution of income post taxes and transfers for the entire population. The specification includes a number of controls directly drawn out of the literature on inequality in advanced industrial societies: (a) political and institutional factors that affect redistribution other than decentralization, reflective of the alternative accounts available in the literature; (b) variables conditioning the distribution of disposable income that relate to demographic processes, general economic conditions, and the structure and organization of the labor market (which are known to be major determinants of wage inequality: Rueda and Pontusson 2000; Wallerstein 1999; and (c) the effects of previous redistributive policies on pre-tax income inequality (Beramendi 2001). The inclusion as explanatory variables of the incumbent's ideology and the level of economic coordination, along with the level of decentralization of redistribution, satisfy the controls required in (a). As an indicator of government partisanship, I use a scale ranging between 1 and 4, with higher values indicating incumbency by left parties or coalitions (for details see Cusack and Engelhardt 2002). In turn, I use the indicator constructed by Hall and Gingerich as a measure of economic coordination (2009). This is a time invariant scale ranging between 0 and 1 that captures coordination within the labor market, within capital, and between labor and capital. Values closer to 1 indicate higher levels of coordination. The specialized literature has consistently shown

TABLE 8.5. *Does Inequality Reproduce Itself? Determinants of Overall Economic Inequality in OECD Countries (1980–2000)*

	FEVD	
Decentralization of Interpersonal Redistribution	.08*** (.000016)	–
Geographical Disparities in the Incidence of Inequality	–	.04*** (.00006)
Representation	–	.10*** (.00001)
Geographical Disparities in the Incidence of Inequality*Representation	–	−.09*** (.0001)
Market Income	.193*** (.0007)	.232*** (.0001)
Economic Coordination	−.028*** (.0003)	−.068*** (.0005)
Partisanship	−.003*** (.00006)	−.003*** (.0005)
N	53	53
Adj. R-sq	.924	.920

Key: * p < .10, ** p < .05, *** p < .01

these variables to be major determinants of redistribution (Beramendi and Cusack 2009, Huber and Stephens 2001, Kenworthy and Pontusson 2005).[14]

In turn, controlling for market income inequality provides a straightforward solution for (b) and (c). Inequalities of disposable income are a function of market income inequalities and the direct effect of redistributive policies. What is to be assessed in the different specifications is the role of one or more variables that determine the level of redistribution and, through that channel, the distribution of disposable income. This goal makes an indicator of market income inequality a very useful tool. It aggregates the impact of economic, demographic, and labor market related variables. More importantly, it also includes the feedback effects of previous redistributive policies on people's labor market behavior and, subsequently, on the distribution of wages and additional sources other than earnings and welfare state transfers. Finally, the indicators for the decentralization of interpersonal redistribution, the geographic spread in the incidence of income inequality, and political representation are the same as the ones used in the first section.

Because the indicator of economic coordination is time invariant, I report a panel regression with vector decomposition following the procedure developed by Plümper and Troeger (2007).[15] Table 8.5 reports the estimations.

---

[14] For a critical review of this literature, see Stasavage and Scheve (2009).
[15] The estimation also introduces a Prais-Winsten correction for serial correlation of order one and cluster the standard errors by cross-sectional unit.The results reported are robust to other estimation approaches such as panel corrected standard errors with serial correlation of order

The control variables display the anticipated effects. Market inequality is obviously a strong and positive predictor of disposable income inequality. In addition, the indicators of economic coordination and partisanship confirm standard results in comparative political economy. Organized capitalism and left-wing incumbency contribute, even if marginally, to a more egalitarian distribution of resources in society (Beramendi and Anderson 2008; Iversen 2005; Iversen and Soskice 2009; Kenworthy 2004; Pontusson 2005; Rueda 2008; Stasavage and Scheve 2009).

Turning to the central concerns in this book, Table 8.5 indicates a strong and positive effect of the level of decentralization of interpersonal redistribution on the observable amount of disposable income inequality. On the basis of the estimates reported in the first column, a country with a fully centralized system of interpersonal redistribution is predicted to have a level of overall disposable income inequality of 0.21. In contrast, a country with a territorially fragmented system of taxes and transfers is predicted to have a level of inequality of 0.34. In other words, the territorial organization of public insurance systems accounts for a 30% change in the spread of disposable income, even after controlling for all the standard factors in the literature.

On the basis of this result, it would seem tempting to rescue the conventional view (Chapter 1) and elegantly proclaim that decentralization *creates* inequality. A central theme in this study is that such an impulse is misleading in that the conventional view is, at best, incomplete. And this is so because decentralization itself is a function of a politico-economic process determined by the interplay between economic geography and political representation. This being the case, the indicator of decentralization of redistribution and the interaction between geography and representation ought to work as substitutes of one another as predictors of the spread of disposable income in society. A comparison between the two columns in Table 8.5 reveals that this in fact the case. Put simply, the variables capturing the generating process of decentralization itself perform as well in predicting the overall levels of inequality, holding all the other factors driving the latter constant.

This is best illustrated by analyzing the conditional effects of interregional inequalities on the overall level of inequality (Figure 8.7). The core result is clear: the strength of the association between interregional and interpersonal inequality is mediated by political representation. Much like the case of decentralization, higher values of representation mute the link between interregional and interpersonal inequalities. The same conditions that drive the selection of decentralized public insurance systems are associated with larger levels of overall disposable income inequality. Under centrifugal representation, territorial inequalities sustain themselves through their influence in the selection of fragmented welfare systems that, in turn, work to sustain, perpetuate or reproduce inequality. Thus, to the extent that there is an association between inequality

one and a panel tobit approach to account for the fact that the dependent variable is left-censored.

The Legacy of History

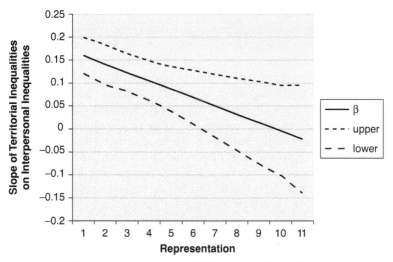

FIGURE 8.7. Representation and the Self-Reproduction of Inequality

and decentralization, it occurs not because decentralization creates inequality, but because, under specific historical, political, and institutional conditions, inequality becomes self-sustaining through the politics of institutional choice. Ultimately, under these conditions, decentralization operates as a transmission mechanism linking different dimensions of inequality. In contrast, there is a broad range of political unions in which territorial inequalities do not reproduce themselves into larger levels of inequality, the same range of unions in which territorial inequalities do not get reflected into extreme levels of welfare state fragmentation, namely those characterized by more centripetal systems of political representation.

In conclusion, these results highlight an important and largely neglected aspect of the politics of redistribution and inequality. I have shown how the territorial organization of fiscal structures, and more specifically the level of decentralization of public insurance systems (taxes and transfers), is a significant determinant of the level of inequality.

INTERREGIONAL REDISTRIBUTION IN POLITICAL UNIONS

One of the guiding themes in this monograph has been to argue that fiscal structures in political unions are bidimensional. That is to say, the distributive conflicts among political actors occur over two policy dimensions, interpersonal (transfers of income between people through taxes and transfers) and interregional redistribution (transfers of resources for discretionary use from rich to poor members of the union). This distinction is not simply definitional. As shown extensively in Chapter 2, depending on their relative position in the union's geography of income, actors' preferences over the size and scope of these tools need not overlap. Which is to say, to a large extent, these two dimensions of fiscal structures in political unions respond to different politico-economic motives. So far this chapter has focused on assessing statistically the hypotheses concerning the determinants of interpersonal redistribution. This section turns to the second dimension of fiscal structures, namely the transfer of resources from wealthier to poorer members of the political union.

Recall that according to the argument developed in Chapter 2 there are two factors driving the emergence of large levels of interregional redistribution. The first one operates through the existence of large cross-regional economic externalities, most notably in the form of labor and/or dependents mobility. To briefly revisit the theoretical efforts developed in Chapter 2, large levels of mobility within any given union have the effect of homogenizing the risk profile of workers and dependants. As a result, and in line with the results reported in Tables 8.1 and 8.3, large levels of mobility reduce the range of geographical income differences among subnational units, thus reducing the incentives that could otherwise exist to pursue a decentralized system of interpersonal redistribution.

Because of its potentially disruptive impact on the workings of regional labor markets or social protection systems, relevant political actors (most notably the political elites of its wealthier members) have incentives to act preventively in the hope of limiting undesired population inflows through the use of interregional redistribution. The intuition behind this claim goes as follows. The interregional transfers of resources will help stabilize the least dynamic regional economies in the union, hence reducing the outflow of its potentially redundant labor force. They will also increase the financial ability of the regional incumbents of the least well off regions to provide services and fund the provision of those welfare transfers (typically minimum income and social assistance programs) they control. This in turn will reduce the outflow of potential benefit hunters, thus limiting the scope for a welfare magnet effect (Peterson 1995; Peterson and Rom 1990). As the comparative analyses of cases as diverse as the European Union, Canada, and Germany reveals, the effect of cross-regional economic externalities seems to be observable across the whole spectrum of systems of representation. The small amount of actual redistribution at work in the EU takes the form of interregional transfers from the wealthier to the relatively poorer members of the union. The empirical analysis in Chapter 4 showed that it is systematically associated with patterns of mobility within the union. Likewise, in the context of a very different system of representation, I have shown that the need to limit the outflow of workers and dependents from Eastern to Western Germany played a key role in politicians' motivations to sustain a massive redistributive effort on both the interpersonal and the interregional dimensions following Reunification.

The fact that the influence of mobility on interregional redistribution appears to be orthogonal to the system of representation does not imply that the latter lacks a role in accounting for observable differences across countries in the size of interregional transfers. What the absence of a conditional relationship between mobility and representation does imply, though, is that the impact of the balance of power on interregional redistribution occurs directly, through a causal chain independent of the scope of cross-regional economic externalities. This alternative causal chain is purely political: it concerns the relative position within the political system of those actors whose optimal choice is a fiscal structure that privileges large levels of interregional transfers at the expense of large scale systems of interpersonal redistribution. The theoretical analysis in Chapter 2 identified those actors as the social and political elites in backward regions. They want to maximize the resources they extract from the rest of the union without giving up control over the tools for interpersonal redistribution and service provision. Backward regions tend to be rural and underpopulated, and therefore these elites would be particularly privileged in systems of representation in which malapportionment empowers them at the national level, both within formal representative institutions and, as importantly, within the organization of countrywide political parties. To the extent that this process is at work, one should expect that in those unions with weaker national party systems in which local elites are directly elected, representatives of relatively poorer and underpopulated regions will be more capable of carrying their preferences through into the design of fiscal structures. In sum, controlling for all other determinants of interpersonal redistribution, more centrifugal systems should facilitate a larger extraction capacity by local leaders. In contrast, in a more centripetal system, local leaders have less leverage vis-à-vis national elites to carry their will through the system. Recent case study analyses of a number of developing federations offer results that are consistent with this expectation (Beramendi and Diaz-Cayeros 2008; Gibson, Calvo and Falleti 2004).

I now offer what, to the best of my knowledge, is the first statistical analysis of the influence of these two factors on the levels of interregional redistribution in political unions around the world. The dependent variable measures the overall amount of transfers between the center and the regions or between the regions themselves as a percentage of the union's GDP. This variable is the result of multiplying two of the variables facilitated in the IMF dataset on decentralization: 1) transfers from other levels of governments as a percentage of total regional revenues, and 2) the value of total regional revenues expressed as a percentage of GDP. Admittedly, these data are less than ideal (Rodden 2004), but for the quantities of interest in this section they constitute the only available source for a large number of countries.[16]

In turn, for the key independent variables of interest (mobility and representation) I use the same two indicators as previously; that is, representation defined as the level of party centralization weighted by the number of directly elected officials (see expression (8.3)), and mobility defined as the elasticity of labor to interregional wage differentials. Again, the use of the latter as a proxy is justified on the idea that production activities tend to be regionally clustered

---

[16] Contrasting these data with national sources in those cases for which these exist, for instance Germany, Canada, the United States or Spain, does substantiate the point that the quality of these data is very uneven. In some cases, the information provided by the IMF data seems accurate whereas in others, like Germany, the gap is significantly larger.

(Krugman 1991). Therefore, to the extent that large levels of interindustry labor mobility are in place, this will imply the existence of larger economic externalities across subnational units.

The in-depth study of the relationship between mobility and interregional redistribution in both the European Union and Germany revealed that these two variables are jointly endogenous. In an effort to isolate the impact of mobility on interregional redistribution I follow a similar econometric strategy as in the previous two sections. In a first equation I instrument mobility using the share of population living in ethnic minority regions. The intuition behind this instrument is that the geography of ethnicity is unlikely to be a function of previous levels of interregional transfers but it is bound to affect directly the patterns of labor mobility. Other things being equal, I expect workers of a particular ethnic background to be less likely to move to other regions dominated by competing ethnic groups. As a result, to the extent that the minority ethnic region(s) harbor(s) large shares of the population, I expect the overall levels of mobility to be lower.[17] All other exogenous variables in the system are used as controls in the first equation. In turn, the predicted values of inter-industry labor mobility are used as an independent variable in the analysis of the following relationship:

$$f(IRR) = \alpha + \hat{mobility}_{it} + bp(R)_{it} + ineq_{it}^{ir} + \theta_{it} + \varepsilon \qquad (8.5)$$

where $bp(R)_{it}$ stands for the measure of representation discussed above, $ineq_{it}^{ir}$ captures the geography of income inequality within the union as defined above, and θ_{it} incorporates the same set of controls included in earlier analyses. In estimating (8.5), I use the same battery of econometric techniques of the previous two sections. Table 8.6 reports the results of the analysis.

The estimates of the determinants of interregional transfers offer a number of interesting insights. Concerning the control variables, the proxies for economic development, international exposure (country size), and quality of democracy fail to show consistent and robust effects across more than one econometric specification. Fortunately, the estimates of other variables' effects offer more assurance. Ethnic fractionalization shows a positive and significant effect on the level of interregional transfers in political unions around the world. This result is consistent with the argument that fiscal transfers contribute to the fiscal appeasement of mobilized minorities in ethnically fragmented societies (Treisman 1999).

In turn, total taxation shows a negative and consistent impact on the level of redistributive transfers of resources between regions. Note that the direction of the effect of this variable is opposite to the one identified when predicting interpersonal redistribution. This contrast between the impact of total

---

[17] Note that this is a measure of the geography of ethnicity and not of overall ethno-linguistic fractionalization. The latter does not pay attention to the regional distribution of ethnic groups. Nevertheless, I keep it as a control variable in equation (8).

The Legacy of History

TABLE 8.6. *Interregional Redistribution in Political Unions*

	PCSE (AR1)	TSIV(2)	FEVD
Mobility	1.40***	.89**	1.6***
(predicted)	(.49)	(.29)	(.30)
Representation	−.62**	−.33	−1.16***
	(.29)	(.48)	(.07)
Interregional	.09	−.39	.18**
Inequality	(.11)	(.26)	(.08)
Country Size	.083	.28*	−.16***
	(.11)	(.16)	(.07)
GDP per	−.011	−.009	−.001
capita (lag)	(.021)	(.039)	(.002)
Ethno-linguisticn	1.86***	2.16***	1.75***
Fractionalization	(.57)	(.82)	(.06)
Total	−.84	−1.16***	−.44***
Taxation	(.14)	(.20)	(.07)
Democracy(Polity)	.006	.021	0.036***
	(.025)	(.039)	(.003)
Intercept	4.68****	3.64*	6.02***
	(1.3)	(1.99)	(.12)
R-squared	.86	.60	.75
N	197	197	197

taxation on interpersonal and interregional redistribution reveals an interesting connection between the two dimensions of redistribution: political unions that collect larger revenues as a share of their economy tend to both decentralize the administration of taxes and transfers and limit the flow of discretionary resources between regions. To the extent that the size of tax revenues is associated with the amount of redistribution in society, this points to an interesting trade-off between interpersonal and interregional redistribution. Using a sample with both developing and developed unions, the negative association between total taxation and interregional transfers suggests that those countries that redistribute more through interpersonal taxes and transfers manage to limit the ability of local lords to extract resources via the system of interregional transfers.

The estimated impact of representation on interregional transfers also generates implications consistent with this view. The left panel in Figure 8.8 displays the predicted value of interregional transfers at different points of the representation scale. *Ceteris paribus*, as local elites lose power relative to national elites (as the system of representation moves from centrifugal to centripetal), the scope of interregional transfers declines significantly. The effect is pretty noticeable, albeit not overwhelming: covering the entire range of the representation scale reduces the predicted level of interregional transfers by about 2% of GDP. Putting together this finding with the ones in the previous section

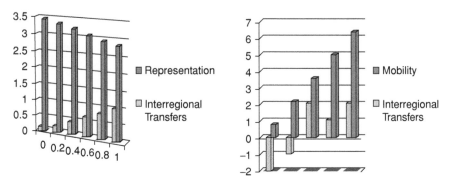

FIGURE 8.8. Impact of Representation and Mobility on Interregional Transfers (predicted values)

on interpersonal redistribution further reinforces the notion of a trade-off. A system of representation that increases the leverage of national political elites versus local political elites is associated with both a more integrated system of interpersonal redistribution through taxes and transfers and less success by local elites in extracting resources from other levels of government. In other words, centripetal representation leads both to a more centralize public insurance system and to a lower share of the economy being devoted to interregional transfers.[18]

The differential impact of representation appears to confirm the idea that, at least partially, interpersonal and interregional redistribution respond to different political logics. However, such is not necessarily the case in every union. As the German experience illustrates, a union with large levels of both interpersonal and interregional redistribution is both conceivable and feasible. What the analysis of over twenty unions presented in this section suggests though, is that these cases tend to be the exception, especially in the developing world (Beramendi and Diaz-Cayeros 2008). While the ultimate reasons behind this divide are yet to be ascertained, the degree of discretion in the use of interregional transfers by local elites emerges as a critical aspect of the problem. The narrative of the German response to Reunification reveals that a large share of transfers to the East were tied to the implementation of specific programs involving interpersonal redistribution (e.g., social assistance, public employment, income support). By implication, in those unions in which this connection is formally recognized and enforced, the two dimensions of fiscal structures tend to converge into one, an image conveyed quite clearly by the analysis of the German experience. By contrast, in those cases in which interregional transfers involve resources to be used at the discretion of local elites, the trade-off between the two ways of organizing and allocating redistributive efforts becomes starker.

---

[18] For a related paper on the relationship between malapportionment and redistribution in federations, see Rodden and Dragu (2010).

The Legacy of History

Last but not least, the results provide strong support for the claim that large levels of mobility are associated with larger levels of interregional transfers. As displayed in the right panel of Figure 8.8, as interindustry wage elasticity increases so does the share of the economy political unions devote to transfers from wealthier to poorer regions. The substantive impact is noteworthy: a 1 point increase in the value of the elasticity implies an increase in interregional redistribution equivalent to about 4% of the union's GDP. This result is consistent with the evidence provided by the previous case studies, and supports the argument that large levels of mobility lead net contributors to accept interregional transfers to ensure themselves against potential disruptions of their labor markets and welfare systems. Furthermore, the strong and direct impact of mobility on interregional redistribution adds to the case that there are two dimensions of redistribution with partially independent politico-economic logics. The last column in Table 8.3 shows that mobility has no direct effect on interpersonal redistribution. Instead, it conditions interpersonal redistribution indirectly, through its impact on the geography of inequality and the level of risk sharing between regions (as illustrated by the Canadian experience as well). By contrast, the results in this section indicate that mobility is a very strong predictor of interregional redistributive efforts.

9

The Political Geography of Inequality
Summary and Implications

As democracy and decentralization spread around the world, the number of people living in democratic political unions continues to increase. Canonical approaches in political economy would predict, either with cheer or concern, a new wave of higher inequalities. This book began with a challenge and a pledge. I challenged the conventional view that decentralized political structures inevitably lead to more inequality and less redistribution. As with other aspects of federalism, such as the macroeconomic consequences of the design of fiscal constitutions (Rodden and Wibbels 2002), the case that motivates the conventional theoretical arguments, namely the United States, is far from being the rule. In fact, in terms of observable outcomes some political unions display very little redistribution and large levels of inequality as a result (United States, Mexico, Argentina, the EU) whereas others show levels of redistribution that challenge the conventional expectation that decentralization breeds poverty and inequality (Canada, Germany, Spain). Why, to borrow the language of Linz and Stepan (2000), are some political unions inequality inducing whilst others are inequality reducing? In addressing this question, I pledged to shed light on a largely overlooked aspect of the politics of inequality: the territorial distribution of conflicting interests over the nature and scope of redistribution.

I have endeavored to show that the key to this task lies in the politics behind the origins and evolution of fiscal structures in political unions. A choice about fiscal structures is a choice about redistribution. More precisely, it is first a choice about the degree of decentralization of taxes and public insurance programs, and, secondly, a choice about the amount of redistribution of resources from wealthier to poorer members of the union. In exploring these choices, I have encountered a few puzzling characters: representatives of poor regions (Southern Democrats in the 1930s) fiercely opposing centralized public insurance programs that would have implied a massive income transfer; and leaders of rich regions (like Ontario or British Columbia in the post-Depression years) begging for the centralization of welfare despite its implications for the regional tax base; or happy to accept significant transfers of resources to their less advantaged counterparts (like Germany in the EU, or the Western Länder after Reunification).

This book has developed a systematic account of these choices and, more broadly, of the observable variation in distributive outcomes in political unions. As I bring this study to a close, let me offer first a summary of the core analytical findings in the book. I will then discuss the implications of the analysis for the problems of political stability in federations. Finally, I draw a number of broader lessons for the study of the links between political institutions and redistribution and outline a number of follow up questions emerging as pointers for future research.

THE POLITICAL GEOGRAPHY OF INEQUALITY: ANALYTICAL SUMMARY OF FINDINGS

As this study draws to a close, let me return to the original question: why do some political unions show less redistribution and more inequality than others? The answer lies in the combined effect of economic geography, political representation, and mobility. The findings in the previous chapters support this contention. In this section, I provide a comparative summary of the key results in this study and how they illuminate the nuts and bolts of the political geography of inequality.

The Origin of Preferences: The Role of Economic Geography (Hypothesis 1)[1]

Economic geography produces a multidimensional set of preferences. At the micro level, the analysis of individual preferences for the centralization of redistribution in the EU has revealed individual income and the aggregate wealth of the society they live in as key factors shaping people's stances regarding policy integration. In line with the premises of the model, welfare recipients in rich countries have been shown to be particularly opposed to the idea of moving social security to Brussels. More generally, citizens' views map onto a bidimensional space defined by individual income and regional wealth. In turn, these dynamics translate directly to the level of elites, in Europe and elsewhere. Ontario's premier was wary at first about the idea of centralizing social insurance due to the fiscal consequences on his province. Middle income workers in Bavaria and Baden-Württemberg see the system of regional transfers with very different eyes than those in Berlin or Brandenburg. And all the left-wing parties in Catalonia supporting an expansion of interpersonal redistribution would like to see it happen within regional boundaries as opposed to in Spain as a whole. Overall, the analysis of specific country experiences brings out a close link between the geography of income inequality and elite's political preferences regarding negotiation of the union's fiscal structure. The more systematic

---

[1] Numbers correspond to the summary of hypotheses at the end of Chapter 2.

statistical scrutiny of the LIS income surveys (Chapter 8) confirms that this link is in fact an empirical regularity: a heterogeneous geography of income drives preferences for fiscal structures apart and tilts politics towards a conflict between regions; a homogenous geography of income implies that the nature of redistributive conflicts is similar across regions and renders politics a conflict between nationwide social groups.

The extent to which the geography of income shapes politics as a conflict between regions or country-wide income classes is, in turn, mediated by two other factors: the degree of regional economic specialization, and the level of mobility of workers and dependents. By fostering a disperse geography of labor market risks, the former reinforces the decentralizing impact of a heterogeneous geography of income. By bridging risk profiles across regions, the latter mutes such an impact. The contrast between the American and Canadian experiences after the Great Depression captured clearly the workings of this tension and its direct political implications.

I have shown that the shape of the American response to the Great Depression is largely the result of efforts of a particular set of units, the Southern states, to protect the peculiarities of their labor market structure (δ) from external influences. The potential demise of the political economy of paternalism was, for the Southern political elites, a much higher price to pay than revenues coming from Washington, regardless of their magnitude, could offset. Obviously, as argued above, they managed to protect their specificities because they enjoyed the institutional capacity to do so by controlling the relevant Committees in the House and the Senate. Yet Canadian provinces enjoyed a similar capacity in that the centralization of redistribution required their consent to amend the British North America Act. Likewise, Canadian provinces also differed largely in their regional labor market structures and, furthermore, the Depression hit the more agrarian economies in the West of the country harder. And even so they renounced their institutional capacity to block centralized unemployment insurance.

The origin of these differences lies in the differing patterns of interregional mobility between units in the two North American federations. While the estimated 100,000 transients in Canada operated as a sort of multiplier effect across provinces, expanding the unskilled workers' unrest through the nation, the whole logic of Southern paternalism was to create a system of mutual dependencies able to prevent tenants and croppers from moving toward the Western and Northeastern industrialized states. As a result Canadian provinces became closer in terms of both the profile of their dependent population and the way in which the Depression affected them. The structure of Ontario and Quebec's incentives changed towards a position less reluctant to embrace a centralized solution. Meanwhile, American states maintained the large distance between them in both respects. In addition, the beginning of World War II operated in Canada as a second shock at the time of designing their response to the Depression, disabling the few remaining pockets of provincial resistance to pooling resources in a centralized solution. To conclude, in Canada the magnitude of the external shocks was enhanced by interterritorial mobility, overcoming inter-provincial disparities in terms of labor market structures. By contrast, in the United States the huge gap between the rural and racial South and the industrialized states, together with the absence of a phenomenon like the transients, rendered the pooling effect of the Depression insufficient to foster a national solution to the problem of unemployment.[2]

From Preferences to Choices: The Role of Political Representation (Hypothesis 2)

The joint effect of income, risk, and mobility determines the map of preferences on the centralization of interpersonal redistribution. Through the systematic analysis of household income surveys I have shown that distributive tensions associated with economic geography are at work in all political unions. Why then the variation in the actual organization of fiscal structures? What makes Germany or Spain more centralized than the United States or the EU?

The findings in this book confirm political representation as the key mediating factor. I have shown the role of political representation to be important in two ways. First, representation shapes the outcome of political conflicts in the event of a sudden exogenous change in economic geography. The contrast between Germany's response to Reunification and America's response to the Depression is particularly informative in this regard, as in both cases representation is given before the exogenous changes in economic geography unfold. Germany is much more centripetal when it comes to the articulation of political will.

Hence, contending preferences fare differently. Whereas those opposed to more comprehensive public insurance efforts in the EU and the United States had the institutional ability to condition the final outcome, the few in Germany in favor of institutionalizing the increase in regional inequalities were overrun by the political incentives of national parties to incorporate the East as quickly and generously as possible. Indeed, Eastern länder were fully incorporated into the system of interpersonal redistribution almost immediately, and Western länder barely managed to postpone the full integration of interregional redistribution into the system for five years. Centripetal representation turned the decentralizing effects of a massive increase in geographic economic disparities into a redistributive effort whose scale lacked precedent in the economic history of advanced industrial societies. Whereas Southern senators and other defenders of specific territorial interests managed to prevent centralization during the process leading up to the Social Security Act, Stoiber failed in his attempts to decentralize unemployment insurance even during the late 1990s.

---

[2] An interesting implication of this finding for the future of the EU is that those programs more likely to see partial integration are those dealing with the more mobile subsector of the union's population (Ferrera 2005: 154–159).

Second, representation matters as a determinant of long-term dynamics. Under centrifugal representation, the economic geography produces very decentralized fiscal structures with a very narrow window for redistributive efforts. As a result, economic geography limits the feasibility of radical alterations of the interpersonal distribution of income via public policy, thus fostering an observable association between decentralized political structures and inegalitarian distributive outcomes. Things work differently under centripetal representation. The disaggregating push of an uneven geography of inequality is contained by a set of political incentives to either build or sustain a proredistributive coalition that cuts across territorial boundaries. This case, broadly substantiated by a stream of research on the relationship between proportional representation and redistribution (Cusack, Iversen and Soskice 2007; Iversen and Soskice 2006), became particularly apparent across the cases in this book.

The comparative analysis of Spain and the EU shows how status quo conditions in terms of representation have a lingering impact on the outcome of distributive conflicts over time. The centrifugal nature of representation in the EU has successfully constrained any attempt to have Social Security systems follow markets on the path to integration. In turn, only the progressive erosion of the centripetal system set up in 1978 facilitated the translation of Catalan demands into the partial decentralization of the income tax. These partial changes notwithstanding, the electoral system remains a powerful constraint on national parties' incentives to entertain demands for the decentralization of Social Security.

Interregional Transfers and Redistribution: Insurance and Capture (Hypothesis 3)

The third set of findings emerging across the cases concerns the interdependence between the decentralization of interpersonal redistribution, mobility, and the scope of interregional redistribution. The argument I have developed suggests that *in anticipation* of an undesired population inflow, wealthier members of the union willingly provide for interregional redistribution to insure themselves. The intuition behind this is that wealthier regions are aware that, should the large population inflow become a reality, the push for either centralization or much larger transfers of resources will be harder to stop, as indeed shown by the process leading to the centralization of unemployment insurance in Canada. The trade-off is particularly intense in those unions where wealthier members have highly specialized economies. Interregional transfers in this situation become a tool not only to protect the local welfare state from excessive demand, but also to protect the local economy from a potential surplus of unskilled (or *wrongly* skilled) workers. I have shown this to be one of the main motivations behind the Structural Funds and other policies intended to bridge the modernization gap between European regions.

Put in comparative perspective, the case of the European Union illustrates a situation in which very low mobility rates trigger very moderate interregional transfers of resources (relative to the union's GDP). These transfers, however moderate, are a significant resource to bolster regional economies in need, which, in turn, further suppresses the migration rates. To the extent that the Structural Funds operate as an insurance device against undesired population inflows, they can be considered a success. At the other end of the spectrum is Germany, where a massive outflow from East to West triggered an equally massive set of transfers, aimed in large part at stopping the population flow into the West. In this case, the results were mixed at best, though to make this claim one would have to somehow imagine a counterfactual reunified German market with no transfers from the West. Undoubtedly, the population outflow would have been much larger under these circumstances. Taken together, these experiences support the claim that higher levels of interregional mobility drive interregional redistributive efforts in political unions upwards, a claim also confirmed by the quantitative analyses presented in Chapter 8.

The findings in this book also point to a complementary mechanism behind the size of interregional transfers: the ability of representatives of different regions to capture rents through the political process. In addition to the quantitative evidence in Chapter 8, the case studies have robust evidence in this regard. South European countries successfully used their veto power to increase interregional transfers during the negotiations leading to the monetary union. Southern Democrats implicitly achieved some interregional transfers without risking autonomy through the tax-offset system of unemployment insurance finally included in the Social Security Act. This ability is readily apparent in centrifugal systems, but at times it is also observable in systems originally designed to be centripetal. I have shown how minority governments at the national level in Madrid almost inevitably imply reforms in the system of interregional transfers to the advantage of regions with pivotal parties. Finally, in Germany the incorporation of the East created a stronghold of potentially pivotal voters. As a result, massive interregional transfers complemented those channeled indirectly through the system of interpersonal redistribution.

The Dynamics of Inequality in Political Unions

This book has explained why some political unions are more egalitarian than others. Those unions with a more heterogeneous economic geography, centrifugal systems of political representation, and low levels of interregional mobility have less integrated fiscal structures and lower levels of redistribution. As a result, they will have higher levels of income inequality. The empirical analyses in this book have also shown how the interplay over time between economic geography, representation, and mobility accounts for the dynamics of inequality in political unions.

Centrifugal representation has emerged as a mechanism that facilitates the direct transmission of interregional income differences into weaker systems of redistribution, in turn reinforcing preexisting inequality patterns. It operates as an important mechanism through which inequality becomes self-sustained over time. The evolution of the EU's fiscal structure and its distributive implications provides a very good illustration of this process. As does the close link between the centrifugal transformation of Spain's party system and the success of partial reforms to limit the scope of redistribution.

Pressure to pursue or sustain decentralized systems of redistribution is lower when cross-regional differences in economic geography are less acute. As shown by the experiences of Social Security reform in Germany and Spain, in the context of such pressures, the dynamic is very different under centripetal representation. I have shown in detail how the latter works to facilitate or sustain cross-regional coalitions along income lines, thereby muting the decentralizing push of economic geography. In turn, the prospect of high levels of mobility fosters interregional transfers, thereby reducing the regional resource gap. As the prospect of mobility becomes less daunting, acceptance of interregional redistribution weakens, and political conflicts over fiscal structures reemerge. The evolution of political contentions in Germany after Reunification provides direct evidence on this. Ultimately, centripetal representation and mobility are the key mechanisms that explain why only some unions are capable of overcoming the trade-off between equality and autonomy.

IMPLICATIONS: INEQUALITY AND STABILITY IN POLITICAL UNIONS

In what follows I address the implications of these findings for some relevant normative contentions about federalism and decentralization. Politically, as well as analytically, fiscal decentralization has been either celebrated or dammed on very similar grounds. For welfare economists and public choice theorists, for the neoclassical right and the jacobine left, subnational governments, in competition for either rents or investments, constrain redistribution and foster efficiency.[3]

What this study suggests is that these expectations, whether in fear or hope, are justified only under specific conditions. For factors to be mobile and redistribution to be constrained, the labor force should have a similar skills composition across regions, with significant differences in average incomes (Cai and Treisman 2005). Only under these conditions is a race to the bottom likely to emerge.

If, alternatively, regions are relatively closer in their average income levels but differ in the degree of specialization of their economic activities, no race to the bottom is likely to emerge for neither capital nor labor are easily mobile. Under these conditions, one could envision a rather different decentralized design, namely one which is compatible with the development of different redistributive strategies tailored towards highly specialized regional labor markets.

Potentially, this could improve the comparative advantage of the different regions and generate efficiency gains. Far from fostering inequality,

---

[3] For sources on these literatures, see Chapter 1. A more detailed review of these literatures is available in Beramendi (2007); Rodden (2007); and Wibbels (2006b).

decentralization would, in such a scenario, enhance efficiency by allowing for different strategies of redistribution rather than by preventing redistribution itself. Put differently, under specific circumstances, decentralization may lock in a more egalitarian structure where regions differ in dimensions other than their average income levels. The implication that emerges from this study is clear: several long term scenarios are feasible. Therefore it is not possible to make normative claims, let alone policy prescriptions, about institutional changes a priori, that is without investigating first the geography of inequality, the patterns of interregional mobility, and the system of political representation at work in the political unions in question.

Moreover, the interplay between these factors offers important insights on the problem of institutional stability in federal polities. Economists and political scientists alike have devoted significant intellectual efforts to ultimately ascertain whether there exists an institutional design such that the federal contract becomes "self-enforcing" (De Figueirido and Weingast 2005). Indeed, the quest for the "robust federation" has rendered major insights on the working of federations, not least the idea that the stability of federal institutions requires a set of complementary institutions (Bednar 2005, 2008).

Central to this approach is the problem of opportunistic behavior in the context of federations (including migration of authority for the *wrong* reasons). Opportunism, Bednar argues, can only be contained, not eliminated, through a set of complementary institutions designed to maximize compliance and minimize opportunism. Among these institutions, particular attention is paid to constitutional safeguards, the party system, and the judiciary.[4] Each of these institutions covers different types of opportunism, thereby reinforcing each other's effectiveness. On their own, they are ineffective as guarantors of federal stability. Yet in conjunction, when properly designed, foster the stability of the federal contract. There is a great deal of insight in this reasoning as well as a fair amount of hope about the potential gains from adequate institutional engineering.

This study raises fundamental questions about the scope of these efforts. To the extent that the "optimality" of any given design is conditional on the economic geography under which it was adopted, any significant change in the latter, whether exogenous or endogenous, creates a new set of conditions that may render the status quo suboptimal but, more importantly, will help to de-stabilize it politically (Hug 2005). In other words, fiscal structures and federal contracts, potentially self-enforcing under a particular set of economic conditions, may unravel into a cycle of contention as a result of changes in economic geography and/or political representation. These changes, as triggers of new party strategies towards institutional reform, render any existing equilibrium between the center and the regions fundamentally unstable, even if not by design.

---

[4] See also Bednar, Eskridge, and Ferejohn (2001).

As the case studies presented in this book have shown, fiscal structures, once adopted, generate distributive effects that feed back into the political process. The analytical framework applied to the Spanish case can apply to other experiences such as Belgium, Italy, or Bolivia, and hints at a number of interesting extensions. The analysis of the Spanish experience illustrates how the framework of this study can easily incorporate experiences in which contentions over the design of fiscal structures emerge endogenously, that is as a result of the distributive consequences of preexisting fiscal structures and not as a result of exogenous shocks.

Laments over the criteria to allocate resources across regions find echoes in every political union. The Catalan nationalists in Spain, the conflict between La Paz and the regions over the control of natural resources in Bolivia, the Lega Lombarda in Italy, and the Flemish political parties in Belgium share a well known *leitmotif*: the central government abuses our wealth to obtain political gains from nurturing inefficiency throughout the rest of the country. Much like in Germany before Reunification, redistribution feeds back grievances among net contributors, paving the way for subsequent conflicts over the rules governing resource allocation. The questioning of existing arrangements becomes a constant in the political process, thus fostering a permanent sense of instability over the existing framework. The scope and ultimate implications of these grievances are likely to vary between the developed and the developing world as many conditioning factors also vary. In Belgium recent challenges to the union by Flemish nationalist reflect directly a concern about economic redistribution between regions without jeopardizing growth or democracy itself. The same sort of tensions in younger democracies are potentially more damaging as they threaten the very stability of the regime (e.g., Bolivia).

Finally, the analysis in this book sheds light on the nature of the responses to the debt crisis in the European Union. As the risk of collapse of the Euro dominates the specialized press, voices crying for a stronger Europe become louder. It remains unclear what specific tools will be put in Europe's hands, from Eurobonds to new taxes on financial transactions. But the message is clear. As in Krugman's opening quote, the only way is forward. But how? Under what conditions is it likely that European incumbents will delegate fiscal sovereignty? This book has offered multiple reasons not to expect a radical overhaul of the EU's fiscal institutions, except under very specific and potentially unfortunate circumstances.

The institutional architecture of the union and the disparities in income, production systems, and welfare states stand as a major political obstacle for fiscal integration. The diversity of preferences is simply too strong to allow for fiscal integration. This is in large part because the economic and social risks within the Union have remained territorialized, that is, largely specific to the different member states. Under these circumstances, incumbents' own electoral survival demands the preservation of fiscal autonomy. Thus, any proposal for Eurobonds, EU-wide taxes, or, more pressingly, for increasing the size of rescue transfers to avert countries defaulting, is bound to meet strong political opposition. German, French, and Dutch core voters, among many others, are unlikely to agree to delegate the management of fiscal policy to an upper body where potential recipients of transfers have a strong political presence. A proper integration of fiscal policy would entail distributive implications that seem, at this point, politically infeasible.

Unless, that is, the short-sighted patches and the lack of medium-term economic strategy in response to the crisis manage to transform the Great recession into a second Great Depression throughout advanced European economies. As this book has shown, the push for fiscal integration derives from major transformative crises, where cross-regional economic and social externalities operate as a risk multiplier across jurisdictions, as a process causing risks to be no longer restricted to subnational entities. Only then, when a majority of German, French, British or Austrian voters, to name just a few, ask for solutions that their governments alone will not be able to provide, will the integration of fiscal policy in the EU become politically feasible. The paradox, central to the strategic interaction among myopic incumbents responsive to their electorates, is that the early adoption of fiscal integration could avoid the very social and economic distress that seems necessary for fiscal integration to become a viable political option.

SOME BROADER LESSONS AND THE ROAD AHEAD

This study of the relationship between fiscal structures and inequality, has shown that the observable associations between institutions and social outcomes result from a process of endogenous self-selection (Przeworski et al. 2000). As stated throughout this research, if an association between decentralization and inequality is observable, it is so because decentralization alters the distribution of income and also because the geography of economic inequality works, (under the specific economic and institutional conditions established above), to produce and sustain specific fiscal structures. This process triggers a dynamic, bidirectional, and at times mutually reinforcing relationship. It follows that the reasons institutions matter are linked to the reasons these institutions came into existence in the first place.

This result bears important implications for ongoing debates on the relationship between political institutions and social outcomes. The institutionalist turn in comparative political science has been very helpful in preventing a sort of naive economic approach according to which politics is just a mere reflection of the working of a number of economic factors. This research has shown that political institutions make a difference to a wide array of political processes taking place under similar economic circumstances (Pierson and Skocpol 2002: 693–722; Thelen 2010).

However, in its efforts to substantiate the impact of institutions, the analysis of the relationship between institutions and social outcomes may have gone too far in the opposite direction. There is a tendency within institutionalist literature to assume that institutions matter, per se, beyond the social and economic dimensions of reality. The absence of a proper theoretical analysis of the relationship of interest leads not only to misconceive correlations as explanations, but also to the understanding of politics as a self-referential realm. This study has illustrated the limitations of such an approach.

A second set of implications concern institutional change. The comparative study of the evolution of fiscal structures suggests that the contrast between punctuated equilibrium theory and historical institutionalism as mutual exclusive models of institutional change is a rather artificial one (Pierson 2004; Thelen 2004). As illustrated by the cases of Germany and North America, sharp breaks and long-term endogenous changes interact and complement each other as sources of change and adaptation. In accounting for change one cannot do without the other: in the absence of exogenous shocks or constitutional moments, causal identification becomes nearly unfeasible; without looking at past political and institutional legacies, reactions to sharp breaks are hard to understand.

Understanding well this interplay is crucial in large part because of another implication of this book: today's income distributions and systems of redistribution are rooted much further in the past than standard datasets allow us to measure or appreciate. In the same way that economic and electoral institutions today project "a shadow of the XIX century" onto the politics of redistribution (Iversen and Soskice 2009), fiscal structures in contemporary political unions often carry the weight of decisions adopted in the very early stages of welfare state development.

The policy differences between Canada and the United States provide one example. In the realm of unemployment insurance, those "small differences that matter" (Banting 1997, Card and Freeman 1993) go back to the New Deal, that is to the process and the logic analyzed in this book. Similarly, the institutional choices underpinning the Treaty of Rome (1957), largely determined by geopolitical considerations at the time (Rosato 2011), cast a shadow over current distributive contentions within the union, and its ability to transform itself from a confederation into a federation. These results imply that the theoretical and empirical investigation of the historical origins of today's links between institutions and inequality should become a top priority in the comparative politics of inequality and redistribution (Beramendi and Anderson 2008; Rogowski and MacRae 2008).

This implication applies to many aspects of the comparative study of distribution and redistribution beyond this book. For instance, the relationship between economic institutions and the distribution of income is worth revisiting from this perspective. From standard analysis in which economic institutions are the primary determinant of wage compression (Wallerstein 1999), the field has evolved. It is now recognized that the decline in inequality might have preceded the adoption of comprehensive collective bargaining systems and employers' coordination (Stasavage and Scheve 2009). The possibility that these institutional arrangements may be a function of pre-existing levels of inequality, either among workers organizations (Iversen 1999) or among employers themselves (Beramendi and Rueda 2010) is also being explored. Overall, the analytical approach developed in this study offers an alternative framework for understanding the long-term relationship between institutions and social outcomes, and is potentially extendable beyond its empirical realm of interest.

A third implication of this study concerns the way redistribution operates and how to conceptualize it. The distinction between interpersonal and interregional as dimensions of redistribution implies that each of these responds to different political logics. Interregional redistribution occurs when interpersonal redistribution is partly decentralized and local elites manage to maximize rent extraction. In turn, interpersonal redistribution is centralized when the will of local elites is overrun by either massive externalities or the political interests of their national counterparts. The interplay between geography and representation on the one hand, and the levels of mobility on the other, matter to explain both of them, but the relative importance of each set of factors seems to differ.

I have provided in depth analyses and econometric results on both of them. The latter suggests that while the design of interpersonal redistribution is mostly driven by the interplay between geography and representation, interregional redistribution responds mostly to the scope of economic externalities created by large levels of geographical mobility. As a result, the EU has some interregional redistribution and virtually no interpersonal redistribution, whereas Germany, for instance, seems to score very high on both dimensions. However, the findings in this book also suggest that the boundaries between these two programs are much more blurred than the sharp distinction I have just drawn.

To begin with, the factors that matter overlap: representation is also an important determinant of the levels of interregional redistribution, as exemplified by Germany's experience with Reunification. Mobility can also affect the incentives to centralize a public insurance program directed to individuals, as exemplified by the analysis of the Canadian response to the Great Depression. Moreover, in many cases, there is a budgetary link between them: the incorporation of the East into the German system of social assistance (a system of transfers to those most in need) required an increase in the interregional transfer of resources. The tax-offset system that accompanied the launching of unemployment insurance in the United States was also a system of interregional redistribution: those states enacting the program would receive their share of the employer's tax collected by the federal government. Otherwise, they would not. To complicate matters further, interpersonal transfers themselves have a nonneutral incidence across territories, mostly dictated by the regional distribution of actual and/or potential recipients. Thus, an increase in the generosity of unemployment benefits in Germany for instance, would automatically imply a flow of resources from East to West.

With these complications in mind, it is hardly surprising that the field treats redistribution as a black box. By either ignoring the territorial aspects of redistribution altogether (Beramendi and Anderson 2008; Beramendi and Cusack

2009; Bradley et al. 2003) or by mixing both actual interregional transfers and the territorial incidence of interpersonal ones into the indicator (Rodden and Dragu 2010), the field continues to neglect the multidimensionality in the architecture of redistribution. However, insofar as the conclusions of this study hold, there is much to gain in the future by analytically decomposing the different tools through which redistribution occurs in both developed and developing nations. This will require not only a massive data collection effort on the territorial incidence of different policy tools but, more importantly, a theoretical effort to better understand the incentives of incumbents in centralized regimes to target funds to different regions and/or population subgroups.

In addition, the full understanding of the multidimensional nature of redistributive conflicts in complex societies requires to take on several other challenges. These relate directly to some of the simplifying assumptions adopted in this study. The first one concerns the interplay between identity and redistribution. In many political unions, identity is a major factor driving political preferences, party alliances, and public policy (Fearon and Van Houten 1998; Horowitz 1985). In the theoretical argument of this book, I have treated identity both partially and indirectly. But this by no means implies that identity based dimensions do not matter. Quite to the contrary, as reflected by a growing literature on the role of second dimensions in the formation of preferences for redistribution (Austen-Smith and Wallerstein 2008; Glaeser 2005; Roemer and Woojin 2006) this is hardly the case. While the need to prevent additional complexities in an argument already involving several dimensions justifies its exclusion from the analysis of the relationship between economic geography and preference formation, a thorough analysis of the interplay between identity and inequality during the process of preference formation for fiscal structures remains a major task ahead in comparative politics.

Identity also matters for the process of preference aggregation through the system of political representation. On this point, I have limited my approach to the assumption that the presence of regional political parties mobilizing ethnic identities is a major factor contributing to the centrifugal nature of political representation. The Spanish experience offers an illustration of how the presence of nationalist parties as major players in the political system triggers and sustains a centrifugal spiral in the representation of contending political views. Identity based parties limit the nationalization of parties and alter the feasible set of political coalitions in the lower house. Moreover, as reflected by the Spanish and other experiences, this tendency tends to reinforce itself over time.

Within such a process, the boundary between contentions about fiscal structures and the politicization of the federal contract itself becomes increasingly blurred. A full grasp of this process requires taking yet another step: tackling the endogenous nature of political representation over time. An important concern in this book was whether political representation was *fixed* at the time an exogenous alteration of the patterns of economic geography triggered the political conflict. This condition determined the extent to which cases provided leverage for causal identification.

Yet, the fact that a particular arrangement is given at the time of a shock does not necessarily shelter it from eventually becoming the object of political contention or, more importantly, for having been in the past. This book has shown how conflicts over fiscal structures and conflicts over political representation of territorial interests condition one another in a dynamic, bidirectional way, often fostering institutional stability in political unions. This line of reasoning brings out one final corollary: the need to better understand the relationship between the distributive tensions emerging from the geography of inequality and labor market risks, and the original constitutional bargains in federations. Constitutions freeze the organization of political representation for long historical periods, thus shaping the dynamics of what Ackerman called "ordinary politics" (Ackerman 1998). Therefore, a full account of the origins of different systems of representation of territorial interests demands a better understanding of the role of distributive conflicts in shaping the original contract of political unions. While some scholarly effort has been devoted to this problem (McGuire 2003; Wibbels 2005a), there is much room to cover, both theoretically and empirically, to fully explain why some federal constitutions are more centrifugal than others and what makes them evolve. Analyzing the representation of territorial interests across constitutional agreements as a function of economic geography is a natural path to follow in our continuing efforts to decipher politics in complex unions around the world.

Appendix A

Chapter 2

THE DECISION TO PURSUE A CHANGE IN THE ORGANIZATION OF FISCAL STRUCTURES

Status Quo 1: The Decision by the National Government (expression 4 in text)

$$U_n^P(D) \leq \alpha(U_n^P(C)) + (1 - \alpha)(U_n^P(D \mid challenge))$$

This can be shown to imply (expression 6 in text):

$$1 \leq \frac{\alpha}{(1-\alpha)} \frac{\left[(\Omega_r - \Omega_n)\lambda_n^P + (1-\Phi)(\varphi_r - \varphi_n)\chi_r^P\right]}{(1-\Omega_r)(1-\mu)\lambda_n^P}$$

Proof:

$$\left[(1-\Omega_r)\lambda_n^P + (1-\Phi)(1-\varphi_r)\chi_r^P\right]$$
$$\leq \alpha \left[(1-\Omega_n)\lambda_n^P + (1-\Phi)(1-\varphi_n)\chi_r^P\right]$$
$$+ (1-\alpha)\left[(1-\Omega_r)\mu\lambda_n^P + (1-\Phi)(1-\varphi_r)\chi_r^P\right]$$
$$\to \left[(1-\Omega_r)(1-\mu)\lambda_n^P\right]$$
$$\leq \alpha \left(\left[(1-\Omega_n)\lambda_n^P + (1-\Phi)(1-\varphi_n)\chi_r^P\right]\right.$$
$$\left.- \left[(1-\Omega_r)\mu\lambda_n^P + (1-\Phi)(1-\varphi_r)\chi_r^P\right]\right)$$
$$\to 1 \leq \frac{\alpha}{(1-\alpha)} \frac{\left[(\Omega_r - \Omega_n)\lambda_n^P + (1-\Phi)(\varphi_r - \varphi_n)\chi_r^P\right]}{(1-\Omega_r)(1-\mu)\lambda_n^P}$$

Status Quo 2: The Decision by the Regional Government (expression 5 in text)

$$U_r^P(C) \leq \beta\left(U_r^P(D)\right) + (1-\beta)(U_r^P(C \mid challenge)).$$

This can be shown to imply (expression 7 in text):

$$1 \leq \frac{\beta}{(1-\beta)} \frac{[\varphi_n - \varphi_r]\lambda_r^P + \Phi(\Omega_n - \Omega_r)\varphi_r^P}{(1-\varphi_n)(1-\mu)\lambda_r^P}$$

249

Proof:

$$[(1-\varphi_n)\lambda_r^P + \Phi(1-\Omega_n)\phi_r^P]$$
$$\leq \beta[(1-\varphi_r)\lambda_r^P + \Phi(1-\Omega_r)\phi_r^P] + (1-\beta)[(1-\varphi_n)\mu\lambda_r^P + \Phi(1-\Omega_n)\phi_r^P]$$
$$\rightarrow [(1-\varphi_n)(1-\mu)\lambda_r^P] \leq \beta[(\varphi_n-\varphi_r)\lambda_r^P + (1-\varphi_n)(1-\mu)\lambda_r^P + \Phi(\Omega_n-\Omega_r)\phi_r^P]$$
$$\rightarrow 1 \leq \frac{\beta}{1-\beta} \frac{[(\varphi_n-\varphi_r)\lambda_r^P + \Phi(\Omega_n-\Omega_r)\phi_r^P]}{(1-\varphi_n)(1-\mu)\lambda_r^P}$$

ECONOMIC GEOGRAPHY AND PREFERENCES FOR REDISTRIBUTION

The Geography of Income and Preferences for Fiscal Structures

As stated in the main text, citizens face a decision about two policy instruments, namely the level of interpersonal redistribution (t), and the level of interregional transfers of resources among members of the union, that is to say the level of interregional redistribution (T). At any given time individuals might be employed with probability α or unemployed with probability $(1-\alpha)$. Individuals maximize consumption across both states. Individual consumption is defined by $c_i = (1-t)w_i$ in the good state of the world and by b in the bad state of the world, where b represents the benefits individuals receive while unemployed. In addition, citizens are affected by an interregional transfer that, when in place, is a function of the regional average income vis-à-vis the union. So, for regions wealthier than the average, the transfer is negative (and vice versa).

Finally, there is a union budget constraint given by $\alpha w^\mu t = (1-\alpha)b$, where w^μ is the average output in the union. The term $\frac{\beta}{2}t^2$ captures the inefficiency cost of taxation, typically assumed to operate through the reduction in supply of labor.

Given these assumptions and a status quo of centralization, citizens in any given region, r, have the following utility:

$$V_{ir} = \alpha(w_{ir}(1-t)) + (1-\alpha)b - \frac{\beta}{2}t^2 - T(w_r - w^\mu)$$
$$\text{s.t. } (1-\alpha)b = \alpha w^\mu t$$
$$\rightarrow V_{ir} = \alpha(w_{ir}(1-t)) + \alpha w^\mu t - \frac{\beta}{2}t^2 - T(w_r - w^\mu)$$
$$\rightarrow \frac{\partial V_{ir}}{\partial t} = \alpha(w^\mu - w_{ir}) - \beta t \geq 0$$
$$\rightarrow 1 \geq t^* = \frac{\alpha}{\beta}(w^\mu - w_{ir}) \geq 0$$

The following insights emerge from this expression:

(i) any citizen in any region with income above w^μ will want zero union-wide income tax rate;

Appendix A Chapter 2

(ii) any citizen anywhere with income at or below $w_{ir} \leq \overline{w}_{ir} \equiv w^u - \frac{\beta}{\alpha}$ will want $t^* = 1$;

(iii) $\frac{\partial t}{\partial w_{ir}} < 0$ for $w^u \geq w_{ir} \geq \overline{w}_{ir}$

(iv) the more citizens below w^u the greater the demand for redistribution;

(v) a rise in average income in the country raises the demand for redistribution $\frac{\partial t}{\partial w_{ir}} = \frac{\alpha}{\beta} > 0$.

(vi) It is also clear that all citizens in regions with $w_r < w^u$ will support the highest value of T feasible, and those where $w_r > w^u$ will want $T = 0$.

In a decentralised world, the solution to the maximization problem yields:

$$1 \geq t_r^* = \frac{\alpha}{\beta}(w_r - w_{ir}) \geq 0$$

and all the corresponding results apply within regions. These results map formally onto the distribution of preferences for citizens in regions A and B reported earlier in Figure 2.2.

THE GEOGRAPHY OF ECONOMIC SPECIALIZATION AND INSTITUTIONAL PREFERENCES

To capture the link between economic specialization and risk, and how they shape preferences for redistribution and fiscal structures, the model of individual preferences includes an additional insurance motive that is assumed to relate directly to the specialization of economic activity across areas. Risks are assumed to behave according to Arrow-Pratt constant relative risk aversion function, by which $(\frac{c_i}{1-\delta})^{1-\delta}$, where c_i represents individual consumption. As a result of these transformations, citizens' utility function becomes:

$$V_{ir} = \alpha \frac{(w_{ir}(1-t) - T(w_r - w^u))^{1-\delta}}{1-\delta}$$

$$+ (1-\alpha) \frac{(\frac{\alpha}{1-\alpha} t w^u - T(w_r - w^u))^{1-\delta}}{1-\delta}$$

$$\rightarrow \frac{\partial V_{ir}}{\partial t} = -\alpha w_{ir}(w_{ir}(1-t^*) - T(w_r - w^u))^{-\delta} + (1-\alpha)$$

$$\times \left(\frac{\alpha}{1-\alpha} t^* w^u - T(w_r - w^u)\right)^{-\delta} \frac{\alpha}{1-\alpha} w^u = 0, 1 > t^* > 0$$

$$\rightarrow (w_{ir}(1-t^*) - T(w_r - w^u))\left(\frac{w_{ir}}{w^u}\right)^{-\frac{1}{\delta}}$$

$$= \left(\frac{\alpha}{1-\alpha} t^* w^u - T(w_r - w^u)\right), 1 > t^* > 0$$

where the last line is the FOC for a unique interior solution of the optimal tax rate, t^*.

A number of interest implications follow from this FOC expression:

(i) The demand for redistribution, t^*, increases with the scope of realized risks, $1 - \alpha$. If the FOC is totally differentiated with respect to t^* and $(\alpha/1 - \alpha)$, the result is:

$$\frac{dt^*}{d\left(\frac{\alpha}{1-\alpha}\right)} = -\frac{t^* w^\mu}{\left(\frac{\alpha}{1-\alpha} w^\mu + \left(\frac{w_{ir}}{w^\mu}\right)^{-\frac{1}{\delta}} w_{ir}\right)} < 0 \rightarrow \frac{dt^*}{d(1-\alpha)} > 0$$

(ii) The demand for redistribution increases with risk aversion. To see this, note that in the solution to the optimization problem, $\frac{\partial t^*}{\partial \delta} > 0$.

(iii) As a result of risk aversion, it is also the case that $t^* > 0$ when $w_{ir} > w^\mu$ (so long as it is not too much greater), whereas with $\delta = 0$ any income above w^μ will prefer $t^* = 0$. To see this note that if $w_{ir} = w^\mu$ then in the FOC $(\frac{w_{ir}}{w^\mu})^{-\frac{1}{\delta}} = 1$, if $\delta > 0$, and the FOC then implies with $w_{ir} = w^\mu$ that $t^* = 1 - \alpha$, which is strictly positive for $\alpha < 1$. Hence a small increase in w_{ir} above w^μ implies a small decrease in t^*, and a small enough increase in w_{ir} implies that t^* must remain positive.

On the basis of these results, the geography of economic specialization and risk produces the following map of preferences in the case of a union where the poor region in the one showing high levels of economic specialization (as reported in Figure 2.3).

Appendix B

Chapter 4

TABLE B.I. *Mixed Level Estimates of Individual Preferences for the Harmonization of Social Welfare Systems within the European Union*

	Full Population	Dependents
Inequality	−12.09***	−10.8***
	(1.27)	(2.24)
GDP-per capita	−.0256***)	−.019**
	(.004)	(.007)
Inequality*GDPpc	.117***	.106***
	(.014)	(.025)
Fiscal Balance	−.001***	−.001***
	(.00001)	(.0002)
Effort in Active Labor Market Policy	.27***	.137
	(.053)	(.097)
Unemployment_95_00	−.019***	−.0178
	(.006)	(.0103)
Dependent vs. Active	−.069*	–
	(.039)	
Age	.0017	.0036*
	(.001)	(.001)
Gender	.078**	.197***
	(.029)	(.051)
Subjective Perception of Economic Situation	.014	−.008
	(.015)	(.026)
Ideology	007	.0059
	(.006)	(.011)

(continued)

253

TABLE B.1 *(continued)*

	Full Population	Dependents
Education	−.048**	−.079**
	(.019)	(.032)
Marital Status	.015**	.016*
	(.006)	(.009)
Urban-Rural	−.0160	−.03
	(.0188)	(.03)
N		
Individuals	16545	5685
Countries	18	18

(Link function: ologit; standard errors in parentheses)
Individual Variables from ICPSR Study 20321: Eurobarometer 65.1: The Future of Europe, February-March 2006.
Key: * p < .10, ** p < .05, *** p < .01

TABLE B.2. *Logit and Probit Estimates of Support for Welfare Centralization Among European Social Democratic Parties and Trade Unions*

	Logit	Probit
Inequality	−243.73**	−142.8**
	(124.06)	(72)
GDP-per capita	−.857**	−.501**
	(.40)	(.22)
Inequality*GDPpc	2.57**	1.50**
	(1.44)	(.71)
Fiscal Balance	.00006	.00004
	(.0002)	(.0001)
Effort in Active Labor Market Policy	−4.20	−2.44
	(4.3)	(2.25)
Unemployment_95_00	−.22	−.121
	(.22)	(.136)
Intercept	84.1**	49.3**
	(41)	(23)
N	38	38
Pseudo-R-Sq.	.53	.54

Data: "European Social and Economic Model", Friedrich Ebert Foundation. My thanks to Marius Busemeyer for sharing the data with me.
Key: * p < .10, ** p < .05, *** p < .01

TABLE B.3. *OLS Estimation of Countries' Position over the EU's role in Social Policy during the Constitutional Convention*

	OLS, robust s.e.	OLS, robust s.e.
Inequality	−87.36**	−.005**
	(35.5)	(.0025)
GDP-per capita	−.20*	.036**
	(.10)	(.013)
Inequality*GDPpc	.833**	−
	(.40)	
Fiscal Balance	.0002	−.00512**
	(.0002)	(.0025)
Inequality*Fiscal Balance	−	.0171**
		(.0077)
Effort in Active Labor Market Policy	−.25	−2.98
	(.45)	(.2.6)
Unemployment_95_00	−.083	−.112
	(.19)	(.161)
Intercept	29.8***	10.40***
	(9.2)	(3.43)
N	24	24
Pseudo-R-Sq.	.40	.46

Data for the dependent variable from the Domestic Structures and European Integration Project (DOSEI). My thanks to Thomas König for sharing the data with me.
Key: * $p < .10$, ** $p < .05$, *** $p < .01$

VARIABLE SOURCES AND DEFINITIONS

Individual Level Variables: Eurobarometer 65.1: The Future of Europe
Age: continuous variable ranging from 15 to 97
Gender: 1: Male 2: Female
Subjective Perception of Economic Situation: Scaled response (1: totally agree-4: totally disagree) to the following statement: "You find it difficult to make ends meet".
Ideology: Left-Right Scale (1: left-10: right)
Education: Age at the time of stopping full time education
Dependent: 1=not working, receiving welfare benefits; 0=working
Marital Status: 1: Married; 0: rest
Urban-Rural: 1: cities, 2: mixed settings, 3: rural

Country Level Variables:
Inequality: Household Disposable Income per Equivalent Adult, Luxembourg Income Study data set. I use the wave/year immediately preceding the observation of the dependent variable.

GDP per capita: Gross Domestic Product per capita in PPS (EU average=100). Source: Eurostat.

Fiscal Balance: Net budgetary balance per capita. Data from European Commission, Budget, several years.

Effort in Active Labor Market Policy: Expenditure in Active Labor Market Policies as a percentage of GDP, 2000–2005 (average): Social Expenditure Database, 2009 Edition.

Unemployment, 1995–2000 (average): OECD Labor Force Statistics, various years.

Internal and Outward Mobility Rates: Huber (2005) and Eurostat, New Cronos Database.

Appendix C

Chapter 7

Interregional Transfers per Capita: Author's calculations on the basis of data from Budesministerium der Finanzen (1960–2004) and the Statistiche Bundesamt (population data, several years).

Mobility: outward mobility rate by land. Source: Heiland (2004) and Statistische Bundesamt, several years.

GDP per capita: Länder's gross domestic product per capita, expressed in Euro 1995. Source: Rodden (1999).

East: categorical variable with value 1 for Eastern länder and 0 otherwise.

Copartisanship: categorical variable identifying whether the regional and the federal governments are controlled by the same party or coalition. Source: Rodden (1999).

Appendix D

Chapter 8 – Sources and Descriptive Statistics

TABLE D.1. *Economic Geography, Interpersonal Redistribution, and Income Inequality in Advanced Industrial Societies (Tables 8.1, 8.2, and 8.5 in text)*

	Mean	Standard Deviation	Range
Decentralization of Interpersonal Redistribution	2.04	3.99	0–17.4
Interregional Differences in Growth	0.10	.04	0.04–0.26
Interregional Differences in the Incidence of Unemployment	.32	.17	0.05–1.23
Trade Openness	63.8	29.5	17.7–148.38
Mobility	.01	.0075	0–.045
Geographical Differences in the Incidence of Inequality	1.2	.25	1–1.9
Representation	.67	.37	.12–1
Heterogeneity of Party Systems across Regions	.24	.44	0–2.94
Country Size (log)	12.9	1.81	10.3–16.11
Ethnic Fractionalization	0.23	0.21	0.022–0.75
Total Taxation	39.24	7.03	23.8–52.21
Economic Growth	2.34	1.45	−1.11–5.7
Overall Economic Inequality (Disposable Income)	0.27	0.043	0.19–0.37
Market Income Inequality	0.39	0.041	0.28–0.47
Partisanship	1.9	.43	1–4
Economic Coordination	0.59	0.30	0–1

TABLE D.2. *Economic Geography, Interpersonal Redistribution, and Interregional Redistribution around the World (Tables 8.3, 8.4 in text)*

	Mean	Standard Deviation	Range
Decentralization of Interpersonal Redistribution	18.37	13.6	.22–73.9
Interregional Redistribution	2.88	1.51	.0006–6.26
Distribution of Ethnic Population across Regions	0.26	0.23	0–0.74
Inter-industry Labor Mobility	–.22	0.92	–2.93–2.70
Interregional Inequality	2.33	1.08	1.12–5.46
Representation	0.51	0.342	0–1
Country Size	10.7	1.26	8.7–13.86
Economic Development (thousands US$ 85)	8.03	5.46	0.32–21.1
Ethno-linguistic Fractionalization	0.483	0.266	0.013–0.886
Total Taxation	3.35	1.20	1.43–7.50
Democracy (Polity)	5.09	6.31	–9–10

Data Sources

TABLE D.3. *Advanced Industrial Societies (Tables 8.1, 8.2, and 8.5 in text)*

	Definition and Sources
Decentralization of Interpersonal Redistribution	OECD data on consolidated central government direct transfers to households (generously facilitated by Thomas Cusack) and regional fiscal autonomy (OECD; Stegarescu 2005). My thanks as well to Dan Stegarescu for generously sharing his data on tax decentralization.
Interregional Differences in Growth	Coefficient of Variation in Regional GDP per capita. Source: OECD territorial database and EUROSTAT-New Cronos Database (NUTS-3 regions); Statistics Canada; Bureau of the Census; Australian Bureau of Statistics; Statistics Finland; Statistics Norway; Statistics Denmark; and Statistics Sweden.
Interregional Differences in the Incidence of Unemployment	Coefficient of Variation in Regional Unemployment Rates (constructed by the author). The term regional refers to a level of government similar to the German länder, the Canadian provinces or the American states. Sources: EUROSTAT-New Cronos Database (NUTS-3 regions); Statistics Canada; Bureau of the Census; Australian Bureau of Statistics; Statistics Finland; Statistics Norway; Statistics Denmark; and Statistics Sweden.
Trade Openness	Sum of total imports and exports on good and services as a percentage of GDP. Source: OECD, National Accounts, Part II: Detailed Tables (various years).

(continued)

TABLE D.3 *(continued)*

	Definition and Sources
Mobility	Rate of inter-industry labor mobility for any given country-year. Data from Hiscox and Rickard 2002, generously facilitated by Michael Hiscox and updated by the author to 2000 on the basis of OECD and Structural Analysis-STAN Databases.
Geographical Differences in the Incidence of Inequality	Ratio of the most to the least unequal region in the union, as measured by the regional Gini coefficient for household market income per equivalent adult. Calculations by the author on the basis of the Luxembourg Income Study and the European Community Household Panel databases.
Representation	Definition in text (expression 8.3). Calculations by the author on the basis of regional and national official electoral results of OECD countries between 1980 and the early 2000s.
Heterogeneity of Party Systems across Regions	Definition in text (expression 8.4). Calculations by the author on the basis of constitutional sources, secondary sources (Watts 2008), and regional and national official electoral results of OECD countries between 1980 and the early 2000s.
Country Size	Data gathered from Geohive: Global Data Index.
Ethnic Fractionalization	Source: 1960 Soviet Ethnographic Atlas. Defined as one minus the sum of squared population proportions in each ethnolinguistic group.
Total Taxation	Source: OECD Government Finance Dataset, collected by Thomas R. Cusack. Science Center, Berlin.
Economic Growth	Inter-annual change in GDP per capita. Source: Penn World Tables.
Overall Economic Inequality (Disposable Income) Market Income Inequality	The Gini Coefficient ranges between 0 (perfect equality) and 1 (perfect inequality). Calculations by the author based on Luxembourg Income Study data and domestic sources for the following income concepts. *Market* = GWS + SEI + CPI, where GWS stands for gross wages and salaries (earnings), SEI stands for self-employment income, and CPI refers to cash property income. *Disposable* = Market + TR-TX, where TR is the sum of all transfers received by the working age population and TX stands for the sum of social security contributions and income tax.
Partisanship	This is an index of cabinet "center of political gravity" developed by Thomas Cusack (see Cusack and Engelhardt 2002).
Economic Coordination	Indicator of overall economic coordination that ranges between 0 and 1 as calculated by Hall and Gingerich (2009).

TABLE D.4. *Sample Including Advanced and Developing Countries (Tables 8.2, 8.4 in text)*

Decentralization of Interpersonal Redistribution	Author's calculations. Product between expenditure decentralization and revenue autonomy (excluding intergovernmental transfers) on the basis of the IMF Government Financial Statistics.
Interregional Redistribution	Author's calculations. Transfers to other levels of government as a percentage of GDP. Original data from IMF Government Financial Statistics and Rodden and Wibbels "States, Rates, and the Fates of Federations: Regional Politics and Fiscal Policy Around the World", NSF Project.
Distribution of Ethnic Population across regions	Share of population living in ethnic minority regions. minority/majority regions are defined as those in which at least half of the population belongs to an ethnic group that is different from the largest ethnic group in the country as a whole. Source: Bakke and Wibbels (2006).
Oil Dependence	Categorical variable indicating whether the union is oil exporting (1) or not.
Inter-industry Labor Mobility	Elasticity of labor to inter-industry wage differentials. Source: Zhou (2009).
Interregional Inequality	P90_p10 ratio in terms of regional GDP per capita. Source: Bakke and Wibbels (2006).
Representation	Same definition as above (expression 8.3). Data necessary to compute the index from Rodden and Wibbels "States, Rates, and the Fates of Federations: Regional Politics and Fiscal Policy Around the World", NSF Project.
Economic Development	GDP per capita. Source: Penn World Tables, various years.
Ethno-linguistic Fractionalization	Same as above.
Total Taxation	Total revenues as a percentage of GDP. Source: IMF Government Finance Statistics.
Democracy (Polity)	Aggregate Index of Democracy as constructed by Polity IV (http://www.systemicpeace.org/polity/polity4.htm)

References

Acemoglu, D., S. Johnson and J. Robinson (2002) "Reversals of Fortune: Geography and Institutions in the Making of the Modern World Income Distribution." *Quarterly Journal of Economics*, 117(4): 1231–1294.

Acemoglu, D. and J. Robinson (2006) *Economic Origins of Dictatorship and Democracy*. Cambridge: Cambridge University Press.

Achembaum, W. A. (1986) *Social Security: Visions and Revisions*. Cambridge: Cambridge University Press.

Ackerman, B. (1998) *We the People: Transformations*. Cambridge, MA: Belknap Press.

Adsera, A. and C. Boix (2002) "Trade, Democracy, and the Size of the Public Sector: The Political Underpinnings of Openness." *International Organization*, 56(2): 229–262.

Adelberger, K. (1999) *Federalism and its Discontents: Fiscal and Legislative Power Sharing in Germany, 1948–1999*. Institute of Governmental Studies. Berkeley, CA: University of California-Berkeley. Pp. 16–99.

Aja, Eliseo (2003)[1999] *El Estado Autonomico: Federalismo y Hechos Diferenciales*. Madrid, Alianza Editorial.

Albertí Rovira, E. (1996) "El Regimen de los Convenios de colaboracion entre administraciones: un problema pendiente" *en Informe de las Comunidades Autonomas*, Barcelona: Instituto de Derecho Publico.

Alesina, A and R. Perotti (1998) "Economic Risks and Political Risks in Fiscal Unions." *The Economic Journal*, 108: 989–1008.

Alesina, A. and E. L. Glaeser (2004) *Fighting Poverty in the US and Europe: A World of Difference*. Oxford: Oxford University Press.

Alesina, A., E. Glaeser and B. Sacerdote (2001) "Why Doesn't the United States Have a European Style Welfare State?" *Brookings Paper on Economic Activity* , (Fall): 187–278.

Alesina, A. and E. Spolaore (2003) *The Size of Nations*. London: MIT Press.

Alesina, A. and R. Wacziarg (1998) "Openness, Country Size and Government." *Journal of Public Economics*, 69: 305–321.

Alston, L. J. and J. P. Ferrie (1999) *Southern Paternalism and the American Welfare State*. Cambridge: Cambridge University Press.

Altmeyer, A. (1968) *The Formative Years of Social Security*, Madison: University of Wisconsin Press.

Amat, F., I. Jurado and S. León (2010) *A Political Theory of Decentralization Dynamics*, Madrid: Juan March Institute, Working Paper 2009/248.

Amenta, E. and B.G. Carruthers, (1988) "The Formative Years of U.S. Social Spending Policies: Theories of the Welfare State and the American States during the Great Depression." *American Sociological Review*, 53: 661–678.

Amenta E., E. Clemens, J. Olsen, S. Parihk and T. Skocpol (1987) "The Political Origins of Unemployment Insurance in Five American States." *Studies in American Political Development*, 2: 137–182.

Anderson, J. (1992) *The Territorial Imperative. Pluralism, Corporatism and Economic Crisis*. Cambridge: Cambridge University Press.

Arriba González de Durana, A. (1999) "Procesos de implantación de políticas de rentas mínimas de inserción en España." CSIC-WP.

Atkinson, A.B. (1995) *Incomes and the Welfare State*. Cambridge: Cambridge University Press.

Atkinson, A.B. (1999) *The Economic Consequences of Rolling Back the Welfare State*. Cambridge, MA: MIT-CES, Cambridge.

Atkinson, A.B. (2002) "Social Inclusion and the European Union", *Journal of Common Market Studies*, 40(4): 625–43.

Austen-Smith, D. and J. Banks (1988) "Elections, coalitions and legislative outcomes." *American Political Science Review*: 82(2): 405–422.

Austen-Smith, D. and M. Wallerstein (2008) "Redistribution and Affirmative Action." In D. Austen-Smith et al. (eds.) *Selected Works of Michael Wallerstein*. Cambridge, Cambridge University Press.

Babones, S. J. (2008) "Standardized Income Inequality Data for Use in Cross-National Research", *Sociological Inquiry*, 77:3–22.

Bakke, K. and E. Wibbels (2006) "Diversity, Disparity and Civil Conflict in Federal States." *World Politics*, 59:1–50.

Baltagi, B. (2008) *Econometric Analysis of Panel Data*. New York: John Wiley.

Banting, K. (1987) *The Welfe State and Canadian Federalism*, Quebec, Mc-Gill-Press University Press.

Banting, K. (1992) "Neoconservatism in an Open Economy: The social Role of the Canadian State", *International Political Science Review*, 13: 149–170.

Banting, K. (1997) "The Social Policy Divide: the welfare state in Canada and the United States." In K. Banting et al. (eds.) *Degrees of Freedom: Canada and the United States in a Changing World*, Kingston-Montreal, McGill-Queens University Press.

Banting, K. (2005) "Canada: Nation Building in a Federal Welfare State." In H. Obinger et al. (eds) *Federalism and the Welfare State*. Cambridge, Cambridge University Press.

Bañón, R. and R. Agranoff (1998) *El Estado de las Autonomias:Hacia un Nuevo Federalismo?* Bilbao IVAP.

Barbe, E. (1999) *La Political Europea de España*. Barcelona, Ariel.

Barr, J.J. (1974) *The Dynasty: The Rise and Fall of Social Credit in Alberta*. Oronto, Maclellan.

Bartomeous, O. (ed.) (2003) *La Competencia Politica en la España de las Autonomias*. Barcelona, ICPS.

Beard, Ch. (1933) [1913] *An Economic Interpretation of the Constitution of the United States*, New York, The Free Press.

Beck, N. and J. Katz (1995) "What To Do (and Not To Do) with Times-Series–Cross-Section Data in Comparative Politics." *American Political Science Review*, 89(3): 634–647.

References

Bednar, J. (2005) "Federalism as a Public Good." *Constitutional Political Economy* 16(2): 189–204.

Bednar, J. (2008) *The Robust Federation*. Cambridge, Cambridge University Press.

Bednar, J., W. Eskridge, Jr., and J. Ferejohn (2001) "A Political Theory of Federalism." In J. Ferejohn, J. N. Rakove, and J. Riley (eds.), *Constitutional Culture and Democratic Rule*. New York, NY: Cambridge University Press, pp. 223–270.

Benz, A. (1989) "Intergovernmental Relations in the 1980s." *Publius: The Journal of Federalism*, 19(4): 199–217.

Beramendi, P. (2001) "The politics of income inequality in the OECD: the role of second order effects." Working Paper 284. Luxembourg Income Study.

Beramendi, P. (2007) "Inequality and the territorial fragmentation of solidarity." *International Organization*, 61: 783–820.

Beramendi, P. (2007b) "Federalism." In C. Boix and S. Stokes (eds.) *Handbook of Comparative Politics*. Oxford: Oxford University Press.

Beramendi, P. and C. J. Anderson (2008) "Inequality and Democratic Representation: the road traveled and the path ahead." In P. Beramendi and C. J. Anderson (eds.), *Democracy, Inequality and Representation: A Comparative Perspective*. Russell Sage Foundation, forthcoming.

Beramendi, P. and T. R. Cusack. (2009) "Diverse Disparities: the Politics and Economics of Wage, Markets, and Disposable Income Inequalities." *Political Research Quarterly*, 62(2): 257–275.

Beramendi, P. and A. Diaz-Cayeros (2008) "Distributive Tensions in Developing Federations." Paper presented at the Annual Meetings of the American Political Science Association.

Beramendi, P. and R. Máiz. (2004) "Spain: Unfulfilled Federalism, 1978–2004." In N. Bermeo and U. Amoretti (eds.), *Federalism and Territorial Cleavages*. Baltimore, John Hopkins University Press.

Beramendi, P. and D. Rueda. (2010) "Inequality and Labor Market Coordination in the Early XXth Century." Mimeo. DPIR University of Oxford.

Beramendi, P. and Wibbels (2010) "Foundational Bargains: Distributive Conflicts and Representation in Federations." Duke University. Unpublished manuscript.

Berkowitz, E. D. (1991) *America's Welfare State. From Roosevelt to Reagan*. Baltimore: The John Hopkins University Press.

Bernacke, B. (2004) *Essays on the Great Depression*. Princeton, NJ: Princeton University Press.

Bewley, T.F. (1981) "A Critique of Tiebout's Theory of Local Public Expenditures" *Econometrica*, 49(3): 713–740.

Biehl, D. and P. Ungar. (1991) "La Distribución de la Renta y el Sistema de Transferencias Intergubernamentales en la República Federal de Alemania." *Hacienda Pública Española*, 118(2): 39–65.

Boix, C. (2003) *Democracy and Redistribution*. New York, Cambridge University Press.

Bolton, P. and G. Roland (1996) "Distributional Conflicts, Factor Mobility and Political Integration." *American Economic Associations Papers and Proceedings* 86(2): 99–104.

Bolton, P. and G. Roland (1997) "The Breakup of Nations: a Political Economy Analysis." *Quarterly Journal of Economics* 112: 1057–1090.

Borkenhagen, F. H. (1990) "Vom kooperativen Föderalismus zum Europa der Regionen." *Aus Politik and Zeitgeschichte*, 4: 36–44.

Börzel, T. (2005) "Mind the Gap! European Integration between Level and Scope." *Journal of European Public Policy*, 12(2): 1–20.

Bosch N. and J.J. Durán. (2005) *La Financiacion de las Comunidades Autonomas: Politicas Tributarias y Solidaridad Interterritorial*. Barcelona, Universidad de Barcelona.

Bradley, D., E. Huber, S. Moller, F. Nielsen, and J. D. Stephens. (2003) "Distribution and Redistribution in Post-industrial Societies." *World Politics* 55: 193–228.

Brancatti, D. (2009) *Peace by Design*. Oxford, Oxford University Press.

Brennan, G. and J. Buchanan (1980) *The Power to Tax*. Cambridge, Mass: Cambridge University Press.

Brinegar, A. S. Jolly and H. Kitschelt (2004) "Varieties of Capitalism and Political Divides over European Integration" in G. Marks and M. Steenbergen (eds.) *European Integration and Political Conflict*, Cambridge, Cambridge University Press.

Brinegar A. and S. Jolly (2005) "Location, location, location" *European Union Politics* 6,2:155–180.

Brinkley, A. (1984) "The New Deal and Southern Politics." In J. Cobb and M.V. Namorato (eds.) *The New Deal and the South*, Jackson, University Press of Mississippi.

Buchanan, J. (1950) "Federalism and Fiscal Equity." *American Economic Review*, 40: 583–599.

Buchanan, J. (1995) "Federalism As an Ideal Political Order and an Objective for Constitutional Reform." *Publius: The Journal of Federalism*, 25(2): 19–27.

Buchanan, J.M. and R.E. Wagner (1970) "An Efficiency Basis for Federal Fiscal Equalisation." In J. Margolis (ed.) *The Analysis of Public Output*, New York. NBER.

Bulmer, S. (1991) "Efficiency, Democracy and West German Federalism." In C. Jeffery and P. Savigear (eds.), *German Federalism Today*, St Martin Press, New York.

Bundesverfassungsgericht; (1999) Pressemitteilung 117/1999: Finanzausgleichsgesetz ist als Übergangsrecht bis Ende 2004 nach bestimmten Maßgaben weiter anwendbar; Accessed Febr. 5th 2008: http://www.bverfg.de/bverfg_cgi/pressemitteilungen/text/bvg117-99.

Busemeyer, M., C. Kellerman, A. Petrig, and A. Stuchlik (2006) *Political Positions on the European Social and Economic Model*. Friedrich Ebert Stifftung.

Cai, H. and D. Treisman (2005) "Does Competition for Capital Discipline Governments? Decentralization, Globalization and Public Policy." *American Economic Review* 95(3): 817–830.

Calderola, C. (1979) "The Social Credit in Alberta, 1935–1971." In Calderola (ed.) *Society and Politics in Alberta*.: 33–48.

Cameron, D. (1978) "*The* Expansion of the Political Economy: A Comparative Analysis." *American Political Science Review* 72: 1243–61.

Campbell, L. (2000) "'We Who Have Wallowed in the Mud of Flanders': First World War Veterans, Unemployment and the Development of Social Welfare in Canada, 1929–39." *Journal of the Canadian Historical Association* 11: 125–149.

Campeau, George (2005) *From Unemployment Insurance to Employment Insurance: Waging War on the Welfare State*. Vancouver, University of British Columbia Press.

Card, D. and R. Freeman (eds.) (1993) *Small Differences that Matter. Labor Markets and Income Maintenance in Canada and the United States*. NBER.

Carrubba, C.J. (1997) "Net Financial Transfers in the European Union: Who gets What and Why." *Journal of Politics*. 59(2): 469–96.

Carty, R.K., W. Cross, and L. Young (2000) *Rebuilding Canadian Party Politics*. Vancouver, UBC Press.

Casella, A. (2005) "Redistribution Policy: A European Model." *Journal of Public Economics*, 89: 1305–1331.
Casella, A. and B. Frey. (1992) "Federalism and Clubs. Towards an Economic Theory of Overlapping Political Jurisdictions." *European Economic Review*, 36: 639–646.
Casella, A. and B. Weingast. (1995) "Elements for a Theory of Jurisdictional Change." In B. Eichengreen, J. Frieden and J. von Hagen (eds.) *Politics and Institutions in an Integrated Europe*. New York: Springer.
Chhibber, P. and K. Kollman (2004) *The Formation of National Party Systems*. Princeton, NJ: Princeton University Press.
Closa C. and P. Heywood (2004) *Spain and the European Union*. Palgrave, McMillan.
Colomer, J. (1998) "The Spanish State of Autonomies: Non Institutional Federalism" in P. Heywood (ed.) *Politics and Policy in Democratic Spain*, London: Frank Cass.
Corcuera, J. (1991) *Politica y Derecho: La Construccion de la Autonomia Vasca*. Madrid, Centro de Estudios Constitucionales.
Courchene, T. (1993) "Canada's Social Policy Deficit: Implications for Fiscal Federalism." In K. Banting, T. Courchene, and D.M. Brown, (eds.) *The Future of Fiscal Federalism*, Queen's University, School of Policy Studies.
Courchene, T. (1994) *Social Canada in the Milenium*, Toronto, C.D.Howe Institute.
Cox, G. (1990) "Centripetal and Centrifugal Incentives in Electoral Systems" *American Journal of Political Science*, 34: 903–35.
Cox, G. (1997) *Making Votes Count*. Cambridge, Cambridge University Press.
Cram, L. (1997) *Policymaking in the EU*, London, Routledge.
Crémer, H. et al. (1996) "Mobility and Redistribution: A Survey." *Public Finance* 51(3): 325–52.
Crémer, J. and T. Palfrey (1999) "Political Confederation." *American Political Science Review*, 93(1): 69–83.
Crémer, J. and T. Palfrey (2000) "Federal Mandates by Popular Demand." *Journal of Political Economy* 108(5): 905–927.
Cruz Villalón, P (1990) "La Doctrina Constitucional sobre el Principio de Cooperacion" In J. Cano Bueso (ed.) *Comunidades Autonomas e Instrumentos de Cooperacion*. Madrid, Tecnos.
Cusack, T., and L. Engelhardt (2002) *The PGL file collection: File structures and procedures*. Paper, Berlin: Science Center.
Cusack, T., T. Iversen, and P. Rehm (2006) "Risks at Work: The Demand and Supply Sides of Government Redistribution." *Oxford Review of Economic Policy*, 22(3): 365–389.
Cusack, T., T. Iversen, and D. Soskice (2007) "Economic Interests and the Origins of Electoral Systems." *American Political Science Review*, 101(3): 373–393.
Czada, R. (1994) "Die Treuhandstalt im politischen System der Bundesrepublik." *Aus Politik und Zeitgeschichte*, 94: 31–42.
Czada, R. (1995) *Die Kampf um die Finanzierung der deutschen Einheit*. Cologne: Max Plank Institute for the Study of Society. Discussion Paper 95/1.
Czada, R. (1999) "Reformloser Wandel: Stabilität und Anpassung im politischen Akteursystem der Bundesrepublik." In T. Ellwein (ed.) *50 Jahre Bundesrepublik Deutschland*. Wiesbaden: Westdeutscher Verlag.
Czada, R. (2004) *The End of a Model? Crisis and Transformation of the German Welfare State*. Working Paper. Osnabrück: University of Osnabrück.

Dahl, R. (1983) "Federalism and the Democratic Process." In J. R. Pennock and J. C. Chapman (eds.) *Nomos XXV. Liberal Democracy*. New York: New York University Press.
De Figueiredo, R.J.P., and B. Weingast. (2005) "Self Enforcing Federalism." *The Journal of Law, Economics and Organization* 21(1): 103–135.
De la Granja J.L., J. Beramendi and P. Anguera (2001) *La España de los Nacionalismos y las Autonomias*. Madrid, Sintesis.
Degg, R. (1996) "Economic Globalization and the shifting boundaries of German Federalism." *Publius: The Journal of Federalism*, 26(1): 27–52.
Department of Manpower and Immigration (DMPI), Canada (1974) *The Immigration Programme*. Berkeley: University of California Press.
Diamond, J. and J. Robinson (2010) *Natural Experiments of History*, Cambridge, MA: Harvard University Press.
Diaz-Cayeros, A. (2006) *Federalism, Fiscal Authority and Centralization in Latin America*. New York: Cambridge University Press.
Dinan, D. (1999) *Ever Closer Union*. London: Palgrave.
Dingledine, G. (1981) *A Chronology of Response. The Evolution of Unemployment Insurance from 1940 to 1980*, Paper prepared for Employment and Immigration Canada.
Dixit A. (1996) *The Making of Economic Policy*. Cambridge, MA: MIT Press.
Dixit, A. and J. Londregan (1998) "Fiscal Federalism and Redistributive Politics." *Journal of Public Economics* 68: 153–180.
Douglas, P.H. (1934) "A National Program of Unemployment Insurance," *The New Republic*, LXXX: 215–216.
Douglas, P.H. (1936) *Social Security in the United States. An Analysis and Appraisal of the Federal Social Security Act*, New York: MacGraw Hill.
Dunning, T. (2008) "Improving Causal Inference: Strengths and Limitations of Natural Experiments." *Political Research Quarterly* 61(2): 282–293.
Durán, J. (2007) "La corresponsabilidad fiscal en la financiación autonomic." *Principios* 7: 109–121.
Eichengreen, Barry (2007) *The European Economy since 1945*, Princeton, NJ: Princeton University Press.
Elazar, D. (1987) *Exploring Federalism*. Tuscaloosa: The University of Alabama Press.
Enkikolopov, R. and E. Zhuravskaya (2003) *"Decentralization and Political Institutions."* Unpublished Paper, Moscow: Center for Economic and Financial Research.
Epple, D. and T. Romer (1991) "Mobility and Redistribution." *The Journal of Political Economy* 99(4): 828–858.
Epstein, Abraham (1936) *Insecurity: A Challenge to America*. New York: Random House.
Espina, A. (2007) *Modernizacion y Estado de Bienestar en España*. Madrid: Siglo XXI.
Esping-Andersen G. (1985) *Politics against Markets: the Social Democratic Road to Power* Princeton, NJ: Princeton University Press.
European Commission (2002) *Standard Eurobarometer 57*, Brussels: European Union Research Group.
European Commission (2003) *Standard Eurobarometer 59*, Brussels: European Union Research Group.
European Commission (2004) *34th Financial Report on the European Agricultural Guidance and Guarantee Fund*, Brussels: Commission of the European Communities.

European Commission (2004b) *Standard Eurobarometer 61*, Brussels: European Union Research Group.
Exler, U. (1991) "Aktuelle Probleme des Finanzpolitik und des Finanzausgleichs." In Hirscher, G. (ed.), *Die Zukunft des kooperativen Föderalismus in Deutschland*. Munich: Hanns-Seidel Stiftung Verlag.
Falleti, T. (2005) "A Sequential Theory of Decentralization: Latin American Cases in Comparative Perspective." *American Political Science Review*, 99(3):327–346.
Fearon, J. (1991) "Counterfactuals and Hypothesis Testing in Political Science." *World Politics*, 43: 169-195.
Ferrera, Maurizio (2005) *The Boundaries of Welfare*. Oxford: Oxford University Press.
Filippov, M., P.C. Ordeshook, and O. Shvetsova (2004) *Designing Federalism*. Cambridge, MA: Cambridge University Press.
Finanzministerium Baden-Wuerttemberg (2007) *Neuregelung seit 2005*; Accessed on Febr. 10th 2008: http://www.fm.baden-wuerttemberg.de/de/Neuregelung_seit_2005/110291.html
Finanzministerium Baden-Wuerttemberg (2007) *Der bundesstaatliche Finanzausgleich*: Kurzuebersich zu den Regelungen fuer die Jahre 2005 bis 2019; Accessed on Febr. 10th 2008: http://www.fm.baden-wuerttemberg.de/fm/2347/brosch%FCre_lfa.427664.pdf
Finanzministerium Bayern (2007) *Der bundesstaatliche Finanzausgleich*: Ueberblick, Zielesetzung, Instrumente; Accessed on Febr. 10th 2008: www.stmf.bayern.de/finanzpolitik/laenderfinanzausgleich/info_finanzausgleich.pdf
Finanzministerium Niedersachsen; *Finanzausgleich*: Funktionen und Funktionsweise; Accessed on Feb. 11th 2008: http://cdl.niedersachsen.de/blob/images/C2320000_L20.pdf
Finegold, K. and Th. Skocpol (1995) *State and Party in America's New Deal*. Madison: The University of Wisconsin Press.
Finkel, A. (1979) *Business and Social Reform in the Thirties*. Toronto, Lorimer.
Finkel, A. (1989) *The Social Credit Phenomenon in Alberta*. Toronto: University of Toronto Press.
Flockton, C. (1999) "Employment, Welfare Support and Income Distribution in East Germany." In C. Flockton (ed.) *Recasting East Germany: Social Transformation after the GDR*. London, Routledge.
Friedman, M. and A.J. Schwartz (1963) *Monetary History of the United States, 1867–1960*. Princeton, NJ: Princeton University Press.
Gallego, R., R. Goma, and J. Subirats (eds.) (2003) *Estado de Bienestar y Comunidades Autonomas*. Madrid: Tecnos.
Garrett, G. and J. Rodden (2003) "Globalization and Fiscal Decentralization." In M. Kahler and D. Lake (eds.) *Globalizing Authority*. Princeton, NJ: Princeton University Press.
Garrett G. and G. Tsebelis (1996) "An Institutional Critique of Intergovernmentalism." *International Organization* 50(2): 269–300.
Gibson E. (2004) *Federalism and Democracy in Latin America*. Baltimore: John Hopkins University Press.
Gibson, E., E. Calvo, and T. Falleti (2004) "Reallocative Federalism: Overrepresentation and Public Spending in the Western Hemisphere." In E.L. Gibson (ed.) *Federalism and Democracy in Latin America*. Baltimore: John Hopkins University Press.
Glaeser, E. L. (2005) "The Political Economy of Hatred." *Quarterly Journal of Economics*, 120(1): 45–86.

Gonzalez J.J. (2004) "Las Bases Sociales de la Politica Española" *Revista Española de Investigaciones Sociologicas* 4: 119–142.

Grabka, M. M., J. Schwarze, and G. G. Wagner (1999) "How Unification and Immigration Affected the German Income Distribution." *European Economic Review* 43: 867–878.

Gramlich, E. (1973) "State and Local Fiscal Behaviour and Federal Grant Policy," In *Selected Essays of Edward M. Gramlich*, Northampton, MA: Edward Elgar: 21–57.

Gramlich, E. (1987) "Cooperation and Competition in Public Welfare Policies," In *Selected Essays of Edward M. Gramlich*, Northampton, MA: Edward Elgar, 1997: 309–327.

Greene, W. (2000) *Econometric Analysis*. New York: Prentice Hall.

Guest, D. (1997) *The Emergence of Social Security in Canada*. Vancouver: UBC Press.

Gunlicks, A. B. (1994) "German Federalism after Unification: The Legal-Constitutional Response." *Publius: The Journal of Federalism* 24: 81–99.

Gunlicks, A. (2001) "A Major Operation or an Aspirin for a Serious Illness? The Recent Agreement Between the Federation and the Länder on Financing the Länder." AICGS Report.

Gunlicks, A. (2003) *The Länder and German Federalism*. Manchester: Manchester University Press.

Gunlicks, A. (2005) "German Federalism and Recent Reform Efforts" *German Law Journal* 6(10): 1283–1296.

Gunlicks, A. (2007) "German Federalism Reform" *German Law Journal* 8(1): 111–132.

Gunther, R., P. N. Diamandouros, and H.-J. Puhle (eds.) (1995) *The Politics of Democratic Consolidation: Southern Europe in Comparative Perspective*. Baltimore and London: The Johns Hopkins University Press.

Hacker, J. and P. Pierson (2002) "Business Power and Social Policy: Employers and the Formation of the American Welfare State." *Politics and Society* 30,(2): 277–325.

Hall, P. and D. Gingerich (2009) "Varieties of Capitalism and Institutional Complementarities in the Macroeconomy: and Empirical Assessment." *British Journal of Political Science* 39: 449–482.

Hall, P. and D. Soskice (2001) *Varieties of Capitalism*. Oxford, Oxford University Press.

Hallerberg, M. (2002) "Fiscal Policy in the European Union." *European Union Politics* 3(2):139–150.

Hantrais, L. (1995) *Social Policy in the European Union*. New York: Palgrave.

Hefeker, C. (2001) "The Agony of Central Power: Fiscal Federalism in the German Reich." *European Review of Economic History* 5(1): 119–142.

Hegelich, S. (2004) "Can Welfare Expansion Result in Disintegration? The Integration of East Germany into the German Pension System." *German Politics* 13(1): 81–105.

Heiland, F. (2004) "Trends in East-West German Migration from 1989 to 2002." *Demographic Research* 11(7): 173–194.

Heller, W. (2002) "Regional Parties and National Politics in Europe." *Comparative Political Studies* 35(6):657–685.

Hicks, A. and L. Kenworthy (1998) "Cooperation and Political Economy Performance in Affluent Capitalism." *American Journal of Sociology* 103(6): 1631–1673.

Hicks, A. and D.H. Swank (1992) "Politics, Institutions and Welfare Spending in Industrialized Democracies 1960–1982." *American Political Science Review* 86(3): 658–674.

Hiscox, M. J. and S. J. Rickard (2002) "Birds of a Different Feather? *Varieties of Capitalism, Factor Specificity, and Interindustry Labor Movements*." Mimeo. Cambridge, MA: Harvard University Press.

References

Hix, S. (2001) "Legislative Behavior and Party Competition in the European Parliament." *Journal of Common Market Studies* 39(4): 663–688.

Hix, S. (2005) *The Political System of the European Union*. New York: Palgrave.

Hobolt, S. and S. Brouard (2010) "Contesting the European Union? Why the Dutch and the French Rejected the European Constitution?" *Political Research Quarterly* 64(2): 309–322.

Hooghe, L. and G. Marks. (2003) "Unraveling the Central State, but How? Types of Multi-level Governance." *American Political Science Review* 97(2): 1118–1140.

Hooghe, L., G. Marks and A. H. Schakel (2008) "Regional Authority in 42 Democracies, 1950–2006: A Measure and Five Hypotheses." *Regional and Federal Studies* 18(2–3): 111–302.

Höpner, M. and A. Schäfer (2010a) "Polanyi in Brussels? Embeddedness and the Three Dimensions of European Economic Integration", Discussion Paper MPISS.

Höpner, M. and A. Schäfer (2010b) "A New Phase of European Integration: Organized Capitalisms in Post-Ricardian Europe" *West European Politics* 33, 344–368.

Horowitz, D. (1985) *Ethnic Groups in Conflict*. Berkeley: University of California Press.

Huber, E. and J. D. Stephens (2001) *Development and Crisis of the Welfare State*. Chicago: University of Chicago Press.

Huber, E., C. Ragin, and J. D. Stephens (1993) "Social Demoracy, Christian Democracy, Constitutional Structure and the Welfare State." *American Journal of Sociology*, 99(3): 711–750.

Huber, P. (2005) "Inter-regional Mobility in the Accession Countries. A Comparison to EU-15 Member States." WIFO Working Papers, No. 249.

Hug, S. (2005) "Federal Stability in Unequal Societies." *Constitutional Political Economy*, 16(2): 113–124.

Inman, R.P. and D.L. Rubinfeld (1997a) "The Political Economy of Federalism." In D.C. Mueller (ed.), *Perspectives of Public Choice*. Cambridge: Cambridge University Press.

Inman, R.P. and D.L. Rubinfield (1997b) "Rethinking Federalism." *Journal of Economic Perspectives* 11(4): 43–64.

Iversen, T. (1999) *Contested Economic Institutions. The Politics of Macroeconomics and Wage Bargaining in Advanced Democracies*. Cambridge: Cambridge University Press.

Iversen, T. (2005) *Capitalism, Democracy, and Welfare*. Cambridge: Cambridge University Press.

Iversen, T. (2006) "Capitalism and Democracy." In B. R. Weingast and D. L. Wittman (eds.), *Oxford Handbook of Political Economy*. Oxford: Oxford University Press.

Iversen, T. and D. Soskice (2006) "Electoral Institutions and the Politics of Coalitions: Why some democracies redistribute more than others." *American Political Science Review* 100(2): 165–181.

Iversen, T. and D. Soskice (2009) "Distribution and Redistribution: The Shadow of the XIX Century." *World Politics* 61(3): 438–486.

Jeffery, Ch. (1995) "The Non-Reform of the German Federal System after Unification." *West European Politics* 18(2): 252–272.

Jeffery, Ch. and P. Savigear (eds.) (1991) *German Federalism Today*, New York: St Martin Press.

Jeffery, Ch. and J. Yates (1993) "Unification and Maastricht: The Response of the Länder Governments." In Jeffery, Ch. and Sturm, R. (eds.) *Federalism, Unification and European Integration*. London: Franck Cass.

Jusko, K. (2006) "Electoral Politics and Poverty Relief: How Changing Electoral Incentives Can Help the Poor." Manuscript. Stanford, CA: Stanford University.
Katzenstein, P. (1987) *Policy and Politics in West Germany: The Growth of a Semisovereign State*. Philadelphia: Temple University Press.
Kenneth, S.A. (1998) *Securing the Social Union A Comment on the Decentralised Approach*. Kingston: Institute of Intergovernmental Relations.
Kenworthy, L. (2004) *Egalitarian Capitalism*. New York: Russell Sage Foundation.
Kenworthy, L. (2008) *Jobs with Equality*. Oxford: Oxford University Press.
Kenworthy, L. and J. Pontusson (2005) "Rising Inequality and the Politics of Redistribution in Affluent Countries." *Perspectives on Politics* 3: 449–471.
Kessing, S., K. Konrad, and C. Kotsogiannis (2007) "Fiscal Decentralization: Vertical Horizontal and FDI." *Economic Policy* January: 5–70.
Key, V.O. (1949) *Southern Politics in State and Nation*. New York: Knopf.
King, D. (1995) *Actively Seeking Work*. Chicago: University of Chicago Press.
King, G., R. Keohane and S. Verba. (1994) *Designing Social Inquiry*. Princeton, NJ: Princeton University Press.
Kitschelt, H. (2004) "Political-Economic Context and Partisan Strategies in German Federal Elections, 1990–2002." In H. Kitschelt and W. Streeck (eds.) *Germany: Beyond the Stable State*. London: Routledge.
König, T. (2005) "Measuring and Analyzing Positions on European Constitution-building." *European Union Politics* 6(3): 259–267.
Kousser, M.J. (1974) *The Shaping of Southern Politics: Suffrage Restriction and the Establishment of One Party South, 1880–1910*. New Haven, CT: Yale University Press.
Krugman, P. (1991) *Geography and Trade*. Boston, MA: The MIT Press.
Krugman, P. (2008) *The Return of Depression Economics*. New York: W.W. Norton.
Lange, P. (1993) "Maastricht and the Social Protocol: Why Did They Do It?" *Politics and Society*, 21(1): 5–36.
Lees, C. (2005) *Party Politics in Germany: A Comparative Politics Approach*. New York: Palgrave.
Lehmbruch, G. (1990) "Die Improvisierte Vereinigung: Die Dritte deutsche Republik." *Leviathan* 18: 462–486.
Lehmbruch, G. (1996) "German Federalism and the Challenge of the Unification." In V. Wright and J.J. Hesse (eds.) *Federalizing Europe?* Oxford: Oxford University Press.
León-Alfonso, S. (2007) *The Political Economy of Fiscal Decentralization*. Barcelona: Institut d'Estudis Autonomics.
León S. (2009) "Why is the System of Regional Financing in Spain Unstable?" *Revista Española de Investigaciones Sociologicas* 128: 57–87.
León S and M. Ferrin (2009) "A Cooperación Intergubernamental no Estado Autonómico." *Escola Galega de Administración Pública*.
Leonardy, U. (1996) "The Political Dimension: German practice and the European Perspective" In Wright, V. and J.J. Hesse (eds.), *Federalizing Europe?* Oxford: Oxford University Press.
Lieberman, R. C. (1998) *Shifting the Color Line*. Cambridge: Harvard University Press.
Lijphart, A. (1999) *Patterns of Democracy*. New Haven, CT: Yale University Press.
Lindert, P. (2004) *Growing Public*. New York: Cambridge University Press.
Linz, J. (1997) *Democracy, Multinationalism and Federalism*. CEACS-Juan March Institute, Working Paper 103.

Linz, J. and J. R. Montero (1999) *The Party Systems of Spain: Old Cleavages and New Challenges*. CEACS-Juan March Institute, Working Paper 138.

Linz, J. and A. Stepan (2000) "Inequality Inducing and Inequality Reducing Federalism." Unpublished paper, IPSA Meetings, Quebec City.

Lowi, Th. (1984) "Why is there no Socialism in the United States? A Federal Analysis." In R.T. Golembiewski, and A. Wildavsky (eds.) *The Costs of Federalism*. Piscataway, NJ: Transaction Books.

Lucas, R.E. (1990) "Why Doesn't Capital Flow From Rich to Poor Countries?" *American Economic Review*, 802: 92–96.

Majone, G. (1996) *Regulating Europe*. London: Routledge.

Maldonado, J.S. and J.S. Gomez-Sala (2003) "Novedades en el sistema de financiación de las Comunidades Autonómas." *Revista de Estudios Regionales, Universidades Públicas de Andalucia* 2: 41–55.

Manow, P. (2005) "Germany: Cooperative Federalism and the Overgrazing of the Fiscal Commons." In H. Obinger, S. Leibfried, and F.G. Castles (eds.) *Federalism and the Welfare State*. Cambridge: Cambridge University Press.

Manski, C. (1995) *Identification Problems in the Social Sciences*. Cambridge, MA: Harvard University Press.

Maravall, J. M. (1997) *Regimes, Politics, and Markets*. Oxford: Oxford University Press.

Maravall, J.M. (1999) "Accountability and Manipulation" in Przeworski, A. et al. (ed.) *Democracy, Accountability, and Representation*. Cambridge: Cambridge University Press.

Mares, I. (2003) *The Politics of Social Risks*. Cambridge: Cambridge University Press.

Marks G. and M. Steenberger (eds.) (2004) *European Integration and Political Conflict*. Cambridge: Cambridge University Press.

Mathias, J. (2003) "Farewell, Welfare State–Hello, Welfare Regions? Chances and Constraints of Welfare Management in the German Federal System." *German Politics* 12(3): 35–65.

Mattila, M. (2004) "Fiscal Redistribution in the European Union and the Enlargement." *International Journal of Organization Theory and Behavior* 7(4): 555–570.

Mattli, W. (1999) *The Logic of Regional Integration*. Cambridge: Cambridge University Press.

McGowan, J.J. (1999) *A History of Unemployment Insurance Legislation in the United States and the New York State, 1935–1998*. New York: New York State Department of Labor.

McGuire, R. (2003) *To Form a More Perfect Union*. Oxford: Oxford University Press.

McIntosh, T. and G. Boychuk (2001) "Dis-Covered: EI, Social Assistance and the Growing Gap in Income Support for Unemployed Canadians." In T. Mcintosh (ed.) *Federalism, Democracy and Labor Market Policy in Canada*. Montreal: McGill-Queen's University Press and Queen's University School of Policy Studies.

MEDEF (2005) "L'essentiel de la proposition de directive sur les services," Paris, http://www.medef.fr/medias/upload/76710_FICHIER.pdf.

Meltzer, A.H. and S.F. Richard (1981) "A Rational Theory of the Size of Government." *Journal of Political Economy*, 89: 914–927.

Mettler, S. (2002) "Social Citizens of Separate Sovereignties: Governance in the New Deal Welfare State." In S. M. Milkis and J. M. Mileur (eds.) *The New Deal and the Triumph of Liberalism*. Amherst: University of Massachussets Press.

Michaelopoulos, S. (2008) "The Origins of Ethnolinguistic Diversity: Theory and Evidence.". Unpublished manuscript. Boston: Tufts University.
Moene, K.O. and M. Wallerstein. (2001) "Inequality, Social Insurance, and Redistribution." *The American Political Science Review* 95(4): 859–874.
Monasterio C. (1995) *Informe sobre el Actual Sistema de Financiacion y sus Problemas*. Madrid: Instituto de Estudios Fiscales.
Montero J.R. (1998) "Stabilising the Democratic Order: Electoral Behavior in Spain" in P. Heywood (ed.) *Politics and Policy in Democratic Spain*. London: Frank Cass.
Moore, C., W. Jacoby, and A. Gunlicks (2008) "German Federalism in Transition?" *German Politics* 17,4: 393–407.
Moravcsik, A. (1998) *A Choice for Europe*. Ithaca, NY: Cornell University Press.
Moravcsik, A. (ed.) (1998) *Centralization or Fragmentation? Europe Facing the Challenges of Deepening, Diversity, and Democracy*. New York: Council on Foreign Relations.
Moreno L (1997) *La Federalizacion de España*. Madrid, Siglo XXI.
Moreno, L. (2007) "The Nordic Path of Spain's Mediterranean Welfare," Center for European Studies, WP-163.
Moreno, L. and N. McEwen (2005) "Exploring the territorial politics of welfare." In N. McEwen and L. Moreno (eds.) *The Territorial Politics of Welfare*. New York: Routledge.
Musgrave, R. (1997) "Devolution, Grants and Fiscal Competition." *Journal of Economic Perspectives* 11(4): 65–72.
Nelson, D. (1969) *Unemployment Insurance. The American Experience 1915–1935*. Madison: The University of Wisconsin Press.
Noble, Ch. (1997) *Welfare as We Knew It. A Political History of the American Welfare State*. Oxford: Oxford University Press.
Nogera, J. and G. Ubasart (2003) "Las Politicas de Rentas Minimas de las Comunidades Autonomas" en R. Gallego et al. (ed.) *Estado de Bienestar y Comunidades Autonomas*. Madrid: Tecnos.
Oates, W. (1972) *Fiscal Federalism*. New York: Harcourt.
Oates, W. (1991) *Studies in Fiscal Federalism*. Cheltenham, UK: Edward Elgar.
Oates, W. (1999) "An Essay on Fiscal Federalism." *Journal of Economic Literature* XXXVII: 1120–1149.
Oates, W. and Ch. Brown (1987) "Assistance to the Poor in a Federal System." *Journal of Public Economics* 32: 307–330.
Obinger, H., S. Leibfried, and F. Castles,(eds.) (2005) *Federalism and the Welfare State*. Cambridge: Cambridge University Press.
OECD (1991) *Economic Survey of Germany, 1990–1991*, Paris: OECD.
O'Neill, K. (2005) *Decentralizing the State*. Cambridge: Cambridge University Press.
Orloff, A. (1988) "The Political Origins of America's Belated Welfare State." In M. Weir, A. Orloff and T. Skocpol (eds.) *The Politics of Social Policy in the United States*. Princeton, NJ: Princeton University Press.
Orriols L. (2009) *Social Policies and Vote Choices in OECD Democracies*. Madrid: Juan March Institute.
Pal, L. (1988) *State, Class and Bureaucracy: Canadian Unemployment Insurance and Public Policy*. Montreal: McGill Queen's University Press.
Panizza, U. (1999) "On the Determinants of Fiscal Centralization: Theory and Evidence." *Journal of Public Economics* 74: 97–139.
Parikh, A. and M. Van Leuvensteijn (2002) *Internal Migration in Regions of Germany: A Panel Data Analysis*. ENPRI, Working Paper.

Patterson, J. T. (1969) *The New Deal and the States. Federalism in Transition*. Princeton, NJ: Princeton University Press.

Patterson, J. (1986) *America's Struggle against Poverty, 1900–1985*. Cambridge, MA: Harvard University Press.

Peffekoven, H. (1990) "Finanzausgeich in vereinten Deutschland." *Wirtschaftsdienst* 7: 346–352.

Perotti, R. (2001) "Is a Uniform Social Policy Better? Fiscal Federalism and Factor Mobility." *American Economic Review*, 91(3): 596–610.

Persson, T. and G. Tabellini (1996a) "Federal Fiscal Constitutions: Risk Sharing and Redistribution." *Journal of Political Economy* 104(5): 979–1009.

Persson, T. and G. Tabellini (1996b) "Federal Fiscal Constitutions: Risk Sharing and Moral Hazard." *Econometrica* 64(3): 623–646.

Persson T. and G. Tabellini (2003) *The Economic Effects of Constitutions*. London: MIT Press.

Peterson, P. (1995) *The Price of Federalism*, Washington, DC: The Brookings Institute.

Peterson, P. and M. Rom (1990) *Welfare Magnets. A New Case for a National Standard*, Washington DC: The Brookings Institute.

Peterson, P., M. Rom, and K.F. Scheve (Jr) (1998) "Interstate Competition and Welfare Policy." *Publius: The Journal of Federalism* 28: 17–37.

Petite, M. (1998) *The Treaty of Amsterdam*, Harvard Jean Monnet Chair Working Papers Series No. 2/98.

Pierson, P. (1995) "Fragmented Welfare States: Federal Institutions and the Development of Social Policy." *Governance* 84: 449–478.

Pierson, P. (2004) *Politics in Time*. Princeton, NJ: Princeton University Press.

Pierson, P. and S. Leibfried (1995) "The Dynamics of Social Policy Integration." In S. Leibfried and P. Pierson (eds.) *European Social Policy*. Washington, DC: The Brookings Institute.

Pierson, P. and T. Skocpol (2002) "Historical Institutionalism in Contemporary Political Science." In I. Katznelson and H. V. Milner (eds.), *Political Science. State of the Discipline*. New York: Norton & Company.

Plümper, T., C. Schneider and V. E. Troeger (2005) "The Politics of EU Enlargement: Evidence from a Heckman Selection Model." *British Journal of Political Science* 36: 17–38.

Plümper, T. and V. Troeger. (2007) "Efficient Estimation of Time-Invariant and Rarely Changing Variables in Finite Sample Panel Analyses with Unit Fixed Effects." *Political Analysis* 15(2): 124–140.

Pollack, M. A. (2003) *The Engines of European Integration: Delegation, Agency and Agenda Setting in the EU*. New York: Oxford University Press.

Pontusson, J. (2005) *Inequality and Prosperity: Social Europe vs. Liberal America*. Ithaca, NY: Cornell University Press.

Prud'homme, R. (1995) "The Dangers of Decentralization." *The World Bank Research Observer* 10(2): 201–220.

Przeworski, A. (2004a) "*Some Historical, Theoretical, and Methodological Issues in Identifying the Impact of Political Institutions*." Unpublished manuscript. New York University.

Przeworski, A. (2004b) "The Last Instance: Are Institutions the Primary Cause of Economic Development." *European Journal of Sociology* 45(2): 165–188.

Przeworski, A. (2004c) "Institutions Matter?" *Government and Opposition* 39(2): 527–540.

Przeworski, A. (2007) "Is the Science of Comparative Politics Possible." In C. Boix and S. C. Stokes (eds.), *Oxford Handbook in Comparative Politics*. Oxford: Oxford University Press.

Przeworski, A., M.E. Alvarez, J.A. Cheibub and F. Limongi. (2000) *Democracy and Development*. Cambridge: Cambridge University Press.

Qian, Y., and B. Weingast. (1997) "Federalism as a Commitment to Preserving Market Incentives." *Journal of Economic Perspectives* 11(4): 83–92.

Quadagno, J. (1994) *The Color of Welfare*. Oxford: Oxford University Press.

Ray, L. (2004) "Don't Rock the Boat: expectations, fears, and opposition to EU level policy making" in G. Marks and M. Steenbergen (eds.) *European Integration and Political Conflict*, Cambridge: Cambridge University Press.

Rehm, P. (2009) "Risks and Redistribution." *Comparative Political Studies* 42(7): 855–881.

Renzsch, W. (1989) "Föderale Finanzbeziehungen im Pateienstaat. Eine Fallstudie zum Verlust politischer Handlungsmöglichkeiten." *Zeitschrift für Parlamentsfragen* 3: 331–345.

Renzsch, W. (1994) "Föderale Problembewältigung: Zur Eibeziehung der neuen Länder in einem gesamtdeutschen Finanzausgleich ab 1995." *Zeitschrift für Parlamentsfragen* 1: 116–138.

Renzsch, W. (1995) "Konflictlösung im parlamentarischen Budesstaat: zur Regelung finanzpolitischer Bund-Länder Konflikte im Spannungsfeld von Administration und Politik-Vorläufige Überlegungen." In R. Voigt (ed.), *Der kooperative Staat*, Munchen Nomos Verlagsgesellschaft.

Renzsch, W. (1998) "Financing German Unity: Fiscal Conflict Resolution in a Complex Federation." *Publius: The Journal of Federalism* 28(4): 127–146.

Renzsch, W. (2001) The Dispute on the Financial Equalisation. The Financial Constitution as a Problem of the Federal State, In Financing Local Self Government. Case-Studies from Germany, Slovenia and Croatia, hrg. von der Friedrich-Ebert-Stiftung, Zagreb Office.

Rhodes M. (1997) "El Futuro de la Dimensiòn Social Europea," in L. Moreno (ed.), *Uniòn Europea y Estado del Bienestar*, Madrid: CSIC.

Riker, W.H. (1964) *Federalism*. Boston: Little Brown and Company.

Rittberger, B. (2005) *Building Europe's Parliament*. Oxford: Oxford University Press.

Ritter, Gerdhard (2006) *Die Wiedervereinigung und die Krise des Sozialstaates*. Munchen: C.H. Beck.

Rodden, J. (1999) "And the Last Shall Be First: Federalism and Soft Budget Constraints in Germany." Stanford University. Unpublished paper.

Rodden, J. (2002) "Strength in Numbers? Representation and Redistribution in the European Union." *European Union Politics* 3: 151–175.

Rodden, J. (2004) "Comparative Federalism and Decentralization: On Meaning and Measurement." *Comparative Politics* 36(4): 481–500.

Rodden, J. (2006) *Hamilton's Paradox: The Promise and Peril of Fiscal Federalism*. Cambridge: Cambridge University Press.

Rodden, J. (2007) "The Political Economy of Federalism." In B. Weingast and D. Wittman (eds.) *Oxford Handbook of Political Economy*. Oxford: Oxford University Press.

Rodden, J. (2008) "Why Did Western Europe Adopt Proportional Representation? A Political Geography Explanation." *Paper presented at the Annual Meetings of the American Political Science Association*, Boston MA.

Rodden, J. and T. Dragu (2010) "Representation and Regional Redistribution in Federations". Mimeo. Stanford, CA: Stanford University.

Rodden, J. and E. Wibbels (2002) "Beyond the Fiction of Federalism: Macroeconomic Management in Multi-tiered Systems." *World Politics* 54(July): 494–531.

Rodden, J. and E. Wibbels (2010) "Dual Accountability and the Nationalization of Party Competition." *Party Politics* 17: 629–654.

Rodrik, D. (1998) "Why Do More Open Economies Have Bigger Governments?" *Journal of Political Economy* 106(5): 997–1032.

Rodrigo, F and J.I. Torreblanca (2001) "Germany on My Mind? The Transformation of Germany and Spain's European Policies" in Heinrich Schneider, Mathias Jopp and Uwe Schmalz (eds.), *Germany's (new) European Policy – External Perception* Berlin: Institut für Europäische Politik, Europa Union Verlag.

Roemer, J. and L. Woojin (2006) "Race and Redistribution: A Solution to the Problem of American Exceptionalism." *Journal of Public Economics* 90: 1027–1052.

Rogowski, R. and D. MacRae (2008) "Does Inequality Determine Institutions? What Theory, History and (Some) Data Tell Us." In P. Beramendi and C. J. Anderson (eds.) *Democracy, Inequality and Representation: A Comparative Perspective.* New York: Russell Sage Foundation, forthcoming.

Room, G. (1991) "Towards a European Welfare State?" In G. Room (ed.) *Towards a European Welfare State?*. Bristol: SAUS Publications.

Rosato, S. (2011) *Europe United.* Ithaca: Cornell University Press.

Rose-Ackerman, S. (1983) "Beyond Tiebout: Modelling the Political Economy of Local Government." In G.R. Zodrow (ed.) *Local Provision of Public Services: the Tiebout Model after Twenty-Five Years.* New York: Academic Press.

Rosenbloom J.L. and W. Sundstrom (2004) "The Decline and Rise of Interstate Migration in the United States: Evidence from the IPUMS, 1850–1990." *Research in Economic History* 22: 289–325.

Rueda, D. (2008) "Left Government, Policy, and Corporatism: Explaining the Influence of Partisanship on Inequality." *World Politics,* 60(3): 349–389.

Rueda, D. and J. Pontusson (2000) "Wage Inequality and Varieties of Capitalism." *World Politics* 52(3): 350–383.

Ruiz-Huerta, J. and López Laborda, J. (1996) "Catorce preguntas sobre el nuevo sistema de financiación autonómica." In *Informe Comunidades Autónomas,* Universitat de Barcelona, ed., Barcelona: Instituto de Derecho Público.

Saalfeld, T. (2002) "The German Party System – Continuity and Change." *German Politics,* 11(3): 99–130.

Sahner, H. (1999) "Zur Entwicklung ostdeutscher Städte nach der Wende: nicht nur "dem Tod von der Schnippe gesprungen." *Aus Politik und Zeitgeschichte* 5: 26–37.

Sally, R. and D. Webber (1994) "The German Solidarity Pact: A Case Study in the Politics of Unified Germany" *German Politics* 31:18–46.

Sambanis, N. and B. Milanovic (2009) "Explaining the Demand for Sovereignty." Unpublished manuscript. New Haven, CT: Yale University.

Sánchez-Cuenca, I. (2002) "The Political Basis of Support for European Integration." *European Union Politics* 3(4): 387–413.

Scharpf, F. (1988) "The Joint Decision Trap: Lessons From German Federalism and European Integration." *Public Administration* 66(3): 239–278.

Scharpf, F. (1997a) "Economic Integration, Democracy and the Welfare State." *Journal of European Public Policy* 4(1): 18–36.

Scharpf, F. (1997b) "Introduction: The Problem Solving Capacity of Multi-Level Governance." *Journal of European Public Policy* 4(4): 520–538.
Scharpf, F. (1998) *Governing in Europe. Effective and Democratic?* Oxford: Oxford University Press.
Scharpf, F. (1999) *Föderale Politikverflechtung: Was muß man ertragen- was kann man ändern?*, MPIfGF, WP-3.
Scharpf, F. (2002) "The European Social Model. Coping with the Challenges of Diversity." *Journal of Common Market Studies* 40(4): 645–670.
Scharpf, F.W. (2007) "No Exit from the Joint Decision Trap? Can German Federalism Reform Itself?" Max Plank Institute for the Study of Societies. Working Paper 05/8.
Schimmelfennig, F. (2001) "The Community Trap: Liberal Norms, Rhetorical Action, and the Eastern Enlargement of the European Union." *International Organization* 55(1): 47–80.
Schmidt, M. G. (1992) "Political Consequences of German Unification." *West European Politics* 15(4): 1–15.
Schmidt, M. (2003) *Political Institutions in the Federal Republic of Germany.* Oxford: Oxford University Press.
Schneider, C.J. (2007) "Enlargement Processes and Distributional Conflicts: The Politics of Discriminatory Membership in the European Union." *Public Choice* 132: 85–102.
Schneider, C.J. (2009) *Conflict, Negotiations, and EU Enlargement.* Cambridge: Cambridge University Press.
Schwarze J. (1996) "How Income Inequality Changed in Germany following Reunification: And Empirical Analysis Using Decomposable Inequality Measures." *Review of Income and Wealth* 42: 1–11.
Seabright, P. (1993) *Making Sense of Subsidiarity: How Much Centralization for Europe?* London: CEPR.
Singleton, J. (2000) *The American Dole. Unemployment Relief and the Welfare State in the Great Depression.* London: Greenwood Press.
Sinn, H.W. (2002) "Germany's Economic Unification: An Assessment after Ten Years." *Review of International Economics* 10(1): 113–128.
Skocpol, Th. (1992) *Protecting Soldiers and Mother. The Political Origins of Social Policy in the United States.* Cambridge, MA: Harvard University Press.
Skocpol, Th. and J. Ikenberry (1983) "The Political Formation of the American Welfare State in Historical and Comparative Perspective." *Comparative Social Research* 6: 87–148.
Skocpol, T. and A.S. Orloff (1984) "Why not Equal Protection? Explaining the Politics of Public Social Spending in Britain, 1900–1911, and the United States, 1880s-1920." *American Sociological Review* 49: 726–750.
Snower, D. and G. De la Dehesa (eds.) (1997) *Unemployment Policy. Government Options for the Labour Market.* Cambridge: CEPR-Cambridge University Press.
Soskice, D. (1990) "Wage Determination: The Changing Role of Institutions in Advanced Economies." *Oxford Review of Economic Policy* 6: 36–61.
Spahn, P.B. (1993) "The Design of Federal Fiscal Constitutions in Theory and Practice." *European Economy, The Economics of Community Public Finance, Reports and Studies*, Commission of the European Communities, Directorate-General for Economic and Financial Affairs 5: 63–100.

Spahn, P.B. and O. Franz (2002) "Consensus Democracy and Interjurisdictional Fiscal Solidarity in Germany." In E. Ahmad and V. Tanzi (eds.) *Managing Fiscal Decentralization*. New York: Routledge.
Springer, B. (1992) *The Social Dimension of 1992. Europe Faces a New EC*. London: Praeger.
Stasavage, D. and K. Scheve (2009) "Institutions, Partisanship, and Inequality in the Long Run." *World Politics* 61(2): 215–252.
Steckel, R. (1983) "The Economic Foundations of East-West Migrations During the Nineteenth Century." *Explorations in Economic History* 20(1): 14–36.
Stegarescu, D. (2005) "Public Sector Decentralization: Measurement Concepts and Recent International Trends." *Fiscal Studies* 26(3): 301–333.
Stegarescu, D. (2009) "The Effect of Economic and Political Integration on Fiscal Decentralization: Evidence from OECD Countries." *Canadian Journal of Economics* 42(2): 694–718.
Stepan, A. (2001) *Arguing Comparative Politics*. Oxford: Oxford University Press.
Stewart, B. (1930) *Unemployment Benefits in the United States. The Plans and their Setting*. New York: Industrial Relations Counselors.
Stiglitz, J. E. (1983) "The Theory of Local Public Goods Twenty-Five Years after Tiebout: A Perspective." In G. Zodrow (ed.) *Local Provision of Public Services: the TieboutModel after Twenty-Five Years*. New York: Academic Press.
Streeck, W. (1995) "From Market to State Building? Reflections on the Political Economy of European Social Policy." In P. Pierson and A.S. Liebfried (eds.) *European Social Policy*. Washington, DC: The Brookings Institution.
Streeck, W. (2009) *Reforming Capitalism: Institutional Change in the German Political Economy*. Oxford: Oxford University Press.
Struthers, J. (1983) *No Fault of Their Own: Unemployment and the Canadian Welfare State 1914–1941*. Toronto: University of Toronto Press.
Sturm, R. and Ch. Jeffery. C (1993) "German Unity, European Integration and the Future of the Federal System: revival or permanent loss of substance?" In Ch. Jeffery and R. Sturm (eds.), *Federalism, Unification and European Integration*. London, Franck Cass.
Subirats, J. and R. Gallego (2002) *Veinte Años de Autonomias en España*. Madrid: CIS.
Sundquist J. L. (1983) *Dynamics of Party System*. Washington, DC: The Brookings Institute.
Temin, P. (1976) *Did Monetary Forces Cause the Great Depression?* New York: Norton.
Thaysen, U. (1994) "The Bundesrat, the Länder and German Federalism." *German Issues*, 13, Baltimore: John Hopkins University Press.
Thelen, K. (2004) *How Institutions Evolve*. Cambridge: Cambridge University Press.
Thelen, K. (2010) *Beyond Comparative Statics: Historical Institutional Approaches to Stability and Change in the Political Economy of Labor, in the Oxford Handbook of Comparative Institutional Analysis*. Oxford: Oxford University Press.
Thomson, R. and M. Holsi (2006) "Explaining Legislative Decision-Making in the European Union." In R. Thomson, F. N. Stokman, C. H. Achen, T. König (eds.) *The European Union Decides*. Cambridge: Cambridge University Press.
Thomson, R. et al. (2006) *The European Union Decides*, New York; Cambridge: Cambridge University Press.
Ticchi, D. and A. Vindigni (2003) "Endogenous constitutions." WP 726. Stockholm: Institute for International Economic Studies, Stockholm University.

Tiebout, C. (1956) "A Pure Theory of Local Expenditures." *Journal of Political Economy* 64: 416–424.
Torreblanca, J.I. (1998) "Overlapping Games and Cross-Cutting Coalitions in the European Union." *West European Politics* 21(2): 134–153.
Treisman, D. (1999) *After the Deluge: Regional Crises and Political Consolidation in Russia*. Ann Arbor: University of Michigan Press.
Treisman, D. (2004) "*Decentralization, Fiscal Incentives and Economic Performance: A Reconsideration*." Unpublished manuscript. Los Angeles, CA: UCLA.
Treisman, D. (2007) *The Architecture of Government. Rethinking Political Decentralization*. Cambridge: Cambridge University Press.
Tsebelis, G. (2002) *Veto Players*. Princeton, NJ: Princeton University Press.
Tsebelis G. and G. Garrett (2001) "The Institutional Foundations of Intergovernmentalism and Supranationalism in the European Union." *International Organization*, 55(2): 357–390.
Uhlig, H. (2006) *Regional Labor Markets, Network Externalities and Migration: The Case of German Reunification*. Berlin: SFB-Humboldt University.
Urbanos, R. and A. Utrilla (2001) "El Nuevo Sistema de Financiacion Sanitaria y sus Implicaciones economicas en las Comunidades Autonomas" *Revista de Administracion Publica* 20: 10–12, 25–48.
Valle, V. (1996) "La hacienda pública de la democracia española: principales rasgos." *Papeles de Economía Español* 68: 2–26.
Van Houten, P. (2009) "Multi-level Relations in Political Parties: A Delegation Approach," *Party Politics* 15(2): 137–156.
Vandenbroucke, F. (2002) "The EU and Social Protection: What Should the European Convention Propose." Lecture. Max Planck Institute for the Study of Societies, Bonn.
Varian, H. (1980) "Redistributive Taxation as Social Insurance." *Journal of Public Economics* 14: 49–67.
Venables, A.J. (2001) "Geography and International Inequalities : The Impact of New Technologies." *Journal of Industry, Competition and Trade* 1(4): 135–159.
Venables, A.J. (2007) "Trade, Location, and Development: An Overview of Theory." In D. Lederman and W.F. Maloney (eds.) *Natural Resources: Neither Curse nor Destiny*. Stanford, CA: Stanford University Press.
Volden, C. (1997) "Entrusting the State with Welfare Reform." In J. Ferejohn and B. Weingast, (eds.) *The New Federalism: Can the States Be Trusted?* Stanford, CA: Hoover Institution Press.
Volden, C. (2004) "The Politics of Competitive Federalism: A Race to the Bottom in Welfare Benefits?" *American Journal of Political Science* 46(2): 352–363.
Volden, C. (2005) "Intergovernmental Political Competition in American Federalism." *American Journal of Political Science* 49(2): 327–343.
Wallerstein, M. (1999) "Wage-Setting Institutions and Pay Inequality in Advanced Industrial Societies." *American Journal of Political Science* 43(3): 649–680.
Wallis, J. and W. Oates (1988) "Decentralization in the Public Sector: An Empirical Study of State and Local Government." In H. Rosen (ed.) *Fiscal Federalism: Quantitative Studies*. Chicago: University of Chicago Press.
Watts, R.L. (2008) *Comparing Federal Systems*, Third Edition. Kingston, Ontario: Institute of Intergovernmental Relations, Queen's University.
Webber, C. and A. Wildavsky (1986) *A History of Taxation and Expenditure in the Western World*. New York: Simon and Schuster.

Weber, D. (1999) *The Franco–German Relation in the European Union.* London: Routledge.
Weingast, B. (1993) "Constitutions as Governance Structures: The Political Foundations of Secure Markets." *Journal of Institutional and Theoretical Economics* 149(1): 286–311.
Weingast, B. (1995) "The Economic Role of Political Institutions: Market Preserving Federalism and Economic Development." *The Journal of Law, Economics and Organization* 11(1): 1–31.
Weingast, B. (2006) "Second Generation Fiscal Federalism: Implications for Decentralized Democratic Governance and Economic Development." Paper presented at the Annual Meetings of the American Political Science Association.
Weingast, B., G. Montinola, and Y. Qian (1995) "Federalism, Chinese Style: The Political Basis for Economic Success in China." *World Politics* 48(1): 50–81.
Weir, M. (1988) "The Federal Government and Unemployment: The Frustration of Policy Innovation from the New Deal to the Great Society." In M. Weir, A. Orloff and T. Skocpol (eds.) *The Politics of Social Policy in the United States.* Princeton, NJ: Princeton University Press.
Whatley, W. C. (1983) "Labor for the Picking: The New Deal in the South." *Journal of Economic History* 43: 905–930.
Whitaker, R. (1977) *The Government Party: Organizing and Financing the Liberal Party in Canada, 1930–58.* Toronto: University of Toronto Press.
Wibbels, E. (2001) "Federal Politics and Market Reform in the Developing World." *Studies in Comparative International Development,* 36(2): 27–53.
Wibbels, E. (2005a) *Federalism and the Market.* Cambridge: Cambridge University Press.
Wibbels, E. (2005b) "Decentralized Governance, Constitution Formation, and Redistribution." *Constitutional Political Economy* 16(2): 161–188.
Wibbels E. (2006a) "Dependency Revisited: International Markets, Business Cycles and Social Spending in the Developing World." *International Organization* 60(2): 433–469.
Wibbels E. (2006b) "Madison in Baghdad? Decentralization and Federalism in Comparative Politics," *Annual Review of Political Science* 9(1): 165–190.
Wibbels, E. and E. Godberg (2010) "Natural Resources, Trade and Development: The Questions for Mechanisms." Duke University. Unpublished manuscript.
Wiesenthal, H. (1995) "East Germany as a Unique Case of Societal Transformation: Main Characteristics and Emergent Misconceptions." *German Politics* 4(3): 49–74.
Wiesenthal, H. (1996) "Die Transition Ostdeutschlands: Dimensionen und Paradoxien eines Sonderfalls." In H. Wiesenthal (ed.) *Einheit als Privileg. Vergleichende Perspektiven auf die Transformation Ostdeutschlands.* Frankfurt/New York: Campus.
Wiesenthal, H. (2003) "German Unification and Model Germany: An Adventure in Institutional Conservatism." *West European Politics* 26(4): 37–58.
Wildasin, D. (1991) "Income Redistribution in a Common Labor Market." *American Economic Review* 81(4): 757–774.
Wildasin, D. (1995) "Factor Mobility, Risk and Redistribution in the Welfare State." *Scandinavian Journal of Economics* 97: 527–546.
Wildavsky, A. (1984) "Federalism means Inequality." In R.T. Golembiewski and A. Wildavsky (eds.) *The Costs of Federalism.* Piscataway, NJ: Transaction Books.
Williams, E. (1939) *A Federal Aid for Relief.* New York: Columbia University Press.

Witte, E. (1962) *The Development of the Social Security Act.* Madison: The University of Wisconsin Press.

Witte, J. and G. Wagner (1995) "Declining Fertility in East Germany After Unification: A Demographic Response to Socioeconomic Change." *Population and Development Review* 21(2): 387–397.

Zhou, Q. (2009) "Research Note: A New Measure of Interindustry Labor Mobility." Unpublished.

Ziblatt, D. (2002) "Recasting German Federalism? The Politics of Fiscal Decentralization in Post-Unification Germany" *Politicsche Vierteljahrenscrift* 43(4): 424–652.

Index

Aberhart, William (Canadian politician), 118, 122
Acemoglu and Robinson (2006), 6, 19
Acemoglu, Johnson and Robinson (2002), 16
Achembaum (1986), 109
Ackerman (1998), 247
Adelberger (1999), 155
Adenauer, Konrad (first post-WWII German Chancellor), 137
Adsera and Boix (2002), 76
Aja (1999), 177, 183, 190
Aja (2003), 182
Albertí Rovira (1996), 182
Alesina and Glaeser (2004), 4, 5, 6
Alesina and Perotti (1998), 12, 35, 37
Alesina and Spolaore (2003), 6, 47, 134, 216
Alesina and Wacziarg (1998), 216
Alesina, Glaeser, and Sacerdote (2001), 6
Alston and Ferrie (1999), 4, 6, 107, 111, 113, 130, 132, 133
Altmeyer (1968), 128, 131
Amat, Jurado and León (2010), 15, 198
Amenta and Carruthers (1988), 6
Amenta et al. (1987), 120
Amsterdam Treaty (1999), 69, 82
Anderson (1992), 141
Arriba (1999), 14
Asset specificity, 14
Atkinson (1995), 2, 34, 65
Atkinson (1999), 34

Atkinson (2002), 83
Austen-Smith and Banks (1988), 13, 41, 58
Austen-Smith and Wallerstein (2008), 246
Australia, 136
Autonomous Communities (Spain), 177, 178, 184
Aznar, José Maria (Spanish PM), 197, 199
Aznar, José Maria (Spanish PM), 98

Babones (2008), 6
Bakke and Wibbels (2006), 47, 261
Baltagi (2008), 212
Bañón and Agranoff (1998), 177
Banting (1987), 6, 8, 61
Banting (1992), 6
Banting (1997), 244
Banting (2005), 8
Barbe (1999), 98
Barr (1974), 118
Bartomeous (2003), 198
Basque Country (Spain), 53, 54, 58, 176, 177, 179, 183, 186, 188, 189, 190, 191, 192, 195, 196, 197, 203, 205
Basque Nationalist Party (PNV), 180
Beard (1913), 48
Beard (1933), 50
Beck and Katz (1995), 211
Bednar (2005), 241

283

Bednar (2008), 21, 241
Bednar, Eskridge, and Ferejohn (2001), 241
Bennett, Richard Bedford (Prime Minister of Canada), 117, 118, 120, 121, 122
Bennett, Richard Bedford (Prime Minister of Canada), 117
Benz (1989), 142
Beramendi (2001), 224
Beramendi (2007), 6, 12, 35, 40, 134, 240
Beramendi (2007b), 15
Beramendi and Anderson (2008), 19, 226, 244, 245
Beramendi and Cusack (2009), 136, 225, 246
Beramendi and Diaz-Cayeros (2008), 8, 42, 229, 232
Beramendi and Máiz (2004), 15, 54, 196
Beramendi and Rueda (2010), 245
Beramendi and Wibbels (2010), 17, 48
Beramendi et al. (2004), 177
Berkowitz (1991), 119, 127
Bernacke (2004), 51
Beveridge, William (British social reformer), 105
Bewley (1981), 5
Biedenkopf, Kurt (German CDU politician), 160
Biehl and Ungar (1991), 141, 143, 152
Bismarck, Otto von, 136
Blair, Tony (British PM), 82
Boix (2003), 6, 14, 19, 34
Bolton and Roland (1996), 38
Bolton and Roland (1997), 19, 20, 40, 47, 134, 173
Bolton, Patrick and Gerard Roland (1997), 6
Borkenhagen (1990), 142
Börzel (2005), 67, 68, 69
Bosch and Durán (2005), 191, 194, 195
Bradley et al. (2003), 246
Brancatti (2009), 15
Brazil, 4, 7
Brennan and Buchanan (1980), 4
Brinegar and Jolly (2005), 85, 87, 88
Brinegar et al. (2004), 86
Brinegar, Jolly and Kitschelt (2004), 79, 87

Brinkley (1984), 130
British North America Act (1867), 49, 104, 106, 107, 118, 121, 236
British Poor Laws, 105
Buchanan (1950), 4, 5
Buchanan (1995), 4
Buchanan and Wagner (1970), 5
Bulmer (1991), 142
Bundesbank, 74, 97
Bundesrat (Germany), 63, 64, 138, 143, 149, 153, 155, 159, 160, 162, 169, 174, 279
Bundestag (German parliament), 63, 149, 167
Bundesverfassungsgericht (1999), 170
Busemeyer, et al. (2006), 88

Cabré-Durán (2007), 194
Cai and Treisman (2005), 4, 34, 133, 240
Calderola (1979), 118
Cameron (1978), 209
Campbell (2000), 117
Campeau (2005), 124
Canada
  and centralization, 65, 132
  and centrifugal political will, 63
  and decentralized federalism, 106
  and externalities, 116
  and interterritorial mobility, 236
  and the distributive curse, 8
  and the Great Depression, 61, 62, 64, 65, 111, 117, 236
  contrast with the U.S., 60
  formation of, 48
  immigration to, 111, 112, 113
  in contrast with the U.S., 103
  labor mobility in, 236
  macroeconomy of, 123
  mobility patterns in, 111
  national unemployment insurance, 2
  parliamentary system in, 104, 106
  response to unemployment, 120
Card and Freeman (1993), 8, 244
Carruba (1997), 74, 77
Carty, Cross and Young (2000), 62
Case selection, 17, 48
Casella (2005), 76
Cassella and Frey (1992), 76
Cassella and Weingast (1995), 76

Index

Catalonia, 14, 53, 54, 58, 59, 176, 177, 179, 180, 183, 186, 188, 189, 191, 194, 195, 196, 197, 199, 200, 201, 202, 203, 204, 235
  autonomy of, 179
Causal identification, 46, 50, 51, 55, 60, 207, 244, 247
  conditions for, 47
Centralization of redistribution
  preferences for, 67
Centralized redistributive systems, 33, 43, 79, 80
Centrifugal representation, 12, 13, 40, 41, 42, 43, 67, 77, 132, 223, 226, 238
Centripetal representation, 12, 13, 14, 19, 40, 41, 42, 43, 44, 50, 59, 66, 67, 168, 169, 175, 177, 204, 211, 215, 223, 238, 240
Chhibber and Kollman (2004), 15, 55, 106
Christian Democratic Union (CDU), 150, 155, 160, 161, 162, 164, 172
Class interests, 13, 40, 90
Closa and Heywood (2004), 96
Coalitions
  and the median voter, 41
  centrifugal formation, 40
  centripetal formation, 40
  cross-regional, 240
  electoral, 10, 13, 15, 35, 40, 41, 58, 112, 149, 246
  redistributive, 6, 14, 32, 79, 238
  redstributive, 37
  regional cross-class, 36
Colomer (1998), 182
Common Agricultural Policy (EU), 70, 74, 100
Common market (EU), 74, 82, 98
Community Charter of the Fundamental Social Rights of Workers (EU), 82
Constitution of Catalonia, 176, 194, 197, 200, 202, 204
Constitutional choice, 6
Constitutional Convention, 255
Constitutional Convention (EU), 17, 93
Constitutional Court (German), 142
Constitutional Court (Spain), 182, 190
Coolidge, Calvin, 127

Corcuera (1991), 179
Courchene (1993), 6
Courchene (1994), 6
Cox (1990), 12
Cox (1997), 12
Cram (1997), 68, 81, 82
Crémer and Palfrey (1999), 35, 40, 58
Crémer and Palfrey (2000), 37, 40
Crémer, et al. (1996), 5
Cruz Villalón (1990), 182
Cusack and Engelhardt (2002), 224, 260
Cusack, Iversen and Rehm (2006), 35, 84
Cusack, Iversen and Soskice (2007), 6, 238
Czada (1994), 156
Czada (1995), 151
Czada (1999), 151
Czada (2004), 151

D'Hondt Law (Spanish electoral law), 180
Dahl (1983), 221
De Figueirido and Weingast (2005), 241
De la Granja, Beramendi and Anguera (2001), 177
Decentralization, 2, 4, 6, 7, 8, 9, 10, 13, 14, 21, 22, 24, 25, 27, 28, 32, 39, 43, 44, 50, 51, 52, 53, 54, 55, 56, 59, 60, 65, 66, 68, 133, 143, 154, 168, 173, 176, 177, 178, 180, 181, 184, 185, 189, 190, 191, 196, 197, 198, 203, 204, 205, 208, 211, 213, 214, 215, 216, 217, 218, 219, 221, 223, 224, 225, 226, 227, 229, 234, 238, 240, 241, 243
  and fiscal policy, 188
  fiscal, 7, 33, 42, 54, 55, 59, 135, 175, 189, 192, 196, 211, 214, 240
  political, 175
  of public insurance, 188
  of representation, 59
Degg (1996), 141, 142
Delors, Jacques
  French President of the EC, 82
Delors, Jacques
  French President of the EC, 57
Demand
  for redistribution, 18
Demand for insurance, 34, 35

Democracy, 19, 22, 29, 52, 55, 106, 112, 176, 177, 189, 221, 230, 234, 242
Democratic Party (U.S.), 62, 107, 119
Democratic transition, 10, 199
Diamond and Robinson (2010), 22
Diaz-Cayeros (2006), 59
Dinan (1999), 57
Dingledine (1981), 124
Distributive curse, 8
Distributive outcomes, 6, 7, 13, 19, 20, 235, 238
Distributive tensions, 8, 9, 13, 19, 27, 40, 52, 60, 65, 78, 80, 81, 111, 135, 162, 163, 175, 185, 189, 209, 237, 247
Dixit (1996), 177
Dixit and Londregan (1998), 58
DMPI (1974), 111
Domestic Structures and European Integration Project (DOSEI), 101
Domestic Structures and European Integration Project (DOSEI), 91
Douglas (1934), 127
Douglas (1936), 119, 126, 127, 128, 129, 131
Dunning (2008), 18
Durán (2007), 191, 194
Dysart, A. Allison (Canadian politician), 107, 122

Economic geography, 3, 4, 10, 11
  and centrifugal representation, 13
  and fiscal structures, 13
  and political incentives, 76
  and political representation, 13
  and representation, 15
Economic specialization, 12, 17, 29, 34, 35, 36, 75, 88, 120, 146, 216, 240
  logic of, 216
  model, 251
  regional, 38, 39, 44, 65, 68, 78, 85, 103, 105, 116, 236
Edinburgh Summit (1992), 97
Efficiency, 5, 240
  administrative, 124
  gains, 240
  gains associated with decentralization, 216
Eichengreen (2007), 98
Elazar (1987), 61, 181

Elites, 23
  local, 24
  national, 24
  regional, 13
  regional balance of power, 12
Employment and Social Insurance Act (Canada) (1935), 121
Employment Service (Canada), 105
Endogeneity, 15, 19, 21, 22, 51, 54, 55, 56, 58, 59, 60, 134, 212, 220, 230, 241, 242, 243, 244, 246
  endogeneity problem, 212
  endogenous decentralization, 189
  endogenous institutions, 9, 15, 16, 20, 133
  endogenous processes, 46, 53, 55, 56, 57
  joint, 59
Enikolopov and Zhuravskaya (2003), 62
Enlargement, 52, 53, 73, 94, 95, 97, 98
Epple and Romer (1991), 5
Epstein (1936), 108
Equal Opportunity Act (1964), 133
Equality
  equality-autonomy trade-off, 3
Espina (2007), 9
Esping-Andersen (1985), 204
Euro, the, 1, 73, 242
European Agricultural Guidance and Guarantee Fund (EAGGF), 71, 72
European Commission, 71, 90, 92, 99
European Commission (2002), 75
European Commission (2003), 75
European Commission (2004), 71
European Commission (2004b), 75
European Constitution (2004), 67, 69, 91
European Court of Justice, 90
European Economic Community, 9, 49, 57, 71, 95
European monetary crisis (1930–1931), 108
European Monetary Union, 73, 74, 97, 98
European Parliament, 91, 92
European Social Fund (ESF), 99
European Union
  agricultural policy in, 71
  and policy integration, 68, 69

budget, 67, 70, 72, 74
budget of, 74
distributive conflicts within, 93
fiscal structure, 68
geography of income in, 87
harmonization of welfare systems, 85, 87
institutional design of, 77
lack of redistributive policies, 13
policy realms, 67
political fragmentation, 79
redistribution in, 70
redistributive efforts, 67
Exler (1991), 142, 143
Exogeneity, 6, 15, 21, 47, 53, 58, 59, 64, 111, 163, 212, 224, 241
exogenous changes, 17
exogenous institutions, 16
exogenous shocks, 56, 108, 122, 242, 244, 246
in economic geography, 19, 47, 51, 53, 144, 206, 237
in institutions, 19
in natural experiments, 19, 56
variables, 230
Expectations, 60
about distribution, 10, 61, 108, 119, 245
about institutions, 16
agricultural, 71, 72, 80, 96
by government, 70
Expenditures, 121, 184, 185
agricultural, 71
by government, 184
in the EU, 70
expenditures side, 175
for relief, 123, 124
health, 184
needs, 141, 142, 202
regional, 183
social, 214
Externalities, 43, 75, 86, 116, 124, 230, 245
and market integration, 76
and mobility, 245
cross-jurisdictional, 4, 5
cross-provincial, 124
cross-regional, 11, 23, 36, 37, 75, 80, 101, 103, 124, 134, 174, 209, 220, 228

cross-regional economic, 10
in the EU, 76
interprovincial, 132
interregional, 104, 132, 133, 209
interstate, 133
reducing negative, 99, 100, 101, 146, 150, 163

Factor mobility, 5, 11
labor, 14
labor, interregional, 18
Falleti (2005), 56
Fearon (1991), 16, 46
Fearon and Van Houten (1998), 246
Federalism, 4, 5, 6, 9, 16, 20, 21, 56, 61, 63, 64, 106, 133, 136, 155, 168, 169, 172, 180, 181, 190, 197, 234, 240
fiscal, 54, 55, 176, 182, 183
functional theories of, 76
Ferrera (2005), 20, 237
Filippov, Ordeshook and Shvetsova (2004), 56
Finanzverfassungsreform (Germany) (1969), 138
Finegold and Skocpol (1995), 62, 106
Finkel (1979), 117, 118, 123
Finkel (1989), 118
Fiscal
policy, 1
structures, 2
Fiscal asymmetry, 182
Fiscal autonomy, 43, 192, 195, 196, 198, 199, 200, 203, 204, 205, 214
Fiscal capacity, 3, 140, 142
in Spain, 198
of the Canadian provinces, 111
of the German länder, 141
of the German länder, 141
Fiscal centralization
and regional risk-sharing, 76
Fiscal discipline, 61
Fiscal independence
preference for, 79
Fiscal institutions, 21, 22, 34, 76, 83, 134, 245
and economic geography, 135
endogenous, 20
federal, 21
Fiscal integration, 9, 12

Fiscal policy, 12
  autonomy in, 74
  decentralization, 9
  Fiscal structures, 3
Fiscal structure
  and redistribution, 32
  centralized, 24, 32
  decentralized, 24
  hybrid system, 24
  in Germany, 136, 137, 140, 143, 144
  in Spain, 176, 183, 201, 202
  in the EU, 68, 70, 74, 101, 102, 240
  of Germany, 135
  of the EU, 53
  preferences for, 229
  vertical integration, 74
Fiscal structures, 2, 3, 6, 7, 8, 9, 10, 11, 12, 13, 14, 15, 16, 17, 18, 19, 20, 21, 22, 23, 24, 27, 29, 33, 34, 36, 37, 39, 41, 42, 43, 46, 47, 48, 49, 50, 51, 52, 53, 55, 58, 59, 60, 64, 75, 133, 135, 195, 196, 199, 205, 206, 207, 223, 224, 227, 228, 232, 234, 237, 239, 241, 242, 243, 244, 246
  and centrifugal representation, 67
  and distributive conflicts, 56
  and economic geography, 15, 29, 47, 60, 183, 196, 205, 236
  and electoral survival, 40
  and inequality, 223, 243
  and mobility, 18, 20, 43, 51
  and redistribution, 52
  and representation, 59
  and the median voter, 40
  and union formation, 47
  as outcome of political agency, 21
  centralization, 21, 31, 32, 33
  centralized, 10, 38
  choice of, 29
  conflicts over, 240, 247
  cross-regional, 37
  decentralization, 25
  decentralization of, 26, 215, 216
  decentralized, 10, 11, 13, 19, 42, 238
  design of, 50, 56, 133, 136, 206, 223, 229
  distributive effects, 242
  fragmented, 41
  in Germany, 158, 168, 173
  in political unions, 23
  in Spain, 54, 176, 177, 184, 188
  in the EU, 66, 75
  integrated, 37, 43
  integration of, 75
  organization of, 36
  origin of, 24
  origins of, 28, 48
  politics of, 64
  preferences for, 17, 23, 25, 29, 31, 33, 34, 35, 39, 208, 210, 246, 251
  under centripetal representation, 135
Fiscal transfers, 11, 54, 230
Flockton (1999), 138, 152
Fondo de Compensacion Interterritorial (FCI) (Spain), 184
Franco, Francisco, 49, 54, 177
Free Democratic Party (FDP), 156, 160, 167
Friedman and Schwartz (1963), 51

Gallego, Goma and Subirats (2003), 9
Garrett and Rodden (2003), 209
Garrett and Tsebelis (1996), 57
Geography, 3
  economic, 17
  of economic specialization, 11
  of income, 11
  of income and labor markets, 9
  of inequality, 9
  of risk, 12
German Constitution (1949), 137
German Reunification, 9, 18, 19, 22, 46, 50, 52, 56, 60, 64, 65, 66, 98, 135, 136, 138, 140, 144, 146, 148, 149, 150, 153, 155, 156, 157, 158, 159, 160, 161, 162, 163, 167, 168, 169, 171, 173, 206, 211, 228, 232, 235, 237, 240, 242, 245
German Unity Fund (1990), 152, 153, 160, 170
Germany
  and incorporation of the East, 52, 146, 151
  and unitarian federalism, 63
  as semi-sovereign state, 63
  centripetal system of representation in, 143

constitutional court of, 169
contribution of to the EU budget, 98
economic geography of, 52
federalism in, 9
fiscal constitution of, 138
fiscal structure of before, 1990, 141, 159
political representation in, 161
regional patterns of inequality in, 155
role of in the creation of the SCF, 97, 98
Gibson (2004), 13
Gibson, Calvo and Falleti (2004), 42, 229
Gini coefficient, 6
Glaeser (2005), 246
Gonzalez (2004), 204
Gonzalez, Felipe (Spanish socialist politician), 190, 195
Grabka, Schwarze and Wagner (1999), 148
Gramlich (1973), 4
Gramlich (1987), 4
Great Depression, 1, 8, 18, 19, 22, 37, 46, 50, 51, 52, 53, 56, 60, 61, 62, 63, 64, 65, 66, 103, 104, 105, 106, 107, 108, 109, 110, 111, 113, 114, 115, 116, 117, 118, 120, 122, 123, 124, 125, 130, 132, 206, 234, 236, 237, 243, 245
Greene (2000), 212
Greif and Laitin (2004), 15
Guest (1997), 109, 110, 117
Gunlicks (1994), 153, 159
Gunlicks (2001), 170
Gunlicks (2003), 64, 149
Gunlicks (2005), 168, 172
Gunlicks (2007), 172
Gunther, Diamandouros and Puhle (1995), 52

Hacker and Pierson (2002), 63, 119
Hall and Gingerich (2009), 224, 260
Hall and Soskice (2001), 81
Hallerberg (2002), 74
Hantrais (1995), 81
Hefeker (2001), 137
Hegelich (2004), 156
Heiland (2004), 164, 257

Heller (2002), 198
Hepburn, Michael (Premier of Ontario), 107, 122
Hicks and Kenworthy (1998), 6
Hicks and Swank (1992), 6
Hiscox and Rickard (2002), 260
Hix (2001), 68
Hix (2005), 57, 58, 70, 71, 73
Hobolt and Brouard (2010), 75
Holt, Elmer (Montana Governor), 119
Hooghe and Marks (2001), 68
Hooghe, Marks and Schakel (2008), 56
Hoover, Herbert, 51
Höpner and Schäfer (2010a), 90
Höpner and Schäfer (2010b), 90
Horowitz (1985), 246
Huber (2005), 256
Huber and Stephens (2001), 6, 225
Huber, Ragin and Stephens (1993), 4, 6
Hug (2005), 241

Income transfers, 10, 12, 146, 184
    demand for, 144
    interregional, 95
    passive, 157
    short-term, 159
Inman and Rubinfield (1997a), 4, 5
Inman and Rubinfield (1997b), 4
Institutional design, 16
    and electoral coalitions, 35
    distributive implications of, 10
    endogenous theory of, 134
    of American social policy, 133
    of social security, 104
    of the German federation, 135
Interpersonal redistribution, 2, 3, 4, 6, 7, 8, 10, 11, 12, 13, 14, 18, 21, 22, 24, 30, 31, 32, 33, 35, 36, 37, 38, 39, 41, 42, 43, 44, 45, 51, 54, 58, 60, 65, 66, 67, 68, 70, 74, 75, 76, 77, 80, 81, 85, 86, 91, 92, 93, 94, 101, 137, 148, 149, 151, 155, 175, 176, 208, 209, 210, 211, 213, 216, 217, 218, 219, 220, 221, 223, 224, 225, 226, 228, 229, 230, 232, 233, 235, 237, 238, 239, 245, 250
    centralized systems of, 80
    decentralized, 70
    in the EU, 70

Interregional redistribution, 2, 3, 4, 7, 8, 9, 10, 11, 13, 14, 15, 17, 18, 19, 21, 22, 23, 24, 30, 36, 38, 39, 41, 42, 43, 45, 52, 58, 65, 66, 67, 68, 69, 71, 74, 75, 77, 84, 93, 95, 97, 100, 101, 133, 136, 140, 146, 149, 151, 152, 153, 155, 159, 160, 162, 168, 169, 171, 172, 173, 184, 185, 188, 208, 227, 228, 229, 230, 231, 232, 233, 237, 238, 240, 245, 250
and mobility, 68
and risk reduction, 77
Interregional transfers, 3, 13, 14, 30, 31, 37, 38, 39, 42, 43, 66, 68, 77, 94, 95, 96, 97, 98, 99, 100, 101, 146, 152, 159, 172, 173, 176, 184, 195, 214, 228, 229, 230, 231, 232, 233, 239, 240, 246, 250
Interterritorial redistribution, 142
Iversen (1999), 244
Iversen (2005), 19, 80, 226
Iversen (2006), 6, 19, 20
Iversen and Soskice (2006), 12, 35, 41, 93, 238
Iversen and Soskice (2009), 226, 244

Jeffery (1995), 142, 154
Jeffery and Savigear (1991), 64
Jeffery and Yates (1993), 142
Johnson, Lyndon, 133
Jusko (2006), 149

Katzenstein (1987), 63, 159
Kenneth (1998), 6
Kenworthy (2004), 226
Kenworthy (2008), 81
Kenworthy and Pontusson (2005), 225
Kessing, Konrad and Kotsogiannis (2007), 216
Key (1949), 62, 63, 107
King (1995), 130
King, Keohane, and Verba (1994), 212
King, William Lyon Mackenzie, 107, 117, 121, 122, 123
Kitschelt (2004), 158
Kohl, Helmut, 97, 150, 153, 155, 157, 162
König (2005), 91
Kousser (1974), 107

Krugman (1991), 12, 14, 34, 81, 133, 220, 230
Krugman (2008), 51
Krugman, Paul, 1, 9

La Follette Jr., Robert (Wisconsin Senator), 120, 130, 132
Labor mobility, 12, 14
Lafontaine, Oskar (German SPD politician), 160
Lange (1993), 74, 77, 97
Lees (2005), 149
Lehmbruch (1990), 64, 154
Lehmbruch (1996), 153, 154, 155, 159, 160
León (2007), 9
León (2009), 196, 198, 205
León and Ferrin (2009), 182
León-Alfonso (2007), 53, 54, 194, 196, 198
Leonardy (1996), 138
Liberal Party (Canada), 106, 107
Lieberman (1998), 8, 130
Lijphart (1999), 63
Lindert (2004), 7, 19, 104, 133
Linz (1997), 216
Linz and Montero (1999), 181, 195
Linz and Stepan (2000), 7, 234
Lisbon Summit (2000), 83
Local economies, 11, 12, 18, 35, 37, 90, 96, 99, 119, 238
Low income regions, 8
Lowi (1984), 4, 6
Lucas (1990), 14

Maastricht Treaty (1992), 69, 73, 82, 97
Madison, James, 4
Majone (1996), 68
Malapportionment
and legislative chambers, 215
and proportional representation, 177
in legislative chambers, 12, 25, 42, 61
Malaysia, 7
Maldonado and Gomez-Sala (2003), 194
Manow (2005), 9, 136, 137
Manski (1995), 46, 212
Maragall, Pasqual (Catalonian politician), 199
Maravall (1997), 49

Index

Maravall (1999), 195
Mares (2003), 12, 136
Marks and Steenberger (2004), 86
Marx, Karl, 4
Mathias (2003), 138, 151, 157, 158
Mattila (2004), 74, 77
Mattli (1999), 74, 75, 76
McGowan (1999), 106, 120
McGuire (2003), 48, 50, 247
McIntosh and Boychuk (2001), 106
MEDEF (2005), 90
Medicare, 1
Meltzer and Richard (1981), 20
Mettler (2002), 8
Mexico, 4, 7, 234
Michaelopoulos (2008), 220
Mobility
  and incentives to redistribute, 18
  cross-regional, 15
Moene and Wallerstein (2001), 2, 12, 34, 35
Monasterio et al. (1995), 183
Montero (1998), 58, 180
Moore, Jacoby and Gunlicks (2008), 172
Moravcsik (1998), 57, 74, 77, 94
Moreno (1997), 177
Moreno (2007), 184
Moreno and McEwen (2005), 9
Multidimensionality, 6
  and redistribution, 246
  in preferences, 235
  of political institutions, 56
Musgrave (1997), 4

National Employment Commission (NEC) (Canada), 121
Nationalist Party of Catalonia (CiU), 180
Natural experiments, 19
  and causal mechanisms, 19
Navarra (Spanish region), 53, 54, 176, 177, 183, 186, 192, 195, 196, 197, 205
Nebaümer (1996), 152
Nelson (1969), 120, 128
Nice Treaty (2001), 69
Noble (1997), 104, 127
Nogera and Ubasart (2003), 184

O'Neill (2005), 10, 20

Oates (1972), 4, 5
Oates (1991), 4, 5, 216
Oates (1999), 4
Oates and Brown (1987), 4
Obinger, Leibfried and Castles (2005), 7, 20, 133, 136
OECD (1991), 151
Open method of coordination (OMC), 83
Orloff (1988), 106, 125, 128
Orriols (2009), 204

Pal (1988), 117
Panizza (1999), 5, 216
Parikh and Van Leuvensteijn (2002), 164
Party competition, 26, 169, 172, 221
Patterson (1969), 119
Patterson (1986), 111
Peffekoven (1990), 146
Perotti (2001), 35, 38
Persson and Tabellini (1996a), 134
Persson and Tabellini (1996b), 134
Persson and Tabellini (2003), 5, 216
Peterson (1995), 4, 6, 38, 134, 228
Peterson and Rom (1990), 4, 38, 228
Peterson, Rom and Scheve (1998), 6
Petite (1998), 82
Pierson (1995), 6
Pierson (2004), 15, 59, 244
Pierson and Leibfried (1995), 9
Pierson and Skocpol (2002), 243
Plümper and Troeger (2007), 212, 225
Plümper, Schneider and Troeger (2005), 53
Polarization, 192
Political autonomy, 11
Political unions, 2, 3, 4, 6, 7, 8, 10, 11, 17, 18, 19, 20, 21, 30, 46, 47, 50, 51, 60, 66, 103, 134, 207, 208, 211, 217, 219, 221, 227, 228, 229, 230, 231, 233, 234, 235, 237, 239, 241, 244, 246, 247
  elites in, 23
  fiscal structure in, 75
  versus centralized democracies, 3
Pollack (2003), 68, 77
Pontusson (2005), 81, 226
Portugal
  EU accession of, 95, 96
Privy Council (U.K.), 121

Progressive Party (Canada), 106, 112
Progressive Party (U.S.), 120
Prud'homme (1995), 4
Przeworski (2001), 49
Przeworski (2004a), 16
Przeworski (2004b), 16
Przeworski (2004c), 16
Przeworski (2007), 16
Przeworski et al. (2000), 243
Public choice theory, 5, 240
Public good provision, 4, 19, 32
Public insurance, 8, 11, 12, 20, 35, 51, 53, 60, 63

Qian and Weingast (1997), 4, 5
Quadagno (1994), 6, 104, 112, 133
Quebec, 107, 124
  autonomy of, 107

Race to the bottom, 240
  as outcome of factor mobility, 14
Ray (2004), 87
Rehm (2009), 35
Rents, 11
Renzsch (1989), 143
Renzsch (1994), 153, 154, 159
Renzsch (1995), 144
Renzsch (1998), 144, 153, 160
Renzsch (2001), 169
Representation, 3, 10, 12, 15, 16, 18
  centrifugal, 68
  centripetal systems of, 19
Reverse causality, 15. (see endogeneity)
Rhodes (1997), 82
Riker (1964), 16, 48
Riker, William, 16
  neo-Rikerianism, 16
Risk aversion, 34, 35
Risk differentials, 35
  across regions, 39, 132
Rittberger (2005), 57
Ritter (2006), 150
Rodden (1999), 257
Rodden (2002), 74, 77
Rodden (2004), 56, 214, 229
Rodden (2006), 4, 13, 15, 61, 64
Rodden (2007), 240
Rodden (2008), 12
Rodden and Dragu (2010), 232, 246

Rodden and Wibbels (2002), 42, 62, 234
Rodden and Wibbels (2010), 42
Rodrigo and Torreblanca (2001), 98
Rodriguez-Ibarra, Juan Carlos (Spanish politician), 204
Rodrik (1998), 209
Roemer and Woojin (2006), 246
Rogowski and MacRae (2008), 6, 244
Romany, the, 77, 99
Room (1991), 82
Roosevelt, Franklin D., 1, 2, 8, 117, 119, 120, 122, 125, 127, 128, 130
Rosato (2011), 49, 57, 244
Rose-Ackermann (1983), 5
Rosenbloom and Sundstrom (2004), 51, 115
Royal Commission on Dominion-Provincial Relations (Canada), 109
Royal Commission on Industrial Relations (Canada), 106
Rueda (2008), 226
Rueda and Pontusson (2000), 224
Ruiz-Huerta and López Laborda (1996), 192

Saalfeld (2002), 64
Sahner (1999), 151
Sally and Webber (1994), 153, 154, 155, 156, 159
Sambanis and Milanovic (2009), 6
Sánchez-Cuenca (2002), 75
Scharpf (1988), 64
Scharpf (1997a), 155
Scharpf (1997b), 97
Scharpf (1998), 9, 83
Scharpf (1999), 137
Scharpf (2002), 83
Scharpf (2007), 155, 169, 172
Schimmelfennig (2001), 53
Schmidt (1992), 151
Schmidt (2003), 63, 64
Schneider (2007), 53
Schneider (2009), 52, 95, 97, 98
Schroeder, Gerhard (German Bundeskanzler, 170
Schwarze (1996), 148
Seabright (1993), 83
Service Directive (EU), 90

Index

Single European Act (1987), 69, 82
Single European Market, 77
Singleton (2000), 125
Sinn (2002), 151
Skocpol (1992), 6, 61, 104, 105
Skocpol and Ikenberry (1983), 120
Skocpol and Orloff (1984), 6
Snower and De la Dehesa (1997), 80
Social Credit Movement (Canada), 118, 122
Social Democracy, 93
Social Democratic Party (SPD), 150, 155, 159, 160, 164
Social insurance, 3
Social policy
  European, 67
Social security, 9, 54, 80, 81, 89
  in Spain, 18
Social Security, 1
Socialism
  specter of, 118
Socialist Party (PSOE) (Spain), 176
Solidarity Pact (Germany) (1993), 153, 155, 159, 160, 162, 163, 170, 277
Soskice (1990), 82
South Africa, 7
Southern Paternalism, 113, 116
Spahn (1993), 138
Spahn and Franz (2002), 138
Spain
  as centripetal political union, 58, 60
  decentralization in, 175
  economic geography of, 201
  EU accession of, 95, 96
  fiscal federalism in, 176, 182
  high levels of redistribution in, 185
  inequality in, 188, 192
  plurinational character of, 196
  provinces of, 180
  social and territorial cohesion of, 203
  under Franco, 177
  unitary social security in, 204
Spanish Constitution (1978), 59, 177, 179, 180, 197
Spanish Constitution (1987), 182
Specialization
  economic, 3
Springer (1992), 82

Stasavage and Scheve (2009), 225, 226, 244
Steckel (1983), 113
Stegarescu (2005), 259
Stegarescu (2009), 216
Steinbeck, John, 116
Stepan (2001), 216
Stewart (1930), 127
Stiglitz (1983), 5
Stoiber, Edmund (German CDU politician), 168, 237
Streeck (1995), 9
Streeck (2009), 52, 146, 150, 154, 160
Structural and Cohesion Funds (SCF), 70, 72, 73, 74, 97, 98, 100
Struthers (1983), 62, 107, 109, 114, 117, 118, 121, 122, 124
Sturm and Jeffery (1993), 142
Suarez, Adolfom (Spanish CDS politician), 180
Subirats and Gallego (2002), 9
Subnational governments, 2, 3, 10, 61, 103, 107, 110, 116, 119, 138, 240
Sundquist (1983), 62
Supreme Court (Canada), 121
Supreme Court (U.S.), 107, 127, 128

Talmadge, Eugene (American Democratic politician), 119
Tax and transfer policies, 10
Temin (1976), 51, 108
Territorial interests, 5, 13, 40, 41, 182, 237
  and economic geography, 201
  cleavages across, 58
  representation of, 58, 61, 247
Thaysen (1994), 155
Thelen (2004), 15, 244
Thelen (2010), 243
Thomson and Holsi (2006), 57
Thomson et al. (2006), 58
Tichi and Vindigni (2003), 6
Tiebout (1956), 5
Torreblanca (1998), 96
Transition to capitalism, 150
Treaty of Lisbon (2009), 67
Treaty of Paris (1783), 48
Treaty of Rome (1957), 59, 67, 69, 71, 244

Treisman (1999), 230
Treisman (2004), 4
Treisman (2007), 4
Trennsystem (Germany), 138
Treuhandanstalt (German restructuring agency), 151, 156
Tsebelis (2002), 57
Tsebelis and Garrett (2001), 57

U.S. Social Security Act (1935), 8, 12, 103, 117, 119, 120, 125, 126, 127, 128, 129, 130, 135, 237, 239
Uhlig (2006), 151
Unemployment insurance, 2, 8, 64, 65, 81, 103, 104, 105, 106, 107, 111, 116, 117, 120, 121, 122, 123, 124, 126, 127, 128, 129, 130, 132, 133, 137, 152, 156, 157, 158, 168, 169, 236, 237, 238, 239, 244, 245
Unemployment Insurance Act (Canada) (1940), 104, 112, 118, 121, 122, 123, 124
Union of the Democratic Center (UCD) (Spain), 179
United States, the
  and centrifugal political will, 63
  and fiscal decentralization, 7
  and inequality, 4
  and states' rights, 107
  and the Great Depression, 8, 18, 22, 61, 62, 64, 65, 111
  anti-centralization in, 8
  as welfare laggard, 104
  Constitution of, 50
  contrast with Canada, 60, 103, 104
  economic geography of, 22, 60, 112
  Electoral College, 60
  fiscal policy in, 3
  formation of, 48
  government expenditure in, 70
  immigration to, 113
  in contrast with Canada, 8
  labor mobility in, 116
  malapportionment in, 61
  mobility patterns in, 111
  presidential system of, 106
  relationship between states and federal government in, 116
  the dole system in, 61

Urbanos and Utrilla (2001), 198

Valle (1996), 183
Van Houten (2009), 198
Vandenbroucke (2002), 83
Varian (1980), 2, 12, 34, 65
Venables (2001), 34, 133
Venables (2007), 133
Venezuela, 7
Verbundsystem (Germany), 138
Veto points, 5, 41, 103
  and elite power, 43
  in fiscal structures, 59
  in the EU, 53
  in the Weimar constitution, 137
Volden (1997), 6
Volden (2004), 14
Volden (2005), 14

Wagner, Robert (American Senator), 106, 128
Wagner-Lewis Bill (1934), 126, 127, 128
Wallerstein (1999), 224, 244
Wallis and Oates (1988), 221
War on Poverty, 133
Watts (2008), 260
Webber and Wildavsky (1986), 103
Weber (1999), 74, 77
Weigel, Theo (German CDU politician), 159, 160
Weigel, Theo (German CDU politician), 156
Weimar Germany, 136, 137
Weingast (1993), 5
Weingast (1995), 4
Weingast (2006), 20
Weingast, Montinola and Qian (1995), 5
Weir (1988), 120
Welfare economics, 5
Welfare state, 5, 6, 9, 79, 85, 86, 87, 106, 134, 136, 141, 175, 184, 227, 238, 244
Whatley (1983), 130
Whitaker (1977), 62
Wibbels (2001), 62
Wibbels (2005a), 4, 13, 48, 134, 247
Wibbels (2005b), 6
Wibbels (2006a), 8
Wibbels (2006b), 15, 240

Index

Wibbels and Goldberg (2010), 220
Wiesenthal (1995), 52, 151
Wiesenthal (1996), 52, 151
Wiesenthal (2003), 146, 150, 160
Wildasin (1991), 4, 133
Wildasin (1995), 133
Wildavsky (1984), 4
Williams (1939), 132

Witte (1962), 126, 128, 131, 132
Witte and Wagner (1995), 151

Zapatero, Jose Luis Rodriguez (Spanish PM), 54, 93, 198, 199, 201, 203
Zhou (2009), 220, 261
Ziblatt (2002), 168, 169

Other Books in the Series (continued from page iii)

Catherine Boone, *Merchant Capital and the Roots of State Power in Senegal, 1930–1985*
Catherine Boone, *Political Topographies of the African State: Territorial Authority and Institutional Change*
Michael Bratton, Robert Mattes, and E. Gyimah-Boadi, *Public Opinion, Democracy, and Market Reform in Africa*
Michael Bratton and Nicolas van de Walle, *Democratic Experiments in Africa: Regime Transitions in Comparative Perspective*
Valerie Bunce, *Leaving Socialism and Leaving the State: The End of Yugoslavia, the Soviet Union, and Czechoslovakia*
Daniele Caramani, *The Nationalization of Politics: The Formation of National Electorates and Party Systems in Europe*
John M. Carey, *Legislative Voting and Accountability*
Kanchan Chandra, *Why Ethnic Parties Succeed: Patronage and Ethnic Headcounts in India*
Eric C. C. Chang, Mark Andreas Kayser, Drew A. Linzer, and Ronald Rogowski, *Electoral Systems and the Balance of Consumer-Producer Power*
José Antonio Cheibub, *Presidentialism, Parliamentarism, and Democracy*
Ruth Berins Collier, *Paths toward Democracy: The Working Class and Elites in Western Europe and South America*
Christian Davenport, *State Repression and the Domestic Democratic Peace*
Donatella della Porta, *Social Movements, Political Violence, and the State*
Alberto Diaz-Cayeros, *Federalism, Fiscal Authority, and Centralization in Latin America*
Thad Dunning, *Crude Democracy: Natural Resource Wealth and Political Regimes*
Gerald Easter, *Reconstructing the State: Personal Networks and Elite Identity*
Margarita Estevez-Abe, *Welfare and Capitalism in Postwar Japan: Party, Bureaucracy, and Business*
Henry Farrell, *The Political Economy of Trust: Institutions, Interests, and Inter-Firm Cooperation in Italy and Germany*
Karen E. Ferree, *Framing the Race in South Africa: The Political Origins of Racial Census Elections*
M. Steven Fish, *Democracy Derailed in Russia: The Failure of Open Politics*
Robert F. Franzese, *Macroeconomic Policies of Developed Democracies*
Roberto Franzosi, *The Puzzle of Strikes: Class and State Strategies in Postwar Italy*

Timothy Frye, *Building States and Markets After Communism: The Perils of Polarized Democracy*
Geoffrey Garrett, *Partisan Politics in the Global Economy*
Scott Gehlbach, *Representation through Taxation: Revenue, Politics, and Development in Postcommunist States*
Miriam Golden, *Heroic Defeats: The Politics of Job Loss*
Jeff Goodwin, *No Other Way Out: States and Revolutionary Movements*
Merilee Serrill Grindle, *Changing the State*
Anna Grzymala-Busse, *Rebuilding Leviathan: Party Competition and State Exploitation in Post-Communist Democracies*
Anna Grzymala-Busse, *Redeeming the Communist Past: The Regeneration of Communist Parties in East Central Europe*
Frances Hagopian, *Traditional Politics and Regime Change in Brazil*
Henry E. Hale, *The Foundations of Ethnic Politics: Separatism of States and Nations in Eurasia and the World*
Mark Hallerberg, Rolf Ranier Strauch, and Jürgen von Hagen, *Fiscal Governance in Europe*
Stephen E. Hanson, *Post-Imperial Democracies: Ideology and Party Formation in Third Republic France, Weimar Germany, and Post-Soviet Russia*
Gretchen Helmke, *Courts Under Constraints: Judges, Generals, and Presidents in Argentina*
Yoshiko Herrera, *Imagined Economies: The Sources of Russian Regionalism*
J. Rogers Hollingsworth and Robert Boyer, eds., *Contemporary Capitalism: The Embeddedness of Institutions*
John D. Huber and Charles R. Shipan, *Deliberate Discretion? The Institutional Foundations of Bureaucratic Autonomy*
Ellen Immergut, *Health Politics: Interests and Institutions in Western Europe*
Torben Iversen, *Capitalism, Democracy, and Welfare*
Torben Iversen, *Contested Economic Institutions*
Torben Iversen, Jonas Pontussen, and David Soskice, eds., *Unions, Employers, and Central Banks: Macroeconomic Coordination and Institutional Change in Social Market Economies*
Thomas Janoski and Alexander M. Hicks, eds., *The Comparative Political Economy of the Welfare State*
Joseph Jupille, *Procedural Politics: Issues, Influence, and Institutional Choice in the European Union*
Stathis Kalyvas, *The Logic of Violence in Civil War*
David C. Kang, *Crony Capitalism: Corruption and Capitalism in South Korea and the Philippines*
Junko Kato, *Regressive Taxation and the Welfare State*

Orit Kedar, *Voting for Policy, Not Parties: How Voters Compensate for Power Sharing*
Robert O. Keohane and Helen B. Milner, eds., *Internationalization and Domestic Politics*
Herbert Kitschelt, *The Transformation of European Social Democracy*
Herbert Kitschelt, Kirk A. Hawkins, Juan Pablo Luna, Guillermo Rosas, and Elizabeth J. Zechmeister, *Latin American Party Systems*
Herbert Kitschelt, Peter Lange, Gary Marks, and John D. Stephens, eds., *Continuity and Change in Contemporary Capitalism*
Herbert Kitschelt, Zdenka Mansfeldova, Radek Markowski, and Gabor Toka, *Post-Communist Party Systems*
David Knoke, Franz Urban Pappi, Jeffrey Broadbent, and Yutaka Tsujinaka, eds., *Comparing Policy Networks*
Allan Kornberg and Harold D. Clarke, *Citizens and Community: Political Support in a Representative Democracy*
Amie Kreppel, *The European Parliament and the Supranational Party System*
David D. Laitin, *Language Repertoires and State Construction in Africa*
Fabrice E. Lehoucq and Ivan Molina, *Stuffing the Ballot Box: Fraud, Electoral Reform, and Democratization in Costa Rica*
Mark Irving Lichbach and Alan S. Zuckerman, eds., *Comparative Politics: Rationality, Culture, and Structure, second edition*
Evan Lieberman, *Race and Regionalism in the Politics of Taxation in Brazil and South Africa*
Pauline Jones Luong, *Institutional Change and Political Continuity in Post-Soviet Central Asia*
Pauline Jones Luong and Erika Weinthal, *Oil Is Not a Curse: Ownership Structure and Institutions in Soviet Successor States*
Julia Lynch, *Age in the Welfare State: The Origins of Social Spending on Pensioners, Workers, and Children*
Lauren M. MacLean, *Informal Institutions and Citizenship in Rural Africa: Risk and Reciprocity in Ghana and Côte d'Ivoire*
Doug McAdam, John McCarthy, and Mayer Zald, eds., *Comparative Perspectives on Social Movements*
Beatriz Magaloni, *Voting for Autocracy: Hegemonic Party Survival and Its Demise in Mexico*
James Mahoney, *Colonialism and Postcolonial Development: Spanish America in Comparative Perspective*
James Mahoney and Dietrich Rueschemeyer, eds., *Historical Analysis and the Social Sciences*
Scott Mainwaring and Matthew Soberg Shugart, eds., *Presidentialism and Democracy in Latin America*

Isabela Mares, *The Politics of Social Risk: Business and Welfare State Development*
Isabela Mares, *Taxation, Wage Bargaining, and Unemployment*
Anthony W. Marx, *Making Race, Making Nations: A Comparison of South Africa, the United States, and Brazil*
Bonnie M. Meguid, *Party Competition between Unequals: Strategies and Electoral Fortunes in Western Europe*
Joel S. Migdal, *State in Society: Studying How States and Societies Constitute One Another*
Joel S. Migdal, Atul Kohli, and Vivienne Shue, eds., *State Power and Social Forces: Domination and Transformation in the Third World*
Scott Morgenstern and Benito Nacif, eds., *Legislative Politics in Latin America*
Layna Mosley, *Global Capital and National Governments*
Layna Mosley, *Labor Rights and Multinational Production*
Wolfgang C. Müller and Kaare Strøm, *Policy, Office, or Votes?*
Maria Victoria Murillo, *Labor Unions, Partisan Coalitions, and Market Reforms in Latin America*
Maria Victoria Murillo, *Political Competition, Partisanship, and Policy Making in Latin American Public Utilities*
Monika Nalepa, *Skeletons in the Closet: Transitional Justice in Post-Communist Europe*
Ton Notermans, *Money, Markets, and the State: Social Democratic Economic Policies since 1918*
Aníbal Pérez-Liñán, *Presidential Impeachment and the New Political Instability in Latin America*
Roger D. Petersen, *Understanding Ethnic Violence: Fear, Hatred, and Resentment in Twentieth-Century Eastern Europe*
Simona Piattoni, ed., *Clientelism, Interests, and Democratic Representation*
Paul Pierson, *Dismantling the Welfare State? Reagan, Thatcher, and the Politics of Retrenchment*
Marino Regini, *Uncertain Boundaries: The Social and Political Construction of European Economies*
Marc Howard Ross, *Cultural Contestation in Ethnic Conflict*
Lyle Scruggs, *Sustaining Abundance: Environmental Performance in Industrial Democracies*
Jefferey M. Sellers, *Governing from Below: Urban Regions and the Global Economy*
Yossi Shain and Juan Linz, eds., *Interim Governments and Democratic Transitions*
Beverly Silver, *Forces of Labor: Workers' Movements and Globalization since 1870*

Theda Skocpol, *Social Revolutions in the Modern World*
Regina Smyth, *Candidate Strategies and Electoral Competition in the Russian Federation: Democracy Without Foundation*
Richard Snyder, *Politics after Neoliberalism: Reregulation in Mexico*
David Stark and László Bruszt, *Postsocialist Pathways: Transforming Politics and Property in East Central Europe*
Sven Steinmo, *The Evolution of Modern States: Sweden, Japan, and the United States*
Sven Steinmo, Kathleen Thelen, and Frank Longstreth, eds., *Structuring Politics: Historical Institutionalism in Comparative Analysis*
Susan C. Stokes, *Mandates and Democracy: Neoliberalism by Surprise in Latin America*
Susan C. Stokes, ed., *Public Support for Market Reforms in New Democracies*
Duane Swank, *Global Capital, Political Institutions, and Policy Change in Developed Welfare States*
Sidney Tarrow, *Power in Movement: Social Movements and Contentious Politics, revised and updated third edition*
Kathleen Thelen, *How Institutions Evolve: The Political Economy of Skills in Germany, Britain, the United States, and Japan*
Charles Tilly, *Trust and Rule*
Daniel Treisman, *The Architecture of Government: Rethinking Political Decentralization*
Lily Lee Tsai, *Accountability without Democracy: How Solidary Groups Provide Public Goods in Rural China*
Joshua Tucker, *Regional Economic Voting: Russia, Poland, Hungary, Slovakia, and the Czech Republic, 1990–1999*
Ashutosh Varshney, *Democracy, Development, and the Countryside*
Jeremy M. Weinstein, *Inside Rebellion: The Politics of Insurgent Violence*
Stephen I. Wilkinson, *Votes and Violence: Electoral Competition and Ethnic Riots in India*
Jason Wittenberg, *Crucibles of Political Loyalty: Church Institutions and Electoral Continuity in Hungary*
Elisabeth J. Wood, *Forging Democracy from Below: Insurgent Transitions in South Africa and El Salvador*
Elisabeth J. Wood, *Insurgent Collective Action and Civil War in El Salvador*

For EU product safety concerns, contact us at Calle de José Abascal, 56–1°,
28003 Madrid, Spain or eugpsr@cambridge.org.

www.ingramcontent.com/pod-product-compliance
Ingram Content Group UK Ltd.
Pitfield, Milton Keynes, MK11 3LW, UK
UKHW040414060825
461487UK00006B/505